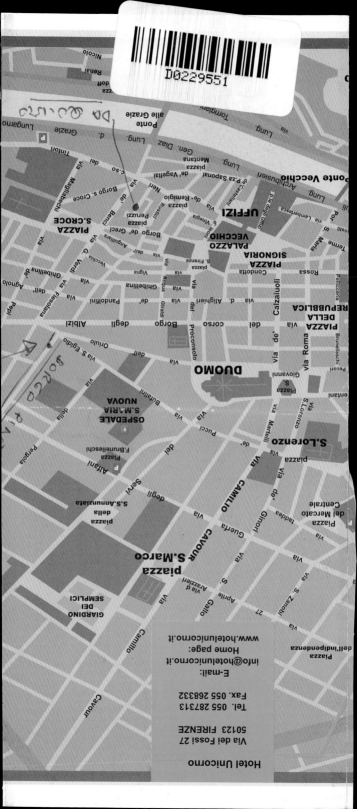

L'Hotel Unicorno é situato in posizione strategica su una strada di antichi negozi nel cuore di Firenze.

L'Hotel é stato rinnovato (l'ultima ristrutturazione é del 1997) combinando lo stile originale del '600 con un'ottica più semplice e moderna, il cui risultato e un interno caldo e confontevole, con camere individualizzate.

A due passi da Santa Maria Novella e a 5 minuti dalla stazione ferroviaria si trovano il centro congressi e la Fortezza da Basso,

sede di mostre ed esibizioni internazionali.

Anche i maggiori musei ed i più importanti monumenti si trovano nelle vicinanze, tutti raggiungibili a piedi.

Tutte le camere sono dotate di: vasca da bagno/doccia, aria condizionata, linea telefonica, frigo bar, TV satellite, cassaforte, asciugacapelli e presa telefonica RJ11 per connettere un computer portatile ad internet.

The city's finest hotels are on streets, such as the Lungarno Corsini, along the banks of the Arno. These have always been popular places for a stroll.

The Piazza della Signoria contains Cellini's famous statue of *Perseus*, which is overshadowed by a column of the Loggia dei Lanzi.

The *renaioli* (sand gatherers) were among the workmen who made a living on the Arno. They dredged sand from the river bed and used it to build up the banks.

The bridges of Florence and the banks of the Arno were constantly being rebuilt. The chapels, shops and houses which grew up over the centuries on the Ponte alle Grazie, still visible in this illustration, were demolished in 1876 to widen the road. The construction of fine palaces that began in the 13th century gradually brought the Lungarno Acciaioli to its present form. Major rebuilding was necessary after the German bombardments of 1944.

This ghetto was once part of the old center of the city. It was considered dilapidated and unhealthy, and so was demolished at the end of the 19th century.

The Loggia dei Pesci housed the fishmongers' stalls of the long-gone Mercato Vecchio. At the end of the 19th century it was moved to the Piazza dei Ciompi.

CONTENTS

PONTE VECCHIO, *141*

BARGELLO, *185*

PIAZZA STROZZI, *195*

SAN MARCO, *227*

SANTA CROCE, *253*

SANTA TRINITA, *269*

BOBOLI, *285*

SANTO SPIRITO, *299*

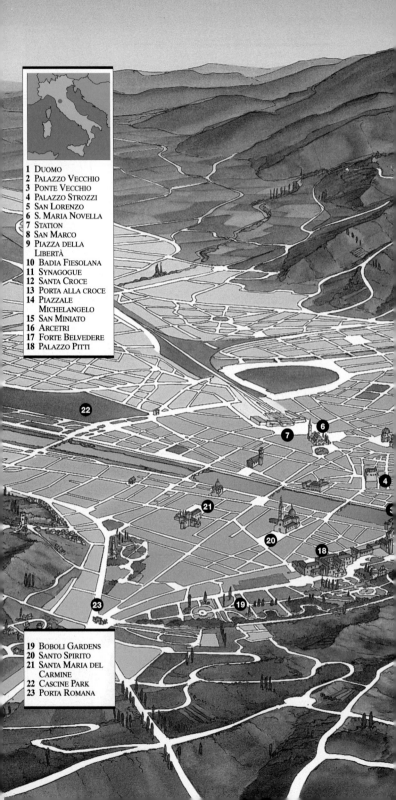

Florence

1 Duomo
2 Palazzo Vecchio
3 Ponte Vecchio
4 Palazzo Strozzi
5 San Lorenzo
6 S. Maria Novella
7 Station
8 San Marco
9 Piazza della Libertà
10 Badia Fiesolana
11 Synagogue
12 Santa Croce
13 Porta alla croce
14 Piazzale Michelangelo
15 San Miniato
16 Arcetri
17 Forte Belvedere
18 Palazzo Pitti

19 Boboli Gardens
20 Santo Spirito
21 Santa Maria del Carmine
22 Cascine Park
23 Porta Romana

HOW TO USE THIS GUIDE

The symbols at the top of each page refer to the different parts of the guide.

■ NATURAL ENVIRONMENT

● UNDERSTANDING VENICE

▲ ITINERARIES

◆ PRACTICAL INFORMATION

The itinerary map shows the main points of interest along the way and is intended to help you find your bearings.

The mini-map locates the particular itinerary within the wider area covered by the guide.

The gateway to Venice, after all, is neither the station nor the Piazzale, but the Grand Canal before us, thronged, turbulent as a great river.
Fernand Braudel, *House*

Santa Lucia Station.

★ The star symbol signifies that a particular site has been singled out by the publishers for its special beauty, atmosphere or cultural interest.

At the beginning of each itinerary, the suggested means of transport to be used and the time it will take to cover the area are indicated:

🚢 By boat
🚶 On foot
🚲 By bicycle
⏱ Duration

● ▲ ■ ◆
The symbols alongside a title or within the text itself provide cross-references to a theme or place dealt with elsewhere in the guide.

THE GATEWAY TO VENICE ★

PONTE DELLA LIBERTA. Built by the Austrians 50 years after the Treaty of Campo Formio in 1797 ● *34,* to link Venice with Milan. The bridge ended the thousand-year separation from the mainland and shook the city's economy to its roots as Venice, already in the throes of the industrial revolution, saw

🚶 Half a day

BRIDGES TO VENICE

NATURE

■ THE STONES OF FLORENCE

Every year, about fifty thousand tons of marble are quarried in the Apuan Alps.

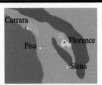

Paisine
Serpentine (*Verde di Prato*)
Pietra serena
Marbles and breccias

The buildings of Florence were traditionally constructed from brick and stone. Religious and civic architecture made full use of the rich variety of handsome and decorative local stones. Two kinds of sandstone, *pietra forte* and *pietra serena*, were the most popular for building and decorative work, since they were particularly easy to cut. Their gentle gray and ocher tones contrasted with the more vivid polychrome work that used serpentine, marble and breccia from the Apuan Alps. Many artists came to Florence in order to find the finest white Carrara marble for their statues, paisine for mosaic work, and good quality clay.

"PIETRA SERENA"
A relatively soft mica schist much used for building.

The clays found around Florence are extremely fine and lend themselves to the ancient and still flourishing tradition of terracotta work.

CARRARA MARBLE
The marble found around Carrara is famous for its purity and translucent quality.

CLAY
A stiff, sedimentary earth which can be molded and which hardens when fired.

"PIETRA FORTE"
A detrital rock. A micaceous sandstone that is used mainly for building.

The sculptor cuts the marble following a drawing made on the block.

Pietra forte can also be sculpted.

Pietra serena can be used to emphasize a feature.

Pietra serena rustication of the Palazzo Pitti ▲ 288.

Both Giotto's campanile ▲ *132* and the Badia Fiesolana arcades ▲ *327* have polychrome decorations, predominantly of gray and white marble.

The marble is attached by spreading the surface with a thin layer of cement and then fixing each section with iron pegs.

The rich colors and varied patterns of local breccias and marbles have provided mosaicists and architects with a broad palette with which to work.

COMPACTED LIMESTONE

The traditional Florentine designs of inlaid *pietra dura* were inspired by the variety of colors that could be found locally.

PRIMORDIAL LIMESTONE   **COMPACT LIMESTONE**

Limestone	Granite dome	Limestone
	Marble	

HOW MARBLE IS FORMED
Marble is a calcareous rock. It is limestone that has recrystallized due to pressure or heat. If the calcite contains no impurities it is white, but often accessory minerals occur to give patterns and colors.

TALCIFEROUS LIMESTONE   **SERPENTINE**

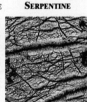

SERPENTINE   **GREEN SERPENTINE**

BRECCIA LIMESTONE   **TALCIFEROUS LIMESTONE**

Specialized tools are necessary to sculpt the marble.

CARRARA MARBLE   **PAISINE**

Florence lies in an alluvial plain and is surrounded by hills.

The Florentine hills, although intensely cultivated, offer a variety of natural habitats for wildlife. Wooded areas contain a mixture of deciduous trees, like chestnuts and various species of oak (common oak, holm oak and durmast oak), along with Mediterranean plants such as white heath, myrtle, rockrose and the pistachio tree. The hills to the south are covered with forests of umbrella pine and pinaster, which were once exploited for their cones, resin and timber. Villas and small farmhouses sit upon the cultivated hillsides. The agriculture remains mixed, with vegetables and cereal crops predominating, and organized as it has been for centuries on the *mezzadria* (share-cropping) system.

COMMON BUZZARD
A bird of prey that hunts for small rodents and lizards.

COMMON LIZARD
It basks in the sunshine on walls and paths.

HOODED CROW
The commonest member of the crow family in Italy is found in both woods and open countryside. It is a scavenger.

GOLDEN ORIOLE
From April its "wheela-wheeo" cry is often heard in Tuscany, but this shy bird is seldom seen.

LESSER KESTREL
Ruined buildings or the old nest of a hooded crow are its usual choice of nesting place.

TAWNY OWL
Its characteristic hoot is heard at night in the oak woods.

CYPRESS
A tree that can grow to well over 50 feet in height. It was introduced to Italy from eastern Europe by the Romans.

COMMON OAK
A magnificent tree found all over Europe which likes a dry environment.

SPANISH CHESTNUT
A tree that thrives on poor land. The chestnuts were ground to make flour by poorer families.

UMBRELLA PINE
The nuts are used in a number of Italian dishes, as well as for cakes and sweets.

PINASTER
Essence of turpentine is extracted from its resin.

19

THE IRIS AND THE OLIVE TREE

OLIVE OIL

SCENTED OIL
(extracted from the iris bulb)

Olive trees dominate the countryside around Florence. Small, hardy and deep-rooted, with twisted trunks and silvery leaves, they line the hillside terraces. The olive does best in mild climates and is sensitive to dramatic changes in temperature. It has been cultivated in the Mediterranean basin for thousands of years but was brought originally from Asia Minor. The harvest begins late in the fall. The fruits are pressed to give a greeny-golden oil that has a flavor so delicious it can be savored like a wine. In May bright patches of violet appear on the Tuscan hills: this is the flowering of the *giaggiolo*, the *Iris florentina*, a particular species that is used in the manufacture of scent.

THE OLIVE TREE
A tree that can continue to produce fruit for several hundred years.

GRINDER

PRESS CLOTHS

A PRESS

The olive blossoms from April onwards, and the fruits begin to appear in early summer. They can be picked green for the table, but those used for oil must ripen to become black and wrinkled.

OLIVE OIL
The olives are picked, washed in cold water, crushed in grinders, and the pulp wrapped in press cloths. Oil is then separated from the water by decanting or centrifugal force. It takes about 5 or 6 lbs of olives to produce a pint of oil.

THE FLORENCE IRIS
It has long been cultivated
alongside the olive tree.

Iris bulbs supply
the local perfume
industry.

"IL GIAGGIOLO"
Also known as the flower-de-luce, it
was the model for the French royal
emblem, the *fleur de lys*. The purple
flower has a scent of violets.

SWALLOW
In summer swallows are
seen swooping in
and out of the
olive trees in
search of flying
insects.

PORCUPINE
A large rodent that
eats roots, and
particularly enjoys
those of the iris. It is
a solitary creature
and will make a show
of its spines if
threatened.

21

CHIANTI

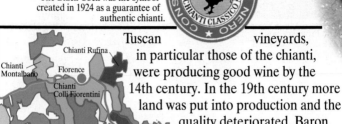

Chianti Rufina

Chianti Montalbano

Florence

Chianti Colli Fiorentini

Chianti Colline pisane

Siena

Chianti Colli Senesi

Chianti Colli Aretini

Chianti Colli Senesi

■ Chianti classico
■ Chianti

Tuscan vineyards, in particular those of the chianti, were producing good wine by the 14th century. In the 19th century more land was put into production and the quality deteriorated. Baron Bettino Ricasoli took matters in hand in 1932, and regulations came into force defining areas of production and varieties of vine. This created the *denominazione di origine controllata* (D.O.C.), the equivalent of the French *appellation d'origine contrôlée.* Chianti classico comes from 170,000 acres of vineyards at the heart of the chianti area. Other wines under the chianti classification are Colli Aretini, Colli Fiorentini (around Florence), Colline Pisane (Pisa), Colli Senesi (Siena), Montalbano and Rufina.

The grape harvest is from late September to late October, depending on the altitude of the vineyard.

TREBBIANO
Its acidity helps chianti to retain its taste for longer.

CANAIOLO
The grape that gives chianti its rounded flavor.

MALVASIA
A white variety of grape that softens the taste of the wine.

The vine is trained on wires and grown high off the ground.

SANGIOVESE
The principal variety, it gives the full flavor and fine bouquet.

One thousand million bottles of chianti are produced each year.

Among such an enormous range of chianti labels, a chianti classico provides a guarantee of quality.

CHIANTI "RISERVA"
This wine remains in casks to mature and develop a fuller flavor for about three years. The very best chianti is now usually sold in a claret bottle; the traditional straw-covered flagon is fast becoming a thing of the past.

THE BOBOLI GARDENS

HORSE CHESTNUT LEAVES

During spring the gardens are full of birdsong. The pure notes of the blackbird, the rich song of the blackcap, and the insistent chirp of the flycatcher contrast with the sharp twittering and cheeping sounds of serin and grey wagtail. The Boboli Gardens ▲ 294 are the largest in Florence and they contain native varieties of tree that have adapted to the city, along with a number of imported species. Common varieties of oak stand alongside cedar of Lebanon, lemon tree and magnolia. There is also plenty of wildlife: jays are common, while red squirrels frisk among the cypresses, and other nocturnal mammals such as hedgehogs and martens find plenty of places to hide.

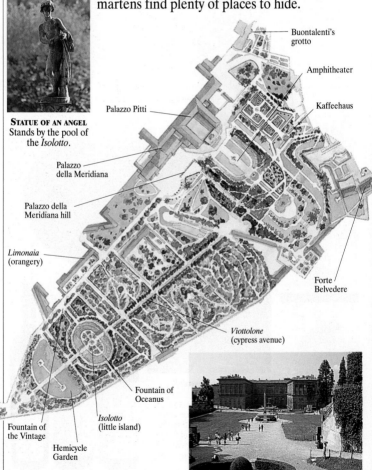

STATUE OF AN ANGEL
Stands by the pool of the *Isolotto*.

Buontalenti's grotto

Amphitheater

Kaffeehaus

Palazzo Pitti

Palazzo della Meridiana

Palazzo della Meridiana hill

Limonaia (orangery)

Forte Belvedere

Viottolone (cypress avenue)

Fountain of Oceanus

Isolotto (little island)

Fountain of the Vintage

Hemicycle Garden

PLANE TREE LEAF

BAY LEAF
The bruised leaf gives off a heavy scent.

LEMON TREE LEAF
The tree keeps its shiny leaves through the winter.

LEAF AND ACORN OF THE HOLM OAK
One of the rare evergreen species of European oak.

GREY WAGTAIL
Nests close to the water and can often be seen on the paths wagging its tail.

Head of an Italian sparrow

House sparrow

ITALIAN SPARROW
The sparrow to be found all over Italy. Unlike the house sparrow, it has a brown cap.

SPOTTED FLYCATCHER
A shy bird that does not arrive from equatorial Africa until mid-May.

STARLING
In winter these birds gather together in the evenings to sleep.

JAY
A shy but colorful bird with a distinctive, piercing cry.

BLACKBIRDS
In spring they eat insects and worms, while in fall their diet changes to berries.

MAGPIE
A bold and predatory bird. It starts to build its nest in February.

The hoopoe chooses fissures in old walls for its nest. In flight it resembles a huge butterfly.

HOOPOE
Its numbers are declining throughout Europe.

An alley of plane trees borders the Garden of Columns.

HEDGEHOG
By nature a shy and cautious creature, it only comes out into the gardens at night.

WOODMOUSE
A nocturnal rodent that spends its days in a well-concealed nest.

RED SQUIRREL
The grace and energy of these creatures, bright chestnut in color, is marvelous to watch as they jump about the branches. They spend most of their time in the trees and live on acorns, nuts, shoots and buds.

MARTEN
By night this predator hunts small rodents. By day it stays hidden in attics and unused buildings.

25

BLACK-HEADED GULL
The smallest of the common gulls comes far inland in winter to search for food along the Arno.

Today Florence suffers from severe problems of pollution, but there is still a certain amount of wildlife to be found, even in the city center. Bats can be seen flitting over the river at dusk, and rock-dwelling swifts and house martins nest as happily on the façade of a monument as they do on a cliff face. The river Arno, so often praised in Italian literature for its beauty, has also become severely polluted, and its fauna is threatened.

SWIFT

The Arno is an unruly river which can flood suddenly and violently; it did so to terrible effect in 1966 ▲ 176.

COYPU
Escapees from farms north of Florence are now living and breeding close to the city. They are sometimes seen on the riverbanks in the very center of Florence.

KINGFISHER
A sensitive ecological indicator, it disappears with the first trace of pollution.

HOUSE MARTIN
Returning from Africa early in April, these birds like to build or repair nests underneath an old bridge using mud from the banks.

HISTORY AND LANGUAGE

● THE HISTORY OF FLORENCE

DISTANT ORIGINS

Fiesole, below, and, right, an Etruscan vase.

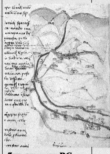

THE FOUNDATION OF THE CITY. Between the 10th and the 8th centuries BC, Italic tribes from what is now the Emilia settled on this site. There is no archeological evidence to suggest the involvement of the Etruscans, who founded many other towns in Tuscany including nearby Fiesole. The Romans chose this site for a *castrum*, and Caesar's army established a colony in 59 BC. It was probably called *Florentia* after the season in which the *Ludi Floreales* (Floral Games) were held in honor of the goddess Flora. The population grew as commerce developed; trade expanded with Greek or Syrian merchants, who introduced the Christian faith. Among them was Minias, who was martyred in AD 250 ▲ *320*.

7TH CENTURY BC
With strongholds in Tuscany, the Etruscans move south to Latium.

509–527 BC
Founding of the Roman republic.

402
The first invasions by barbarian tribes.

A DARK AND TROUBLED TIME. From the 4th to the 9th centuries, a succession of hostile barbarian tribes invaded northern Italy and Tuscany. The town was taken by the Lombards, but in the 7th and 8th century it ceased to interest them. Perhaps it was too close to Ravenna, a stronghold of their Byzantine enemies. They favored towns further west, including the Tuscan capital of the Lombard dukes at Lucca.

THE CAROLINGIANS. Legend has it that Charlemagne "refounded" Florence. This is an exaggeration, but under Carolingian domination it regained importance and prosperity. The town was elevated to the status of a diocese with its own count, then merged with Fiesole in 854 to become the most important domain in Tuscany. It extended from the Apennines to Siena, and the area was known as the *contado* of Florence. When Ugo

OBIIT AÑO SALVTIS MILLESIMO P XII KAL IANVARIAS

The tomb of Margrave Ugo of Tuscany.

568
Lombard rule (lasting until 774).

(953–1001) was Margrave of Tuscany he transferred his residence here from Lucca. The town began to expand rapidly, thanks to a general growth in commerce and consequently in the population.

774–814
Charlemagne conquers the north of Italy.

1076–1122
The investiture controversy and its resolution by the Concordat of Worms, which decided the rights of church and emperor over the bishops and their possessions.

Matilda of Canossa, right.

CHURCH AND EMPIRE. A number of Florentine dignitaries, both clerics and laymen, played an important part in the reform of the church. They defended the Pope in his struggle against the secular authorities, who were meddling in church affairs and encouraging corruption. It was to the castle of Matilda of Canossa, Countess of Tuscany (1046–1115), that the excommunicated Henry IV came in 1077 to ask the pardon of Pope Gregory VII.

A NEW INDEPENDENCE. Florence was becoming gradually more autonomous, freeing itself from the rule of the Holy Roman Empire. In 1082 the imperial

REX ROGAT ABBATEM. M̄

The Battle of Montaperti (1260).

army laid siege to the city. The Florentines held out for ten days and survived. In 1125 they attacked and destroyed Fiesole. During the 12th century the nobles of the province were brought under control and made to live within the city.

THE FOUNDATIONS OF COMMUNAL RULE

INSTITUTIONS EMERGE. The first signs of a developing political autonomy appeared in 1138, and in 1154 the emperor granted Florence the right to administer justice throughout its *contado*, a right which was confirmed and extended in 1183. From then on the Comune was ruled by nobles and wealthy merchant families. The power of the twelve consuls was regulated by the council of Credenza, a senate numbering a hundred men, and the *parlamentum* to which all citizens were summoned four times a year.

THE PODESTÀ. Commerce flourished in the 13th century, and Florence gained a tighter grip over the surrounding province. It was now as powerful as Siena or Pisa. But the constant feuds between the city's important families led to a podestà being put in charge. This was a nobleman brought in from outside and made responsible for the administration of justice. He held a great deal of executive and military power.

THE "PRIMO POPOLO". With law and order restored, the city prospered and the power of the merchants grew. They organized themselves into *Arti*, or guilds ● *52*, ▲ *198*, and took an active part in communal affairs. In October 1250, with the support of the Guelf faction, they assumed power and installed the regime of the *primo popolo*, taking over existing institutions and modifying them to their own ends.

GUELFS AND GHIBELLINES. Hostility continued towards the Ghibellines and cities which, like them, supported the emperor. Pistoia, Siena and Pisa were defeated one by one. Defeat at Montaperti in 1260 in a second war with Siena, this time backed by the Ghibellines, put a stop to Florentine ambitions. The houses of noble Guelf families were destroyed, and the institutions of the *primo popolo* were disbanded.

THE "SECUNDO POPOLO". In 1267 the Florentine Guelfs, now allied to the king of France, made a triumphant return when Charles of Anjou took the city and was made podestà for seven years. The city was now under the thumb of the Guelf nobles, but rivalry between Ghibellines and Guelfs continued. After a few years, the wealthy business classes, or *popolo grasso*, got the upper hand and between 1284 and 1292 the guilds evolved a new system of government. The city was ruled by a Signoria of six priors from the Arti Maggiori, the principal guilds ● *52*. Two other councils also shared power. The Ordinamenti di Giustizia (the Orders of Justice) put the finishing touches to these reforms in 1293 by

c. 1080
The major towns of northern-central Italy become self-governing.

1176
Emperor Frederick Barbarossa is defeated at Legnano by the comuni, *the civic republics of Lombardy.*

1183
The comuni *are liberated by the Peace of Constance.*

1220–50
The reign of Emperor Frederick II.

1236–37
Frederick II attempts to quell the rebellious Lombard cities.

1266–68
A series of victories for the Italian Guelfs, aided and commanded by Charles of Anjou, who takes the throne of Naples.

1282
The Sicilian Vespers. The House of Anjou loses Sicily to the House of Aragon.

1309–77 *The Pope in Avignon.*	excluding the nobles from public office. Peace was shortlived, and by 1300 new disputes had broken out. Two years later the "White" Guelfs were exiled by the "Blacks" ● *34*.

FROM THE TURBULENT 14TH CENTURY TO THE AGE OF THE MEDICIS

1337
The beginning of the Hundred Years' War.

1348
The Black Death in Europe.

1378–1418
The Great Schism.

LATE 14TH CENTURY
The alliance with Venice against the Visconti of Milan.

The Medici coat of arms.

At the Battle of San Romano in 1432 Florence was fighting both Sienese and Visconti troops.

A FLOURISHING CITY. Florence, whose population was nearing 100,000, was by now probably the wealthiest city in the civilized world. Her merchants traded with France, Germany and the Orient, and her bankers financed the Christian monarchs. The gold florin was international currency, and the Italian spoken in Florence was understood throughout the rest of Italy. Between 1331 and 1338 Florence subdued Pistoia and Arezzo; but Lucca, Siena and Pisa, though weak, managed to fight off her armies. The city asserted its independence and proud republican status.

A CITY IN CRISIS. Continually threatened by internal conflict as well as by her powerful neighbors, Florence next fell prey to dictatorship – first Charles of Calabria (1326–28), then Walter of Brienne, Duke of Athens (1342–43). This form of government did not suit the great families of Florence at all. Between 1341 and 1346 several of them were forced into bankruptcy ▲ *200*. The economic crisis worsened with the Black Death of 1348, which claimed half the city's population.

ARTI MAGGIORI VERSUS ARTI MINORI. The depression resulted in labor unrest, and in 1378 caused the rising of the Ciompi, the lowest paid workers in the wool industry who wanted the right to form their own guild. But the Arti Minori, or lower guilds, were soon able to channel this first urban workers' rebellion to their own ends. By 1382 the leaders of the Arti Maggiori had re-established their hold on power and retained it until 1434.

EXPANSION. With the return of prosperity came the renewed desire for more land, both towards the Apennines and the coast. Florence joined with other Tuscan cities to oppose the expansionist maneuvers of the duke of Milan, Gian-Galeazzo Visconti. Pisa was finally taken in 1406, giving Florence its own seaport.

Lorenzo the Magnificent
(1449–92).

RULERS IN DISGUISE. Undermined once more by internal disputes, the ruling oligarchy of wealthy families lost its hold on power. In 1434, after a year's exile, Cosimo de' Medici (1389–1464) made a triumphant return to Florence and from then on took gradual control of the city. The Medicis dominated Florence until 1494 ● *36*, without making any official changes to the existing republican system of government. Lorenzo (1449–92) followed Cosimo and, escaping the Pazzi conspiracy's attempt to assassinate him in 1478 ▲ *131*, increased his control over elections to high office and so gathered further power into his own hands.

A GOLDEN AGE OF PEACE AND PATRONAGE. Under the Medicis, Florence became the capital of Italian humanism. Painters, sculptors, architects, poets and men of letters gathered at the Medici court from all over Italy. The signing of the Treaty of Lodi in 1454 initiated a long period of peace in which the arts could flourish undisturbed. Lorenzo was an astute politician, but also a wise and respected arbiter whose influence was felt all over Italy. His son Piero, however, abandoned the traditional alliance with the French, and his indecision when Charles VIII crossed the Alps in 1494 nearly brought about the downfall of Florence. He was hounded out of office.

ITALY TORN APART BY WARS

SAVONAROLA'S FLORENCE. With his tireless oratory, the Dominican Girolamo Savonarola urged the citizens of Florence to adopt a pious life. In 1494 he also took a hand in politics, reviving the republic under a Grand Council accessible to the people. He was brought down by the powerful wealthy families and merchants who feared interference by the Pope. On May 23, 1498, he was burned at the stake in the Piazza della Signoria ▲ *143*.

THE PEOPLE VERSUS THE MEDICIS. The republic continued for more than ten years under Piero Soderini, who was elected "gonfaloniere for life" in 1502. But in 1512 the Spanish took the city and brought back the Medicis, who abolished the Grand Council but left the patricians in place. After the sack of Rome (1527) they were again removed from power, and a republic with a Grand Council was reinstated. In 1530 the republic held out in a heroic eight-month siege by the Spanish army, but on their surrender the Spaniards reinstated the Medicis. When Alessandro (1510–37) was assassinated by his cousin Lorenzino ● *37* Florence fell into the hands of Cosimo (1519–74).

1414–18
The Council of Constance ends the Great Schism of the West.

1447–50
Milan becomes a republic, and from 1450 the Sforza dynasty comes to power.

1453
Constantinople falls to the Turks.

1454
The Italian states make peace at Lodi.

1494
Charles VIII of France sparks off a series of wars in the Italian peninsula in his attempt to conquer Naples.

Left, Bernardo Baroncelli, hanged after the Pazzi conspiracy.

1513–21
The pontificate of Leo X (Giovanni de' Medici).

Savonarola at the stake.

1523–34
The pontificate of Clement VII.

1527
The sack of Rome.

1530
Clement VII names Charles V emperor of the Romans at Bologna.

THE GRAND DUKES OF FLORENCE (1537–1860)

The Medici-Lorraine coat of arms.

1545–63
The Council of Trent.

1556
The abdication of Charles V. Italy is left to the Spaniards.

1559
The Peace of Câteau-Cambrésis. France renounces all claim to Italy.

1701–13
The War of Spanish Succession between France and a coalition of European powers.

1706–7
France suffers defeats. Austria conquers the Milanese and the kingdom of Naples.

THE END OF THE CITY STATE. The city leaders thought Cosimo would do what they wanted, but they were wrong. He soon held most of the power. With the support of the emperor Charles V, he transformed Florence into a virtual principate. The conquest of Siena in 1555 united the region into one state. Cosimo was duke of Florence and became grand duke of Tuscany in 1569.

POLITICAL NEGLIGENCE AND DIMINISHING FORTUNE. Unfortunately, Cosimo's successors were not of his caliber apart from Ferdinando I (1587–1609). They formed alliances to strengthen their position, in particular with the kings of France. But they paid a high price for such support as trade in agricultural produce was strictly limited, hindering economic development. There was also new competition from the north in all areas of trade, especially textiles. Under Ferdinando II (1621–70) and Cosimo III (1670–1723) Florence suffered hardship and poverty among the lower classes. Despite his record of banishing the Jesuits, and abolishing the death penalty and secret police, Giovanni Gaston (above, 1723–37) showed little interest in public affairs, and died without an heir.

AN AGE OF REFORM. The grand duchy passed into the hands of imperial Austria in the form of Francesco of Lorraine (1737–65). The Age of Enlightenment had dawned, and he and his successor Pietro Leopoldo (1765–92) did much to modernize the Tuscan economy and bring in social reforms. Ferdinando III was removed by Napoleon's troops in 1799, and the city was given to Napoleon's sister Elisa Baciocchi, then brought into the empire in 1807. On Ferdinando's return in 1814 he upheld many Napoleonic reforms and ruled much as his father had done. His son Leopoldo II began in the same spirit, but the revolution of 1848 frightened him into a dictatorial style of government.

Elisa Baciocchi.

FLORENCE BECOMES THE CAPITAL OF ITALY

1736
The House of Lorraine exchanges Lorraine for Tuscany.

1797
The Treaty of Campo Formio. Napoleon expels the Austrians.

European society had already begun to converge on Florence during the Hapsburg-Lorraine rule. British culture had a strong influence, and the city kept up with the latest Parisian fashions. It also had its own group of intellectuals, a circle of free-thinking liberals. Certainly it was the cultural capital of an Italy that was now verging on unification. In 1859 the citizens of Florence expelled Grand Duke Leopoldo II and opted by plebiscite to join with Piedmont and Sardinia, soon

Uniforms of the
Grand-Ducal
army.

to be part of the newly united Italy. In 1865 Florence was chosen as temporary capital of the new country. Only Rome was still in the hands of the Pope. The city incurred enormous

debts during its five years as capital, and when Rome resumed the position, Florence subsequently fell into a long period of recession.

1801
Tuscany becomes the kingdom of Etruria.

1804–5
Napoleon crowned emperor and king of Italy.

1814–15
The Congress of Vienna brings back the Austrians.

1848–9
Revolutions throughout Europe. The first uprisings for Italian independence are put down by the Austrians.

1859
The second revolution in Italy.

FLORENCE IN MODERN TIMES

UP TO THE LIBERATION. At the beginning of the 20th century Florence once again became the center of Italian cultural activity. With the coming of Benito Mussolini and his particularly violent brand of Fascism, Florence was quick to react by both covert and overt opposition, which eventually developed into active resistance. A massive popular uprising in August 1944 liberated the city before the Allies got there, but not before the Germans had destroyed all the city's bridges except the Ponte Vecchio.

FROM THE END OF THE WAR TO THE PRESENT DAY.
From 1951 to 1966 the popular Christian Democrat mayor Giorgio La Pira exercised an enormous influence on the life of the city of Florence. There was some terrible unemployment after the war, but the state took over a good many businesses in order to create jobs, and it also subsidized the building of much new housing. The traditional Florentine community spirit emerged once again when the river Arno broke its banks on November 4, 1966, and flooded much of the city ▲ 173. However, in the decades that followed, Florence made the mistake of over-exploiting its enormous cultural heritage and obvious attraction for tourists at the expense of its own industry. Despite its substantial population (more than 400,000 inhabitants) Florence has lost ground to smaller but more dynamic towns in the region, such as Prato, which are now important centers of activity.

1861
Italy is proclaimed a kingdom.

1915
Italy enters the First World War on the side of the Allies.

1922
The March on Rome. The beginning of the Fascist era.

1946
Italy becomes a republic.

The hostility between Guelfs and Ghibellines had its origins in the German conflict between the dukes of Bavaria and the imperial family of Hohenstaufen. As enemies of the emperor, the dukes and their allies sided with the Pope in the Investiture Controversy. Later, when the Italian *comuni* ● *28* stood up to the Hohenstaufens, the same conflict spread to Italy, where it degenerated into family rivalries and wars between the *comuni*.

THE INVESTITURE CONTROVERSY ● *28*
In 1059 Pope Nicholas II issued a decree which forbade the investiture of bishops by any secular powers. This ruling was upheld by his successors, and Emperor Henry IV responded by declaring Pope Gregory VII deposed. Henry was excommunicated and then pardoned at Canossa, but he finally forced Gregory to leave Rome. The conflict was eventually resolved in 1122 by the Concordat of Worms.

THE ORIGINS OF THE NAMES
The term "Ghibelline" came from Weiblingen, the name of the Hohenstaufen castle in Germany. "Guelf" goes back to Welf, the family name of the dukes of Bavaria, who took the side of the Pope against the imperial family.

1076–1122. The Investiture Controversy.
1138–1254. The imperial throne returns to the Hohenstaufens, who are kings of Sicily from 1195–1266.
1154–83. Emperor Frederick Barbarossa and the Italian *comuni* at war.
1167. With support from Pope Alexander III, the *comuni* of Lombardy form a league against Barbarossa.
1216. The war reaches Florence.
1226. The civic republics of Lombardy reform their alliance.
1237. Frederick II defeats the united troops.
1237–40. The Ghibellines govern Florence.
1240–60. The Guelfs govern Florence.
1250. The Guelf standard, a red lily on a white background, becomes the emblem of Florence. The Ghibelline standard was the same with colors reversed.
1258. Manfred, illegitimate son of Frederick II, usurps the throne of Sicily from his cousin Conradin, and reopens the Ghibelline conflict across Italy.
1260. The Battle of Montaperti. Manfred leads the Ghibellines to victory over Florence.
1260–8. The Ghibellines govern Florence once more.
1265. The Pope summons Charles of Anjou into Italy to make war on the Hohenstaufen faction.
1266. The Battle of Benevento. Aided by the Guelfs, Charles of Anjou defeats Manfred, who is killed in battle. In 1268 he defeats and executes Conradin, and takes the throne of Sicily.
c. 1300. The Guelfs split into Whites and Blacks.

FARINATA DEGLI UBERTI

After the victory at Montaperti, Manfred wanted Florence destroyed. Farinata, although leader of the victorious Ghibellines, declared that he would stand against them. He saved the city.

THE BATTLE OF MONTAPERTI

In 1260 the Sienese, with Manfred, his troops and the Ghibellines (including some Florentines), inflicted a crushing defeat on Florence. On Farinata's orders, the Florentine Ghibellines re-entered their city.

CITIES AT WAR

United at first against the emperor, the *comuni* next began to fight among themselves. What was worse, within each city rivalries developed between individual Guelf and Ghibelline families. Florence was, on the whole, a Guelf city.

WHITE AND BLACK GUELFS

Once the Ghibellines had been expelled, the Guelf faction divided into Whites, hostile to papal supremacy, and Blacks, who supported the Pope. The Whites were banished in 1302 but most returned in 1311. Dante ▲ *107* was one of the few who did not.

A BLOODY EASTER

In 1216 a quarrel developed between two Florentine *consorterie* (groups of noble families). To avoid punishment by the *comune*, they turned the dispute into a political matter involving the entire ruling class. A marriage was set up between a Fifanti and a Buondelmonte in an attempt to reconcile two key families. But the Buondelmonte husband was lured into marrying a Donati, a bitter insult to his bride and all the Fifanti-Amidei. That Easter, in revenge, the *consorteria* had him murdered. This started the conflict between the Guelfs and Ghibellines.

THE COAT OF ARMS
Palle, palle, palle was the war cry of the Medicis, a reference to the balls (*palle*) on their armorial bearings. These were in fact bezants, coins originally from Byzantium. The arms seem to have been inspired by those of the Guild of Money-changers ▲ 199 to which the Medicis belonged.

The Medicis originally came from Mugello. They settled in Florence in the 12th century. Their rise to wealth and power began in the mid-14th century, and they gradually amassed an immense fortune. One of them, Salvestro, supported the rising of the Ciompi ● *30*, earning his descendants a reputation as defenders of the common people. But Giovanni di Bicci was the true founder of the dynasty. Within a century and a half these newly rich merchants were on familiar terms with the royal families of Europe. The family provided two popes and two queens of France.

GIOVANNI D'AVERARDO, KNOWN AS DI BICCI (1360–1429)

COSIMO IL VECCHIO (1389–1464)
An astute businessman who kept personal control of the companies in which he had a main share, and multiplied his fortune by ten. He led the opposition to the ruling elite and then, with popular support, he ruled Florence in all but name. He was a great patron of the arts.

PIERO IL GOTTOSO (1416–69)
Gifted in business like his father, he took over leadership of the republic (1464–9).

GIOVANNI (1421–63)

CARLO († 1492)

LORENZO IL MAGNIFICO (1449–92)

GIULIANO (1453–78)

PIETRO II (1472–1503)
Lacking wealth to back his power, and political ability to secure his position, he was driven out of Florence.

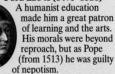

GIOVANNI DE' MEDICI, POPE LEO X (1475–1521)
A humanist education made him a great patron of learning and the arts. His morals were beyond reproach, but as Pope (from 1513) he was guilty of nepotism.

GIULIANO, DUKE OF NEMOURS (1479–1516)

IPPOLITO, CARDINAL (1511–35)

GIULIO (1478–1534), POPE CLEMENT VII FROM 15
His refusal to cooperate wi Charles V caused the Medic to be removed from power after the sack of Rome.

LORENZO II, DUKE OF URBINO (1492-1519)

ALESSANDRO (1511–37)
Pope Leo X made him Duke of Urbino, and he governed Florence from 1530 to 1537. He asked Cellini to cast a new coin with his image to replace the old republican florin. Young and impressionable, Alessandro allowed Leo X and other powerful men to make his decisions for him. He was murdered by his cousin Lorenzino.

CATARINA DE' MEDICI (1519–89)
Wife of King Henry II of France, in 1560 she became regent when her second son, Charles IX, inherited the French throne. After he came of age, and then later under the reign of a third son, Henry III, she continued to wield considerable influence. Royal power was severely threatened during the French religious wars, but her political cunning kept the unstable monarchy in place.

LORENZO IL MAGNIFICO
His humanist education made him not only a patron of the arts, but a true intellectual. He was not good at business, but his genius for diplomacy proved crucial in negotiations between the various Italian powers. He wanted to found a royal dynasty and married into the ancient and noble Roman family of Orsini. But his key move for the future of the Medici family was to make his son Giovanni a cardinal at the age of 14.

Maria de' Medici became the second wife of Henry IV of France in 1600.

MARIA DE' MEDICI
When the king died in 1610, she became regent and assumed full control. But Maria put the monarchy in great danger by handing over the reins of power to her minister Concini. Her son, Louis XIII, had Concini assassinated in 1617, and was forced to exile his mother, who twice joined with rebellious nobles to take up arms against him.

married Piccarda di Odoardo Bueri

LORENZO (1395–1440)

PIER-FRANCESCO († 1467)

LORENZO († 1503), LORD OF PIOMBINO

GIOVANNI (1467–98)

PIER-FRANCESCO (1487–1525)

GIOVANNI DELLE BANDE NERE (1498–1526)
On the death of Leo X, he took the black banner and led the papal armies against the imperial forces. Admired by Machiavelli ● 39 and his friend Aretino as the greatest Italian condottiere of the time. Wounded by the Duke of Ferrara's troops, his leg was amputated and he died aged 28.

LORENZINO (1514–47)
He may have murdered Alessandro for a political motive, as in de Musset's play, or for personal reasons, because Alessandro had caused the ruin of his family. Whatever the motive, it was a deranged and pointless act.

COSIMO I (1519–74)
Imposing order on turbulent Florence, he said "I would rather lose people than lose the city". A despot, but an enlightened one, he commissioned Vasari to decorate the Palazzo Vecchio and to build the Uffizi. He was the first grand duke of Tuscany.

FRANCESCO I, GRAND DUKE (1541–87)

FERDINANDO I, GRAND DUKE (1549–1609)

MARIA DE' MEDICI (1575–1642)

COSIMO II, GRAND DUKE (1590–1621)

CARDINAL LEOPOLDO (1617–75)

FERDINANDO II, GRAND DUKE (1610–70)

COSIMO III, GRAND DUKE (1642–1723)

GIAN GASTONE (1671–1737)
The last Medici grand duke. He was not interested in politics, although he did abolish the death penalty and the secret police. He agreed to the succession of Francesco I of Lorraine.

ANNA MARIA-LUDOVICA (1667–1743)

● LANGUAGE AND LITERATURE

The Tuscan language was the predecessor of the language now known as Italian. It gained much of its importance through its literature. For two and a half centuries Florence dominated the cultural life of the peninsula, and by the 16th century its language was accepted as the language of literature. But it was not until the 19th century that the language spoken by educated Tuscans spread to become the language of a new nation.

THE FIRST TEXTS: THE 13TH CENTURY

In the first half of the 13th century Florence was preoccupied with the development of trade. Then interests began to broaden, especially under the lively influence of Latini.
BRUNETTO LATINI (1220–94). Latini was exiled to Paris from 1260 to 1266 and became a link between France and Tuscany. He wrote the *Trésor* (in French) and the *Tesoretto* and contributed to the development of allegorical and didactic poetry, along with a tradition of rhetoric upon which the "dolce stil nuovo" and *Divine Comedy* were based.
THE "DOLCE STIL NUOVO" (1270–1310) ● *204*. Although in theory they continued the Provençal tradition and counted themselves members of the Sicilian School of Frederico II's reign, the Florentine writers went their own way. They used all their knowledge of science and philosophy in a delicate and detailed analysis of love. Among them were Guido Cavalcanti and the young Dante.
THE CHRONICLERS. These were men of the merchant class whose involvement in city affairs inspired them to write tales in the vulgar tongue. Some, such as Dino Compagni (d. 1324), wrote about local conflicts and rivalries; others, like Giovanni Villani (d. 1348), took much wider European events as their subject.

THE THREE JEWELS IN THE CROWN

DANTE ALIGHIERI (1265–1321). Dante's *Divine Comedy* is one of the great works of world literature, and it was also proof that in literature the vulgar tongue could rival Latin. He had already defended his argument in two unfinished treatises, *De vulgari eloquentia* and *Convivio*. But to prove his point it needed the *Divine Comedy*, "this masterpiece in which Italians rediscovered their language in sublime form" (Bruno Migliorini).
PETRARCH (1304–74). Francesco Petrarca was born in Arezzo, since his father was in exile from Florence. He was a passionate admirer of ancient Roman civilization and one of the great early Renaissance humanists, creating a Republic of Letters. His philological work was highly respected, as were his translations from Latin into the Vulgate, and also his own Latin works. But it is his love poetry, written in the vulgar tongue, that keeps his name alive

D A N T E

Lorenzo the Magnificent surrounded by artists, scholars and philosophers.

today. His *Canzoniere* had enormous influence on the poets of the 15th and 16th centuries.

BOCCACCIO (1313–75). This was a man from the rising commercial classes, whose *Decameron* has been described as a "merchant's epic". It consists of one hundred stories told by characters who are also part of a story that provides the setting for the whole, much like *The Arabian Nights*. The work was to become a model for fiction and prose writing. Boccaccio was the first to write a commentary on Dante, and he was also a friend and disciple of Petrarch. Around him gathered enthusiasts of the new humanism.

A scene from Boccaccio's *Decameron*.

HUMANISM

CIVIC HUMANISM. Florentine men of letters living in the late 14th- and early 15th-century republic had a strong sense of civic responsibility. Men such as Coluccio Salutati (1331–1406) and Leonardo Bruni (1370–1444) believed that knowledge of classical civilization was vital to the defense of the *florentina libertas* ● *30*.

PHILOSOPHICAL HUMANISM. After 1434 the atmosphere changed ● *31* as Lorenzo centered the cultural life of the city on his court. Marsilio Ficino (1433–99), who translated Plato into Latin, formed a Platonic Academy (1463). Cristoforo Landini and Pico della Mirandola were other exponents of this neo-Platonism that attempted to combine Greek thought with Christianity, and which spread throughout Europe. The eminent Greek scholar and man of letters Angelo Ambrogini, known as Poliziano, wrote poems in the Vulgate, as did Lorenzo himself. However, Luigi Pulci, author of the humorous courtly poem *Morgante*, was rather out of place in these refined circles. Latin returned to favor under the humanists, some of them rejecting outright the great writers of the 14th century. But thanks to Lorenzo and those close to him this attitude fell out of fashion as the 15th century progressed. In the last decades the vulgar tongue regained ascendance over Latin, and the battle was won. In fact, in the 16th century the language used by the major writers was not very different from that which could be heard in the streets of Florence.

LEON BATTISTA ALBERTI (1404–72) Born at Genoa into a great Florentine family in exile, Alberti is best known for his work as an architect and for his theoretical writings on art (especially *Della Pittura*). He was also a writer on more general, moral topics. Author of the first Italian grammar, he defended the Vulgate at a time when Latin ruled supreme, and he wrote in both tongues. His major work, *I Libri della famiglia*, combines both Latin and Tuscan terms.

INSTABILITY AND SPLENDOR: THE 16TH CENTURY

POLITICAL THINKERS. The instability that followed the death of Lorenzo stimulated intense political discourse. In *The Prince*, NICCOLÒ MACHIAVELLI (1469–1527) argued in favor of political autonomy. In his *Discourses on the First Decade of Titus Livius* he defended the republican ideal, and in *Florentine Histories* he took a critical look at the history of his city. He

● LANGUAGE AND LITERATURE

RENAISSANCE ARTISTS
At the beginning of the 15th century a number of respected artists tried their hand at writing. It was a sign of their changing status. Michelangelo wrote sonnets, Leonardo da Vinci was the author of scientific works, sonnets and tales, Benvenuto Cellini's autobiography is famous; and Giorgio Vasari's history of art, *Lives of the Great Painters, Sculptors and Architects,* was the first great work on the subject, and was unsurpassed until the 19th century. These men were not primarily writers, but they helped fashion the new written Italian.

"LA CRUSCA"
The name "Crusca" was metaphorical. The Academy's goal was to sift the wheat from the chaff (*crusca*), in other words to purify the Italian language.

also wrote biting comedies like *La Mandragola*. FRANCESCO GUICCIARDINI (1483–1540) was also a political writer, but firmly unaligned. He wrote a brief criticism of Machiavelli, but is remembered as Italy's first modern historian for his *History of Italy*.

PIETRO BEMBO (1470–1547). The most important literary event of the 16th century did not actually take place in Florence. In 1525 the Venetian Pietro Bembo set out his proposals for a standardized language and style: Petrarch and Boccaccio were his models and thus became the modern classics. So the language of Italian literature is modeled on that spoken in Florence in the 15th century.

FLORENCE UNDER THE GRAND DUKES (1634–1860)

Florence gradually withdrew into itself, although Giovanni della Casa's manual of etiquette *Galateo* was read all over Europe. Leonardi Salviati founded his Accademia della Crusca, which in 1612 published a gigantic dictionary setting down rules for written Italian and taking its examples exclusively from writers of the 14th and 15th centuries. As a result the language of Italian literature remained frozen until the 19th century. One man came to the fore in the decadent years of the 17th century – the great astronomer Galileo Galilei (1564–1642), who began writing about science in a new way. The 18th and 19th centuries produced little literature of note.

TUSCAN BECOMES THE NEW ITALIAN. The standardization of Italian based on the language of the 14th-century masters was a purely literary phenomenon. Italy was still a land of regional dialects. When the Milanese author Alessandro Manzoni (1785–1873) wrote his epic *The Betrothed* he became seriously worried by the lack of a unifying language, a thing writers elsewhere took for granted. Once again he took Tuscan as his model and spent time there absorbing the spoken language. "Thus the living breathing language of a city became the living, breathing language of a nation" (Gian Luigi Beccaria).

LA "GORGIA TOSCANA"

The Italian spoken in Florence has a particular distinguishing feature. The hard "*c*" between two vowels is aspirated. Thus *amico* (friend) becomes "amiho"; *domenica* (Sunday) is

another example. This is also the case if the hard "*c*" comes at the beginning of a new word preceded by an article ending in a vowel, as with la *casa* (house) or *i cavalli* (horses). The Tuscans also employ several old-fashioned terms that have fallen out of use elsewhere.

ARTS AND TRADITIONS

In the Palazzo Davanzati ▲ *205*, the so-called *Pappagalli Room* (the Room of Parrots) is a rare surviving example of a 14th-century painted room.

In the 14th century the walls of the rooms in some grand houses began to be decorated. They were painted with geometrical designs, false curtains, flowers, fruit and so forth. During the following century the furniture became steadily more ornate, and a large chest would often provide the centerpiece of a room. The walls were panelled, and above them ran a decorative feature that Vasari called the cornice. Like the cornices and the chests, the panelling was decorated with figurative scenes, sometimes the work of a famous artist of the day.

A LARGE BED
Beds grew in size during the 15th and 16th centuries. The boxed sides disappeared, and the medieval canopy no longer enclosed the whole. Instead, beds were left open to the surrounding room, and so became a decorative feature.

WEDDING CHESTS

On her wedding day, a young bride from a rich or noble family would arrive at her husband's house, followed by these large chests (*cassone*) containing her trousseau.

IMPASTO

Impasto became an alternative to painting as a technique for decorating furniture in the 15th century. The wood was covered with a fine cloth which was then coated with several layers of a paste made of plaster, powdered marble and glue.

A TUSCAN BUFFET

Several woods could be used to make a single piece of furniture. Walnut (good for inlays), cherry, beech and even pine were popular. In the buffet below, the columns at the corners rest on a high projecting base.

Relief-work was made with the same mixture, following the outlines of a design. A wash of oil and glue was then applied before the final gold leaf or color. Any extra decoration was done with a fine chisel. Shown above is an early 15th-century chest decorated with three scenes that depict the history of Paris.

AN "ARMADINO"
(SMALL CUPBOARD)

Inlaid furniture from the 14th century was often of eastern appearance. The designs were usually geometric and made of wood, bone or mother-of-pearl. Painted decoration became more common in the 15th century, followed by inlaid figurative designs. The 16th century brought cunning tricks using perspective. Scenes were often copied from cartoons and even used light and shade effects.

A TRADITIONAL BENCH SEAT

From the basic, heavy Tuscan chest came the bench chest, complete with back and arms, and from this the straightforward bench. The shape gradually became more elegant and lighter, decorated with a frieze or coat of arms.

Florentine dress in the 14th century was of near-monastic simplicity, but toward the end of this period sumptuary laws regulating private expenditure brought about a major change. Elegant clothes began to appear in the city, though the sober-minded Florentines were always opposed to too much eccentricity. The fashion grew in the second half of the 15th century, but fifty years of conflict were soon to put Italy under foreign domination. The fall of the last Florentine republic in 1530 ● *31* marked the beginning of a new era, with the city open to foreign influences.

THE "LUCCO" AND THE TUNIC

Older men and those with an important position in society wore the *lucco*, a long gown of black or purple cloth with wide sleeves and a hood, buttons down the front and no belt. Well-off young men preferred to dress in short tunics, with a belt knotted at the waist and woollen, silk or velvet hose, the legs of which could be of different colors, and sheepskin or chamois boots.

THE DRESS OF A 15TH-CENTURY LADY

Noble ladies wore flowing silk dresses trimmed with gold, leather or soft skin slippers, linen purses decorated with embroidery or appliqué work, and costly jewelry.

THE DRESS OF A 16TH-CENTURY LADY

Eleanor of Toledo, wife of Cosimo I de' Medici, loved dresses of "velvet pricked with gold". In accordance with contemporary fashion, she wore jewelry, carried accessories like a handkerchief, fan and scented gloves, and had her hair in a pearl net.

Cosimo I de' Medici (1519–74), the first grand duke of Tuscany, wore clothes no less elegant than those of his wife.

FOREIGN INFLUENCES

As a young man, Cosimo I "liked to dress in Florentine style, with coat and cape rather after the Spanish fashion." As he grew older, he preferred "reddish-brown or beige colors", and wore a French-style knee-length coat over a gathered tunic, stockings and short, wide trousers.

During the Renaissance, great artists would spend time and effort designing theater costumes and even some new fashions.

COURT FASHIONS

Lorenzo de' Medici (1449–92), dressed in an embroidered tunic stitched with pearls and precious stones. He wears his hair long and curled in the fashion then current among the Florentine youth, who used curling tongs and bleached their hair blond. The men around him are wearing quilted doublets and tabards lined with silk or fur.

Sketch for a dress by Pisanello (1395–1455).

HEADGEAR

There was a variety of head coverings available to men of rank. The man in the center wears a *cupolino tondo* (little round dome), usually made of red, black or brown felt. The flanking figures each wear a *mazzocchino*, a woollen cloth rolled into a crown with the free end drooping down. Less important men also wore pointed caps called "cut cones".

45

CARNIVAL
In 1886 the young people of Florence decided to transform the old ghetto into an oriental bazaar, for an "Arabian Night".

On the face of it, the festival spirit seems more in keeping with a light-hearted and eccentric city like Venice than with sober Florence. And yet few places have indulged in ceremony and display to the extent that was once the case here. There was a succession of religious, civil and military ceremonies, along with popular festivals and sporting events. Solemn processions, religious spectacles and performances, firework displays, horse races, ball games and dances all became vehicles for public rejoicing and spontaneous fun, and served to strengthen the vital link between the city and its people.

THE "PALIO DEI COCCHI"
This chariot race, modeled on the games in ancient Rome, was inaugurated by Cosimo I in 1563. Each chariot was drawn by a pair of horses, and the course was three circuits of the Piazza Santa Maria Novella. The winner was presented with a banner (*palio*) of silk or velvet.

The "Joust of the Saracen", which used to take place in Florentine piazzas, still goes on in Arezzo and other Italian towns.

"GIOSTRA DEL SARACINO"
A knight in armor had to hit the head or heart of the "Saracen", a wooden effigy of a Moor. If he missed, he could well end up being unseated.

"LA RIFICOLONA"
This festival, imported from the Austrians, is still celebrated each September 7.

"CALCIO STORICO"
This game, with two teams of twenty-seven men each, goes right back to antiquity. It was played in streets and squares at times of public celebration and important marriages. It is still played in medieval costume in the Piazza della Signoria.

On that day each window is lit by a lamp in honor of the Virgin, while other lamps, on very long poles, are taken around the city streets in procession. These simple paper lanterns containing a candle, called *rificolone,* are designed in imaginative and unusual shapes.

THE "PALIO DEI BARBERI"
This ancient horse race was one of the great Florentine spectacles until 1858.

"SCOPPIO DEL CARRO" OR "THE EXPLODING WAGON"
The origins of this ceremony go back to the 12th century. In 1101 Pazzo de' Pazzi, the first crusader to plant the Christian flag on the walls of Jerusalem, brought three stones from Christ's tomb back to Florence. Sparks were struck from these to relight lamps that had been extinguished on Good Friday, in celebration of Christ's resurrection. On each Easter Saturday since the 16th century (now Easter Day) the custom is to set fire to a cart loaded with fireworks in front of the church of Santa Maria del Fiore. An artificial dove slides down a wire from the high altar and ignites the firecrackers.

Along with racing, jousting and other sports that were features of the city's festivals and celebrations, there were also the regular pastimes enjoyed by the common people. Many were played by youths from all over the city who kept the old traditions alive. Some games had a definite fighting spirit, such as *sassaiole*, which involved throwing volleys of stones at rival gangs. Other less violent pastimes pandered to the Florentine fondness for practical jokes, like the game of Ladders which was played during Lent. The aim was either to draw or to fasten a ladder onto the back of a passer-by. But there were many gentler games as well, and group recreations for all ages that the family could play together in the open air or when gathered around the fireside.

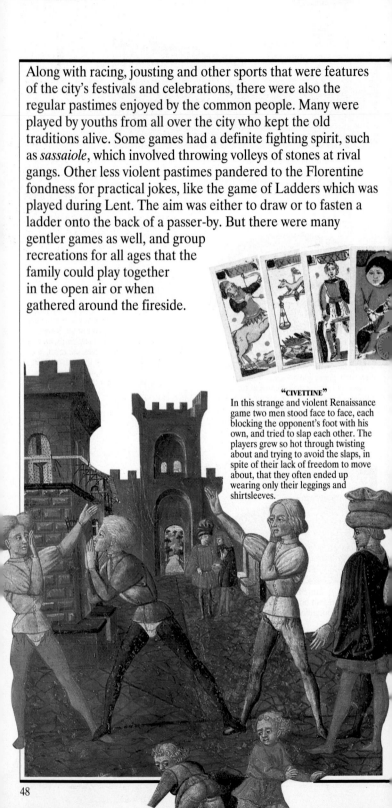

"CIVETTINE"

In this strange and violent Renaissance game two men stood face to face, each blocking the opponent's foot with his own, and tried to slap each other. The players grew so hot through twisting about and trying to avoid the slaps, in spite of their lack of freedom to move about, that they often ended up wearing only their leggings and shirtsleeves.

THE GAME OF BOWLS OR "PALLOTTOLE"

March 21 was the feast day of St Benedict, to whom the Florentines were particularly devoted. Close to the parish church consecrated in his name was the square known in the 17th century as *Pallottole*, after a game which had already been popular for more than two centuries. According to some historians, this kind of bowling, an ancestor of skittles, originated in Florence.

"MINCHIATE"

The game of *minchiate*, a Florentine version of Tarot, used a pack of seventy-eight cards (14 coins, 22 trophies, 14 cups, 14 swords and 14 sticks), each with different values. The trophy cards were particularly interesting since they featured pictures of people or objects. There was the emperor and the empress, the pope, the hanged man, the house, the sun, the moon, and the stars. The designs on some of the more ancient packs provide invaluable information about the Florentine history of costume. The game is for three or four people, the first player to score 100 points being the winner. As with Tarot packs, the cards were also used to predict the future.

Card games, especially *minchiate*, were popular by the start of the 15th century. Card-playing is still a favorite pastime in many Florentine families today.

● MUSIC AND DANCE

Francesco Landini (1325–97), the city's virtuoso organist.

By the 15th century Florence was one of the most important musical centers in Europe. In addition to the tradition of vocal music, under the inspiration of Lorenzo the Magnificent instruments such as the harpsichord, organ, viols, lute, harp and horn became fashionable. Around the year 1600, thanks to a society of Florentine intellectuals, an entirely new art form emerged – opera. There was also a flourishing tradition of popular music, which developed between the 15th and 18th centuries, and expanded into the production of all kinds of festive and dance music to enliven public celebrations.

THE "CAMARETA FIORENTINA" OR "CAMARETA DI CASA BARDI"

Founded in 1576 under the patronage of Giovanni de' Bardi, the society numbered among its members the composers Vincenzo Galilei, Jacopo Peri and Emilio de' Cavalieri, and the poet Ottavio Rinuccini. Inspired by Plato's writings (whose aim was to elevate the listener's soul) and by Greek tragedy, the *Camerata* set out to change the language of music. Theirs was essentially a declamatory style, with words having to be clearly audible above the music that supported them.

THE "CALENDIMAGGIO" OR SPRING FESTIVAL

During the Renaissance the spring was the season for light-hearted singing and dancing of all kinds. In the second half of the 14th century Florentine youths and maidens took part in daily *cocchiate* ● 46, where singers and musicians paraded on illuminated wagons. Then they competed among themselves, singing verses accompanied on a lute or *calascione* (an early popular string instrument).

CARNIVAL SONGS

In the time of Lorenzo Florence's carnival was an event of unrivalled magnificence. Lorenzo devised spectacles of ever-increasing complexity, with parades and processions of breathtaking splendor and extravagance. In place of the old *canzone di ballo* (songs to be danced to) came carnival songs written either by himself or by Poliziano ● *39*. These were songs in three or four parts alternating homophony and counterpoint. Their texts were amorous, sometimes to the point of indecency, with classical and topical allusions.

MUSIC IN MAYTIME FLORENCE

Florence's great musical traditions continue to flourish. The home of classical music is the Teatro Communale, but the reason the city is musically so important today is the *Maggio Musicale*, founded in 1933 to promote the classical repertoire. The most celebrated conductors and companies still perform there today.

THE ANCIENT COURT DANCES

The Renaissance standardized what was to become a long musical tradition of formal court dances, the most important of which was the *bassa danza*. These generally had a lute accompaniment, and the intricate formal steps only added to the fun. Many were evolved at the court of Lorenzo the Magnificent, such as the *Pavane* (a solemn stately dance), the *Galliard* (a lively dance in triple time) and the *Allemande* (a moderately fast dance of German origin – as its name implies).

● THE "ARTI", OR GUILDS

Tradesmen, such as the grain merchants (above), were excluded from the guilds since membership entailed payment of high fees that were beyond the means of the more modest businesses and craftsmen.

These organizations had important legal powers and existed to protect the interests of certain professions, and to define their codes of practice. They grew out of the *Societas Mercatorum*, which was founded in the 12th century. At first this was a general merchants' guild, but toward the end of the century it broke into different groups with a total of seven *Arti Maggiori*, or Greater Guilds. Alongside these were the Lesser Guilds. The former represented the wealthy businessmen and the professions, while the latter protected the interests of the better-off tradesmen. Their political power was in direct relation to their economic stature.

THE GUILD OF PHYSICIANS AND APOTHECARIES
With the proclamation of the "Orders of Justice" (1293) ● *29*, anyone wishing to take part in political life and hold public office had to be a member of the Guelf party, and also belong to a guild. Mastery of the trade was not necessary. Dante was of noble birth and chose the Guild of Physicians; Giotto was a member of the same fraternity because apothecaries sold pigments and spices as well as medicinal herbs.

THE GUILD OF WOOL WEAVERS
By 1340 this guild had overtaken the Calimala ▲ *201* as the foremost of the *Arti*. More than a third of the city's population was connected with the trade, and the guild controlled the import of raw materials. Its supremacy continued until the end of the 16th century. Like other guilds, it guaranteed its members the monopoly of a specific product or business, maintaining high standards of workmanship and honesty. Like them, too, it was headed by two consuls in a six-month term of office, aided by two councils.

The goldsmith was more an artist than a mere craftsman, highly respected by his clients and generally well rewarded for his work. Depicted right is Benvenuto Cellini (1500–71) at work.

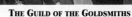

THE GUILD OF JUDGES AND NOTARIES

This guild was highly revered. The other guilds relied on its services as it had the authority to try, judge and condemn anyone contravening their articles of association. Notaries assisted judges during trials, and drew up contracts and articles of association, as well as ensuring that these were not infringed.

THE GUILD OF THE CALIMALA

As the first guild to be formed, the Calimala combined manufacture with lucrative trade (cloth was refined in Florence and exported throughout the civilized world, together with exotic goods of all kinds). Due to its foreign contacts and skill at financial transactions, it also became a guild of bankers ▲ 199.

THE GUILD OF THE GOLDSMITHS

The goldsmiths could manufacture a luxury version of anything, from swords to salvers. They cut gemstones, designed gold plate, and even decorated furniture and chimney-pieces. Donatello, Lucca della Robbia and Benvenuto Cellini all began work as goldsmiths.

THE LEATHERWORKERS

Before they merged into the Guild of Master Leatherworkers in 1534, there were three separate guilds serving different parts of the leather trade – tanners, curriers and shoemakers. Membership rose to more than 2,800. Shoe production remains an important trade in Florence, especially for export.

RESTORATION WORK, OR THE OPIFICIO DELLE PIETRE DURE

L'Opificio delle Pietre Dure ▲ *239* originated in the workshops founded in 1588 by the Grand Duke Ferdinando I de' Medici. Their original function was to restore *pietra dura* mosaics (a fine variety of mosaic using hard and often precious stones, such as agate, amethyst and cornelian). A workshop for picture restoration was added later, under the guardianship of the Superintendent of Florentine Galleries, and from 1975 it began accepting all kinds of restoration work. The Institute is now housed in several buildings, with a world-famous teaching department and a modern laboratory. Works of art are sent here from all over the world, and the restorers may travel anywhere in Italy to work on objects too big or too fragile to be moved.

TAPESTRIES AND OTHER TEXTILES
The tapestry is first immersed in a weak detergent solution, and then stretched out to dry on a perforated surface. Pieces of material can be applied to the back of the tapestry to help reinforce it, or it may even have to be rewoven.

Repairs to textiles of all kinds – they are first vacuum-cleaned and then washed in plain water – are effected by stitching or using adhesive patches. It may sometimes prove impossible to weave replacement parts if the original is made of very fine thread.

CARVED AND PAINTED WOOD
The type of wood used and the manner in which it was worked before being painted determines the appropriate method of restoration. Biological damage, such as mold or woodworm, calls for a thorough cleansing by coating with a volatile liquid, or by a spell in a vacuum chamber. Badly rotted wood may require injections of resin to harden it.

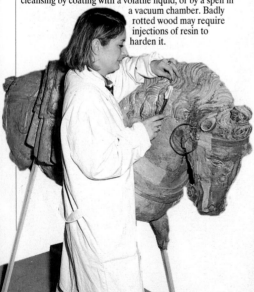

FURNITURE
Liable to warp, crack, break or simply come apart, woodwork often requires the aid of a master carpenter. Cracks are repaired by inserting small triangular pieces of wood across the grain. Pieces that have fallen apart are reassembled using mortise and tenon joints.

A mosaic in *pietra dura*.

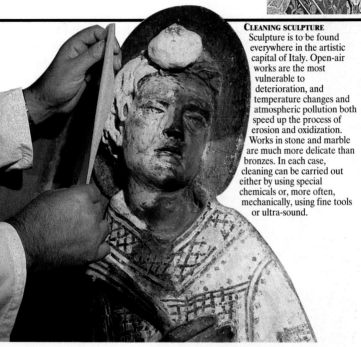

CLEANING SCULPTURE

Sculpture is to be found everywhere in the artistic capital of Italy. Open-air works are the most vulnerable to deterioration, and temperature changes and atmospheric pollution both speed up the process of erosion and oxidization. Works in stone and marble are much more delicate than bronzes. In each case, cleaning can be carried out either by using special chemicals or, more often, mechanically, using fine tools or ultra-sound.

STONE, MARBLE AND BRONZE

Once the corrosion has been completely removed, the work of restoration can begin. Last of all, in order to minimize future corrosion, a protective coating is applied which helps to preserve the natural patina.

PAINTING

The original painting may be given an additional canvas backing to help reinforce it. The colors are chemically revived and preserved. Cleaning is carried out either using solvents, or with the aid of an extremely fine blade.

RETOUCHING

Missing patches of color on a work of art can be filled in by a meticulous process of retouching (the joins are carefully tapered). This is possible thanks to a technique known as *tratteggio*, inspired by an early Italian practice.

"TRATTEGGIO"

This process takes place on a white mastic base. Fine lines of pure colors are painted in vertical and horizontal strokes to blend with the original. A modified *tratteggio* uses subtler tones to replace missing outlines and give a three-dimensional effect.

The ceramic industry in Florence expanded rapidly during the 15th century, starting with articles for medical use and developing into a broader range to produce goods for private customers. But in the second half of the century the city allowed its lead to pass to small towns in the surrounding countryside, such as Montelupo. This resulted in a wider variety of shapes and colors. The so-called Cafaggiolo School, which started in the early 16th century, produced pieces that were particularly elegant in shape.

JUG FROM MONTELUPO

Between the end of the 15th century and the first decades of the 16th the pottery industry at Montelupo came to the fore, and its workshops attracted some important clients. The Medicis and other noble Florentine families ordered jugs, plates and bowls decorated with their armorial bearings. The jugs, which came in different sizes, had a neck shaped like a clover-leaf and were decorated predominantly in blue, green and orange. The designs usually consisted of rhomboid geometric shapes inside a circle.

LARGE MEDICI BOWL

Certain large bowls made in the workshops of Francesco I de' Medici are outstandingly fine, delicate objects. Made of soft porcelain paste largely composed of white clay, they still win the admiration of experts in the field. Here, the center bears a painting of an Evangelist, surrounded by fluted decoration derived from classical models. The characteristic turquoise color is quite without precedent.

CAFAGGIOLO POTTERY
Production probably began here at the end of the 15th century in response to the initiative of a branch of the Medici family. The decorations used were drawn from allegorical or mythological subjects.

**MONTELUPO PLATE
(17TH CENTURY)**

CAFAGGIOLO JUG
Some of the finest objects to come out of the Medici workshops at Cafaggiolo were the two-handled jugs, both large and small. Pieces from the period 1600–30 have distinctive twisted handles, patterns of leaves in relief, and grotesque masks. Favorite colors were turquoise, bright yellow and orange.

PLATE WITH PORCELAIN-STYLE DECORATION
Designed for everyday use, a plate like this with a large flat surface could be decorated in a variety of ways, often with floral or geometric patterns.

MEDICI PORCELAIN
At the end of the 16th century, Francesco I de' Medici commissioned craftsmen from Urbino and Faenza to create a precious porcelain unlike any that already existed. This was the origin of "Medici porcelain", the first soft-paste porcelain in the West, and the result of a process of precise and delicate firing.

The cuisine of Tuscany is essentially a rustic style of cooking, and one which makes much use of olive oil and white haricot beans. Tuscans rely on their superb olive oil to bring out the flavor in a dish, and beans are so much a part of their food that Tuscans are known as *mangiafagioli*, or "bean-eaters". *Ribollita* uses both these ingredients. Using vegetables in season, peasants would make a pot of soup that would last the week, to be heated up afresh each day – hence its name, which literally means "recooked".

2. Coarsely chop the carrot, celery, tomato and leek, and add to the onions.

3. When they are lightly browned, add the beans, the ham and about 4 pints of water.

6. Press the beans through a sieve, so that you obtain a thick purée.

7. Add the purée to the other ingredients, together with the roughly sliced cabbage leaves. Cook for a short time over a gentle heat.

10. Ladle the soup over the slices of garlic toast in individual bowls. Sprinkle plenty of grated Parmesan over the top.

INGREDIENTS (for 6 to 8 people)
2½ lbs white haricot beans (soaked)
1 lb red cabbage
3½ oz Tuscan olive oil
2 slices of ham
3 onions (red if available)

1 stick of celery, 1 carrot, 1 leek, 1 tomato,
2 or 3 cloves of garlic, thyme and rosemary,
6 to 8 slices of bread (1 for each person)
grated Parmesan, salt, pepper (optional)

1. Chop the onions and half a clove of garlic. Put into a large frying pan with 4 tablespoons of oil. Heat gently until softened.

4. Add salt and pepper. Keep the pan on a low heat, stirring frequently until the beans are cooked and some water has evaporated.

5. Remove the ham, and take out about 5 tablespoons of the beans.

8. Meanwhile, pour the rest of the oil into a saucepan, and heat for about 5 minutes with a branch of rosemary, a pinch of thyme and 2 or 3 crushed cloves of garlic. Add the mixture to the soup.

9. Toast the slices of bread, rub them well with a clove of garlic and place in the bottom of a serving dish.

"RIBOLLITA"
If there is any of the mixture left over, it can be served the following day in a different way. Put the soup into an ovenproof glass dish, then cover the surface with sliced onion and add 1½ oz of olive oil. Put the dish into a medium oven until the onions form a golden crust. Serve immediately.

● FLORENTINE SPECIALTIES

TUSCAN SAUSAGE
There are many types of hard sausage to be found. Among the best known is *finocchiona*, made with pork and flavored with fennel seeds.

THE "RIFICOLONA"
On September 7, the feast of the Virgin Mary, Florentines walk the streets carrying lighted paper lanterns.

TREATS
Cantuccini, dry almond cakes from Prato; crisp *brigidini* biscuits made with egg; and *schiacciata*, a sweet flavored style of bread particular to Florence.

VINO SANTO
A sweet white wine in which *cantuccini* are soaked.

OIL AND VINEGAR
Tuscany has about 40 varieties of olive oil.

CHIANTI. Over one thousand million bottles a year are produced. The better quality wine is labeled *classico*.

Products from the Farmacia di Santa Maria Novella ▲ *216*.

THE PRESS
La Nazione is the city's oldest daily newspaper. National papers such as *l'Unità* have local pages.

60

ARCHITECTURE

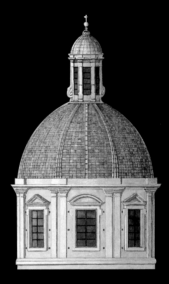

The Convent of San Marco
in the 13th century.

Santo marcho

The square shape (*castrum*) of the Roman
town ● *28* can still be discerned on a map
of modern Florence. The forum (now the
Piazza della Repubblica) stood at the
crossroads of the *cardo maximus* (Via Roma
and Via Calimala) and the *decumanus
maximus* (Via Strozzi and Via del Corso), which split the town
into four. *Florentia* was a port on the north bank of
the Arno, at the junction of several Roman roads.
It became the center of trade and commerce in
Etruria. In the 2nd century, a bridge
was built across the river.

THE EARLY MIDDLE AGES
In the 6th century the city
withdrew into a much smaller
fortified area, but three hundred
years later it had expanded to its
original limits once more. In
1078 a new wall was built
reaching down to the Arno.

▬▬▬	Roman walls
●●●●●	6th-century Byzantine wall
▬▬▬	First medieval wall
▬▬▬	Second medieval wall
▬ ▬ ▬	Extensions to second wall
▬▬▬	Third medieval wall
▬▬▬	16th-century fortifications
▬▬▬	19th-century developments

**THE LATE MIDDLE
AGES**
During the Commune
● *29* Florence grew
rapidly. A second wall
built between 1173
and 1175 tripled the
size of the city. Three
new bridges improved
links with the far side
of the Arno
(Oltrarno) which also
began to expand. In
1258 the walls had to
be moved to make
room for new
districts.

**ARNOLFO DI
CAMBIO**
With the building
of the third wall
(1284–1333) the
city reached a
size and shape
that went
unchanged until
the 19th century.
Arnolfo di Cambio
focused city life
around two points –
religion, centered on
the cathedral, and
political power at the
Palazzo Vecchio.

MEDICI FLORENCE
Thanks to the Medicis ● *36*, Florence was the
birthplace of the Renaissance. Arnolfo was
followed by Brunelleschi ● *88*, who built
palaces and put the dome on the cathedral. The
power of the state was displayed by the Uffizi
▲ *153* and huge defenses ● *65* of the 16th
century. Below, *The Siege of Florence* by Vasari.

THE 17TH AND 18TH CENTURIES

Alterations made in the 17th century were mostly decorative. although the religious orders commissioned a number of Baroque chapels. Under Pietro Leopoldo of Lorraine ● *32*, Florence became a modern city. He organized health and social welfare, which were formerly provided by the convents. Street lighting was also installed, and new parks were opened.

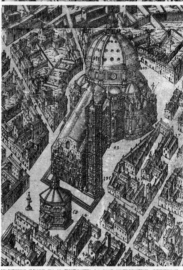

Right, details from Buontalenti's 1584 plan showing the three different centers: San Lorenzo for culture, the Duomo for religion and the Palazzo Vecchio and Uffizi for government.

THE 19TH AND 20TH CENTURIES

The early 19th century saw the growth of many new residential areas. Giuseppe Poggi instituted vast changes with his project of 1865. He replaced the city ramparts with *viali* (boulevards), rebuilt the Piazzale Michelangelo ▲ *319*, and then, in 1888, demolished the ghetto ▲ *209*. During the 20th century the city's suburbs have continued to spread outward.

● CITY DEFENSES AND FORTIFIED DWELLINGS

As the medieval city grew, a new wall was required. Begun in 1284, it was not completed until 1333. The 40-foot high defenses extended for nearly 5 miles round the city, with outworks, 75-foot towers and a wide ditch beyond. The size of the city was restricted in the interests of defense, and there were some fortified towers within the walls as well. But medieval battlements proved to be useless against cannonballs. With the coming of artillery, therefore, the city's defenses had to be altered. They were redesigned by Michelangelo and Antonio da Sangallo (1455–1534).

PORTA ROMANA ▲ *305*
This gate defended one of the main routes through Florence – the road to Siena and Rome. Such gates and towers placed at entrances to the city were of great significance, both real and symbolic. This one was built between 1326 and 1328 to a design by Andrea Orcagna.

PORTA SAN GIORGIO
A gate dating from 1224 that formed a part of both the second and the third medieval walls. In the decoration above the arch can be seen St George fighting the dragon ▲ *298*.

PORTA SAN NICCOLÒ ▲ *318*
This high tower is still standing. It was built around 1324 and is the only one left from the third medieval wall. Like the Zecca tower on the opposite bank, it defended the river.

PORTA SAN GALLO
In 1526, under Pope Clement II, the new system of artillery was adopted. Many 13th-century structures had to be destroyed and this gate was among them.

VILLA CAREGGI

A Medici villa built as a fortified house in the 14th century and altered by Michelozzo around 1457. It retains an original defensive feature – the top floor of overhanging battlements, which are now roofed over.

DELLA CASTAGNA, MARSILI AND AMIDEI TOWERS

The Della Castagna tower is a good example of a medieval fortified town house ▲ 194. It dates from the Romanesque period (1038), as can be seen from the irregular windows. The 13th-century Marsili and Amidei towers appear far more symmetrical.

THE CITY WALL OF 1333

The fortifications designed by Arnolfo di Cambio included 73 high towers, 15 small forts and 4 main gates.

During the 16th century two fortresses were added – the Forte Belvedere ▲ 297, and the Fortezza da Basso.

Although the towers lost their defensive role, the battlements remained to symbolize the power of their noble owners.

FORTEZZA DA BASSO

A huge fort built on a revolutionary plan to ensure it could be defended by a minimum of men. It was virtually impregnable.

The Fortezza di San Giovanni or da Basso (1533–5) was designed by Antonio da Sangallo with ingenious features to make attack extremely difficult. It was built to protect the city from invasion, but was often used by the government as a refuge in times of civil unrest.

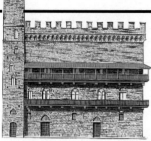

BARGELLO ▲ 188
The oldest seat of Florentine government was built between 1255 and 1261 and altered between 1295 and 1345. Its ocher color shows the use of *pietra forte* ■ 16.

In the 14th century public buildings and the homes of wealthy merchants still had plain, fortified exteriors: only their loggias were richly decorated. Tuscan buildings were of a particular style, known as Communal Gothic. Their austerity was accentuated by a rough stone surface, sometimes with projections, and only simple architectural features such as thin cornices separating the stories, a few ground-floor windows, ogival windows set on narrow sills for the upper floors, and an overhanging parapet walk supported by consoles and topped with "Guelf"-style crenellation. The high tower, a relic from an earlier age, was square, and an interior courtyard provided light and air.

PALAZZO DAVANZATI
▲ 205
The plan of this building (c. 1350) is that of a traditional house with courtyard ● 76. Three large arches open on to the street, with small windows above, after the manner of a medieval Florentine palazzo. The ground floor originally contained shops and storerooms, the floor above housed the main apartments, the next floor, less important members of the family, and beneath the roof were utility rooms including the kitchens.

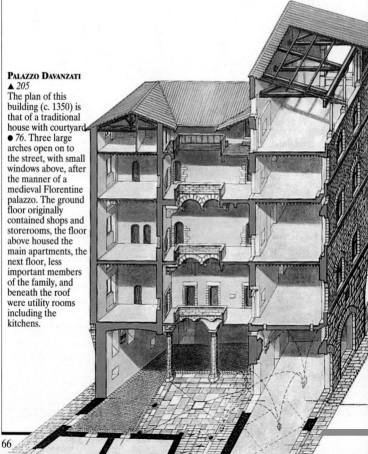

LOGGIA DEL BIGALLO (c. 1352) ▲ *140*
Loggias were an indication of the social standing of a noble family or company, and were an important meeting place for those in public life.

THE BELFRY
The bell tower has a defensive military design, with three rows of square "Guelf" crenellations and a parapet walk. It was intended as a symbol of the city state's power, the arms of which (as well as those of its possessions) are displayed between the supporting consoles of the corbeling.

PALAZZO VECCHIO
Begun by Arnolfo di Cambio in 1299, Florence's city hall ▲ *147* has a solid yet elegant clarity of design. Its fortress-like appearance is relieved by the twin bays of its mullioned windows.

During the 16th century a graceful loggia replaced the crenellation on the Palazzo Davanzati.

PALAZZO DA CINTOIA
The characteristic medieval corbelling of this 14th-century dwelling has been preserved. Made of stone or wood, such overhangs were later forbidden by the city authorities. They were considered to be obstructions which blocked out the light from the city's streets.

67

After he rejected Brunelleschi's design, Cosimo il Vecchio commissioned Michelozzo to build the palazzo on the Via Larga, which then became the model for noble Florentine houses in the 15th century. It was copied (with variations) in Tuscany, Rome, and then all over Italy. Its layout is based on the traditional medieval palazzo, but the spaces are arranged to admit as much light as possible. Four three-story wings form a square enclosing a colonnaded courtyard, whose graceful design contrasts strongly with the rugged exterior façade. During the 17th century the palace was altered and enlarged by the Riccardi family. It increased in size by more than a third.

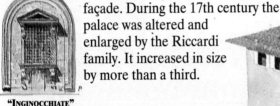

"INGINOCCHIATE" WINDOWS
Michelangelo sealed off the loggia arches on the ground floor with gabled windows in 1517. The sills are supported on stone brackets.

CONTRASTS
Contrast dominates the architecture of the palazzo, both in materials and design. It is evident in the structure at every level. Note the rusticated, almost rough, stonework of the exterior ground floor, the tidily dressed stone of the floor above, and the completely smooth surface of the top floor. These details combine to accentuate the horizontal divisions of the façade, which is topped off with a massive cornice. The openings in the façade are also dominated by a desire for contrast – the small grilles on the ground floor are the stylistic antithesis of the elegant double-bay windows above.

THE CORNICE

At about the time this palazzo was built, the canopy roof of the medieval house was being replaced by a classical cornice. The cornice and its coping were designed to be in proportion to the height of the building (a ratio of 1:9 produced an impressive cornice).

THE CORTILE

The layout of the interior courtyard, like the façade, was based on the desire for symmetry and achieved through mathematical principles. Michelozzo's peristyle was modeled on Brunelleschi's entrance to the Ospedale degli Innocenti ● 71 – a colonnade with arches beneath a medallioned frieze which supports the windows of the floor above. But the architect failed to solve the problems presented by the corners of the courtyard, where the arches and windows are so close that they disturb the balance of the whole.
Below, an oculus in the cortile.

master of the house, reached by a monumental staircase (an important status symbol, but in this case relatively subdued). The upper floor contained storerooms and the quarters of less important family members. The loggias were used for drying grain or linen.

THE LAYOUT

The ground floor was devoted to shops, offices, staff quarters and reception rooms. On the next floor (*piano nobile*) were the apartments of the

THE WINDOWS

The twin bays linked by a single arch, accentuated by fanned stonework or by molded window frames, represent a clean break with the traditional Gothic arches.

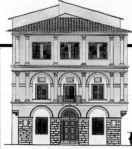

The distinctive feature here is the progressive expansion of the façade.

PALAZZO COCCHI SERRISTORI ▲ *254*
(1469–74), attributed to
Baccio d' Agnolo.

During the period known as the "Early Renaissance" many buildings were constructed or restored, thanks to the influence of Lorenzo the Magnificent ● *31*. The design of the Medici Palace and its component parts set trends to be followed elsewhere. Variations in palazzo design are really only differences in detail – the eaves, decorations on the walls, the number and style of the windows or shape of the entrance – but the bays of the Medici and Pitti Palaces remained the models for this type of building throughout the 15th century.

PALAZZO ANTINORI ▲ *212*
Attributed to Giuliano da Maiano, this palazzo (1461–9) has an austere façade with strict proportions and a carefully crafted smooth stone facing.

PALAZZO RUCCELLAI (below) ▲ *276*
Built around 1460 by Rossellino to Alberti's designs, it represents with its false pilasters the first tentative modern attempts to apply the classical system of orders to a domestic façade.

PORTICO OF THE INNOCENTS' HOSPITAL ▲ *244*
This design by Brunelleschi (c. 1419) shows the new architectural syntax of the Renaissance, with its strict geometric lines and other elements reclaimed from classical antiquity (Corinthian columns and fluted pilasters).

These features articulate a surface design of which the structure is accentuated by the use of contrasting materials – *pietra serena* ■ *16* for the structural lines and pale plaster for the walls. In this building, Brunelleschi created one of the masterpieces of the 15th century.

PALAZZO STROZZI ▲ *208*
The largest in all Florence, this palazzo was begun in 1489 by Benedetto da Maiano and continued by Simone del Pollaiuolo. It has the bold bossed stonework seen on the Palazzo Gondi. Its great stone blocks, diminishing in depth as the building rises, give an impression of strength, lending a monumental character to this mighty structure. The impression is heightened by the massive cornice copied from a Roman model.

CORTILE OF THE PALAZZO STROZZI
(1505, 1533–6)
This blends Early Renaissance style with the new classical innovations, apparent in the outline of the windows and the use of balustrades.

PALAZZO GONDI ▲ *186*
In this design (c. 1490) Giuliano da Sangallo rejected the rugged style of the Medici and Pitti Palaces to achieve smoother, simpler, delicate lines of great refinement.

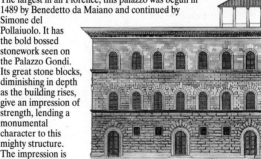

PALAZZO PAZZI-QUARATESI ▲ *190*
Built between 1458 and 1469 by Giuliano da Maiano, this palazzo has a façade after the Medici model, exploiting the contrast between the rusticated stonework base and the smooth rendering of the upper floors. In addition, the flat surface of the walls above the upper bays is relieved by a row of bull's eye windows.

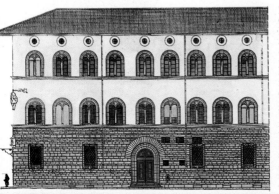

PALAZZO PANDOLFINI ▲ *240*
Built in classical Roman style
and attributed to Raphael.

**PALAZZO DI BIANCA
CAPPELLO** ▲ *311*
The Mannerist style
was the work of
Buontalenti and
Poccetti.

After 1520 the classical Roman style of
Bramante and Raphael was used as a model, just
as the ruins of classical antiquity had inspired the
Early Renaissance builders. At the same time,
Michelangelo was also reinterpreting the rules
of ancient architecture and applying them to
new shapes, opening the way to the
Mannerism of the "Late Renaissance" and
the Baroque. Such freedom with
order, proportion and tradition
were to characterize the work
of the great Florentine
Mannerist architects
Vasari, Ammannati,
Buontalenti and
Antonio da Sangallo
the Younger.

PALAZZO BARTOLINI SALIMBENI
The novelty of this palazzo
(1517–20) ▲ *271*, inspired by
Roman architecture, is evident
in the rectangular bays
decorated with classical motifs.

PALAZZO GRIFONI ▲ *242*
Designed by Ammannati in 1577
after a first attempt by Baccio
d'Agnolo around 1560, the
façades have sculptured motifs
that are very Mannerist in style
(powerful *inginocchiate* windows,
strongly projecting corbels).
There is also a brick frontage
which was an unusual feature
in Florence and was of
Roman influence.

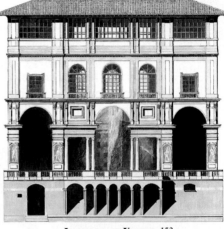

THE UFFIZI ▲ *153*
Organizing and coordinating the offices for maximum efficiency was the logic behind this design, begun by Vasari in 1559 and completed by Buontalenti and Parigi in 1580. The result is a remarkably unified urban development.

LOGGIA OF THE UFFIZI ▲ *153*
The contrasts of light and shade are strongly marked in Vasari's design, which opens on to the Arno.

LAURENTIAN LIBRARY ▲ *221*
The columns of the vestibule are set well back and do not appear to bear any weight; the roof seems to rest simply on the projecting parts of the wall. In fact, the foundations were not strong enough for them to be placed any further forward. Rather than concealing the problem, Michelangelo used it to explore space in a new way. This innovative approach and the creative use of classical elements characterize a masterpiece that was begun in 1523.

PALAZZO UGUCCIONI ▲ *146*
The classical Roman style derives from elements revived by Bramante and Raphael.

The structuring of the upper floors in Doric style and the stonework of the ground floor show the direct link with the Early Renaissance.

Ground-floor window of the Palazzo Nonfinito.

Florence went into an economic and political decline during the 17th century, and fewer new buildings were constructed. The Baroque influence was therefore mild in comparison with Italian cities such as Rome or Turin. With the exception of some late Mannerist designs, there was an austere style, based on classical models, first used by Giovanni Antonio Dosio (1533–1609). Decorative fantasy and rococo ornament hardly feature on Florentine palazzos, which adhered to their traditional long rows of windows, loggias and massive porticos.

PALAZZO NONFINITO ▲ *190*
As its name implies, this palazzo (built between 1593 and 1612) was never completed. The ground floor was the work of Bernardo Buontalenti. Its windows, portico with pilasters and projecting cornerstones are all highly original, and with the curved tympanums show late Mannerism at its most imaginative.

GRANARY OF COSIMO III
The elegant, austere façade of this late 17th-century storehouse, with its massive entrance and fastidiously symmetrical windows, derives from the plain exteriors of earlier 15th-century palazzos.

PALAZZO STROZZI DI MANTOVA ▲ *140*
Designed at the beginning of the 17th century by Gherardo Silvani (1579–1675), the façade of this palazzo features windows like miniature door-ways, and a rusticatedentrance inspired by the courtyard of the Pitti Palace ▲ *288*.

SAN CLEMENTE O DEL PRETENDENTE ▲ *245*
This palazzo was built around 1650 by Gherardo Silvani. The originality of the design lies in the way the terrace is built into the main fabric, relieving the density of the structure. The windows and doors of the courtyard façade are strictly classical in style, with the details deriving from 15th-century models.

PALAZZO CORSINI (above) ▲ *277*
This enormous U-shaped structure, built by Pier Francesco Silvani between 1648 and 1656, consists of two wings linked by a taller central building. Its shape is accentuated by the balustrades and Grecian statuary. Its imposing form, as well as its interior, owe much to Baroque theatrical design.

PALAZZO DELLE MISSIONI ▲ *311*
The palazzo was begun in 1640. It was designed by Bernardino Radi, who had worked in Rome and brought the High Baroque style to Florence. The doorway has numerous decorative features, such as scrollwork, pilasters and a curved broken pediment. The extravagant Baroque style is emphasized by windows surmounted by oval niches, and the elaborately carved ground-floor windows below them.

SANTA MARIA NUOVA HOSPITAL ▲ *248*
The portico and right wing of this massive, forbidding façade were built in 1612 by Giulio Parigi (1571–1635), probably to plans by Buontalenti. The building was completed between 1707 and 1710, although a few final touches were added in 1957. The symmetry of the façade, featuring alternate curved and triangular pediments, is ingeniously relieved by the addition of a few broken pediments.

VILLA CORSINI AT CASTELLO
Antonio Ferri's façade (c. 1690) is a highly decorated example of ornamental Baroque style.

The design of the typical stone Florentine house evolved between the 12th and the 14th centuries, replacing earlier wooden buildings. Its chief characteristic is its double function, with commercial premises such as shops, workshops or warehouses on the ground floor and apartments on the upper floors. It was carefully designed to blend in with its urban surroundings ● 62, and was generally one of two basic types – a house with a courtyard (*casa a corte*) or a terraced house (*casa a schiera*).

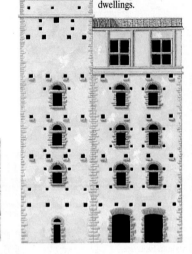

EXPANSION
Over the years, towers were often absorbed into adjacent houses to form larger dwellings.

GALLERIES ("SPORTI")
These walkways were about 3 feet wide. The wooden structure fitted into holes in the wall and was supported on projecting stones.

GROUPS OF HOUSES
The grouping of similar houses was a dominant theme of Florentine construction in the 14th century, and lent continuity to urban development of the period ● 62. Houses with courtyards are the most common type. These varied in size and layout, similar models being set in a row or clustered in a group. The shape of the houses changed as they took over adjacent buildings, and they sometimes came to occupy an entire block. Communication was by means of the galleries.

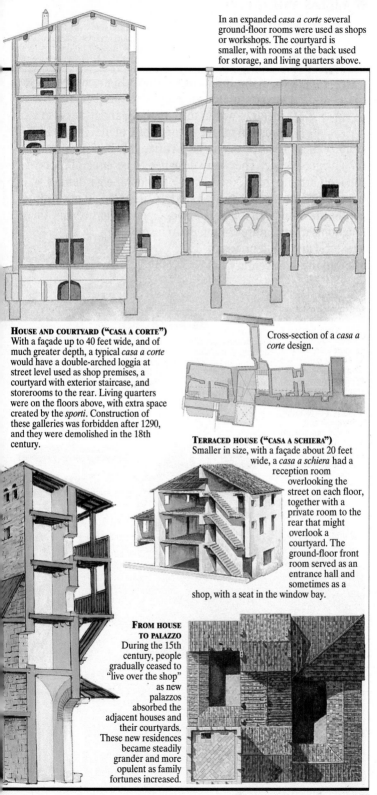

In an expanded *casa a corte* several ground-floor rooms were used as shops or workshops. The courtyard is smaller, with rooms at the back used for storage, and living quarters above.

HOUSE AND COURTYARD ("CASA A CORTE")
With a façade up to 40 feet wide, and of much greater depth, a typical *casa a corte* would have a double-arched loggia at street level used as shop premises, a courtyard with exterior staircase, and storerooms to the rear. Living quarters were on the floors above, with extra space created by the *sporti*. Construction of these galleries was forbidden after 1290, and they were demolished in the 18th century.

Cross-section of a *casa a corte* design.

TERRACED HOUSE ("CASA A SCHIERA")
Smaller in size, with a façade about 20 feet wide, a *casa a schiera* had a reception room overlooking the street on each floor, together with a private room to the rear that might overlook a courtyard. The ground-floor front room served as an entrance hall and sometimes as a shop, with a seat in the window bay.

FROM HOUSE TO PALAZZO
During the 15th century, people gradually ceased to "live over the shop" as new palazzos absorbed the adjacent houses and their courtyards. These new residences became steadily grander and more opulent as family fortunes increased.

● VILLAS AND GARDENS

FOUNTAIN IN THE CASCINE ▲ *284*
One of many neo-classical features (left)
built in the early 19th century for this
Florentine park.

From the 15th century onwards, a country house
was considered an important complement to a
palazzo within the city walls, and it was also a
useful refuge in times of trouble. In the 16th
century these villas ceased to be fortified and became mansions
on a princely scale. They were designed to be integral parts of
the land around them, and the art of landscape gardening
developed into a sophisticated study. Carefully laid out with
geometric designs in topiary, terraces, pools and streams, these
kingdoms in miniature continued to inspire
a tasteful and opulent way of
life into the 19th century.

LA PETRAIA ▲ *325*
Constructed in the
hills to the northeast
of Florence during
the 13th and 14th
centuries, the Villa
La Petraia was a
feudal manor, in turn
the property of the
Brunelleschis, the
Strozzis and the
Medicis. Ferdinando
I commissioned
Bernardo Buontalenti
to rebuild it. He also
laid out the gardens,
which were much
altered by subsequent
generations.

Buontalenti retained
the original medieval
structure, and around
it placed formal
gardens with shrubs
and potted plants in
the Tuscan style.

POGGIO A CAIANO ▲ *336*
Built around 1480 for Lorenzo the
Magnificent by Giuliano da Sangallo, this
was the first Medici villa to look like an
elegant palazzo rather than a fortress.

VILLA GAMBERAIA ▲ *331*

This 14th-century farm at Settignano was transformed into a villa three centuries later. The gardens blend into the setting perfectly, thanks to the natural contours of the landscape.

ORNAMENTS FOR THE CASCINE
The Cascine was an ancient private garden of the Medicis, opened to the public by the Lorraine rulers ● *32*. As an urban park, various features were added between 1796 and 1817, such as this pyramid and the Fountain of Narcissus (right), as well as the fountain opposite. These were executed by G. Manetti, whose work marks the transition from 18th- to 19th-century styles.

TOWER FROM THE TORRIGIANI GARDEN (1821)
Gaetano Baccani's medieval folly is one of the earliest experiments in neo-Gothic architecture in all Italy, coming from the Romantic age of Florentine garden design.

KAFFEHAUS DI BOBOLI (1775)
Del Rosso's design illustrates the 18th-century fashion for the exotic.

GROTTO BY BUONTALENTI (1583-5)
Combining architecture with painting and sculpture, the grotto in the Boboli Gardens is a monument to Mannerist fantasy. Streams of water used to ripple down the rock faces, bringing this extraordinary flight of fancy to life.

Buontalenti was commissioned to design the Villa Pratolino in 1569.

The Villa Cafaggiolo, an old fortress of the Republic, was altered by Michelozzo in 1451.

Van Utens' painting of the Villa Petraia ● *78* was based on a project which was never realized.

At the end of the 16th century the Grand Duke Ferdinando I de' Medici commissioned the Flemish artist Justus van Utens, already living in Carrara, to paint views of the Medici villas ▲ 323. The lunettes he produced were put in the Villa d'Artimino, and all fourteen of them are now preserved in the Topographical Museum (Museo di Firenze com'era), which tells the story of Florence.

Lappeggi was the summer residence of Francesco, first grand duke of Tuscany.

The villa and gardens of Castello were altered in 1537 to designs by Tribolo.

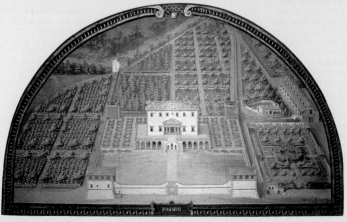

The Villa di Poggio a Caiano ● 78 is a typical summer residence of a 15th-century nobleman.

Florence's Romanesque buildings are remarkable for their proportion, sobriety, geometric clarity and purity of line. They are sometimes described as "proto-Renaissance" structures, because they illustrate the continued use of ancient classical elements such as semicircular arches, columns and pediments through to the 15th century. In the 13th and 14th centuries they were sometimes mistaken for Roman remains. Yet their decoration of green and cream-colored marble is pure Tuscan.

SAN MINIATO AL MONTE ▲ *320*
Begun in 1018, the church is laid out like a basilica with three naves under a sloping roof. The central nave ends in an apse with a half-dome, a widespread feature in the early 13th century.

Beneath the raised chancel is a crypt containing the tomb of the martyr Minias. The proportional size of the central nave to the others points to a study of early Christian monuments, and some of the columns and capitals were clearly taken from earlier buildings. The nave and side aisles are broken at regular intervals by triumphal arches resting on half-columns between alternating supports .

SAN SALVATORE AL VESCOVO ▲ *139*
The marble decoration of the façade (c. 1220), modeled on that of the Baptistery, is absolutely typical of Florentine polychrome design.

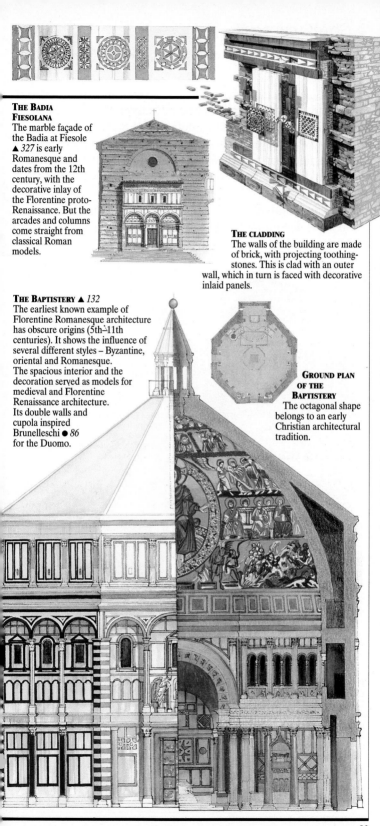

THE BADIA FIESOLANA

The marble façade of the Badia at Fiesole ▲ 327 is early Romanesque and dates from the 12th century, with the decorative inlay of the Florentine proto-Renaissance. But the arcades and columns come straight from classical Roman models.

THE CLADDING

The walls of the building are made of brick, with projecting toothing-stones. This is clad with an outer wall, which in turn is faced with decorative inlaid panels.

THE BAPTISTERY ▲ 132

The earliest known example of Florentine Romanesque architecture has obscure origins (5th–11th centuries). It shows the influence of several different styles – Byzantine, oriental and Romanesque. The spacious interior and the decoration served as models for medieval and Florentine Renaissance architecture. Its double walls and cupola inspired Brunelleschi ● 86 for the Duomo.

GROUND PLAN OF THE BAPTISTERY

The octagonal shape belongs to an early Christian architectural tradition.

It was the French Cistercians who introduced the Gothic style to Italy in 1218 at San Galgano (southwest of Siena). Their churches were built on a new plan, with nave, side aisles, transept, and chancel with chapels. But, like other Italian cities, Florence did not take advantage of the possibilities of these French innovations. Florentine Gothic was not dominated by vertical lines and, unlike Northern Gothic (or Flamboyant), Florentine decoration, and Italian decoration in general, was not integrated into the structure of the building.

SANTA MARIA NOVELLA ▲ 213
Begun in 1246 and completed in 1360, this church has a vaulted roof, and a basilical design with three naves and a transept. The building does not simply rest on pillars – the walls have a major structural part to play. The relatively low height of the nave and its modest length of 92 feet (compared with 125 feet at Santa Croce), gives it a rather squat appearance, while at Santa Croce the use of a wooden roof lightened the structure, allowing a second floor to be built.

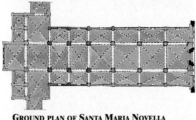

GROUND PLAN OF SANTA MARIA NOVELLA
Preaching was of paramount importance, and the three naves were designed to hold as large a congregation as possible, while the transept was small with just four chapels.

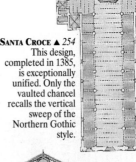

SANTA CROCE ▲ 254
This design, completed in 1385, is exceptionally unified. Only the vaulted chancel recalls the vertical sweep of the Northern Gothic style.

THE BEAMED ROOF OF SANTA CROCE
The large size of the church called for a wooden beamed roof, which has polychrome trusses (above). The great strength of Italian pine-wood enabled it to cover enormous spaces. The Northern Gothic pitch of the roof was rejected in favor of a rather less steeply inclined angle which was more suitable for a warm climate.

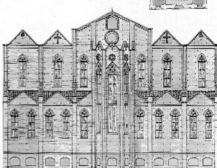

The lunettes of Orsanmichele feature typical Gothic decoration – rose windows with colonnettes, leaflike tracery and overlapping arches.

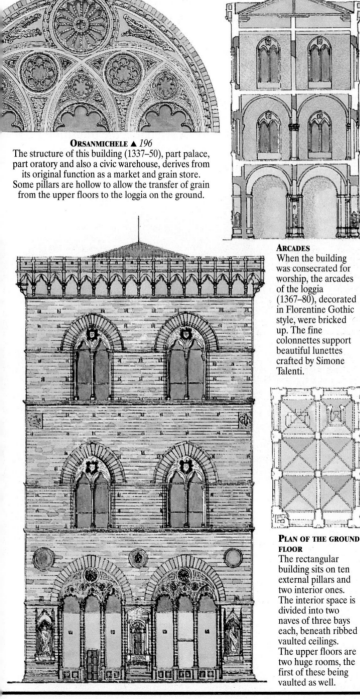

ORSANMICHELE ▲ *196*
The structure of this building (1337–50), part palace, part oratory and also a civic warehouse, derives from its original function as a market and grain store. Some pillars are hollow to allow the transfer of grain from the upper floors to the loggia on the ground.

ARCADES
When the building was consecrated for worship, the arcades of the loggia (1367–80), decorated in Florentine Gothic style, were bricked up. The fine colonnettes support beautiful lunettes crafted by Simone Talenti.

PLAN OF THE GROUND FLOOR
The rectangular building sits on ten external pillars and two interior ones. The interior space is divided into two naves of three bays each, beneath ribbed vaulted ceilings. The upper floors are two huge rooms, the first of these being vaulted as well.

By the 15th century this vast but incomplete cathedral called for something equally grand to crown it. It was to be a symbol of the city's cultural and technical superiority, and Brunelleschi's cupola built between 1420 and 1436 is one of the greatest achievements of the Renaissance. Not since the Pantheon in Rome had an architect constructed a dome of such magnitude. Brunelleschi studied the techniques of ancient classical buildings and Islamic mosques, which had already inspired the Baptistery. A symbol of the transition from the Gothic spirit to the advancing Renaissance, the Duomo had a profound influence on the development of civic architecture as well.

THE CAMPANILE
▲ *132*
Giotto's original design incorporated a spire, but the final result was very different. It was less high (275 feet) when completed by the architects Pisano and Talenti. The impression of lightness comes from the skillful distribution of the openings on the various floors.

PLAN OF THE DUOMO
Taking the form of a Latin cross, the design has three naves which are each divided into four bays. But the transepts and the apse are built to a centralized plan in order to incorporate the cupola. The octagonal chancel is flanked by three polygonal apses, each with five chapels.

CRANES
Brunelleschi was certainly not short of resources to help him cope with the inevitable problems that were posed by such a gigantic undertaking. In particular he used special systems of geared hoists, cranes and scaffolding to speed up the lifting and carrying of building materials.

BUTTRESSES
To strengthen the cupola and to help balance its enormous bulk, Brunelleschi devised a scheme of three solid semicircular buttresses which were each decorated with niches and had shell-shaped half-dome tops.

THE LANTERN
The lantern sits on the cupola 348 feet above the ground and prevents it moving under the force of its ribs. This device also catches the eye with its resemblance to a miniature Greek temple.

THE CUPOLA ▲ *130*
The cupola has a skeleton consisting of eight main ribs at the corners of an octagon, reinforced by another sixteen lesser ribs, all of which are braced by stone arches.
The lateral thrust is absorbed by horizontal rings of stonework which bind the ribs together. Brunelleschi decided to build a double shell and, though the work was begun in stone, the upper part was completed in brick, which for reasons of lightness was laid in a herringbone pattern using an oriental technique. Scorning the support of a wooden frame, Brunelleschi raised his dome over empty space in a series of concentric, self-supporting rings. Layers of stone and brick were constructed in a series of cones all of which converge toward a common center.

● RENAISSANCE CHURCHES

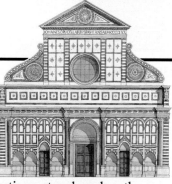

Inspired by classical sources, the 15th-century Florentine architects Brunelleschi (1377–1446), Michelozzo (1396–1472) and Alberti (1404–72), developed a new theory of geometry and proportion, together with a perspective system based on the humanist canon of architectural beauty. As the Flamboyant Gothic style began to degenerate into pure formalism, the Renaissance affirmed the primary importance of simple geometric forms.

SAN LORENZO ▲ *220*
When Brunelleschi began work on San Lorenzo (c. 1421–5), the church already had a transept crossing and chancel. Yet it was here that Brunelleschi first chose to apply his system of harmonious and rational proportions. He based his design for the rest of the church on the geometric module formed by the square of the transept crossing.

Multiplied by four, the module gave the length of the nave; divided by two, the width of the bays in the side aisles.

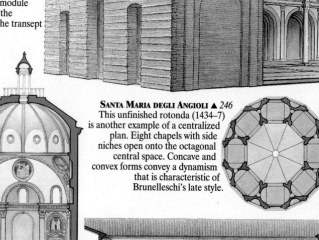

SANTA MARIA DEGLI ANGIOLI ▲ *246*
This unfinished rotonda (1434–7) is another example of a centralized plan. Eight chapels with side niches open onto the octagonal central space. Concave and convex forms convey a dynamism that is characteristic of Brunelleschi's late style.

THE OLD SACRISTY OF SAN LORENZO
Brunelleschi designed the Sacristy c. 1420. The juxtaposed cubes and spheres create a harmonious impression that was perfectly in tune with contemporary ideals of beauty.

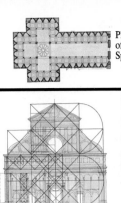

Plan of Santo Spirito.

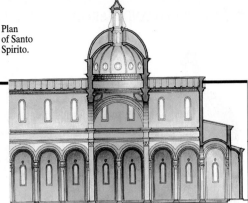

FAÇADE OF SANTA MARIA NOVELLA ▲ 213
The whole is inscribed in a vast square subdivided into basic geometrical forms, which are strictly in proportion with each other (1:1, 1:2 and 1:4). Alberti shared Brunelleschi's precision.

SANTO SPIRITO ▲ 302
Begun in 1444 by Brunelleschi, two years before his death, this building was constructed, according to typical Early Renaissance principles, by multiplying basic metrical quantities. In this case all the measurements were based on the radius of the nave arcades.

The church took a long time to construct and the rather squat cupola, which has no supporting drum, was not finished until 1602.

PAZZI CHAPEL ▲ 261 (c. 1429–44)
This building represents a logical progression from the Old Sacristy of San Lorenzo. The same ground plan of a central square surmounted by a cupola is now augmented by two barrel-vaulted bays.

CLOISTER OF SAN MARCO ▲ 229
(left) Perfect clarity and purity of line indicate the Renaissance restructuring of this building by Michelozzo (1437–43).

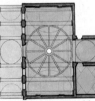

Here, once more, with the aid of a classical vocabulary, Brunelleschi seeks to create a perfect balance between the walls surrounding the space and the vaults above.

The façades of many early 17th-century Florentine churches are designed in a late Mannerist style (sometimes known as post-Mannerism), later followed by a pure Baroque that shows no trace of the anguished style of some Roman architects. Church and chapel interiors were altered to suit current taste, while the late Baroque style was introduced to Florence by Giovanni Battista Foggini (1652–1725).

THE NEW SACRISTY ▲ 223
Michelangelo was in charge of the architecture and decoration of the New Sacristy of San Lorenzo (1520–34). He took his inspiration from the structure of the Old Sacristy, but introduced niche windows and a panelled cupola and put much more emphasis on the statuary.

SANTA TRINITÀ ▲ 273
Buontalenti's sober façade (1593–4) was built at the end of the Mannerist period. It is articulated by smooth pilasters on two levels. The central relief is the only pronounced Baroque feature.

PORTICO OF SAN DOMENICO DI FIESOLE
Nigetti's expressive façade of 1635 features niches suspended from above.

The interior of San Gaetano was modeled on the Gesù Church in Rome.

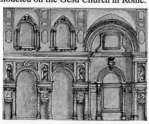

SAN GAETANO ▲ 212
Gherardi Silvani's façade (1648) for Matteo Nigetti's church (begun in 1604) has a graceful vigor that is unmatched in the city's other Baroque buildings.

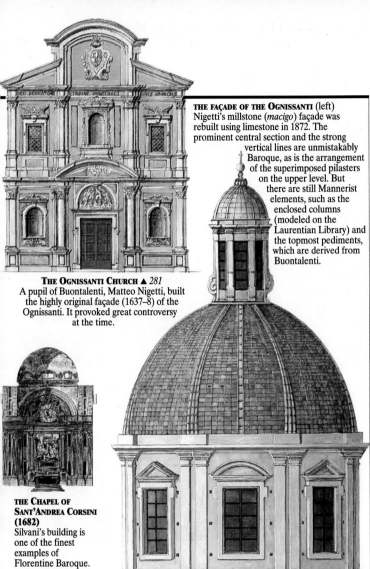

THE FAÇADE OF THE OGNISSANTI (left)
Nigetti's millstone (*macigo*) façade was rebuilt using limestone in 1872. The prominent central section and the strong vertical lines are unmistakably Baroque, as is the arrangement of the superimposed pilasters on the upper level. But there are still Mannerist elements, such as the enclosed columns (modeled on the Laurentian Library) and the topmost pediments, which are derived from Buontalenti.

THE OGNISSANTI CHURCH ▲ *281*
A pupil of Buontalenti, Matteo Nigetti, built the highly original façade (1637–8) of the Ognissanti. It provoked great controversy at the time.

THE CHAPEL OF SANT'ANDREA CORSINI (1682)
Silvani's building is one of the finest examples of Florentine Baroque. Its forceful character serves to intensify Foggini's sculpture and Giordano's painting.

SAN FREDIANO IN CESTELLO ▲ *310*
Antonio Ferri's pilasters and windows around the drum below the cupola (1698) are a graceful variation on the Roman model.

SAN FIRENZE ▲ *186*
This huge façade unites the earlier buildings of the Church of San Filippo Neri (1715), left, and Sant'Apollinare (1772–5), right. Although this is the grandest example of the Florentine Settecento, there are still Mannerist elements, such as the broken pediments and colossal pilasters.

FROM NEO-CLASSICISM TO ART NOUVEAU: THE 19TH CENTURY

A detail from the Mercato Centrale.

During its five years as capital of Italy ● *32* Florence embarked on a number of public works and architectural projects. Many buildings of the time combined an eclectic classicism with a poetic neo-Renaissance style, while there was also a vogue for cast iron and glass. In the late 19th century, the fantasies of Art Nouveau arrived (called Liberty or Floreale in Italy). The leading architect was Michelazzi (1879–1920).

POGGIO IMPERIALE (1806–23)
The impressive neo-classical façade was the work of two men – Pasquale Poccianti (who built the rusticated ground floor), and Giuseppe Cacciali, who built the first floor and pediment.

PALAZZO BORGHESE ▲ *140*
Designed by Gaetano Baccani, the palazzo (1821–2) is one of the finest neo-classical buildings in Florence. Its frontal projection has a substantial loggia with an Ionic colonnade. The rusticated stonework on the ground floor (central section and one at either end) is in traditional Florentine style.

VILLINO LAMPREDI (1905–7)
To cope with an awkward juxtaposition of styles, Michelazzi used delightful curved decorations that disguise the villa's traditional outline (below). To round it off he added dragons, carved with their mouths open wide.

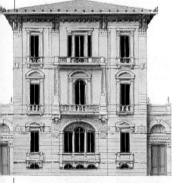

VILLINO UZIELLI (1904–6)
Art Nouveau and 16th-century styles are combined in this elegant villa designed by Paolo Emilio Andre. Note the projecting roof and the window pediments in a late Renaissance style.

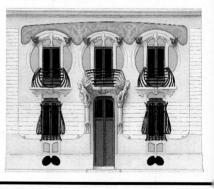

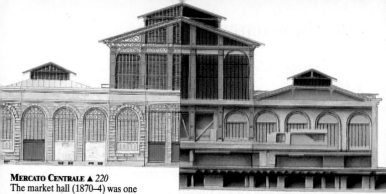

MERCATO CENTRALE ▲ 220
The market hall (1870–4) was one
of the first in Italy to combine stone
with cast iron and glass. Architect Giuseppe Mengoni (from Milan) was
inspired here by the market of Les Halles in Paris, and in particular by the
interior design, the metal framework and the massive neo-classical façade.

Empire style blends here with elements of
Renaissance Mannerism.

VILLA FAVARD ▲ 282
In his design for this villa (built in
1847), Giuseppe Poggi produced one of
the most beautiful 19th-century
buildings in Florence. The perfectly
balanced neo-Renaissance style of the
façade contrasts with the richly
decorated interior to form a typical
example of the eclecticism of
the period.

VILLINO BROGGI-CARACENI ▲ 252
The extravagant curved lines and floral
decoration of Giovanni Michelazzi's 1911
design are continued inside the house. It is
one of the purest and most successful
"Liberty" designs in the whole of Florence.

**CASA GALLERIA
▲ 280**
This house by
Michelazzi, also
from around 1911,
is a superb example
of the "Liberty"
style. Graceful
windows and
sinuous lines
disguise the
traditional
proportions of
successive stories to
breathe life into the
design. The central
feature is a
reworking of the
Mannerist broken
pediments which
were much used by
Buontalenti – an
echo of the great
heritage of
Florentine
architecture.

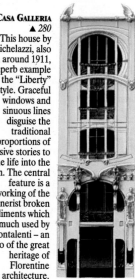

Between the wars, the dramatic designs of Pier Luigi Nervi (1891–1979) dominated Florentine architecture, barely touched by Fascist-style projects. The city also escaped the influence of post-war transatlantic design, and developed an expressive "organic" approach to building, shown by the Tuscan Group, notably Leonardo Savioli (1917–83), Stefano Ricci (b. 1918) and Giovanni Michelucci (1891–1990).

SANTA MARIA NOVELLA RAILWAY STATION (1932–4)
Designed by the Tuscan Group, this was one of Italy's first buildings in modern style. It is a masterpiece of "organic" Italian Rationalism, fitting in unselfconsciously with its historical surroundings.

SIGNAL BOX FOR SANTA MARIA NOVELLA STATION (1931–2)
Angiolo Mazzoni, a key figure in the Futurist school, designed this dynamic building, which combines straightforward geometric forms.

STADIUM (1931)
The imaginative design of the stadium, using reinforced concrete, illustrates Nervi's keen aesthetic sensibilities.

CHURCH OF SAINT JOHN THE BAPTIST (1960–4)
Michelucci's impressive building demonstrates his understanding of Expressionism and sculptural form. Its outlines show a masterly control of spatial unity, and the materials used underline the dignity of the structure.

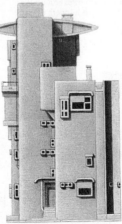

APARTMENT BLOCK (1964–7)
Built by Savioli and Santi, this complex on the Via Piagentina is an exercise in dynamic contrasts which are particularly marked in the projecting roof with its two opposing convex curves.

VILLA BAYON (1964–6)
Leonardo Savioli and Danilo Santi designed this villa with a sculptural feel, continuing the explorations of organic architecture. The concrete roof is independent of the house, and the various extensions are freely arranged.

FLORENCE AS
SEEN BY PAINTERS

« THERE ARE FLOWERS AND GRAPES AND OLIVE
LEAVES, THE SHARP POINTS OF CYPRESSES AND
THE FLAT TOPS OF PINES, ALL SHARPLY DEFINED
AGAINST THE SKY. »   FELIX MENDELSSOHN

Joseph Mallord William Turner (1775–1851) worked for an English publisher called Charles Heath during the 1830's. After the success of a book of *English and Welsh Lanscapes*, Heath decided to produce a companion volume about Italy. Turner painted several pictures for the book: his *View of Florence from San Miniato* (1) shows his mastery of light in what John Constable called Turner's "visions of

tinted steam". Even if the painting is marred by certain academic clichés, the composition is nevertheless daring, with one large cypress tree splitting the picture in half, though the whole retains its overall unity thanks to the shared perspective view of the background. This may not be a revolutionary painting, but it does demonstrate the artist's fresh way of looking at the world. *View over the Arno with the Ponte alle Grazie* (1868) (2) by EMILIO BURCI (d. 1879) is an attractive painting, but academic in approach, especially in its golden tone. The inspiration of GIOVANNI SIGNORINI (1808–c. 1858) (3) is of a rather conventional kind – golden light over a panoramic view with figures, framed on the left by a terrace and on the right by vegetation.

FLORENCE AS SEEN BY PAINTERS

J ean-Baptiste Corot (1796–1875) loved the light in Italy. In 1834 he traveled to northern Italy and Tuscany, where he produced his *Florence seen from the Boboli Gardens* (1). It shows the artist's skill at painting a gentle diffused light, contrasting a dark green foreground with the city bathed in shades of ocher and brown.

Ultimately the picture fails to satisfy, however, since the view is so conventional. Corot's visit to Florence was too short to allow him time for the unhurried reflection that would have added depth to his vision. Corot tended to observe the artistic conventions, producing some studied and superficial work that is inferior to his less formal French landscapes.

The Italian genre painter FILADELFO SIMI (1849–1923) painted landscapes, portraits, and was also a sculptor. His work became popular thanks to the air of poetic melancholy that pervades his sensitive paintings, such as this view of *Dusk over the Arno* (2).

1

2

«I OFTEN GO OUT AFTER TEA IN A WANDERING
WALK TO SIT IN THE LOGGIA AND LOOK
AT THE PERSEUS.»

ELIZABETH BARRETT BROWNING

John Singer Sargent (1856–1925) was an American painter who was born in Florence. He studied there and also in Paris, where Carolus-Duran taught him how to paint society portraits. But he also painted a number of watercolors, such as this *View of the Boboli Gardens* (1).

JULES-LOUIS MACHARD (1839–1900) was a historical painter and portraitist: his *Perseus in the Loggia dei Lanzi* (2) exaggerates the contrast formed by the shadows to enhance the great power of this heroic mythological figure. The architect LE CORBUSIER (1887–1965, see photograph below) was also a painter and founded the Purist movement in 1918. This was an attempt to preserve and to stress the architectural simplicity of objects. In his watercolor *Impression of Fiesole* (3) he seeks to underline the relationship between natural and architectural forms.

Ottone Rosai (1895–1957) started out as a Futurist between 1913 and 1915, before turning to "metaphysical" painting in the wake of Giorgio de' Chirico. In addition, he took part in the experiments of the Florentine "Strapaese" group, who looked for their inspiration to popular art. In Rosai's case this led to a simplification of shapes, the omission of much detail and an approach that was frankly naïve. He became known as the "Italian Douanier Rousseau". His landscapes of Florence and its surroundings have a bitter-sweet wistfulness about them, as seen in this *View of Florence* (1). In 1933 Rosai decorated Florence Railway Station with large murals.

Giuseppe Abbati (1836–68) was a member of the Macchiaioli group, and rose to become one of its leading lights. He was trained in the Venetian studio of the academic painter Michelangelo Grigoletti and then in his father Vincenzo's studio in Naples. Abbati abandoned painting to take part in the political upheavals going on in Italy. He was one of Garibaldi's "thousand heroes" in the Sicilian expedition of 1860, after which he settled in Florence and resumed his work with the Macchiaioli. The cloisters of Santa Croce, where his picture *Chiostro* (2) was painted in 1861, allowed him to explore various shades of white and brighten his palette. In his exceptionally subtle works, Abbati succeeded in capturing the ever-changing qualities of light. Some of his pictures seem to anticipate abstract art, such as this one resembling the 20th-century work of Nicolas de Staël. Abbati liked to paint structures from an angle that accentuated their strong lines, contrasting light and shade, surfaces splashed with brightness. His masterly way of applying paint, in thick soft slabs, shows Abbati to be one of the great landscape artists of the 19th century.

| 1 |

| 2 |

FLORENCE
AS SEEN BY PAINTERS

Telemaco Signorini (1835–1901) was also a member of the Macchiaioli. In his crowded and colorful street scenes, he painted the world that he loved. This picture of 1882, the *Via degli Speziali*, recalls the old Florence before "urban improvements" took place.

THE CITY OF THE LILY

THE ROOTS OF DISCORD

Secretary to the Republic of Florence, Niccolò Machiavelli (1469–1527) is now chiefly remembered for his masterpiece "The Prince". In his role as diplomat he traveled extensively through Italy and Europe, picking up a fund of ideas through his observations of the political scene. "The Florentine Histories" were his final work. Commissioned by Giulio Medici, the future Pope Clement VII, the book is a detailed chronicle of the history of Florence from its earliest origins up to the death of Lorenzo the Magnificent in 1492. This excerpt tells of the death of Buondelmonte in 1216, which marked the beginning of the calamitous split of the great Florentine families. The feud between the Guelf and the Ghibellines ● 34 was originally German, and had spread into Italy as early as the 11th century. It grew into an intense political rivalry, which is why this incident acquired an importance and is often quoted as the birth of the Guelf and Ghibelline factions in Italy.

❝The most powerful Florentine families were the Buondelmonti and the Uberti, and after them the Amidei and the Donati. Among the Donati was a rich widow who had a beautiful daughter, and she planned to marry her off to the young knight Buondelmonte, head of the family of that name. Whether through negligence or through leaving matters too late, she still hadn't told anyone her plan when she found out that Buondelmonte had become engaged to a daughter of the Amidei family. The widow was angry at this news, but still hoped that her daughter's beauty would be enough to end the betrothal before the date fixed for the wedding. Seeing Buondelmonte one day walking by her house, she went out followed by her daughter just as he was passing and said, 'I am overjoyed to hear the news of the wife you have chosen, even though I was keeping my own daughter for you.' Then opening her door a little way she allowed him to set eyes upon the girl. The youth was overcome by the maiden's beauty and, seeing that she was just as well-born as his betrothed, was filled with such a passion that he answered hurriedly, mindless of the promises he had made, the insult he would cause and the serious implications of his action: 'Then you have been keeping her for me, and I would indeed be ungrateful if I failed to accept your offer while there is still time.' And without any further delay he married her. The news of this filled the Amidei family and their allies the Uberti, with wrath. In a meeting togther with many elders of both families they resolved that such an insult required vengeance, which could only be expiated by Buondelmonte's death. Some spoke of all the troubles that might follow such an act; but Mosca Lamberti answered that those who thought too much about the consequences never accomplished anything, and quoted the old proverb: He who hesitates is lost. Accordingly Lamberti, Stiatta Uberti, Lambertuccio Amidei and Oderigo Fifanti were given the job of carrying out the assassination. These men shut themselves up on Easter Day in the house of the Amidei, which is between the Ponte Vecchio and the church of Santo Stefano. That same day Buondelmonte, obviously thinking that it was as easy to forget a grievance as to break off an engagement, was crossing the bridge mounted on a white horse when he was attacked and murdered at one end of it, close to a statue of Mars. The killing at

once divided the whole city, some siding with the Buondelmonti and the rest with the Uberti. As both sides had many fortified buildings and soldiers too between them, they continued fighting for years without either faction gaining the upper hand. Without finding any solution to their quarrels they would eventually call a truce, only to take up arms again whenever the occasion demanded**"**

MACHIAVELLI, *FLORENTINE HISTORIES*, 1520–5

THE DIVIDED CITY

In the first part of his "Divine Comedy", Dante Alighieri (1265–1321) visits the Underworld, which he finds divided into different hells for lost souls according to the gravity of their sin. In the third Hell, Dante finds the Florentine Ciacco among the gluttons, and questions him about the future of Florence. In 1300, at the time of Dante's imaginary journey, Florence had long been in a state of chaos thanks to the quarrels between Guelfs and Ghibellines ● 34. With the Guelfs ultimately the victors, the city was again split between the White Guelfs (moderates, in favor of civic self-government) and the Black Guelfs (who wanted to extend the city's power). Ciacco speaks of the defeat and humiliation of the Whites, whose side Dante took in the quarrel. The Black Guelfs had enjoyed the support of Pope Boniface VIII, whose intervention served to conceal territorial ambitions in Tuscany. Referring indirectly to his exile (to which he was sentenced in 1302), Dante reflects on the underlying causes of Florence's misfortunes.

"Citizens, you called me Ciacco; and for the baneful crime of gluttony you see I languish in the rain;
And mine is not the only wretched spirit here, since all those for like crime suffer like punishment'; and he said no more.
I answered him: 'Ciacco, your sore distress weighs heavy on me and causes me to weep, but tell me if you can, what shall become of the citizens of the divided city, if there is any justice there? And tell me the reason why such discord has assailed it.'
And he replied: 'After much argument will come much blood, and the party of the woods shall rout the other with much suffering.
'And this shall come to pass within three years, then the others shall prevail through the force of one who now bides his time.
'And it shall stay victorious for a long time, ruling the conquered with a heavy hand however much they weep and suffer.
Two men are just, but are not listened to there; Pride, Envy and Avarice are the three sparks that have set the hearts of all on fire.'**"**

DANTE, *THE INFERNO*, CANTO VI, 1314?–21

THE PLAGUE

Like Dante and Petrarch, Boccaccio (1313–75), the third great Italian writer of the Middle Ages, was born in Tuscany. Part of his youth was spent at the court of Naples, until he returned to Florence in 1340 determined to become a writer and with many tales and poems already written. "The Decameron" is a collection of one hundred tales told in a ten-day period by a group of Florentines taking refuge in the country when their city fell victim to the Black Death of 1348.

"I say, then, that the sum of thirteen hundred and forty-eight years had elapsed since the fruitful Incarnation of the Son of God, when the noble city of Florence, which for its great beauty excels all others in Italy, was visited by the deadly

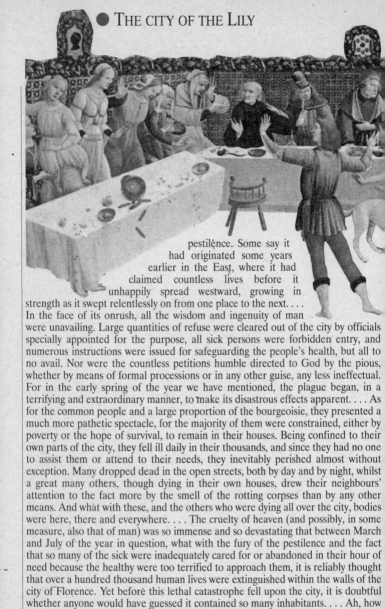

pestilence. Some say it had originated some years earlier in the East, where it had claimed countless lives before it unhappily spread westward, growing in strength as it swept relentlessly on from one place to the next. . . . In the face of its onrush, all the wisdom and ingenuity of man were unavailing. Large quantities of refuse were cleared out of the city by officials specially appointed for the purpose, all sick persons were forbidden entry, and numerous instructions were issued for safeguarding the people's health, but all to no avail. Nor were the countless petitions humble directed to God by the pious, whether by means of formal processions or in any other guise, any less ineffectual. For in the early spring of the year we have mentioned, the plague began, in a terrifying and extraordinary manner, to make its disastrous effects apparent. . . . As for the common people and a large proportion of the bourgeoisie, they presented a much more pathetic spectacle, for the majority of them were constrained, either by poverty or the hope of survival, to remain in their houses. Being confined to their own parts of the city, they fell ill daily in their thousands, and since they had no one to assist them or attend to their needs, they inevitably perished almost without exception. Many dropped dead in the open streets, both by day and by night, whilst a great many others, though dying in their own houses, drew their neighbours' attention to the fact more by the smell of the rotting corpses than by any other means. And what with these, and the others who were dying all over the city, bodies were here, there and everywhere. . . . The cruelty of heaven (and possibly, in some measure, also that of man) was so immense and so devastating that between March and July of the year in question, what with the fury of the pestilence and the fact that so many of the sick were inadequately cared for or abandoned in their hour of need because the healthy were too terrified to approach them, it is reliably thought that over a hundred thousand human lives were extinguished within the walls of the city of Florence. Yet before this lethal catastrophe fell upon the city, it is doubtful whether anyone would have guessed it contained so many inhabitants. . . . Ah, how great a number of splendid palaces, fine houses, and noble dwellings, once filled with retainers, with lords and ladies, were bereft of all who had lived there, down to the tiniest child! How numerous were the famous families, the vast estates, the notable fortunes, that were seen to be left without a rightful successor! How many gallant gentlemen, fair ladies, and sprightly youths, who would have been judged hale and hearty by Galen, Hippocrates and Aesculapius (to say nothing of others), having breakfasted in the morning with their kinsfolk, acquaintances and friends, supped that same evening with their ancestors in the next world! **99**

BOCCACCIO, *THE DECAMERON*, 1349–51, TRANSLATED BY G.H. McWILLIAM

THE GLORY OF FLORENCE

The English novelist Charles Dickens (1812–70) made a tour of Italy in 1844 just after the completion of his Anglo-American story "Martin Chuzzlewit". Lovers of his books will know Dickens as the man with an eye for the telling detail, seeking out one seemingly trivial image that he then reveals as a

microcosm of the whole scene. But a reading of his collected writings from this tour, "Pictures From Italy", seems to find him a little overwhelmed by the constant beauty and magnificence of all he saw. Instead he adopts a symphonic style of writing, letting his majestic prose fill the reader's mind just as his view of Florence fired his imagination.

❝ What light is shed upon the world, at this day, from amidst these rugged Palaces of Florence! Here, open to all comers, in their beautiful and calm retreats, the ancient Sculptors are immortal, side by side with Michael Angelo, Canova, Titian, Rembrandt, Raphael, Poets, Historians, Philosophers – these illustrious men of history, beside whom its crowned heads and harnessed warriors show so poor and small, and are so soon forgotten. Here, the imperishable part of noble minds survives, placid and equal, when strongholds of assault and defence are overthrown; when the tyranny of the many, or the few, or both, is but a tale; when Pride and Power are so much cloistered dust. The fire within the stern streets, and among the massive Palaces and Towers, kindled by rays from Heaven, is still burning brightly, when the flickering of war is extinguished and the household fires of generations have decayed; as thousands upon thousands of faces, rigid with the strife and passion of the hour, have faded out of the old Squares and public haunts, while the nameless Florentine Lady, preserved from oblivion by a Painter's hand, yet lives on, in enduring grace and youth. . . . Let us look back on Florence while we may, and when its shining dome is seen no more, go travelling through cheerful Tuscany, with a bright remembrance of it; for Italy will be the fairer for the recollection. ❞

CHARLES DICKENS, *PICTURES FROM ITALY*, 1844

THE COLD WIND OF CHANGE

D.H.Lawrence (1885–1930) was devoted to Florence, lived there on several occasions and had numerous acquaintances among its English literary set, such as Rebecca West, Bernard Berenson, Reggie Turner (an old disciple of Oscar Wilde), and the amusingly outrageous novelist Norman Douglas. It was the latter who commented that as soon as Lawrence arrived anywhere he would start writing about it. The excerpt below, however, is rather different. It is from the suppressed "Epilogue" to a rather unusual school textbook, "Movements in European History" (1924), that he had written under the pseudonym Lawrence H. Davison.

❝ In Italy, in Florence, there was the same lingering ease and goodwill in 1919 as before the War. By 1920 prices had gone up three times, and socialism was rampant. Now we began to be bullied in every way. Servants were rude, cabmen insulted one and demanded treble fare, railway porters demanded large sums for carrying a bag from the train to the street, and threatened to attack one if the money were not paid. The train would suddenly come to a standstill in the heat of the open country: the drivers had gone on strike for a couple of hours. . . . If in the country you asked at a cottage for a drink of wine, worth a penny, the peasant would demand a shilling, and insult you if he did not get it. . . . This was all pure bullying. And this was socialism. True it was the bad side of socialism, the hatred of 'superiors' or people with money or education or authority. But socialism it was. . . . In the summer of 1920 I went north, and Florence was in a state of continual socialistic riot: sudden shots, sudden stones smashing into the restaurants where one was drinking coffee, all the shops suddenly barred and closed. When I came back there was a great procession of Fascisti and banners: Long Live the King. . . . This was the beginning of Fascism. It was an anti-socialist movement started by the returned soldiers in the name of Law and Order. And suddenly, it gained possession of Italy. Now the cabs had a fixed charge, a fixed charge for railway porters was placarded in the railway stations, and trains began to run punctually. But also, in Fiesole near Florence the Fascisti suddenly banged at the door of the mayor of the village, in the night when all were in bed. The mayor was forced to get up and open the door. The Fascisti seized him, stood him against the wall of his house, and shot him under the eyes of his wife and children, who were in their night dresses. Why? Because he was a socialist. . . . That is Fascism and Law and Order. Only another kind of bullying. **"**

D.H. LAWRENCE, *MOVEMENTS IN EUROPEAN HISTORY*, 1921

THE CITY OF ARTS

POST WAR BLUES

By the time Sinclair Lewis (1885–1951) completed his last (and twenty-second) novel "World So Wide" (1951), his work was all but forgotten. Yet Minnesota-born Lewis was a writer of great power and subtlety, and had enjoyed a brilliant rise to fame. As publisher Bennett Cerf said of him: "Lewis began his literary career in the publicity department of Frederick L. Stokes and Company, publishers. At the end of his second year he was making $23 a week and had the temerity to demand a two-dollar raise. Old Mr Stokes gave it to him, with the comment, 'You're a bright young fellow, Lewis, but you want raises too often. This is the top salary for the job you're doing. I'll never pay you any more.' Less than fifteen years later the same gentleman offered Lewis a $75,000 advance on a new novel, "Sight unseen". His most famous and successful books were "Main Street" (1920) and "Elmer Gantry" (1927). "World So Wide" is a story of Americans in Italy, finished at Sir Harold Acton's beautiful house outside Florence. The novel's hero, Hayden, is seeing Florence for the first time.

" The railway station at Florence had a fine, flaring Mussolini touch, very spacious and inclined to marble and wood panels, but the piazza in front of it was of a suburban drabness, and the back of the church of Santa Maria Novella was a mud-coloured bareness, sullen with evening. He would not be staying here long! His taxi-driver was learning English, and he was willing to make it a bi-lingual party, but as Hayden's Italian was limited to bravo, spaghetti, zabaglione and the notations on sheet music, this promising friendship did not get far, and he went to bed blankly at the Hotel Excelsior. But in the bright morning of late autumn he looked from his hotel and began to fall in love with a city. He saw the Arno, in full brown tide after recent mountain rains, with old palaces along it and cypress-waving hills beyond. On one side was the Tower of Bellosguardo and a fragment of the old city wall, and on the other the marvel of the church of San Miniato, white striped with a green that seemed black from afar. Hayden saw a city of ancient reticences and modern energy, with old passageways, crooked and mysterious, arched over with stone that bore carven heraldic shields. 'I like this! Maybe I'll stay out the week.' "

SINCLAIR LEWIS, *WORLD SO WIDE*, 1951

A FLORENTINE LADY

The Venetian Lorenzo da Ponte (1749–1838) is remembered today as the librettist of three of Mozart's operas: "The Marriage of Figaro", "Don Giovanni" and "Cosi Fan Tutte". But in his witty and scurrilous autobiography from which this passage is taken, his collaboration with Mozart is dealt with very briefly. He is much more concerned with relationships that he considered more important – and sometimes more intimate. At this point in the narrative Da Ponte is in Florence to find singers for the opera in London.

" There are hundreds and hundreds of women in Florence who, in grace of mind and manner and all those merits and virtues which especially adorn their sex, can vie, without fear, with the most cultivated and aimiable ladies of the world. I have found them hospitable without ostentation, educated without pedantry, affable without frowardness, interesting without pretense, courteous without immodesty, good-mannered without affectation. Add to such admirable qualities the sugar of a 'speech that is felt in the soul' and try if you can to suppress a longing to live and die in Florence! . . . What struck me above all was the manner of 'conversation' practised by many of the most illustrious ladies in Florence. I was invited one evening to the conversazione of one of the leading matrons. To nobility of birth this lady coupled all the graces of a cultivated and natively superior mind. She was a widow, rich, young, beautiful. Her house was always open to foreigners of distinction, but along with these, and with princes, dukes and peers from all parts of the world, she received, feasted and honored all people of talent, particularly poets, painters, sculptors, historians, physicians, lawyers and so on. There was music only once a week, saving special occasions, such as the first reception to some eminent musician. Dancing was permitted only once a month. Politics were rarely discussed; and cards were entirely banished. The principal topic of that assembly was literature. Every evening there were readings of poetry, learned papers, essays in light vein, and, two or three times a week, comedies or tragedies, the parts for men and women being assigned by lot . . . I said to myself at that time: 'If certain English ladies were here, who spend so much time in kicking their heels and legs to the ugly music of a bad violin, what idea would they get of the ladies of Italy, and what would they say of themselves?' What I said to myself of English women then, might I dare now, respectfully, reverently whisper in the ears of my still more beloved Americans? **"**

LORENZO DA PONTE, *MEMOIRS*,
TRANSLATED BY ELISABETH ABBOTT, 1880

A VIEW OF THE CASCINE

The Irishman Charles Lever (1806–72) was a novelist of lively and considerable wit, and also of great talent, if not real genius. Like Wilkie Collins, he is yet another of those sadly neglected writers whose books can nevertheless still be read with great enjoyment. They all lived in the shadow of Charles Dickens, certainly a very hard act to follow. Lever was also a practising physician, and on arriving in Italy he settled for a while in Florence before moving on to La Spezia as vice-consul. Then in 1867 the British Foreign Secretary Lord Derby offered him the post of consul at Trieste: "Here is £600 a year for doing nothing; and you, Lever, are the very man to do it."
Lever eventually died while still in Trieste, but in his last years he still liked to return to his beloved Florence after the summer was over.

"Although a choice military band was performing with exquisite skill the favourite overtures of the day, the noise and tumult of conversation almost drowned their notes. In fact, the Cascine is to the world of society what the Bourseis is to the world of trade. It is the great centre of all news and intelligence, where bargains of intercourse are transacted, the scene of past pleasures is revived, and where the plans of future enjoyment are canvassed. . . . Scandal holds here its festival, and the misdeeds of every capital of Europe are now being discussed. The higher themes of politics occupy but few: the interests of literature attract still less. It is essentially of the world they talk, and it must be owned that they do it like adepts. The last witticism of Paris – the last duel at Berlin – who has fled from his creditors in England – who has run away from her husband at Naples – all are retailed with a serious circumstantiality that would lead one to believe that gossip maintained its own correspondent in every city of the Continent. Moralists might fancy, perhaps, that in the tone these subjects are treated there might mingle a reprobation of the bad . . . but no. Never were censors more lenient – never were critics so charitable. The trangressions against good breeding, the gaucheries of manner, the solecisms in dress, language or demeanour do indeed meet with sharp reproof and cutting sarcasm; but in recompense for such severity, how gently they deal with graver offences. **"**

CHARLES LEVER
THE DODD FAMILY ABROAD,
1854–6

SHELLEY APPROACHES FLORENCE

Percy Bysshe Shelley (1792–1822) fell in love with Italy when he arrived in 1818. That was the year he first saw Florence as well, and he was fortunate to be adequately equipped to enjoy it, having recently inherited £1,000 a year from his grandfather. But fate has a familiar habit of compensating for good fortune with misfortune, and it was Shelley's fate never to leave Italy. He perished four years later in a boating accident off Livorno at the age of twenty-nine. One of England's greatest poets, Shelley reveals himself rather unsurprisingly as a first-class writer of descriptive prose in this extract from a letter to his second wife Mary.

❝ As we approached Florence, the country became cultivated to a very high degree, the plain was filled with the most beautiful villas, and, as far as the eye could reach, the mountains were covered with them; for the plains are bounded on all sides by blue and misty mountains. The vines here are trailed on low trellises or reeds interwoven into crosses to support them, and the grapes, now almost ripe, are exceedingly abundant. You everywhere meet those teams of beautiful white oxen, which are now labouring the little vine-divided fields, and their Virgilian ploughs and carts. Florence itself, that is the Lung' Arno (for I have seen no more), I think is the most beautiful city I have ever yet seen. It is surrounded with cultivated hills, and from the bridge which crosses the broad channel of the Arno, the view is the most animated and elegant I ever saw. You see three or four bridges, one apparently supported by Corinthian pillars, and the white sails of the boats, relieved by the deep green of the forest, which comes to the water's edge, and the sloping hills covered with bright hills on every side. Domes and steeples rise on all sides, and the cleanliness is remarkably great. On the other side there are the foldings of the Arno above; first the hills of olive and vine, then the chestnut woods, and then the blue and misty pine forests, which invest the aerial Appenines, that fade in the distance. I have seldom seen a city so lovely at first sight as Florence. ❞

PERCY BYSSHE SHELLEY, *LETTER TO MARY SHELLEY*, 1818

A RELUCTANT SIGHTSEER

The novels of Edward Morgan Forster (1879–1970) are filled with shrewd observations on late Victorian England and its strict conventions. In the first part of "A Room With A View" these conventions are personified in Charlotte, accompanying her young cousin Lucy on a visit to Florence. In this passage Lucy escapes from her chaperone for a morning to discover the City of the Lily with Miss Lavish, an ageing lady novelist staying in the same pension. And just like every other English tourist in Florence, Lucy has not forgotten her Baedeker! But before long, in front of Santa Croce she gets lost: Miss Lavish is nowhere to be seen, and Lucy is all alone . . .

❝ Tears of indignation came to Lucy's eyes – partly because Miss Lavish had jilted her, partly because she had taken her Baedeker. How could she find her way home? How could she find her way about in Santa Croce? Her first morning was ruined, and she might never be in Florence again. A few minutes ago she had been all high spirits, talking as a woman of culture, and half-persuading herself that she was full of originality. Now she entered the church depressed and humiliated, not even able to remember whether it was built by the Franciscans or the Dominicans. . . . Of course, it must be a wonderful building. But how like a barn! And how very cold! Of course, it contained frescoes by Giotto, in the presence of whose tactile values she was capable of feeling what was proper. But who was to tell her which they were? She walked about disdainfully, unwilling to be enthusiastic over monuments of uncertain authorship or date. There was no one even to tell her which, of all these pulchral slabs that paved the nave and transepts, was the one that was really beautiful, the one that had been most praised by Mr Ruskin. Then the pernicious charm of Italy worked on her, and, instead of acquiring information, she began to be happy. She puzzled out the Italian notices – the notice that forbade people to bring dogs into the church – the notice that prayed people, in the interests of health and out of respect to the sacred edifice in which they found themselves, not to spit. She watched the tourists: their noses were as red as their Baedekers, so cold was Santa Croce. She beheld the horrible fate that overtook three Papists – two he-babies and a she-baby – who began their career by sousing each other with the Holy Water, and then proceeded to the Machiavelli memorial, dripping but hallowed. Advancing towards it very slowly and from immense distances, they touched the stone with their fingers, with their handkerchiefs, with their heads, and then retreated. What could this mean? They did it again and again. Then Lucy realized that they had mistaken Machiavelli for some saint, and by continual contact with his shrine were hoping to acquire virtue. **99**

E.M. FORSTER, *A ROOM WITH A VIEW,* 1908

THE REVERSE OF THE MEDAL

"The Innocents Abroad" made its author famous. Samuel Clemens (1835–1910) was a river pilot on the Mississippi turned goldminer turned journalist. He adopted the pseudonym Mark Twain from the cry of the boatman sounding the depth of the river, and used it for his first book "The Jumping Frog of Calaveras County" (1867). This was a success, though it was his next book that made his name as one of the all-time great humorists. "The Innocents Abroad" is an account of a package tour to the Mediterranean that Twain made in 1867. It is to be hoped that he enjoyed himself more than some of the book suggests.

66 We went to the Church of Santa Croce from time to time, in Florence, to weep over the tombs of Michael Angelo, Raphael, and Machiavelli (I suppose they are buried there, but it maybe that they reside elsewhere, and rent their tombs to other parties – such being the fashion in Italy), and between times we used to go and stand on the bridges and admire the Arno. It is popular to admire the Arno. It is a great historical creek, with four feet in the channel and some scows floating around. It would be a very plausible river if they would pump some water into it. They call it a river, and they honestly think it is a river, do these dark and bloody Florentines. They even help out the delusion by building bridges over it. I do not see why they are too good to wade. How the fatigues and annoyances of travel fill one with bitter prejudices sometimes! I might enter Florence under happier auspices a month hence, and find it all beautiful, all attractive. But I do not care to think of it now at all, nor of its roomy shops filled to the ceiling with snowy marble and alabaster copies of all the celebrated sculptures in Europe – copies so enchanting to the eye, that I wonder how they can really be shaped like the dingy petrified nightmares they are the portraits of. . . .My experiences of Florence were chiefly unpleasant. I will change the subject. **99**

MARK TWAIN, *THE INNOCENTS ABROAD,* 1869

A RELUCTANT SIGHTSEER

The English organist and musicologist Dr Charles Burney (1726–1814) was in his mid-forties when he visited the Continent to collect material for his mighty "General History of Music". He seems to have been a man of great charm, numbering among his friends such charismatic figures as David Garrick, Samuel Johnson, Haydn and King George III. The extract below is from the journal he kept on his travels, later published as "Music, Men, and Manners in France and Italy".

[6 September 1770]

❝I yesterday saw the famous chapel of St. Laurence, the mausoleum of the Medici family, but as its chief merit lies in the materials it struck me so little that I forgot to mention it. However as a building 'tis fine. It is of an octagonal figure, vaulted on the top like a cupola, but what it is chiefly admired for is its being incrusted all over with porphyry, agate, touch-stone, jasper, lapis lazuli, oriental alabaster and other very rich materials. . . . There is a statue of the Virgin weeping for the death of Christ by Mich. Angello, very expressive. This seems the place to see the works of Mich. Angello, John di Bologna and Bandinelli. The former was brought up at the expense of one of the grand dukes – they shew in the gallery his 1st attempt at sculpture at 14. It is a grinning head, which so struck the duke that he sent him to Rome to study. It is astonishing how gutterally the Florentines speak particularly words with a hard C or Q. Instead of cor-horr, contra-hontra etc. for qui-huigh. Fruit is not so good or so plentiful as at Venice or Bologna. I suppose the cold from the neighbouring hills prevents it from ripening or at least as early as at those 2 places. The grapes are not yet ripe and the melons have little taste. One seldom hears music in the streets here, and never good, as at Venice and Bologna. The best I have heard yet is that of the *laudisti*. The weather is still hot here and no rain has fallen for some time. There have been showers on the mountains which have disturbed but not filled the Arno. I shall not go on to Rome till it is cooler. I find my blood inflamed – my legs swell and I have a general pruriency in my skin and yet I have such a bad opinion of Italian surgeons I want courage to let 'em bleed me, tho' I believe it would do me a great deal of good. I know not the names or qualities of medicines here or I would take a rumbling purge – a strong dose of jallop if in England. Indifferent food and wine, heat of climate and fatigue have all contributed, I believe to boil my blood.❞

CHARLES BURNEY, *MUSIC, MEN, AND MANNERS IN FRANCE AND ITALY*

THE ARNO, A YELLOW RIVER

In his long poem "Childe Harold's Pilgrimage", Lord Byron (1788–1824) sends his misanthropic hero on a journey through Europe and the near East, meditating on the evils of his past life. By the time the poet got as far as the fourth Canto, from which these verses are taken, he abandoned the pretence of having a fictional hero at all, and muses instead on the glories of the places he visits in Italy.

❝But Arno wins us to the fair white walls,
Where the Etrurian Athens claims and keeps
A softer feeling for her fairy walls.
Girt by her theatre of hills, she reaps
Her corn, and wine, and oil, and plenty leaps
To laughing life, with her redundant horn.
Along the banks where smiling Arno sweeps

Was modern luxury of commerce born,
And buried learning rose, redeem'd to a new morn.

There too, the goddess loves in stone, and fills
The air around with beauty; we inhale
The ambrosial aspect, which, beheld, instils
Part of its immortality; the veil
    Of heaven is half undrawn: within the pale
    stand, and in that form and face behold
    What mind can make, when nature's self would fail;
    And to the fond idolaters of old
    Envy the innate flash which such a soul could mould.

    In Santa Croce's holy precincts lie
    Ashes which make it holier, dust which is
    Even in itself an immortality,
    Though there were something save the past, and this
    The particle of those sublimities
    Which have relapsed to chaos: - here repose
  Angelo's, Alfieri's bones, and his,
   The starry Galileo, with his woes;
Here Machiavelli's earth return'd to whence it rose.

These are four minds, which, like the elements,
Might furnish forth creation: – Italy!
Time, which hath wrong'd thee with ten thousand rents
Of thine imperial garment, shall deny,
And hath denied, to every other sky,
Spirits which soar from ruin: – thy decay
Is still impregnant with divinity,
Which gilds it with revivifying ray:
    Such as the great of yore, Canova is to-day. **"**
        BYRON, *CHILDE HAROLD'S PILGRIMAGE*, 1812–17

CRIMINAL PURSUITS

THE BARGELLO

Augustus William Hare (1792–1834) was a biographer and compiler of travel books. Here he describes the palace of the chief criminal magistrate of Florence.

" The greater part of the palace is due to *Arnolfo di Lapo*. Upon the outside of the older tower, facing the Via del Palagio, were frescoes of the Duke of Athens and his associates, hanging, but they are no longer visible. The bell within, called the *Montanara*, obtained the name of *La Campana delle Armi*, because it was the signal for citizens to lay aside their weapons and retire home. The street below the Bargello witnessed, August 1, 1343, one of the most frightful scenes of Florentine history. The Duke of Athens had taken refuge in the fortress, and the members of the noble Florentine families, Medici, Rucellai, and others, who had suffered from his tyranny, were besieging him. They demanded, as the price of his life, that the Conservatore

Guglielmo d'Assisi and his son, a boy of eighteen, who had been the instruments of his cruelty, should be given up to them. Forced by hunger, he caused them to be pushed out of the half-closed door to the populace, who tore them limb from limb, hacking the boy to pieces first before his father's eyes, and then parading the bloody fragments on their lances through the streets. 99

AUGUSTUS HARE, FLORENCE, 1884

REVENGE

Benvenuto Cellini (1500–71) was an Italian sculptor, gold- and silversmith and engraver. His patrons included two popes, Clement VII and Paul III, and King Francis I of France. A Florentine of a violent and homicidal disposition, he was the most skillful metalworker of his day.

66 A few days afterwards we set out on our return to Florence. We lay one night at a place on this side Chioggia, on the left hand as you go toward Ferrara. Here the host insisted upon being paid before we went to bed, and in his own way; and when I observed that it was the custom everywhere else to pay in the morning, he answered: 'I insist on being paid overnight, and in my own way.' I retorted that men who wanted everything their own way ought to make a world after their own fashion, since things were differently managed here. Our host told me not to go on bothering his brains, because he was determined to do as he had said. Tribolo stood trembling with fear, and nudged me to keep quiet, lest they should do something worse to us; so we paid them in the way they wanted, and afterwards we retired to rest. We had, I must admit, the most capital beds, new in every particular, and as clean as they could be. Nevertheless I did not get one wink of sleep, because I kept on thinking how I could revenge myself. At one time it came into my head to set fire to his house; at another to cut the throats of four fine horses which he had in the stable; I saw well enough that it was easy for me to do all this; but I could not see how it was easy to secure myself and my companion. At last I resolved to put my things and my comrade's on board the boat; and so I did. When the towing-horses had been harnessed to the cable, I ordered the people not to stir before I returned, for I had left a pair of slippers in my bedroom. Accordingly I went back to the inn and called our host, who told me he had nothing to do with us, and that we might go to Jericho. There was a ragged stable-boy about, half asleep, who . . . asked me for a tip, and I gave him a few Venetian coppers, and told him to make the barge man wait till I had found my slippers and returned. I went upstairs, took out a little knife as sharp as a razor, and cut the four beds that I found there into ribbons. I had the satisfaction of knowing I had done a damage of more than fifty crowns. Then I ran down to the boat with some pieces of the bed-covers in my pouch, and bade the bargee start at once without delay. We had not gone far before my gossip Tribolo said that he had left behind some little straps belonging to his carpet-bag, and that he must be allowed to go back for them. I answered that he need not take thought for a pair of little straps, since I could make him as many big ones as he liked. He told me I was always joking, but that he must really go back for his straps. Then he began ordering the bargee to stop, while I kept ordering him to go on. Meanwhile I informed my friend what kind of trick I had played our host, and showed him specimens of the bed-covers and other things, which threw him into such a quaking fright that he roared out to the bargee: 'On with you, on with you, as quick as you can!' and never thought himself quite safe until we reached the gates of Florence. 99

BENVENUTO CELLINI, AUTOBIOGRAPHY,
FIRST PUB. 1558–62

GRAVE ROBBERS

H.V. Morton's "A Traveler in Italy" provides a wealth of detail of the kind not usually discovered by the average visitor to Florence.

❝ The Grand Dukes of Tuscany had a reluctance to be crowned with the regalia of their predecessors, or perhaps it would be more accurate to say that each Grand Duke was buried with his own crown and sceptre and new ones were made for his successor. The presence of so many bejewelled bodies in the vaults of Florence was an invitation to the tomb robber rarely exceeded in promise since the days of the Pharoahs. Accordingly, in 1857 the Government decided to find out how much theft had gone on, and how many of the Grand Dukes still retained their crowns and sceptres. The Pope, Pius IX, visited the mausoleum and inaugurated the Government Commission with special prayers. Forty-nine coffins were opened and examined under the eyes of armed sentries, who were present to see that the workmen employed by the commissioners did not pocket any of the remaining jewels. The report of these proceedings must be the most macabre Government publication ever issued, rivalling in necrophilic appeal the revelations of the royal vaults, which form a gruesome appendix to Dean Stanley's book on Westminster Abbey. When the coffin of Giovanni delle Bande Neri was opened, his bones were found inside a suit of his famous black armour, the visor down. Doctors who saw how his right leg had been amputated were not surprised that he had expired. It is recorded that the surgeons asked for ten men to hold him down while they sawed off his leg, but he scornfully said that twenty could not hold him if he did not wish it, and bore the operation alone, only crying out twice. When he knew he could not recover he cried, 'I will not die amongst all these poultices', so he was moved to a camp-bed, where he died. ❞

H.V. MORTON, *A TRAVELER IN ITALY*, 1964

THE FLORENTINE CHARACTER

CHATTERING VAGABONDS

John Ruskin (1819–1900) spent much of his life traveling in Europe and was particularly attached to northern Italy. His preference was for the landscapes, arts and architecture, however, rather than the people to be found there.

❝ Florence is the most tormenting and harassing place to lounge or meditate in that I have ever entered . . . everybody here is idle, and therefore they are always in the way. The square is full of listless, chattering, smoking vagabonds who are always moving every way at once, just fast enough to make it disagreeable and inevitable to run against them. They are paving, repairing, gas-lighting, drumming from morning to night, and the noise, dirt, tobacco smoke, and spitting are so intolerable in all the great thoroughfares that I have quite given up looking about me. In fact, it is dangerous to do so, for the Italian carts always drive at anyone who looks quiet. . . .In the galleries you can never feel a picture, for it is surrounded, if good, by villainous copyists, who talk and grin, and yawn and stretch, until they infect you with their apathy, and the picture sinks into a stained canvas.One sometimes gets a perfect moment or two in the chapels or cloisters of the churches, but the moment anyone comes it is all over. If monk, he destroys all your conception of monks; if a layman, he is either a French artist with a peaked hat and a beard for two, or a lazy Florentine, who saunters up to look at what you are doing, smokes in your face, stares at you, spits at what you are studying, and walks away again; or perhaps – nearly as bad as any – it is an English cheesemonger and his wife, who come in and remark, – as happened to me the other day while I was looking at the gates of Ghiberti, those which Michelangelo said were fit for the gates of Heaven, two English ladies came and stopped before them. 'Dear me', said one, 'how dirty they are!' 'Oh, quite shocking!' said the other, and away they went.**"**

JOHN RUSKIN, *LETTER TO HIS FATHER,* JUNE 17, 1845

NOBLE WINE MERCHANTS

Tobias Smollett (1721–71) was known for his caustic and satiric writings, earning him the nickname of 'Smelfungus' from his contemporary Laurence Sterne. From 1763 to 1765 he lived in France and Italy with his wife and in 1766 he published "Travels through France and Italy".

"With all their pride . . . the nobles of Florence are humble enough to enter into partnership with shop-keepers, and even to sell wine by retail. It is an undoubted fact, that in every palace or great house in this city, there is a little window fronting the street, provided with an iron-knocker, and over it hangs an empty flask, by way of sign-post. Thither you send your servant to buy a bottle of wine. He knocks at the little wicket, which is opened immediately by a domestic, who supplies him with what he wants, and receives the money like the waiter of any other cabaret. It is pretty extraordinary, that it should not be deemed a disparagement in a nobleman to sell half a pound of figs, or a palm of ribbon or tape, or to take money for a flask of sour wine; and yet be counted infamous to match his daughter in the family of a person who has distinguished himself in any one of the learned professions.**"**

TOBIAS SMOLLETT, *TRAVELS THROUGH FRANCE AND ITALY,* 1776

A CITY OF STONE

Mary McCarthy (1912–92), the American novelist, critic and short story writer wrote with much insight about the city and its people in the 20th century in "The Stones of Florence".

"Many Florentine palaces today are quite comfortable inside and possess pleasant gardens, but outside they bristle like fortresses or dungeons, and, to the passing tourist, their thick walls and bossy surfaces seem to repel the very notion of hospitality. From the Grand Canal, the Venetian palaces, with their windows open to the sun, offer glimpses of sparkling chandeliers and painted ceilings, and it is not hard for the most insensitive tourist to summon up visions of great balls, gaming, love-making in those brilliant rooms. The Florentine palaces, on the contrary, hide their private life like misers, which in fact the Florentines are reputed to be. Consumption is not conspicuous here; an unwritten sumptuary law seems to govern outward display. The famous Florentine elegance, which attracts tourists to the shops on Via Tornabuoni and Via della Vigna Nuova, is characterized by austerity of line, simplicity, economy of effect. In this spare city, the rule of *nihil nimis* prevails. A beggar woman who stands soliciting in front of Palazzo Strozzi, when offered alms a second time in the same day, absently, by another Florentine, refuses: 'No. You gave me before.' Poverty has its own decorum; waste is frowned on. This is a city of endurance, a city of stone. A thing often noticed, with surprise, by foreigners is that the Florentines love their poor, for the poor are the quintessence of Florence – dry in speech, frugal, pessimistic, 'queer', disabused. *'Pazienza!'* is their perpetual, shrugging counsel, and if you ask them how they are, the answer is *'Non c'è male.'* 'Not so bad.' The answer to a favorable piece of tidings is *'Meno male'*, literally, 'less bad'. These people are used to hardship, which begins with a severe climate and overcrowding.**"**

MARY MCCARTHY, *THE STONES OF FLORENCE,* 1963

THE FOOD OF FLORENCE

CASTAGNACCIO

Edmond(1822–96) and Jules Goncourt(1830–70) were authors and diarists who wrote a book entitled "Notes de Voyages 1855–56", which was originally published in Paris in 1894. The piece quoted below was republished in "Italian Food", by the great 20th-century food writer Elizabeth David (1913-91), with her own commentary added.

❝ 'The basic food of the Florentine populace is a cake of chestnut flour larded with pine kernels, the cake is called *Castagnaccio*, a chocolate-coloured cake, displayed for sale in copper cauldrons.' The Goncourts are sometimes surprising: 'In Florence a winter's day is no colder than a summer's night in Paris', they say. Most Florentines would have been amazed to hear such an opinion of their notoriously awful winters. 'The truffles in Florence are the same price as potatoes,' and 'the officers there eat more whipped cream than anywhere else.' The Goncourts' Italian journal was published long after the event, when they had rashly destroyed all their notes. What survived was a skeleton. Even so, the bones still rattle quite effectively. ❞

ELIZABETH DAVID, *ITALIAN FOOD*, 1954

THE RIPENING SUN

Hester Piozzi (1741–1821), a friend of Dr Johnson's, left England to live in Italy with her second husband, an Italian music teacher. The marriage met with much disapproval from family and friends alike, coming three years after her first husband, Henry Thrale's death. But she threw herself into Italian life and seems to have fallen in love with Florence almost immediately.

❝ The fruits in this place begin to astonish me: such cherries did I never yet see, or even hear tell of, as when I caught the laquais de place weighing two of them in a scale to see if they came to an ounce. These are, in the London street phrase, cherries like plums, in size at least, but in flavour they far exceed them, being exactly of the kind that we call bleeding-hearts, hard to the bite and parting easily from the stone, which is proportionately hard. Figs, too, are here in such perfection, that it is not easy for an English gardener to guess at their excellence; for it is not by superior size, but taste and colour, that they are distinguished – small and green on the outside, a bright full crimson within – and we eat them with raw ham, and truly delicious is the dainty. By raw ham, I mean ham cured, not boiled or roasted. It is no wonder, though, that fruits should mature in such a sun as this is, which, to give a just notion of its penetrating fire, I will take leave to tell my country-women is so violent, that I use no other method of heating the pinching-irons to curl my hair than that of poking them out at a south window, with the handles shut in, and the glasses darkened to keep us from being actually fired in his beams. . . . Here is sun enough to ripen pineapples without hot-houses, I am sure, though they repeatedly told us at Milan and Venice that this was the coolest place to pass the summer in, because of the Apennine mountains shading us from the heat, which they confessed to be intolerable with them.

Here, however, they inform us that it is madness to retire into the country, as English people do, during the hot season; for, as there is no shade from high timber-trees, one is bit to death by animals – gnats in particular – which here are excessively troublesome even in the town, notwithstanding we scatter vinegar and use all the arts in our power; but the ground-floor is coolest, and everybody struggles to get themselves a *terreno*, as they call it. ❞

HESTER PIOZZI, QUOTED IN *GLIMPSES OF ITALIAN SOCIETY IN THE EIGHTEENTH CENTURY*, 1892

A JOURNEY THROUGH FLORENCE

▲ San Miniato al Monte.

The Ponte Vecchio seen from the loggia of the Uffizi. ▼

▲ The *Neptune* fountain, Piazza della Signoria.

Piazza Santo Spirito. ▼

▲ The Ponte alle Grazie (foreground) rebuilt after the German bombardments.

▲ The Ponte Vecchio with its jewelers' shops.　　　　▼ The Arno at dusk.

▲ The Palazzo Pitti and the Boboli Gardens. ▼ The *Jolly Caffè* at Santa Maria Novella.

▼ The *Gilli* café on the Piazza della Repubblica.

▲ La Petraia, a Medici villa.　　　　　　　▼ A Florentine villa.

▼ The Certosa di Galluzzo.

Around the Duomo

CHURCH OF SAN SALVATORE AL VESCOVO
ARCHBISHOP'S PALACE
BAPTISTERY
LOGGIA DEL BIGALLO
MISERICORDIA
CAMPANILE

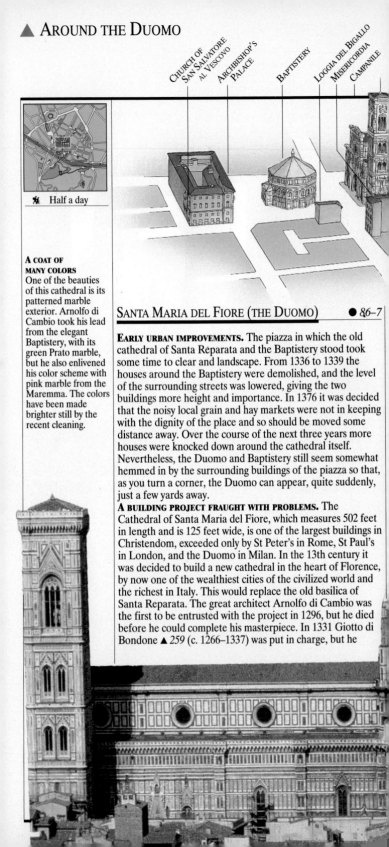

✗ Half a day

A COAT OF MANY COLORS
One of the beauties of this cathedral is its patterned marble exterior. Arnolfo di Cambio took his lead from the elegant Baptistery, with its green Prato marble, but he also enlivened his color scheme with pink marble from the Maremma. The colors have been made brighter still by the recent cleaning.

SANTA MARIA DEL FIORE (THE DUOMO) ● 86–7

EARLY URBAN IMPROVEMENTS. The piazza in which the old cathedral of Santa Reparata and the Baptistery stood took some time to clear and landscape. From 1336 to 1339 the houses around the Baptistery were demolished, and the level of the surrounding streets was lowered, giving the two buildings more height and importance. In 1376 it was decided that the noisy local grain and hay markets were not in keeping with the dignity of the place and so should be moved some distance away. Over the course of the next three years more houses were knocked down around the cathedral itself. Nevertheless, the Duomo and Baptistery still seem somewhat hemmed in by the surrounding buildings of the piazza so that, as you turn a corner, the Duomo can appear, quite suddenly, just a few yards away.

A BUILDING PROJECT FRAUGHT WITH PROBLEMS. The Cathedral of Santa Maria del Fiore, which measures 502 feet in length and is 125 feet wide, is one of the largest buildings in Christendom, exceeded only by St Peter's in Rome, St Paul's in London, and the Duomo in Milan. In the 13th century it was decided to build a new cathedral in the heart of Florence, by now one of the wealthiest cities of the civilized world and the richest in Italy. This would replace the old basilica of Santa Reparata. The great architect Arnolfo di Cambio was the first to be entrusted with the project in 1296, but he died before he could complete his masterpiece. In 1331 Giotto di Bondone ▲ *259* (c. 1266–1337) was put in charge, but he

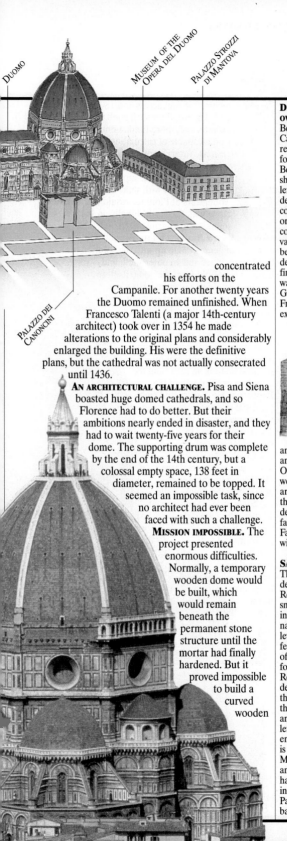

DUOMO

MUSEUM OF THE OPERA DEL DUOMO

PALAZZO STROZZI DI MANTOVA

PALAZZO DEI CANONCINI

concentrated his efforts on the Campanile. For another twenty years the Duomo remained unfinished. When Francesco Talenti (a major 14th-century architect) took over in 1354 he made alterations to the original plans and considerably enlarged the building. His were the definitive plans, but the cathedral was not actually consecrated until 1436.

AN ARCHITECTURAL CHALLENGE. Pisa and Siena boasted huge domed cathedrals, and so Florence had to do better. But their ambitions nearly ended in disaster, and they had to wait twenty-five years for their dome. The supporting drum was complete by the end of the 14th century, but a colossal empty space, 138 feet in diameter, remained to be topped. It seemed an impossible task, since no architect had ever been faced with such a challenge.

MISSION IMPOSSIBLE. The project presented enormous difficulties. Normally, a temporary wooden dome would be built, which would remain beneath the permanent stone structure until the mortar had finally hardened. But it proved impossible to build a curved wooden

DISAGREEMENTS OVER THE FAÇADE
Begun by Arnolfo di Cambio, the façade remained unfinished for several centuries. Below is a drawing showing how it was left at the architect's death. Several competitions were organized to try to complete it, but all in vain as disputes between rival factions defeated all efforts to find a solution. Worse was to follow when Grand Duke Francesco I had the existing part removed

and organized yet another competition. Only a few statues were saved, and these are now preserved in the Museo del Opera del Duomo. The 1887 façade by Emilio de Fabris has been widely criticized.

SANTA REPARATA
The original building, dedicated to Santa Reparata, was far smaller and fitted into what is now the nave. The ground level was raised 6–7 feet for the building of the Duomo, so fortunately Santa Reparata was only demolished down to the foundations of the new cathedral, and there is plenty left to see (the entrance to the crypt is in the nave). Mosaics from the 4th and 5th centuries have been discovered in the remains of the Paleo-Christian basilica.

129

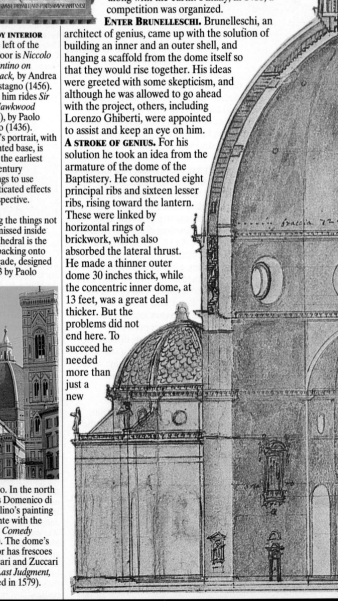

structure 138 feet across and 180 feet above the ground. The wood for such a job could not be found anywhere, and, more fundamentally, the masons proved incapable of calculating the necessary dimensions. Vasari recounts that in their desperation there was even some talk of filling the space beneath the dome with earth to support the construction. It was to be filled with small coins which the youngsters of Florence would then take away, along with the earth! Finally, in 1418, a competition was organized.

ENTER BRUNELLESCHI. Brunelleschi, an architect of genius, came up with the solution of building an inner and an outer shell, and hanging a scaffold from the dome itself so that they would rise together. His ideas were greeted with some skepticism, and although he was allowed to go ahead with the project, others, including Lorenzo Ghiberti, were appointed to assist and keep an eye on him.

A STROKE OF GENIUS. For his solution he took an idea from the armature of the dome of the Baptistery. He constructed eight principal ribs and sixteen lesser ribs, rising toward the lantern. These were linked by horizontal rings of brickwork, which also absorbed the lateral thrust. He made a thinner outer dome 30 inches thick, while the concentric inner dome, at 13 feet, was a great deal thicker. But the problems did not end here. To succeed he needed more than just a new

A SHADY INTERIOR
On the left of the main door is *Niccolo da Tolentino on Horseback*, by Andrea del Castagno (1456). Beside him rides *Sir John Hawkwood* (above), by Paolo Uccello (1436). Uccello's portrait, with its painted base, is one of the earliest 15th-century paintings to use sophisticated effects of perspective.

Among the things not to be missed inside the cathedral is the clock backing onto the façade, designed in 1443 by Paolo

Uccello. In the north aisle is Domenico di Michelino's painting of Dante with the *Divine Comedy* (1465). The dome's interior has frescoes by Vasari and Zuccari (*The Last Judgment,* finished in 1579).

building plan, new lightweight materials and quick-drying mortar. He also had to calculate the position and the angle of each brick. Without the usual wooden framework, the stones could not be tried in place and then cut to fit, so there was absolutely no margin for error. The architect also had to design new tools and special pieces of equipment to complete this revolutionary project. In the end, his theories were proved correct, and work started on August 7, 1420. The dome was completed in 1436. Antonio Manetti described Brunelleschi's method of working: "He persevered in his judgment with great prudence, caution and incredible patience, constantly praising others when he could do so in fairness and rendering honor to those who merited it, holding the esteem of the workmen and the other citizens . . . for the valiant, prudent, ingenious man that he was."

THE HEIGHTS. Ascending the staircase used to climb the dome is a fascinating and exciting experience. It leads round the drum and between the inner and outer shells, giving a first class view of the structure.

ANTONIO ORSO, AN ENLIGHTENED REFORMER. The *Tomb of Bishop Antonio Orso* (backing onto the façade, on the right of the main doors) was made in 1321 by Tino da Camaino (c. 1280–1337), one of the very finest monumental sculptors. Antonio Orso helped to defend the city against the armies of the Holy Roman Emperor, Henry VII of

The interior of Santa Maria del Fiore is awesomely bare.

THE PAZZI CONSPIRACY
The plot's most dramatic events took place inside the cathedral. Pope Sixtus IV had given the Pazzi family the monopoly of alum ▲ 202. Lorenzo retaliated by depriving a Pazzi of his inheritance. The Pazzi decided to murder Lorenzo, with the blessing of the pope, who hoped to extend his power into Tuscany at the expense of the Medicis. After mass on April 25, 1478, Giuliano de' Medici was killed. But Lorenzo was not even wounded, and his revenge was fierce.

Below, a medal commemorating the failure of the conspiracy is inscribed "Salus publica" (for the welfare of the state).

Luxembourg, and was a most important Florentine churchman. Although he led the life of a nobleman, he tried to reform his clergy and stamp out usury. He died in 1321.

THE CAMPANILE ★

PERFECT ELEGANCE. This is one of the most beautiful campaniles in the whole of Italy. Everything about it is refined, delicate and delightful – the fine shaping of the corners running up to the crowning corbel, the exquisite ornamentation of the arched windows, and the charming patterns of colored marble. Yet no fewer than three architects worked on the tower, and their differing styles are quite discernible. The first was Giotto, who began the Campanile in 1334. He died in 1337, having only completed the base, which is decorated with hexagonal bas-reliefs. The decorations were done by Andrea Pisano and Luca della Robbia, and show *Man's Fall from Grace* and his *Redemption through Industry*. On the second level, diamond-shaped bas-reliefs represent the symbolic figures of the planets, the virtues, the arts and the sacraments. Again they are the work of Andrea Pisano, who had also taken over the building of the Campanile itself, which explains the different look of the second story. The last three stories are Talenti's work; he was in charge from 1348 to 1360. There is a staircase to the top with a fine view of the cupola of the cathedral.

THE BAPTISTERY   ● 83

OBSCURE ORIGINS. It was once thought that this building, now consecrated to St John the Baptist, was originally a pagan temple dedicated to Mars. Excavations have since revealed that it was built on Roman foundations dating from the 1st century AD. The oldest parts of the present building go back to the 4th century, when St Ambrose, bishop of Milan, consecrated the first Basilica of San Lorenzo (393). So it was originally a basilica, not a baptistery, and in the 9th century it became a cathedral. Two centuries later it was rebuilt in its present octagonal shape. In 1128 the monument was officially rechristened a baptistery, and it received a beautiful new green and white marble facing.

PERFECTION IN BRONZE. The doors of the Baptistery are among the greatest jewels of Italian Renaissance sculpture. At the beginning of the 14th century it was decided to replace the existing wooden doors, which were considered unworthy of one of Italy's finest religious buildings. Pisa's cathedral had had distinguished sculpted bronze doors since the 11th century, so in 1328 the Florentines called in a Pisan, Andrea Pisano, to complete the job for them. It took him ten years, and his doors were initially installed facing eastward, opposite the Duomo. The motifs were gilded, and this added to their rich appearance. They now hang at the south door.

A RATHER AUSTERE STYLE. Andrea Pisano broke away from the somewhat affected elegance of the late Gothic period. His work is extremely simple, avoiding draped garments and exaggerated poses, and keeping gestures and expressions to the bare minimum. He wanted his compositions uncluttered by insignificant detail.

GHIBERTI'S DOORS. Lorenzo Ghiberti's two doors are utterly different from Pisano's. From 1403 onwards he spent twenty-five years working on the doors for the north entrance, which initially replaced the Pisano doors on the east side. From 1425, and for much of the rest of his life, he worked on those which are now installed at the east door.

THE MUSEUM OF THE OPERA DEL DUOMO

WOOL AND MARBLE. The Opera del Duomo was the administrative body created in 1296 to take charge of the construction and upkeep of the Duomo. In 1331 it was placed under the authority of the Guild of Wool Weavers ▲ *201*, and so it adopted the same emblem – the Agnus Dei. The present building was put up in the 15th century, on the site of a dilapidated old house just next to the furnace and workshop of the sculptor and architect Ghiberti. Brunelleschi, who was then at work on his famous dome, was

FEAST DAYS AND HOLY DAYS
These festivals were of great importance. The *Scoppio del carro* ● *47* still takes place today in the Piazza del Duomo, although it is now on Easter Sunday rather than Holy Saturday. A mechanical dove released from the high altar of the cathedral sets light to a wagon filled with fireworks.

THE CUPOLA OF THE BAPTISTERY
Opposite, a detail from the mosaics that decorate the interior. They took more than a century to complete (1270–30), and show a strong Venetian influence. Cimabue, Coppo and the young Giotto are all thought to have worked on them.

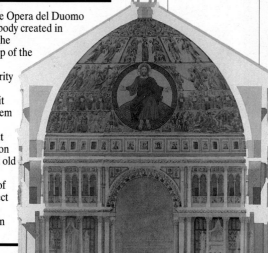

Dividing the doors into panels, as Andrea Pisano had done, Lorenzo Ghiberti (1378–1455) was able to illustrate the life of Christ in a directly narrative fashion. The mass of characters are elegantly and vividly depicted with an originality that makes this a fascinating study of humanity. The influence of antiquity is strong in the garments, attitudes and compositions which are all reminiscent of Roman bas-reliefs.

The Nativity

Jesus Driving the Money Changers out of the Temple

The Adoration of the Magi

The Baptism of Christ

Saint Mark

The Annunciation

"JESUS AMONG THE DOCTORS"
This complex composition shows the maturity of Ghiberti's work. The drapery is especially fine, surging forward in a wave from the figure on the left and swelling as it moves toward the standing figure on the right. The scene is set in a space which is given depth by the expert effects of architectural perspective.

On the right is a detail from one of the bas-reliefs by Andrea Pisano (c. 1290–c. 1348) on the south door. His magnificent work in bronze, done using the process of lost wax casting, contributed to the revival of decorative work in this medium. The gilding of the figures and the frames was a new departure. The doors were cast by Venetians, who had maintained the tradition and the skills of working in bronze.

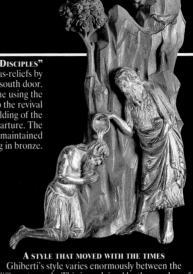

The Temptation of Christ

A STYLE THAT MOVED WITH THE TIMES

Ghiberti's style varies enormously between the different panels. This is explained by the number of years he spent making his doors. *The Annunciation* is somewhat flat, contrasting with the fullness and depth of *The Nativity*, right beside it, which has action on several different planes.

The Crucifixion

Christ Carrying the Cross

GHIBERTI'S CONTRACT

In the terms of this agreement, dated November 1403, Ghiberti undertook to deliver at least three panels a year to the Arte della Calimala ▲ *198*. The faces, hair and trees had to be produced by his own hand, although Donatello and Uccello were among those who helped him on the work.

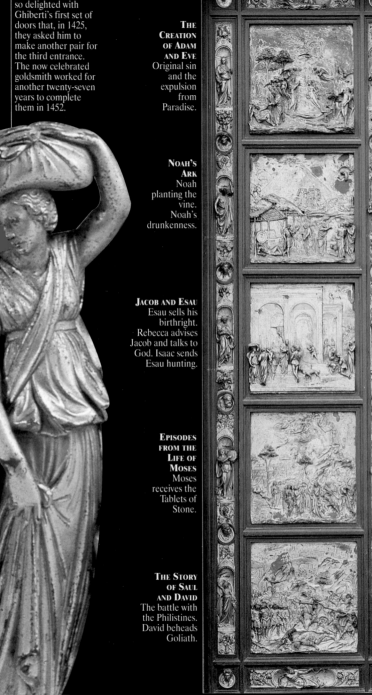

THE CREATION OF ADAM AND EVE
Original sin and the expulsion from Paradise.

NOAH'S ARK
Noah planting the vine. Noah's drunkenness.

JACOB AND ESAU
Esau sells his birthright. Rebecca advises Jacob and talks to God. Isaac sends Esau hunting.

EPISODES FROM THE LIFE OF MOSES
Moses receives the Tablets of Stone.

THE STORY OF SAUL AND DAVID
The battle with the Philistines. David beheads Goliath.

<blockquote>
«FEW THINGS OF IMPORTANCE HAVE BEEN DONE IN OUR LAND WHERE I HAVE NOT HAD A HAND IN THE DESIGN OR THE DIRECTION.»

GHIBERTI
</blockquote>

CAIN AND ABEL
They offer sacrifices. Abel the shepherd and Cain the tiller of land. Cain slays Abel. The wrath of God.

THE STORY OF ABRAHAM
Sarah at the entrance to the tent. The three angels visit Abraham.

THE STORY OF JOSEPH
He is pulled out of the pit and sold to merchants. Joseph explains the Pharaoh's dreams.

THE STORY OF JOSHUA
Joshua at the battle of Jericho. The crossing of the river Jordan.

THE TEMPLE OF SOLOMON
The Queen of Sheba visits King Solomon.

"THE GATES OF PARADISE"
The novelty of this series lay in the new way in which the Old Testament stories were set out. Ghiberti surrounded the panels with a frieze of prophets and sibyls, and within each panel he illustrated several episodes while still maintaining an overall narrative unity. He shows an impressive mastery of architectural perspective, especially in the

Meeting of King Solomon and the Queen of Sheba (bottom right), which proves him to have been one of the great artists of the first half of the Quattrocento (the 1400's). These doors were hung at the eastern entrance, and Michelangelo called them "The Gates of Paradise".

A miniature antiphon (a collection of liturgical choral works) from the 16th century, called *Moses and the Burning Bush*. This is the work of Fra Eustacchio, a Dominican from San Marco.

THE COLLECTON OF RELIQUARIES
Among the fine examples here is the reliquary known as "del Libretto" (below), made by the Florentine Paolo di Giovanni Sogliani (1500). It contains four gold tablets with niches for relics, decorated with miniatures and enamel. In medieval times relics played a very serious part in religious life.

given the job of building a residence for the officials of the Opera. And he was also asked to design a workshop for the marble and stone masons.

A SCULPTURE HAVEN. Since 1891 the Museo dell'Opera del Duomo has gradually accumulated various works of art from the Duomo, Bapistery and Campanile, often pieces that were being damaged by pollution.

REMNANTS OF THE FAÇADE. On the ground floor there are several statues by Arnolfo di Cambio, done for the façade of the cathedral. There is a *Santa Reparata* (on the left with what seems to be a vase but is in fact a glowing brazier), a *Madonna and Child*, also known as the "glass-eyed Virgin" because of this most unusual detail, a *Madonna of the Nativity*, and a remarkable *Boniface VIII*, in stiff, Byzantine style. Although it is not certain in every case exactly who the sculptor was, the statues seem to show di Cambio to be a highly original artist. His huge, priestly figures, although sometimes clearly derived from antiquity, anticipate the work of Giotto.

SELF-PORTRAIT. Halfway up the stairs is a *Pietà*, by Michelangelo, which was once in the cathedral. It is one of his last works, although he had been working on it since 1553. He had intended it for his tomb in Santa Maria Maggiore in Rome, but became very irritated with the piece because of the bad quality of the marble, and broke the left leg of Christ. So he gave it to a friend, and it was then brought to Florence. The Nicodemus would seem to be a self-portrait, and the Mary Magdalene, who looks a little out of proportion, was done by his pupil Tiberio Calcagni.

THE REIGN OF DONATELLO. The museum has a marvellous collection of works by Donato di Betto Bardi, known as Donatello (1386–1466). He spent many years, from 1418 to 1425, making statues for the Duomo and the Campanile. His powerful heroic style, in marked contrast to the elegance of Ghiberti, was utterly new in early 15th-century Florence. His *Habakkuk* is particularly striking – the plain and massive robe is almost crude. The Old Testament prophet looks rugged and unattractive, a simple man but a visionary. The statue was intended for one of the niches of the Campanile, and the Florentines immediately took *lo zuccone* ("marrow-head") to their hearts. It is said that Donatello was so proud of his realism that he gave the finished statue a kick and cried: "Speak, you fool!"

A HAGGARD PENITENCE. In the wooden statue of *Saint Mary Magdalene*, made by Donatello in about 1454, the ugliness is even more exaggerated and verges on the pathetic. Mary Magdalene was reputed to be a sinful woman and was accused of lust.

«THE APOSTLES AND THE MARTYRS [OF DONATELLO] ARE NOT
MEN WHO SUFFER, BUT MEN WHO FIGHT.»

FILARETE

According to some, she used her fortune to help Christ, who accepted her as his only female friend. After the crucifixion she took refuge in Provence where she lived for thirty years in a cave, atoning for her sins. Donatello's statue puts the emphasis on her shame and degradation.

THE "CANTORIE". There are many other works of sculpture in the museum, including two famous *cantorie* (organ lofts) which used to be above the doors of the sacristies. One is a charming, well-balanced piece by Luca della Robbia, the other is a wild dance by Donatello.

THE BRUNELLESCHI ROOMS. These contain models showing how the dome was constructed, with the pulleys, set-squares, and compasses used by craftsmen working on the building in the 15th and 16th centuries. In 1954 a room was opened to display some of the fifty-eight books of choral music (antiphons, graduals and vespers) that remained in use in the cathedral until 1930. Their magnificent illuminations date from the 15th and early 16th centuries. The great flood of November 4, 1966 ● *33,* ▲ *173,* caused the almost total destruction of these documents, and only three escaped serious damage. The parchments swelled and stuck together, and the illuminations ran into blurs of color. The restorers have worked miracles, without which these books would certainly have been lost.

AROUND THE DUOMO

THE ARCHBISHOP'S PALACE. This grand palace was built in the Mannerist style by Andrea de Mozzi, bishop of Florence 1287–95, and a man detested by Dante. Andrea led such a life of scandal that even his own brother was moved to demand his removal. The palace was partially rebuilt by Giovanni Antonio Dosio (1533–1609), who was also responsible for the courtyard, on which he worked between 1573 and 1589. The façade dates from the end of the last century. To visit the CHURCH OF SAN SALVATORE AL VESCOVO ● *82,* ask permission from the custodian. This little 12th-century church with its Romanesque façade faces onto the Piazza del Olio. It was altered in 1221, and then again at the beginning of the 18th century. The frescoes in the chancel are the work of Giovanni Domenico Ferreti (1692–1768), who was a prolific artist.

This early 16th-century mosaic *Bust of Saint Zenobius* is by Monte di Giovanni. The renewed popularity of mosaic work at this time was the result of

Lorenzo the Magnificent's commission for the vault of the San Zanobi chapel in the cathedral.

Below, the *Pietà* by Michelangelo. According to Vasari, *Nicodemus*, holding Christ, is a self-portrait of the master. Opposite, above, are two statues by Donatello – *Habakkuk*, on the left, and *Jeremiah*, on the right.

FILIPPO BRUNELLESCHI
His bust is on the façade of the Palazzo dei Canoncini. His great achievement was to put the cupola on the Duomo.

Members of the Brotherhood of the Misericordia wore dramatic black capes and deep hoods to preserve their anonymity.

Above right, the façade of the Palazzo Strozzi di Mantova and the interior of the Church of San Salvatore al Vescovo. Below, the Loggia del Bigallo.

THE LOGGIA DEL BIGALLO AND MUSEUM ● 67. The fine Gothic loggia was built between 1352 and 1358, probably by Alberto Arnoldi. It was a place where lost and abandoned children were displayed before being fostered. The Compagnia del Bigallo, a charitable brotherhood, is one of the oldest institutions of good works in the city. It grew out of the Company of St Mary the Virgin, founded in 1244 by the Dominican St Peter the Martyr. The name "Bigallo" comes from a hospice he gave to the Company, which still helps children and old people in need. Some rooms in the building are now a museum. In the Sala del Consiglio are the frescoes that used to adorn the façade of the loggia. The *Madonna of the Misericordia* is particularly interesting because it shows Florence as it was in 1342. Other works can be seen in the entrance to the new headquarters of the Misericordia.

THE MISERICORDIA. This building was completely altered at the end of the 16th century by Alfonso Parigi. The Brotherhood of the Misericordia was founded in the 13th century, and today its six thousand members come from every walk of life. All their work is voluntary, giving first aid and caring for the sick at home. In the past they did some gruesome work, accompanying condemned men to their death and burying the victims of epidemics. In their dark, hooded robes, they are still a familiar sight around Florence.

PALAZZO DEI CANONCINI. On the corner of the Via dello Studio is a palace built by Gaetano Baccani (1792–1867), an architect who was frequently employed on various city projects. His other works include the Palazzo Borghese ● 92, and the campanile of Santa Croce ● 84, ▲ 254. The niches of the façade contain busts of Filippo Brunelleschi and Arnolfo di Cambio.

PALAZZO STOZZI DI MANTOVA ● 74. On the ground floor of this palace, formerly known as the "Guadagni dell'Opera" and dating from the 1600's, are windows that are considered to be among the finest in Florence. From here, on the corner of Via dell'Oriuolo and the Piazza del Duomo, there is an excellent view of the cathedral apse, which is all the better at night, when careful lighting brings out the majestic and elegant proportions.

PALAZZO NICCOLINI. Part of this structure, which was once the Palazzo Nardini del Riccio, is thought to be the work of Silvani. It was built in the 17th century on the site of a house that was once occupied by Donatello.

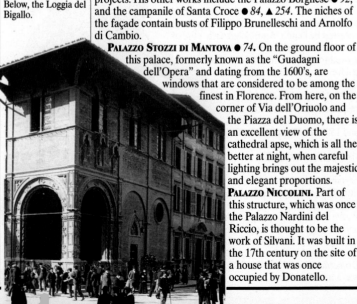

FROM THE SIGNORIA TO THE PONTE VECCHIO

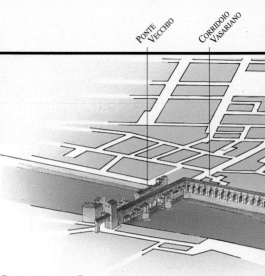

PONTE VECCHIO

CORRIDOIO VASARIANO

🏃 Half a day

THE MISTS OF TIME
The Piazza della
Signoria is of the
greatest significance
in the history of
Florence. For a long
time this quarter was
the nerve center of
Florentine political
life. Remains have
been uncovered that
date from Neolithic
times, and it would
appear that even then
it was an important
center of exchange.
The Romans built an
amphitheater here,
with seats on the site
of the present Via dei
Gondi.

An anonymous
painting of
*Savonarola at the
Stake*. The bonfire
was built on the
Piazza della
Signoria.

PIAZZA DELLA SIGNORIA

POLITICS AND TOWN PLANNING. Many Italian cities were
dominated by their bishop, and the headquarters of civic
government, the cathedral and the bishop's palace all tended
to stand in the same piazza. This was the case in Umbrian
towns that were under the power of Rome, such as Perugia. It
was also the case in those towns further east in the Marche,
and it was true of many Tuscan towns like Volterra, Arezzo
and San Gimignano. There were three cities, however, where
religious and civic life remained separate within the city –
Bologna, Siena and Florence.
DEMOLITION ON A GRAND SCALE. Until the 14th century, this
piazza was quite a modest place. The Uberti, who were
leaders of the local Ghibellines ● *34*, lived here. The defeat
of the imperial faction proved most convenient for, in
revenge, the houses of citizens exiled in 1302 were pulled
down. The Piazza della Signoria was enlarged several more
times during the 14th century and a number of other
buildings were demolished or moved

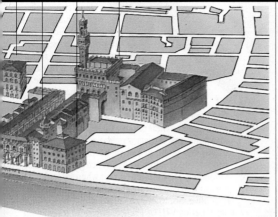

HERCULES AND CACUS
A marble group sculpted by Baccio Bandinelli (1488–1560) in 1533–4. It was intended to rival Michelangelo's *David* (below), the great republican symbol. Commissioned by Alessandro de' Medici, Hercules was supposed to represent the Medici reign. Fierce competition existed between Bandinelli and Michelangelo, and Benvenuto Cellini took the latter's side and was scathing about this piece. The powerful sculpting of anatomy is in typical late Renaissance style.

between 1307 and 1318, while the Uberti quarter was completely destroyed. The church of San Romolo was moved back to stand in line with its neighbors, while the church of Santa Cecilia was knocked down entirely in 1385–8.

OUT WITH UNDESIRABLES. The piazza was the noble and revered seat of government, and so construction standards were set very high. It was paved with more care and expense than any other area. To preserve the dignity of the place, "dishonorable" trades like begging and prostitution were banned, carts and other heavy traffic were also forbidden, and even games of chance were outlawed. Furthermore, any crime would tend to receive harsher punishment if committed in or near the piazza.

PROPHECY, MORALITY AND TERROR. Among the most dramatic stories involving the Piazza della Signoria was that of Girolamo Savonarola (1452–98), a Dominican monk who, with his eloquent and terrifying moral tirades, held the population of Florence in his grip. His message was

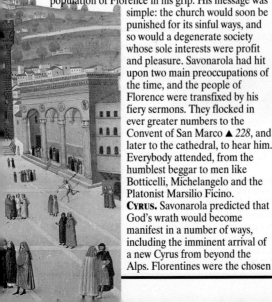

simple: the church would soon be punished for its sinful ways, and so would a degenerate society whose sole interests were profit and pleasure. Savonarola had hit upon two main preoccupations of the time, and the people of Florence were transfixed by his fiery sermons. They flocked in ever greater numbers to the Convent of San Marco ▲ *228*, and later to the cathedral, to hear him. Everybody attended, from the humblest beggar to men like Botticelli, Michelangelo and the Platonist Marsilio Ficino.

CYRUS. Savonarola predicted that God's wrath would become manifest in a number of ways, including the imminent arrival of a new Cyrus from beyond the Alps. Florentines were the chosen

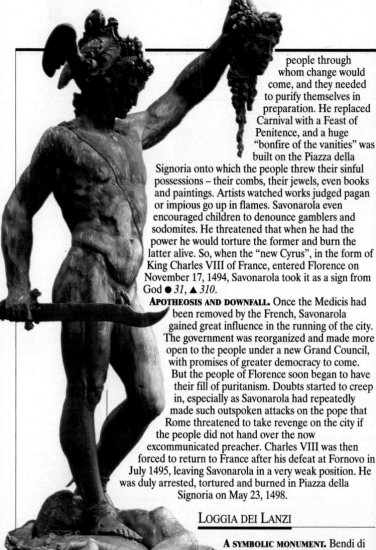

people through whom change would come, and they needed to purify themselves in preparation. He replaced Carnival with a Feast of Penitence, and a huge "bonfire of the vanities" was built on the Piazza della Signoria onto which the people threw their sinful possessions – their combs, their jewels, even books and paintings. Artists watched works judged pagan or impious go up in flames. Savonarola even encouraged children to denounce gamblers and sodomites. He threatened that when he had the power he would torture the former and burn the latter alive. So, when the "new Cyrus", in the form of King Charles VIII of France, entered Florence on November 17, 1494, Savonarola took it as a sign from God ● *31*, ▲ *310*.

APOTHEOSIS AND DOWNFALL. Once the Medicis had been removed by the French, Savonarola gained great influence in the running of the city. The government was reorganized and made more open to the people under a new Grand Council, with promises of greater democracy to come. But the people of Florence soon began to have their fill of puritanism. Doubts started to creep in, especially as Savonarola had repeatedly made such outspoken attacks on the pope that Rome threatened to take revenge on the city if the people did not hand over the now excommunicated preacher. Charles VIII was then forced to return to France after his defeat at Fornovo in July 1495, leaving Savonarola in a very weak position. He was duly arrested, tortured and burned in Piazza della Signoria on May 23, 1498.

LOGGIA DEI LANZI

A SYMBOLIC MONUMENT. Bendi di Cione and Simone Talenti built this loggia between 1376 and 1382, to a design by Orcagna. It was known at first as the Loggia dell'Orcagna, but later came to be called Loggia dei Lanzi (an abbreviation of *Lanzichenecchi* meaning "the halberdiers" of Cosimo I de' Medici's guard). This was the place where the new priors ▲ *148* and *gonfalonieri* of the city were inducted, so that until the 16th century it was also known as the Loggia dei Priori. For a long time it was the symbol of Florentine democracy.

A CHALLENGE. Among the pieces to be seen in this little open-air sculpture gallery are some by Giambologna and Cellini. Giambologna, who was also known as Jean Boulogne (1529–1608), was of Flemish origin. His work is elegant,

CELLINI'S "PERSEUS"
Perseus, son of Zeus and Danaë, beheaded Medusa, a terrifying goddess with a head covered in writhing serpents and a look that turned men to stone.

sensual and strongly Mannerist in flavor. *The Rape of the Sabines* was a magnificent response to a difficult challenge presented by an unshapely piece of marble that no one knew what to do with. It is a composition full of turmoil, yet it still retains a true harmony of line.

LOGGIA DEI LANZI
This also contains the statues of six priestesses, much-restored Roman pieces, as well as *Hercules and the Centaur* (1599) and *The Rape of the Sabines* (below), both by Giambologna.

A REPUTATION AT STAKE. Benvenuto Cellini (1500–71), creator of the famous bronze *Perseus*, was both a sculptor and a goldsmith. He was a proud and violent man, well aware of his own genius. In his autobiography, he told the story behind this famous piece. It had been commissioned by Cosimo I, who was perplexed by the final plaster cast. The head of Medusa, held out at arm's length, seemed too far from the main body of the sculpture for the bronze to reach it in casting. Much offended by this observant criticism coming from a man he despised, Cellini filled his furnace with copper and bronze and stoked up such a blaze that he came near to setting his house on fire. His furious labors brought on a sudden fever, and he went to bed, leaving his assistant with strict instructions to keep an eye on the melting metal, which was nearing the required point of fusion.

A FORCE BORN OF DESPERATION. Alas, things went wrong and the bronze began to cool. Out of bed in an instant, Cellini rushed to take over, regardless of his high fever and also of his roof which was by now on fire. Every piece of metal that he could lay his hands on went into the furnace, right down to the household cutlery and pewter. Nothing mattered any more, his fever was forgotten and his roof was in ashes. At last, the incandescent bronze flowed into the cast, and the piece was finished. Two days later, when it had cooled down, Cellini was slowly able to uncover his statue. The Medusa's head was complete and perfect as was the lithe and vigorous body of Perseus. Only three toes of the right foot were missing, but this was a minor problem. He added them later, along with the statuettes in the niches of the pedestal.

THE DUCHESS THWARTED. When the statuettes were taken to the Palazzo Vecchio to be examined, they so took the fancy of the duchess that she wanted them to decorate her own apartments. Cellini, containing his fury, dared not refuse; but the next day one of his assistants foolishly went ahead and fixed them into their niches. It was a liberty for which the duchess never forgave the great man.

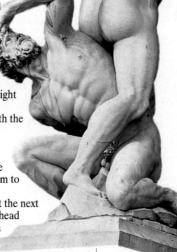

145

Below, the Palazzo Uguccioni.

"CALCIO STORICO" Despite its bloody history, this piazza has always been the scene of festivities. Every year since 1530 the Florentines have played *calcio* (football) ● *47*, here on Midsummer Day to celebrate their brave resistance to a siege by imperial troops. The ceremony never varies. As dusk falls, a solemn procession makes its way into the piazza: first the soldiers of the guard in gold-trimmed uniforms, next the Podestà in scarlet robes, then the trumpeters, the guilds and finally a troop of horsemen. A cannon is fired, and the lights go out. The magic is sustained for a moment longer by burning torches on the

Palazzo Vecchio. Then the lights come up

again and the match begins. It is a wild but basically lighthearted game played in costume.

THE NEPTUNE FOUNTAIN. This rather unmemorable statue of the God of the Deep has been nicknamed *Il Biancone* by the Florentines, a lighthearted allusion to his bright white marble. It was made between 1560 and 1575 by Bartolomeo Ammannati (1511–92), who was also a fine architect. The fountain was first erected, in wood and plaster, in honor of the wedding of Cosimo I's son Francesco to Joanna of Austria in 1565. Neptune was chosen to adorn it in an allusion to Cosimo's naval achievements. The statue is a respectable attempt, but Ammannati seems not to have grasped how to convey power in the human figure, despite the example of Michelangelo's Sistine Chapel in Rome, which was already admired throughout Italy. Michelangelo was actually blunt enough to accuse his fellow sculptor of wasting a good piece of marble! Fortunately, Giambologna had a hand in making the delightful nymphs and satyrs around the basin. The statue of Cosimo I, a few yards away, is also his, with its three bas-reliefs depicting the duke's achievements.

THE MERCHANTS' COURT

The Palace of the Tribunale di Mercanzia was built in 1359 for the Mercanzia, an institution created in 1308 by the Arti Maggiori ● *52*, ▲ *198* to deal with the legal and commercial affairs of the guilds. It was headed by a foreigner, aided by a counsellor from each of the Arti Maggiori, and its function was to deal with fraud, to arbitrate in disputes between members, to uphold the decisions of the guild leaders and to settle matters in cases of bankruptcy. The Mercanzia also ensured the safety of the Arti consuls when traveling abroad. It had its own police and prisons, and methods of interrogation that included torture.

PALAZZO UGUCCIONI

This is a very beautiful palace built between 1550 and 1559 (it is at number 7 in the piazza). The style is extremely unusual for Florence, since it was designed according to rules laid down by Bramante, a Roman architect. The façade is thought to be by Mariotto di Zanobi Folfi.

Left, *Massacre* by Renato Guttoso in 1943. Below right, *Southern Song* by Giorgio de Chirico. Below center, *Still Life* by Giorgio Morandi. Bottom, an anonymous lunette showing a view of the Piazza della Signoria.

PALAZZO LAVISAN

This palace dates from 1871, and is the headquarters of a Venetian insurance company. Its eclectic design derives from a number of sources. The architect, Landi, used medieval features (gemel windows) in a Renaissance context (symmetrical façade, cornice). This is the spot where the Loggia dei Pisani and church of Santa Cecilia once stood.

THE MODERN ART COLLECTION

There is not a lot of modern art in Florence, but this collection, housed at number 5, Piazza della Signoria, was given to the city by Alberto della Raggione from Genoa. Many Italian artists are represented, some much better known than others. Alongside Giorgio de Chirico, Giorgio Morandi and Gino Severini are painters like De Pisis, Giacomo Manzu, Ottone Rosai and Renato Guttoso. Guttoso (1912–87) has a modern, approachable style that combines elements of Cubism and Expressionism. After the war he was co-founder of the *Fronte nuovo dell'arte*, and a leading light of the neo-Realist school, working with the communists to develop an art with strong social ideals. He tended to find his inspiration in the current social struggle, but also took historical events as his subjects.

THE ALBERTO DELLA RAGGIONE COLLECTION OF MODERN ART

Giorgio de Chirico (1888–1978) settled in Paris in 1910 and worked with the avant-garde poets and writers. The enigmatic quality of his work struck a chord with the Surrealists, who included it in the first exhibition of Surrealist art in 1925. Most interesting were his "metaphysical interiors", strange claustrophobic rooms cluttered with symbolic objects that represented an expression of the inner labyrinths of modern man. Giorgio Morandi (1890–1964) came from Bologna. He was a master of still life, his work inspired by a reflective, poetic spirit.

PALAZZO VECCHIO
(OR PALAZZO DELLA SIGNORIA) ● 67

FLORENCE AT ITS PEAK. In the late Middle Ages Florence was one of the major cities of Europe and was in an extremely strong economic position. Siena, its nearby rival, had suffered a serious setback with the bankruptcy of its largest company, the Bonsignori (1309). A short time before Pisa had been defeated by Genoa (1284), and Lucca had been much shaken by the downfall of the Riccardi family.
URBAN IMPROVEMENTS. The city began to see developments of a dramatic kind. Streets were widened, paved and lit, squares were opened up in front of the churches of Santa Maria Novella and Santa Croce, houses and palaces were restored, and villas began to appear on the surrounding hillsides. The finest buildings in the city date from this period. They include the new cathedral of Santa Maria del Fiore (the Duomo, ▲ 128), dedicated to the Virgin Mary (Santa Reparata was not considered important enough for a building which Florentines hoped to see famed throughout the universe); the Palazzo Vecchio, first known as the Priors' Palace; and the churches of

THE PALAZZO VECCHIO Above, the pediment over the entrance. In the oval inset, the view of the Duomo from the tower.

Santa Maria Novella ▲ *213*, Santa Croce ▲ *254*, Santissima Annunziata ▲ *242*, Ognissanti ▲ *281*, Santo Spirito ▲ *302*, and Santa Trinita ▲ *273*. As different religious orders built their churches, they also improved their surroundings, usually creating a large piazza in front of the church. This was not always easy to do in such a densely populated city (see Santa Maria Novella, for example).

THE PRIORS: THE FOUNDING OF THE REPUBLIC. The year 1282 saw the constitution of a new governing body made up of priors. Until then the priors had been the leaders of the guilds ● *52*, ▲ *198*, but now they assumed the highest authority. The number of priors (also called *Signori*) increased as new guilds were created, rising from three to six, then twelve and sometimes reaching sixteen, depending on the politics and economics of the moment. From 1293 a Gonfaloniere di Giustizia presided over the priors. He was also commander-in-chief of the army. "The guilds held the state, a people's state, in their hands, making Florence historically unique", wrote the historian Gino Capponi in 1875. Certainly, the aristocracy could not be elected as governing priors unless they were involved in trade – the world of their social inferiors. Only members of the Arti were eligible, such as Dante ▲ *193*, a prior from June 15 to August 15, 1300. Like other poets, he belonged to the Guild of Physicians and Apothecaries.

AN EXEMPLARY INSTITUTION. The priorate was organized on a strict collegial basis intended to prevent any factional allegiances. The priors lived together day and night, at first in a modest palace owned by the Cerchi family, and from 1302, when it could be used, in the impressive Priors' Palace. Visitors could only be received officially and in public, while priors could only leave the palace for reasons of great importance: the death of a close relative, for example. They had considerable power and were responsible not only for the city's government but also its legal system and diplomatic affairs. The Florentines, ever concerned about security, considered it so

Unfortunately it is hard to obtain admission. Below is a 19th-century engraving showing the splendid Palazzo della Signoria and the open front of the Loggia dei Lanzi facing the piazza. Bandinelli's *Hercules*, decorated with animals (top of facing page), stands at the foot of the palace. The entrance leads into a pretty courtyard which echoes to the splashing of a fountain.

important to have a constant change of leadership that they elected the priors for just two months. They could then not be re-elected for three years. In return, they were supposed to be exempt from prison, torture and exile, but there were many exceptions, the best known being Dante, who was exiled after the defeat of the White Guelfs by the Blacks ● *34*, ▲ *312*.

FROM FORTRESS TO COURT RESIDENCE. The first stone was laid in 1299, and construction took sixteen years. The work is attributed to the architect Arnolfo di Cambio, already at work on the cathedral ▲ *128*. The palace has been altered by a number of building projects over the centuries, particularly under the Medicis. It was Cosimo il Vecchio who first wanted to transform it from a utilitarian seat of government to a comfortable residence. He made several large-scale alterations, instructing his architect Michelozzo to rebuild the 14th-century courtyard, for example.

GLORIFYING THE MEDICIS. A detailed description of all the rich, sometimes over-ornate, decoration of the many rooms in the palace would fill a small volume. Giorgio Vasari (1511–74) and his helpers had one main theme in their work: the glory of the Medicis (and, above all, Cosimo I), either portraying their successes in battle or producing allegorical evocations of their greatness. The immense *Salone dei Cinquecento* (HALL OF THE FIVE HUNDRED) is a very good example. It was built between 1495 and 1496, during the time of Savonarola's republic. When Cosimo I took up residence in the Palazzo Vecchio he wanted it to be a magnificent reception room. He entrusted the work to his faithful Vasari, who immediately covered the walls with grandiose frescoes on such subjects as Florence's victories over Pisa and Siena. In the center of the very elaborately decorated ceiling is the *Apotheosis of Cosimo I*. Opposite the entrance, in the center of the far wall, is Michelangelo's *Victory* (1533–4), which was actually made for the tomb of Julius II.

IN THE "STUDIOLO"
The Alchemist's Laboratory by Stradano, right.

SALA DEGLI ELEMENTI
On the second floor are apartments known as the Quartiere degli Elementi, the first of them consecrated to Air, Earth, Fire and Water. In ancient times it was thought that the universe was composed of these four elements. Not by chance are these rooms directly above those of the Medicis themselves, the symbolic implication being that the family was of equal elemental importance. This idea is pursued in detail room by room. Cosimo I's room is immediately below the Sala di Giove (Jupiter's Room), and allegories of his virtues, *Generosity, Glory, Honor* and *Guile,* surround the

picture of *The Childhood of Jupiter.*

Above, the *Apotheosis of Cosimo I,* in the Salone dei Cinquecento.

AN ALCHEMIST HIDEAWAY. Entering the *Studiolo* of Francesco I de' Medici is like walking into a treasure chest. It was created between 1569 and 1572, and the room was reconstructed in 1920. The young man kept his dearest possessions concealed in the cupboards masked behind the lower line of paintings. These included precious objects and works of art, but also scientific apparatus. The tiny room is covered in decoration by various Mannerist artists (Vasari, Bandini, Santi di Tito and Stradano) with themes such as the triumphs of Prometheus, and the discoveries of science, alchemy and magic – all dear to the heart of the young heir.
BRONZINO PORTRAITS. On the barrel vault are portraits of Cosimo I and Eleanor of Toledo, Francesco's parents. They are by Bronzino (1503–72), then Florence's most sought-after portraitist. His work is stylized, setting subjects against a neutral background and giving the flesh a cold, smooth appearance. This glacial quality was typical of certain Tuscan Mannerists, and was imitated in courts across Europe.
ELEANOR'S CHAPEL. On the second floor is La Cappella di Eleonora, a masterpiecè of Florentine Mannerism. It was decorated by Bronzino in the 1550's. His work has a tremendous power. The colors are strong and bright, the figures combine animation with a studied elegance and a cool, inexpressive look that is particularly impressive in the *Pietà.*

Left, a window of the Palazzo Vecchio with fine loggia dating from the 16th century. Bottom left, one of the doors of the Sala degli Gigli inlaid with a picture of *Petrarch* by Giuliano da Maiano.

There is an interesting medallion on the ceiling, with three faces. It probably represents the Trinity ▲ *233*, with an insistence on the equality of the three divinities.

THE SALA DI GUALDRADA. This room is named after Gualdrada, the daughter of Bellincione Berti, whose portrait is to be seen on the ceiling. She was forced to meet the visiting Holy Roman Emperor, Otto IV of Germany, in the cathedral of Santa Maria Reparata ▲ *129*, and she is remembered, good Guelf that she was, for refusing to greet him with a kiss. Artistically more interesting is the frieze with paintings by Stradano showing aspects of 16th-century Florence: the Piazza della Signoria and the Uffizi; the Piazza del Mercato Vecchio (now the Piazza della Repubblica ▲ *209*); Piazza Santa Croce, complete with jousting, and on the right the houses that were pulled down to make way for the vast façade of the Palazzo dell'Antella ▲ *254* by Giulio Parigi (1619–20); the Ponte Santa Trinita leading into the Oltrarno ▲ *273*; the Via Larga with the Medici palace ▲ *224*, before it was widened; and the façade of the Duomo as Arnolfo di Cambio left it ▲ *128*.

THE "GUARDAROBA", OR MAP ROOM ★. Cosimo I was passionate about geography and astronomy and he had the cupboard doors covered with magnificent maps. They were painted toward the end of the 16th century by Egnazio Danti (1536–86), famous geographer and astronomer of Santa Maria Novella, and by Stefano Bonsignori (d. 1589). In the center is a globe (1564–8) by Danti, which in its day was the largest ever made. The room looks on to an inner courtyard, and the entrance to the Corridoio Vasariano (Vasari's Corridor) ▲ *175* can be seen, as well as Benvenuto Cellini's studio. The latter was often the refuge of Grand Duke Cosimo I. He had a useful peephole from there into the Salone dei Cinquecento.

THE TOWER. This tower appears out of balance with the main body of the façade, one part seeming almost to hang in mid-air. The entrance is through the SALA DEI GIGLI (ROOM OF LILIES). A staircase leads up past the room called, with a certain black humor, the *Alberghettino* ("little hotel"). Cosimo il Vecchio and Savonarola were among the "guests" who stayed here: it was reserved for political prisoners of the highest rank. From the top of the tower the view is superb, but access is strictly limited.

SALONE DEI CINQUECENTO
A medallion from the ceiling

with an allegorical portrayal of one of the districts of Florence.

Below, detail from a painting by Vasari and his school, entitled *The Foundation of Florence*.

151

COATS OF ARMS
Arms took pride of place on palace façades, and were often their only decoration. Between the 11th and 14th centuries people all over Europe began to distinguish their identity in two ways, through the use of the family name and the coat of arms. Michel Pastoureau, an expert on the subject, writes: "Coats of arms were a means of recognition, telling who the bearer was. They served the same purpose as names, and their use quickly extended from the field of battle into civilian life. . . . At first it was only soldiers who used them, but by the 12th century ladies and clerics had adopted the fashion as well. The practice was originally limited to the aristocracy, but in the 13th century it gradually filtered down through the social strata to the patrician classes and then tradesmen, farmers and priests of all ranks."

« THE FINE ARTS ARE VERY REPUBLICAN IN FLORENCE.
THE STATUES AND PICTURES ARE ON SHOW AT ALL HOURS . . .
ATTENDANTS, TRAINED AND PAID BY THE GOVERNMENTS, ARE
ON HAND TO EXPLAIN THE MASTERPIECES.»

MADAME DE STAËL

THE UFFIZI GALLERY ● 73

LA TRIBUNA

An octagonal room of modest dimensions but designed and decorated to have powerful cosmological significance. The weathervane represented Air, the red walls Fire, and the cupola lined with mother-of-pearl was the heavenly vault. The floor of *pietre dure* ● *54*, ▲ *239* symbolized Earth. Works by Raphael and Andrea del Sarto (as the masters of Florentine classicism) used to be shown here, but there are also display cases full of medals and little bronzes by Giambologna.

A VENERABLE INSTITUTION. The Uffizi Gallery is one of the oldest and most famous in the world. Founded in 1581 by Francesco I de' Medici, it occupied the top floor of the building designed by Vasari to house the administrative offices of the state of Tuscany (hence *uffizi*). The building also contains the Medici Theater, part of which has now been incorporated into the rooms that house the COLLECTION OF PRINTS AND DRAWINGS. The gallery first housed antique statues and historical paintings. The great treasures were in the octagonal TRIBUNA. The collection was not originally confined to paintings and statues; a variety of objects were also on display, including scientific instruments, arms, metalwork and pharmaceutical equipment.

THE FOUNT OF ALL ART. The collections of art from the 13th to the 18th centuries attract the most attention today (though the display continues to the 20th century in the CORRIDOIO VASARIANO ▲ *175*). The Florentine art is, of course, outstanding, but there are also many excellent examples from the schools of Siena, Venice, Parma and Mantua along with fine works by German, Flemish and Spanish artists. Paintings that have been restored are marked with a round red label. It is also possible to visit the reserve collection, but by written appointment only.

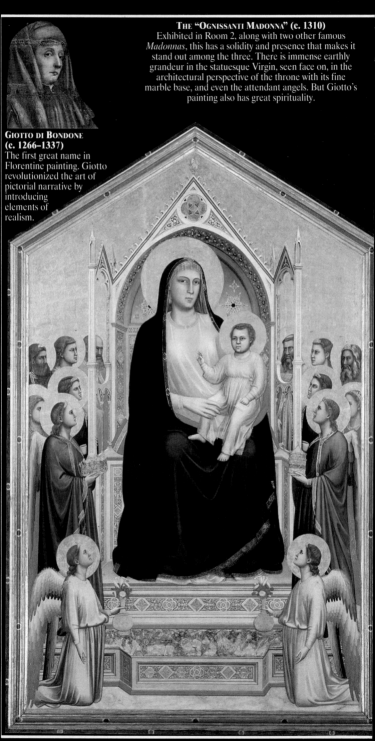

THE "OGNISSANTI MADONNA" (c. 1310)
Exhibited in Room 2, along with two other famous *Madonnas*, this has a solidity and presence that makes it stand out among the three. There is immense earthly grandeur in the statuesque Virgin, seen face on, in the architectural perspective of the throne with its fine marble base, and even the attendant angels. But Giotto's painting also has great spirituality.

GIOTTO DI BONDONE (c. 1266–1337)
The first great name in Florentine painting. Giotto revolutionized the art of pictorial narrative by introducing elements of realism.

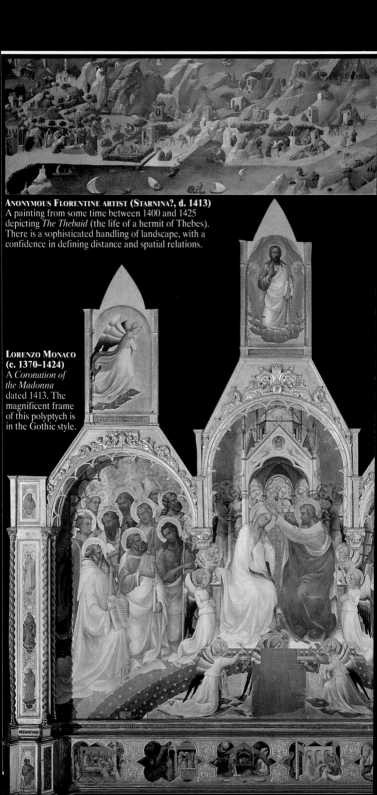

ANONYMOUS FLORENTINE ARTIST (STARNINA?, d. 1413)
A painting from some time between 1400 and 1425 depicting *The Thebaid* (the life of a hermit of Thebes). There is a sophisticated handling of landscape, with a confidence in defining distance and spatial relations.

LORENZO MONACO (c. 1370–1424)
A *Coronation of the Madonna* dated 1413. The magnificent frame of this polyptych is in the Gothic style.

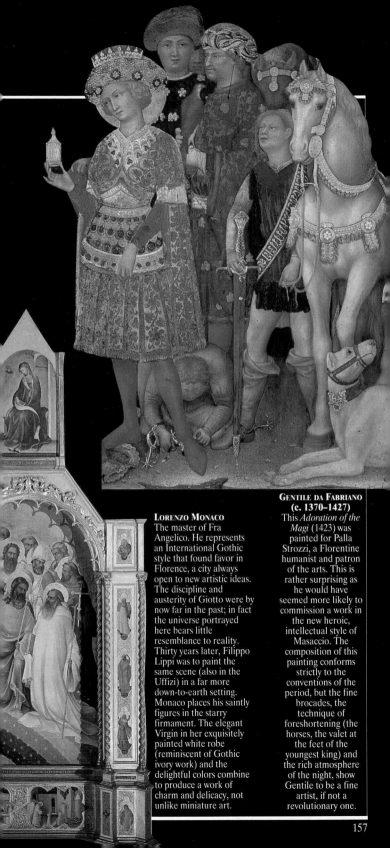

LORENZO MONACO

The master of Fra Angelico. He represents an International Gothic style that found favor in Florence, a city always open to new artistic ideas. The discipline and austerity of Giotto were by now far in the past; in fact the universe portrayed here bears little resemblance to reality. Thirty years later, Filippo Lippi was to paint the same scene (also in the Uffizi) in a far more down-to-earth setting. Monaco places his saintly figures in the starry firmament. The elegant Virgin in her exquisitely painted white robe (reminiscent of Gothic ivory work) and the delightful colors combine to produce a work of charm and delicacy, not unlike miniature art.

GENTILE DA FABRIANO (c. 1370–1427)

This *Adoration of the Magi* (1423) was painted for Palla Strozzi, a Florentine humanist and patron of the arts. This is rather surprising as he would have seemed more likely to commission a work in the new heroic, intellectual style of Masaccio. The composition of this painting conforms strictly to the conventions of the period, but the fine brocades, the technique of foreshortening (the horses, the valet at the feet of the youngest king) and the rich atmosphere of the night, show Gentile to be a fine artist, if not a revolutionary one.

MASACCIO AND MASOLINO DA PANICALE
Madonna and Child with Saint Anne (1424–5). Masolino (c. 1383–c. 1440) was responsible for the overall composition, and for the figures of St Anne and the angels. Masaccio (1401–28) painted the statuesque Virgin, the top right-hand angel and the sturdy Child. This work dates from the same period as the *Adoration of the Magi* by Gentile da Fabriano (previous page). The difference between them is so enormous that it comes as no surprise to learn that Masaccio died practically unknown. His forceful style, with its roots in the work of Giotto, and the severity of his new artistic principles could not be reconciled with contemporary ideas of beauty. Compare this Madonna with any of the numerous Madonnas painted by the very best Florentine artists, like Gentile or Lorenzo Monaco, and the contrast is clear. It is even more marked when comparisons are made with works from the Sienese school.

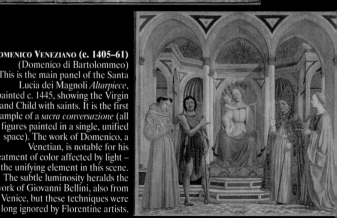

DOMENICO VENEZIANO (c. 1405–61)
(Domenico di Bartolommeo) This is the main panel of the Santa Lucia dei Magnoli *Altarpiece*, painted c. 1445, showing the Virgin and Child with saints. It is the first example of a *sacra conversazione* (all figures painted in a single, unified space). The work of Domenico, a Venetian, is notable for his treatment of color affected by light – the unifying element in this scene. The subtle luminosity heralds the work of Giovanni Bellini, also from Venice, but these techniques were long ignored by Florentine artists.

FRA ANGELICO (c. 1400–55)
Coronation of the Virgin (c. 1430–5) Although
still strongly influenced by his predecessors,
Fra Angelico's handling of the ranks of saints
and angels already shows his mastery of solid
shapes and perspective. Right, by the same
artist, a *Madonna and Child*. The robe is
worthy of Masaccio, but the face of the
Madonna and her long tapering fingers
remain typical of the Trecento tradition.

PAOLO UCCELIO
(Paolo di Dono,
1397–1475)
*The Battle of San
Romano* (c. 1456)
depicts the victory of
the Florentines over
Siena and Milan in
1432. Uccello (his
portrait is to the
right) had a
reputation in
Florence for his

fascination with the
construction of
perspective views.
The painting seems
rather primitive as
there is a certain
confusion in the
composition that
conveys the chaos of
battle. Paolo Uccello
uses the soldiers'
lances, where they
rest upon the ground,

to define the spatial
context of the scene,
but he does not
employ perspective to
open up the
composition. It is
nevertheless a rich
exercise in contrast
and juxtaposition.

159

FILIPPO LIPPI (1406–69)

It is very difficult to define the work of this monk from Santa Maria del Carmine ▲ 306. One need only compare his works in the Uffizi to see how the style changes. It can be solid and realistic (*Coronation of the Virgin*, from which it is clear that he must have seen Masaccio working on the Brancacci Chapel), or much more stylized and spiritual, as in his Nativities. This *Madonna and Child* (right) was painted around 1465. The Madonna is fragile and delicately executed (anticipating Botticelli, Lippi's pupil), while the Christ has the sturdiness of a Masaccio figure. The landscape does not match up to that of Piero della Francesca on the right. Lippi's model was his mistress, which reveals something about his free and independent spirit.

ANTONIO POLLAIOLO (c. 1431–98)

Portrait of a Lady, 1475. There is a clarity and precision about the profile of this young woman, and it is matched by the rich brocade of her sleeve. Antonio del Pollaiuolo, whose portrait is to the left, was also a goldsmith and engraver. He made reliquaries and silver crosses for the Baptistery. There is a magnificent silver reredos by him to be seen in the Museo dell'l Opera del Duomo ▲ 133.

"THE DUKE AND DUCHESS OF URBINO" (c. 1465, or after 1473)

Piero di Benedetto (known as "della Francesca") worked mainly in Arezzo, where he painted a cycle of frescoes for the church of San Francesco. There is a gentle luminosity in these portraits that softens the severity of the profiles.

PIERO DELLA FRANCESCA (c. 1416–92)

A pupil of Domenico Veneziano, whom he helped decorate the Florentine church of Sant'Egidio (of which only fragments remain). He was the only Tuscan artist to understand Veneziano's concern with light and color. He was also one of the great experts on the theory of perspective: he wrote a treatise on it, as well as one on geometry.

ANTONIO POLLAIOLO

In this small panel showing *Hercules Slaying the Hydra* Pollaiuolo pursues Early Renaissance naturalism, attempting, with varying success, to combine carefully observed anatomical detail with the portrayal of violent action. For Pollaiuolo the human body had to radiate energy, resulting sometimes in a certain deformity of the figures. He was an avid student of anatomy, raiding graveyards for examples to satisfy his curiosity and fill his notebooks.

SANDRO BOTTICELLI (1445–1510).
Rightly or wrongly, Botticelli has come to represent Early Renaissance painting more than any other. He worked for the Medicis, although not exclusively. His elegant, archaic, allegorical works often took their themes from ancient mythology. But he was only seven years older than Leonardo da Vinci, who was to turn his world upside-down.

"THE BIRTH OF VENUS" (c.1485)
The first "pagan" nude of the Renaissance. Lorenzo de' Medici's protégé, the philosopher Marsilio Ficino, tried to incorporate ancient beliefs into Christian mysticism. Venus was an incarnation of the Absolute, combining the love of Good with the love of Beauty. The composition is inspired by earlier paintings of the Baptism of Christ.

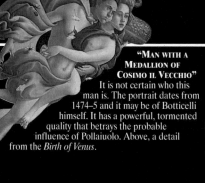

"MAN WITH A MEDALLION OF COSIMO IL VECCHIO"
It is not certain who this man is. The portrait dates from 1474–5 and it may be of Botticelli himself. It has a powerful, tormented quality that betrays the probable influence of Pollaiuolo. Above, a detail from the *Birth of Venus*.

"PRIMAVERA"
(1478). An exquisite painting probably inspired by a work by the scholar Poliziano. However, its exact meaning remains obscure. The young woman in the center may represent Humanity, or Venus, goddess of Spring; on the right Zephyr chases the nymph Chloris, transforming her into Flora; to the left, Mercury waves away the clouds while the Three Graces perform a stately dance. These three figures are still and almost vision-like. The movement is in their transparent garments ruffled by the wind. The unreality of the scene is increased by its lack of depth, rather like a tapestry.

"THE MADONNA OF THE MAGNIFICAT"
The word "Magnificat" is written on the open book. In *Swann's Way* by Marcel Proust, Swann gives his mistress a scarf like that worn by the Madonna. To the right, a self-portrait of the master. Botticelli worked in Florence throughout his career, except in the years 1481–2 when he was painting frescoes for the Sistine Chapel in Rome. At the end of his life he seems to have suffered torments of conscience, possibly inspired by the sermons of Savonarola.

RAPHAEL (1483–1520)
Above, detail of a *Self-portrait* painted around 1506. Right, the *Madonna of the Goldfinch* (c. 1506), symbol of the pure classical art that Raphael was championing at this time, in opposition to the more tormented work of Michelangelo. The painting represents a high point in Florentine classical art: the light is diffused, the landscape is peaceful, and the pyramidal group of figures is powerful but extremely natural.

"ANNUNCIATION"
(1472–5). Leonardo da Vinci and Verrocchio both worked on this painting. Leonardo was responsible for most of the righthand side, while Verrocchio certainly painted the walls; but the overall composition undoubtedly shows the young Leonardo at work.

LEONARDO DA VINCI
Legend has it that when Leonardo painted the lefthand angel (above) for the *Baptism of Christ*, his master Verrocchio was so impressed that he gave up painting. The grace and beauty of the young artist's work were without equal.

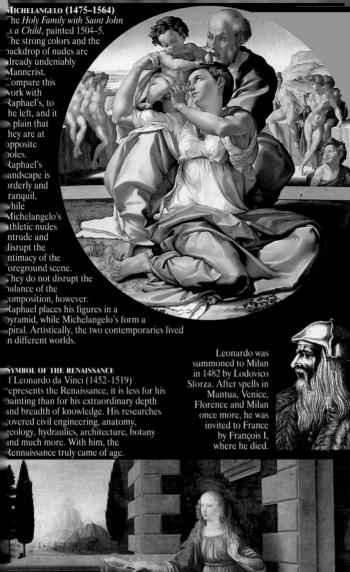

MICHELANGELO (1475–1564)

The *Holy Family with Saint John as a Child*, painted 1504–5. The strong colors and the backdrop of nudes are already undeniably Mannerist. Compare this work with Raphael's, to the left, and it is plain that they are at opposite poles. Raphael's landscape is orderly and tranquil, while Michelangelo's athletic nudes intrude and disrupt the intimacy of the foreground scene. They do not disrupt the balance of the composition, however. Raphael places his figures in a pyramid, while Michelangelo's form a spiral. Artistically, the two contemporaries lived in different worlds.

SYMBOL OF THE RENAISSANCE

If Leonardo da Vinci (1452–1519) represents the Renaissance, it is less for his painting than for his extraordinary depth and breadth of knowledge. His researches covered civil engineering, anatomy, geology, hydraulics, architecture, botany and much more. With him, the Renaissance truly came of age.

Leonardo was summoned to Milan in 1482 by Lodovico Sforza. After spells in Mantua, Venice, Florence and Milan once more, he was invited to France by François I, where he died.

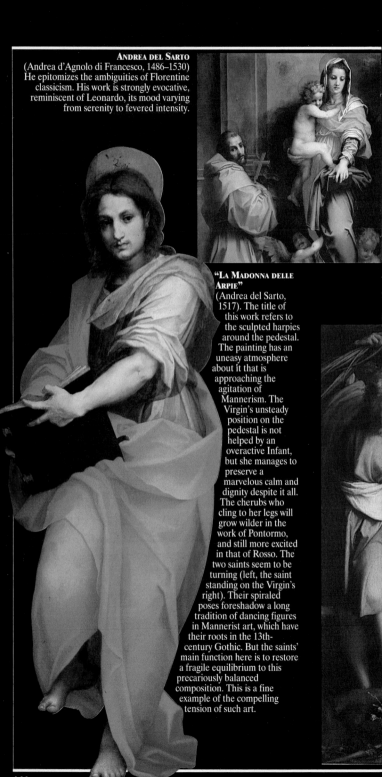

ANDREA DEL SARTO
(Andrea d'Agnolo di Francesco, 1486–1530)
He epitomizes the ambiguities of Florentine classicism. His work is strongly evocative, reminiscent of Leonardo, its mood varying from serenity to fevered intensity.

"LA MADONNA DELLE ARPIE"
(Andrea del Sarto, 1517). The title of this work refers to the sculpted harpies around the pedestal. The painting has an uneasy atmosphere about it that is approaching the agitation of Mannerism. The Virgin's unsteady position on the pedestal is not helped by an overactive Infant, but she manages to preserve a marvelous calm and dignity despite it all. The cherubs who cling to her legs will grow wilder in the work of Pontormo, and still more excited in that of Rosso. The two saints seem to be turning (left, the saint standing on the Virgin's right). Their spiraled poses foreshadow a long tradition of dancing figures in Mannerist art, which have their roots in the 13th-century Gothic. But the saints' main function here is to restore a fragile equilibrium to this precariously balanced composition. This is a fine example of the compelling tension of such art.

«AH, BUT A MAN'S REACH SHOULD EXCEED
HIS GRASP, OR WHAT'S A HEAVEN FOR?»

ROBERT BROWNING

**LUCA SIGNORELLI
(1445–1523)**
His master, Piero della
Francesca, taught him
to convey depth and
perspective. Once
introduced to
Florentine art, he
concentrated on line
and movement. He
learned much from
Pollaiuolo, and painted
some masterful and
vigorous nudes.

MADONNA AND CHILD
(Signorelli, 1495)
This seems to be
influenced by
Michel-
angelo's
Tondo
▲ 165.

CORREGGIO
(Antonio Allegri,
c. 1489–1534)
One of Parma's great
Renaissance painters.
*Rest on the Flight into
Egypt* (c. 1515- 17)
shows Correggio's
soft and sensuous
style. He was much
influenced by
Leonardo's *sfumato*
effects: Da Vinci said
that light and shade
should blend "without
lines or borders, like
smoke". This often
gave Correggio's
paintings a somewhat
mysterious
atmosphere. His
contrasts of light and
shade were later
much admired by the
Baroque artists,
particularly the
paintings done
around 1525 when his
work was stronger in
both line and color.

JACOPO PONTORMO (1494–1556)
Supper at Emmaus (1525). The Mannerism of Michelangelo and Andrea del Sarto was restrained by their respect for certain fundamental rules, but here the last barriers have fallen. The artificial light, the strange shadows, the sharp, pale colors and the facial expressions all combine to produce a work of tormented spirituality that can be compared to paintings by the German Grünewald (the *Isenheim Reredos*, 1505–15, Colmar, France). New ideas from Germany were to have a profound influence on art in the 1520's.

PARMIGIANINO
(Francesco Mazzola, 1503–40) The *Madonna with the Long Neck* (c. 1535). The sinuous elongation of the human form is typical of Mannerism. So too is the Virgin's position (neither sitting nor standing), the columns that support nothing at all, and the imbalance between the overloaded left side of the painting and the empty right. The new Mannerists were blatantly artificial and unashamedly different in their approach. Although the distortion of the Virgin can be disturbing, she has a sensuality and grace that is common to much art from Parma, in particular that of Correggio.

«WORKS OF ART ARE OF AN INFINITE SOLITARINESS, . . .
ONLY LOVE CAN APPREHEND AND HOLD THEM,
AND CAN BE JUST TOWARD THEM.»

RAINER MARIA RILKE

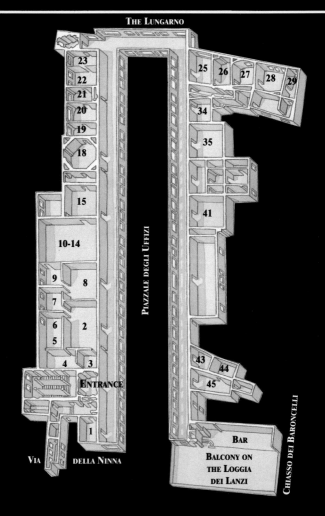

THE ROOMS OF THE UFFIZI GALLERY

1. Antique sculpture.
2. The Duecento. Cimabue, Giotto, Duccio.
3. The Trecento Sienese School. Martini, Lorenzetti.
4. The Trecento Florentine School.
5–6. International Gothic. Monaco, Gentile da Fabriano.
7. Fra Angelico, Uccello.
8. Filippo Lippi.
9. Antonio Pollaiolo.
10–14. Botticelli.
15. Leonardo da Vinci.
16. Map room.
18. La Tribuna. Bronzino, Pontormo, Vasari, Del Sarto, Allori, Rosso, Fiorentino.
19. Perugino, Signorelli.
20. Dürer, Cranach.

21. Bellini, Giorgione.
22. The German school. Holbein, Altdorfer.
23. Correggio.
25. Michelangelo, the Florentine school.
26. Raphael, Andrea del Sarto.
27. Pontormo, Rosso Fiorentino.
28. Titian.
29. Parmigianino.
34. Veronese.
35. Tintoretto.
41. Rubens.
42. Niobe e i Niobidi
43. Caravaggio, Annibale Carracci.
44. Rembrandt.
45. The 18th century. Boucher, Chardin, Goya.

169

Portrait of Galileo, by
Susterman.

**AN ARMILLARY
SPHERE**
This instrument was
made by A. Santucci
in the early 17th
century. It is one of
the most beautiful
objects on display in
the Science Museum.

THE SCIENCE MUSEUM

THE PURSUIT OF KNOWLEDGE. Grand Duke Ferdinando II,
who reigned from 1621 to 1670, did much to encourage
learning and scientific experiment, often to the detriment of
affairs of state. The 17th century saw severe economic
problems, particularly in agriculture and the textile trade. The
arts and sciences flourished, however, and libraries and
academies blossomed. The librarian Antonio Magliabechi
started the collection that became the present Biblioteca
Nazionale ▲ *267*, and the abbot Francesco Marucelli left
twelve thousand volumes as the basis of the Biblioteca
Marucelliana ▲ *238*. Ferdinando, who himself perfected an
early thermometer, created an academy for scientific
experiment, the ACCADEMIA DEL CIMENTO. Based in the
Palazzo Pitti, it brought together gifted
men such as Viviani, Magalotti and
Redi. The Medicis also helped Galileo
when he was in trouble with the papal
Inquisition.

A UNIQUE MUSEUM. The Museo di
Storia della Scienza is a marvelous
place to discover the scientific advances
and excitement of this period, yet it is
rarely visited. It is located in the Piazza
dei Giudici, in the PALAZZO DEI
CASTELLANI which was once the
home of the Accademia della
Crusca, an institute that was founded in 1582 to record
and protect the Italian language, and which is still
the headquarters of the Accademia del
Cimento. In the first room are
mathematical instruments, including
some magnificent astrolabes for
calculating the height of stars
above the horizon. Later, and even
up to the present day, they were
used to calculate times and
latitudes.

**HOMAGE TO AN ENLIGHTENED
GRAND DUKE.** In the second
room are objects showing how
Ferdinando II encouraged the
study of mathematics, paying no
attention to the doubts of those
around him. There are measuring
instruments, a thermoscope, and
some extremely accurate scales which
Ferdinando used for preparing the
medicines he concocted. There is also one of
the first mechanical calculating machines, which
was invented by Sir Samuel Morland and
dedicated to Cosimo III.

GALILEO GALILEI. Room VI is devoted to
Galileo. There is the lens that he
used, late in 1609 or early in 1610, to
discover four satellites of Jupiter. He
diplomatically named them "the
Medici planets". He came to Florence

Left, Galileo's telescope and lenses.

The telescope made by Torricelli (1608–47), a doctor who invented the first mercury barometer.

in September 1610 to be the grand duke's first mathematician and philosopher. In 1633 he was imprisoned by the ecclesiastical authorities.

SATANIC EXPERIMENTS. The story of Galileo's trial and imprisonment is a complicated one. He had the support of influential men in Rome. Pope Urban VIII, a cultured Florentine, was interested in science and also thought well of Galileo. Another Florentine admirer was Giovanni Ciampoli, a sworn enemy of the Jesuits and astronomer at the Vatican. He reorganized the old Roman university, the *Sapienza*, and gave the chair in mathematics to an ex-pupil of Galileo's, Benedetto Castelli. Moreover, the pope enjoyed Galileo's 1623 satire on the Jesuits, *Saggiatore*. But the book actually expounded some dangerous heresies in the way that it explained light and all visible phenomena: it was the theory of atomism in disguise. Feeling that they had been made fools of, the Jesuits replied in 1626 with a paper by Father Orazio Grassi proving that Galileo's atomist theories were a denial of the Eucharist, and therefore more dangerous than even the Copernican astrological system, in which the earth was shown to revolve around the sun.

A CLEVERLY CONDUCTED TRIAL. Urban VIII wanted to keep Galileo alive, so he restricted the 1633 trial to the subject of astronomy. When he appeared before the Inquisition, Galileo knew that he was being tried for the least of his wrongdoings, in the hope of a light punishment. He had never concealed his belief in the Copernican system, for which he could have been burned at the stake. So, on June 22, he was forced to appear on his knees at the church of Santa Maria sopra Minerva in Rome, and he was condemned to prison for life. The punishment was immediately commuted, on the request of Ferdinando II, to permission to reside in Florence. He was protected by the grand duke, but he led the life of a recluse, guarded and watched. Meanwhile his ideas were spreading turmoil among the learned men of Europe. On Galileo's death in 1642, Ferdinando was asked by the Vatican not to give the great man a grand funeral nor to bury him in Santa Croce. He was even denied a funeral oration and epitaph. His body was not moved to Santa Croce until 1734.

LOGIC VERSUS DOGMA. Until the end of the 16th century science remained a branch of philosophy. Scientific theories were constructed with reference to reason and logic, and they could not be tested by experiment. "Research" into the nature of the universe could also be based on information taken from the Bible. From the 17th century onwards, such speculation ceased to satisfy the scientists; they began to check their theories both by observation and calculation. Galileo saw that nature could be understood in terms of mathematics. The church now found that these men were getting beyond its control with their dangerously reliable instruments: the first microscope, for instance, appeared in

He was Galileo's secretary and amanuensis.

PALAZZO DEI CASTELLANI
Also called the Palazzo dei Giudici as the Tribunale della Ruota was based here until 1841. Founded in 1502, it comprised five judges who presided over matters of civil law. They were called the *giudici di Ruota* since they sat in rotation.

LOGGIA DEL GRANO
Built in 1619 by Giulio Parigi (c. 1571 –1635), it was commissioned by Cosimo II, whose bust (left) is at the center of the coat of arms on the façade. The loggia was

originally a corn market, then in 1862 it became part of a theater, and today it is a cinema. It is on the corner of the *Vie* de' Neri and de' Castellani.

171

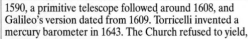

A ROMAN BRIDGE
The Roman town stood only on the

1590, a primitive telescope followed around 1608, and Galileo's version dated from 1609. Torricelli invented a mercury barometer in 1643. The Church refused to yield, remaining stubbornly intolerant: in his *Spiritual Exercises*, Ignatius Loyola, founder of the Jesuits, instructed that "to attain the truth we must believe that what we see as white is in fact black, should the Church decide it is so." The story of Galileo only served to widen and confirm the gap that had now developed between faith and reason.

THE PONTE VECCHIO

A STRATEGIC CROSSING PLACE. The old stone bridge, which had been reinforced in 1170, was carried away in 1333 by one of the worst floods in the turbulent history of the Arno. The bridge was then rebuilt in 1345, after an attempt to contain the river by building the banks up in stone, creating the *lungarni*. It is this same bridge that the tourist walks over today, often unaware of its long and

northern bank of the Arno but it is thought that there was a bridge over the river at its narrowest point, where it is now spanned by the Ponte Vecchio. This bridge would have been the link between north and south Etruria. It remained the only one in Florence until the Ponte alla Carraia ▲ 279 was built in 1218.

In 1900 a bust of Benvenuto Cellini by R. Romanelli was placed on the Ponte Vecchio.

eventful history. These days it is lined with richly stocked jewelers' shops, but during the Middle Ages fishmongers, butchers and leatherworkers all had their businesses here. The atmosphere has changed considerably since the leatherworkers were here, hanging their hides in the water for eight months and tanning them with horse's urine. To make the bridge easier to clean, a gap was created in the row of shops on one side, and on the other there were three arcades. Unsold offal and other waste could then be conveniently thrown into the river.

A SENSITIVE NOSE. These trades were banished from the bridge by Grand Duke Ferdinando I, who was offended by the stench as he crossed over the bridge by the corridor to the Palazzo Pitti. In those days, a busy shopping street would have been a crowded, noisy and extremely smelly place. The shops were tiny and crammed not just with merchandise but also with the tools of the trade, since the work was done on the

premises. The word "bank" comes from the tables (*banchi*) of the moneychangers who would also have been in the street, along with barbers, butchers, cobblers, notaries, blacksmiths, surgeons, painters, tanners and many others, often carrying out their business under awnings, or simply sheltering beneath the overhanging upper stories of the houses. So in 1593 Ferdinando decided to replace the troublesome tradesmen with jewelers and goldsmiths who, as well as being respectable, had the advantage of paying double the rent. Many enlarged their premises by building them out on supporting brackets at the back of the shops.

THE FLOOD OF 1966

A DEVASTATING CYCLONE. Early in November 1966 rain fell very heavily throughout Italy, and on Friday, November 4, a cyclone, very rare in this part of the world, swept across the whole peninsula, inflicting such terrible damage as it did so that it caused a national emergency. The Arno flooded the towns situated along its banks, sweeping all before it in its path. Only when it had receded did the scale of the disaster that had struck Florence become clear. Within just twenty-four hours the city had suffered more damage than had been done to it in the last months of World War Two.

WATERLOGGED. The economic and artistic consequences of this were almost incalculable. Shops on the Ponte Vecchio had been destroyed, carried away by the waters. The basements of the Uffizi, where eight thousand Renaissance paintings had been stored, were under 6 or 7 feet

MURDER AT EASTER
It was at the entrance to the old bridge that Buondelmonte de' Buondelmonti was murdered in 1216. The event sparked off the most bitter civil war in the history of Florence ● *34*, the conflict between the Guelfs and the Ghibellines.

Francis Steegmuller, an American in the city during the flood, described it in *A Letter from Florence*: "[A nightwatchman] telephoned to the homes of those whom he could reach and a number came, unlocked their shops, and filled their suitcases with what they could, the bridge trembling beneath them . . . the water was close, and there were frighteningly sharp reports as though the bridge were cracking . . . .The water continued to rise, and about half the jewelry shops on the Ponte Vecchio are now gaping open – gutted by the force of a torrent."

Top, this 19th-century photo shows the bridge from the lungarno. Above, the *Ponte Vecchio* painted by A. Hollaender. Opposite, jewelers' shops on the bridge.

of water. The restoration workshops were wrecked. The Museo Archeologico ▲ *245* and all its treasures were now deep in mud. The main collection of the Biblioteca Nazionale ▲ *267*, which it had admittedly been rather unwise to house near such a capricious river, was now under water. Hundreds of thousands of volumes, many of them unique and priceless, were either damaged or ruined beyond repair. Precious photographic archives were also lost entirely: they had contained what was often the only record of works of art stolen or destroyed during World War Two. Worst of all was the damage done to the buildings of Santa Croce ▲ *254*, submerged beneath 16 feet of water. The precious Cimabue crucifix was also damaged beyond repair.

MORASS. The streets were left deep in mud, debris and oil from basement storage tanks which had just been filled for winter heating. The slime covered everything – houses, shops, palazzi, churches, up to head-height or even higher, and the mud and water remained for a considerable time, since the gutters and drains were also blocked.

EXTREME CONDITIONS. At night the city was plunged into total darkness, and policemen had to keep up continuous patrols to discourage looting. The inhabitants had no water or heating, and food was in short supply. People stood in line at the Palazzo Vecchio for bread and milk, and waited at the tankers that dispensed drinking water.

A DANGEROUS SITE. The Arno is more like a torrent than a river. Into it flow the waters that run down from the Appenine mountains, and when the rains are heavy the volume of water can double. The threat of flood is ancient, made worse by Florence's geographical position in a low area on the first plane reached by the Arno after it has been joined by its large tributary, the Sieve. Leonardo once studied the possibility of controlling the river by constructing a canal running between Florence and Pisa. But it was never built and in 1966 the Arno swamped the city under a huge flood, while more water poured down from the neighboring hills of San Miniato and Belvedere. Within the city, the Piazza del

174

Duomo itself stands in a slight dip, so that the water continued to flow down into it from Santa Croce even when the main flood subsided.

SHOCK AND TRAGEDY. In the Florentine daily paper *Il Nazione* of November 4, 1971, Piero Bargellini, longtime mayor of Florence, took an emotional look back at the terrible event: "Surrounded by a sea of mud that would discourage even the stoutest heart, the people of Florence did not fail. They set their chins, straightened their shoulders and, with a lot of cursing but joking as well, they got down to work. When Cimabue's *Christ* was carried past, fatally wounded, on a tank going to Limonaia, even the most hardened of the men, the loudest blasphemers, stopped their muddy labors and took off their hats in silence; every woman, however tough or dishonest, crossed herself with sincerity. . . . It was as still and silent as on Good Friday."

THE CORRIDOIO VASARIANO

This famous corridor runs the length of the Ponte Vecchio above the shops. It was built by Vasari in just five months as a private passageway for Cosimo I from the Palazzo Vecchio to the Palazzo Pitti. These elevated escape routes where refuge could be found in times of unrest or conspiracy had long been a feature of Florentine architecture in the Middle Ages and the Renaissance.

THE MANNELLI TOWER
The corridor built by Vasari for Cosimo I was blocked by this tower-house whose owners, the Mannelli, family, would not give way. The only solution was to take the corridor round the tower, supported on brackets.

A FAMOUS GALLERY. The entrance is in the east corridor of the Uffizi Gallery (admittance remains strictly limited while repair work is in progress). The Corridoio Vasariano, over half a mile long, passes through the glazed loggia that links the two wings of the Uffizi. It follows the course of the Arno and then crosses the Ponte Vecchio above the shops and arcades on the righthand side. At the end of the bridge it takes a tortuous route to the Boboli Gardens and the Palazzo Pitti ▲ *288*. There are windows all the way along which give magnificent views over the streets, bridges, and hills of Florence. Cosimo always intended this to be a gallery and so he hung pictures here from the time that it was built.

The people of Tuscany have always feared and respected the Arno. The river had destroyed a number of bridges, including the Ponte Vecchio itself, in 1333. Lorenzo il Magnifico described its floods in his poem *Ambra*. But in the long history of the city the 1966 flood was worst. "Hideously disfigured", "terrifying", "one of the pinnacles of human achievement destroyed" – all attempts to describe it fell short of conveying the dimensions of a tragedy that was not just a loss for Italy but for the whole human race. For the Florentines themselves, life has since been divided into "before" and "after".

CIMABUE'S CRUCIFIX ▲ 261
A Duecento (13th-century) masterpiece that was one of the worst casualties of the flood. The water ate into its surface and, in certain places, the paint was lost forever.

THE MUSEO DELL'OPERA DEL DUOMO ▲ 133
In the courtyard behind the cathedral this marble *Marzocco* was covered in oily mud. Inside the museum, the books of choral works were waterlogged, and their illuminations appeared damaged beyond repair. The model of Brunelleschi's dome had fallen to bits.

A GREY CITY, SODDEN AND DESPAIRING

It is worth comparing this photograph, taken from the Piazzale Michelangelo ▲ 318–319, with the illustration ▲ 318–319. The Florentines contemplated the awful scene, horrified at the disaster that had befallen the city. Around the church of Santa Croce, the spire of which can be seen on the right, the waters rose to more than 16 feet.

THE BAPTISTERY
▲ 132
The force of the water broke open the bronze doors and panels from Ghiberti's masterpiece, the *Gates of Paradise* ▲ 134, were torn off. They were later found, some nearly a mile away.

EVERY CLOUD HAS A SILVER LINING
The disaster did have some fortunate repercussions. During the long period of restoration that followed it, particularly in churches, several new items came to light, such as works of art or architectural features that had previously been hidden. In the church of San Jacopo sopr'Arno ▲ 312 the remains of a Roman building were found; in the badly damaged San Niccolò oltr'Arno ▲ 316, frescoes were discovered beneath 16th-century altar decorations.

▲ The Corridoio Vasariano

It took just five months to build the corridor, from spring to autumn 1565. Vasari designed it and oversaw the works, and he boasted that this was a task which many would not have expected to see finished within five years. Cosimo I, for whom it was built, wanted this to be a safe and private route running between the Palazzo Pitti ▲ 288 and the Palazzo Vecchio ▲ 147, and it was also constructed in honor of the marriage of Francesco, his son and heir, to Joanna of Austria. Cosimo saw it as a marvelous new architectural feature for Florence, but one with strong classical overtones, as it recalled the passageway connecting the palaces of Priam and Hector in ancient Troy.

"ADORATION OF THE INFANT"
by Gerrit van Honthorst (Utrecht, 1590–1656). The painter was a pupil of Caravaggio.

"ALLEGORY OF PAINTING AND ARCHITECTURE"
by Francesco Rustici, known as "Rustichino", who died in 1626 and about whom very little is known, although he was extremely famous in his own lifetime. His work was in the

"ACHILLES WITH CHIRON THE CENTAUR"
(detail), by Pompeo Batoni (Lucca 1708–Rome 1787), an admirer of Raphael and the Carraccis. Batoni's neo-classicism was enlivened with a Baroque sensuality. The French painter David was much influenced by his work.

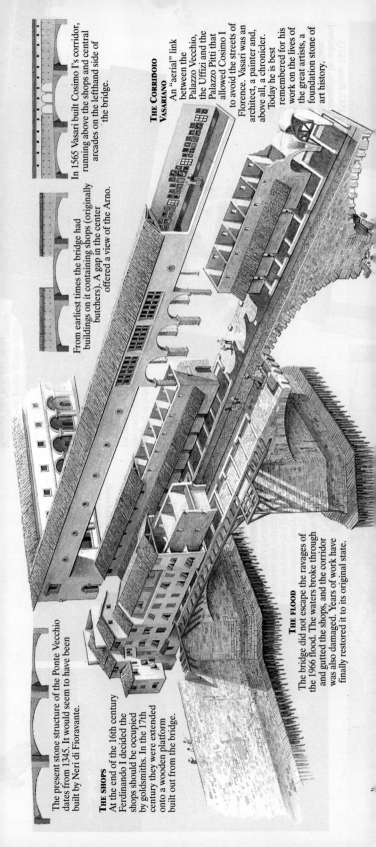

In 1565 Vasari built Cosimo I's corridor, running above the shops and central arcades on the lefthand side of the bridge.

From earliest times the bridge had buildings on it containing shops (originally butchers). A gap in the center offered a view of the Arno.

THE CORRIDOIO VASARIANO

An "aerial" link between the Palazzo Vecchio, the Uffizi and the Palazzo Pitti that allowed Cosimo I to avoid the streets of Florence. Vasari was an architect, a painter and, above all, a chronicler. Today he is best remembered for his work on the lives of the great artists, a foundation stone of art history.

The present stone structure of the Ponte Vecchio dates from 1345. It would seem to have been built by Neri di Fioravante.

THE SHOPS

At the end of the 16th century Ferdinando I decided the shops should be occupied by goldsmiths. In the 17th century they were extended onto a wooden platform built out from the bridge.

THE FLOOD

The bridge did not escape the ravages of the 1966 flood. The waters broke through and gutted the shops, and the corridor was also damaged. Years of work have finally restored it to its original state.

The terrible events of 1944

Gratuitous destruction. As a result of some good fortune, Florence had never suffered serious damage during all its long history. But in the summer of 1944 it seemed that its hour had finally come. Rome had fallen in June, and the country was collapsing before a rapidly advancing American 5th army. The people of Florence feared the worst for their great city when the Germans refused to surrender it to the Allies. The Germans thought of taking a large number of art treasures north with them, but this plan proved impossible due to a lack of vehicles and fuel. Also, Ludwig Heydenreich, the new director of the Kunsthistorisches Institut, the body in

As early as 1940 the Florentines began attempts to protect their heritage from possible bomb damage. Some works were moved to safety, such as the Giambologna statues from around the Neptune Fountain in the Piazza della Signoria ▲ 146.

The brick dome built over Michelangelo's *David* ▲ 234 in the Accademia.

A soldier surveys the destruction from the miraculously spared Ponte Vecchio.

whose care the artistic heritage of Florence had been placed, was a Renaissance specialist and made every effort to keep the art where it belonged. To protect it was a difficult task since Goering and Himmler's vultures were hovering over the town,

spying out last-minute prey for their collections. But disaster was fast approaching. Although the Germans had promised to demilitarize the town as soon as possible, they went back on their word. Adolf Fuchs and his parachutists were given the dreadful task of slowing the Allied advance by destroying the bridges over the Arno, as well as their approach routes. On the night of the August 4, the bridges were blown up. Miraculously, the Ponte Vecchio, although it had been mined, was somehow spared – thanks to Field Marshal Kesselring. It is not known whether this was an order from Hitler or whether Kesselring could not bear to carry out the task. However, the blast of the explosions brought down a number of tower-houses, and the area immediately around the Ponte Vecchio was razed to the ground for strategic reasons that proved of little value compared to the loss of the medieval quarter of the city.

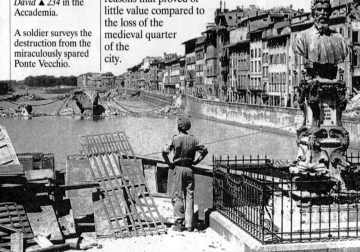

THE MEDIEVAL CITY

▲ THE MEDIEVAL CITY

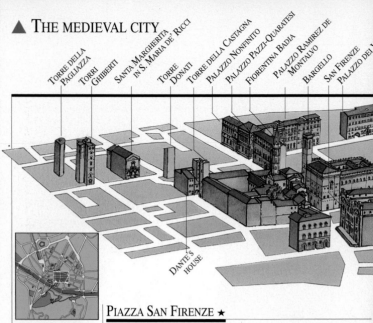

TORRE DELLA PAGLIAZZA · TORRI GHIBERTI · SANTA MARGHERITA IN S. MARIA DE' RICCI · TORRE DONATI · TORRE DELLA CASTAGNA · PALAZZO NONFINITO · PALAZZO PAZZI-QUARATESI · FIORENTINA BADIA · PALAZZO RAMIREZ DE MONTALVO · BARGELLO · SAN FIRENZE · PALAZZO DEI V

DANTE'S HOUSE

✳ Half a day

PALAZZO GONDI
Above, the courtyard. When the Via Gondi was widened the palace was enlarged. Giuseppe Poggi was responsible for the present appearance.

SAINT PHILIP NERI
Born in Florence in 1515, he spent much of his youth at the Convent of San Marco and admired Savonarola. He went to Rome and formed the Congregation of the Oratory. He is seen as a figurehead of the Counter-Reformation.

PIAZZA SAN FIRENZE ★

Just behind the Palazzo Vecchio ▲ *147* lies another spacious piazza, which has the added charm of relative peace away from the tourist crowds. Around it stand some of the buildings that are part of Florence's unforgettable landscape.
PALAZZO GONDI ● *71.* This magnificent building was begun in 1490 by Giuliano da Sangallo but was not completed until 1874. Here, as in the Palazzo Strozzi ▲ *208*, is the final flowering of a style that was typical of the 15th century. The prominent bosses at ground level are of beautifully dressed stone, with more remarkable stonework above and some exquisite windows. Within is a courtyard, a hidden treasure as pretty as any from its period, with its capitals and tall, delicate columns. Giuliano da Sangallo, born in Florence around 1452, was one of Lorenzo the Magnificent's favorite architects.
THE CHURCH OF SAN FILIPPO NERI (OR SAN FIRENZE)
● *91.* This fine, imposing group of buildings, fronted by a single façade, once housed a convent and two churches, Sant' Apollinare to the right and San Filippo Neri to the left. Today only the lefthand side is a church, the rest being occupied by law courts (*Procura*). When the Congregation of the Oratory decided to move to Florence they first approached the great painter and architect Pietro da Cortona, who began work on the project in 1640. But the church of San Filippo Neri was finally completed between 1645 and 1672 by Pier Francesco Silvani (1620–85), no doubt with the help of his father, Gherardo. The façade came later, erected in 1715 by Ferdinando Ruggieri. It was then left for Zanobi Del Rosso to confer a unity on the whole by creating an identical façade for the church of Sant' Apollinare and a connecting palatial frontage between them.
WELL-TEMPERED BAROQUE. In Florence the Baroque style remained austere,

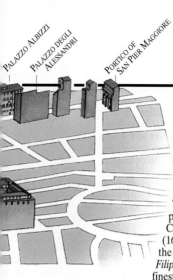

never attaining the extravagance and opulent fantasy that was to be seen in Rome. The church has an elegant and colorful interior without being excessively ornate. The ceiling was painted by Giovanni Camillo Sagrestani (1660–1731), and depicts the *Apotheosis of San Filippo Neri*. One of the finest things to be seen in the church, to the right of the nave, is a *Madonna dei Sette Dolori* by Alessandro Gherardini (1655–1726).

VIA DEL PRONCOSOLO. This narrow and busy street leads to the Piazza del Duomo and offers a fine view of the cathedral ▲ *128*.

THE BADIA FIORENTINA

This Benedictine abbey, whose main doors are opposite the Bargello, was founded in 978 and is Florence's oldest monastery. The church was rebuilt and enlarged in 1285 by Arnolfo di Cambio. During the 17th century it was altered and decorated in the Baroque style, the architect Segaloni actually turning the church round through ninety degrees and transforming the nave into the transept. The campanile was built between 1310 and 1330. Its base is Romanesque, but its upper section is Gothic. It was here that the Signoria

THE "VISION OF SAINT BERNARD"
This painting by Filippino Lippi is in the church of the Badia. It shows the saint interrupted in his writing by the appearance of the Virgin. Bernard of Clairvaux (1090–1153) was one of the great spiritual leaders of the Middle Ages. He was a prelate, a reformer, a theologian and the author of numerous books. He abhorred luxury and "graven images". He exerted strong influence in the development of the Cistercian Order, and also the cult of the Virgin, to whom he directed much of his religious devotion. There are a number of works showing him in the company of the Virgin, the most interesting of them being a statue showing her wetting his lips with a few drops of milk from her breast.

THE PIAZZA
A hand-colored engraving by Giuseppe Zocchi of the Piazza San Firenze in the 18th century. To the left rises the campanile of the Badia Fiorentina and to the right the crenellated tower of the Bargello. The Via del Proconsolo, which leads away into the background, is in fact a good deal narrower.

The *Marzocco*, a lion – the symbol of the city.

instructed the great writer Boccaccio ● *39* (1313–75) to give public readings from Dante's *Divine Comedy*. But the combination of a hostile audience, rheumatism and scabies put a stop to them. The most important work of art in this church is the *Vision of Saint Bernard* by Filippino Lippi (1485), to be found to the left on entering the main door. The left transept is dominated by a minstrels' gallery which was made in Vasari's workshop.

IN MEMORY OF COUNT UGO.
Just beneath this gallery is the monument raised between 1469 and 1489 by Mino da Fiesole to Count Ugo, margrave of Tuscany and founder there of seven Benedictine monasteries ● *28*. Ugo died in 1001, and every year for more than nine hundred years a solemn mass has been celebrated in his memory. Mino da Fiesole (1430–84) was one of the greatest sculptors to work in Florence during the 15th century. His work is delicate and refined. Another example of Mino's work, a marble bas-relief, is to be found opposite the Lippi. The frescoes in the apse with their trompe-l'œil effects are by Giovanni Domenico Ferretti, the man who decorated San Salvatore del Vescovo ▲ *139*.

PALAZZO DEL BARGELLO OR DEL PODESTÀ ● 66

A NEW INSTITUTION. The story of this imposing building begins in 1250 when, after the Guelf uprising and the defeat of the Ghibellines ● *34*, a new governor, the *capitano del popolo*, was put in charge. Chosen anew each year from a noble family of a nearby city with which Florence was on good terms, and aided by two councils, one of ninety and the other of three hundred men, he was to defend the interests of the middle classes against the excesses of the aristocracy, and to command the people's militia, recruited from the working men of the city. This upholder of the rights of the common man needed a suitable headquarters, and in 1255 work began on his palace. The oldest part of the building is on the Via del Proconsolo. It was soon enlarged, and at the end of the 13th century the magnificent *verone*, an arched loggia, was built on the first floor overlooking the *cortile*. Here the leaders of the city guilds held their meetings.

THE PODESTÀ. It was not long before the palazzo became the residence of another important governing magistrate, the

DONATELLO'S "DAVID"
In Renaissance philosophy the body was regarded as the most perfect earthly manifestation of God. A full appreciation of this beauty was considered a philosophical virtue, as it was by the ancient Greeks. According to Marsilio Ficino, the 15th-century Italian Platonist, the love of human beauty, both physical and moral, was an essential part of Platonic thought. In this way he justified a physical attraction to the bodies of young men.

THE INNER COURTYARD OF THE BARGELLO
Right, the splendid *cortile* of the Palazzo del Bargello. Neri de Fioravanti designed the open staircase, and the walls are hung with the coats-of-arms of past Podestà.

A Donatello bas-relief (left), a majolica of Leda (below), and a *Portrait of an Unknown Woman*, from the school of Luca della Robbia (bottom).

Podestà ● 29. This post had been created in 1193, again to be held for a short term of office by a nobleman not native to the city, with the function of keeping the peace between the rival factions.

A SLOW DECLINE. Over the centuries that followed the palazzo served a variety of functions concerned with the rule of law in the city. In the 14th century the bodies of executed criminals and political enemies were displayed there. From the 15th century onwards, when the Podestà declined in importance, it housed the civil and criminal courts, the prison cells and the torture chambers. Under the Medicis it became the headquarters of the leader of their henchmen, the chief of police, or *bargello*, hence its present name. The grand dukes also used the place as a prison, walling up the elegant arches of the loggia and daubing paint over the frescoes in the Cappella della Maddalena and other works of art. At last, in the latter half of the 18th century, the enlightened reformer Grand Duke Pietro Leopoldo of Lorraine had the instruments of torture burnt. The prisons were moved elsewhere, and in 1865 the palazzo became a museum.

A VARIED COLLECTION. The special charm of this museum, which is unique of its kind in Florence, derives from the sheer variety of objects that are on display, in addition to paintings and above all sculpture of the first rank (with several by Donatello in particular).

LA CAPPELLA DI SANTA MARIA MADDALENA. The frescoes depict *Heaven and Hell*. They date from 1330–40 and would seem to be the product of Giotto's school. The chapel was only restored in 1841, after some intense pressure from artists and intellectuals. Until then it had simply been used as two floors of prison cells. The pulpit, lectern and stalls came from San Miniato al Monte and all date from 1483–8.

SALA DELLE MAIOLICHE. This room contains a diverse and fascinating collection of Italian majolica. Italy was one of the first European countries to experiment in the manufacture of

The "recipe" for Medici porcelain ● 56 has been preserved. White clay from Vicenza was mixed with white sand, ground rock crystal, tin and calcinated lead, making a hard, yellowish substance. Next the surface was coated with a white tin oxide glaze. The piece was then painted and fired using the same method as for majolica *alla porcellana*.

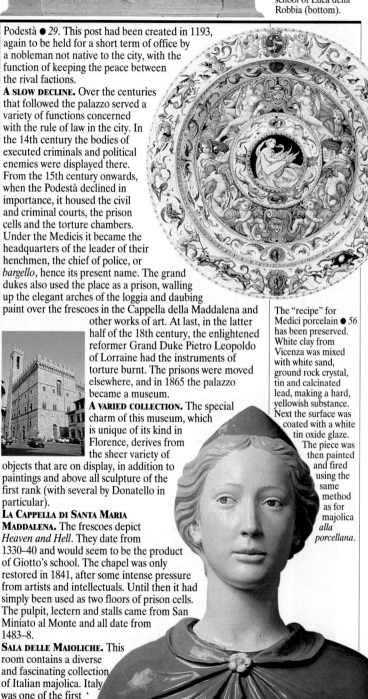

LA SALA DEI BRONZETTI IN THE BARGELLO
During the Renaissance, a number of artists made small bronzes in the antique style. Donatello and Bartoldo were the first to practise the art. Above is one of the finest pieces, a vigorous *Hercules and Antaeus* by Antonio Pollaiuolo. This is a fine example of the exquisite detail that can be obtained in these tiny bronzes. The most famous works in this genre are by Giambologna, notably a figure of *Mercury*.

PALAZZO DEI VISACCI
Below and right are two of the many figures of famous Florentines that adorn the façade of this palazzo on the Borgo degli Albizzi.

porcelain – Renaissance man, with his great interest in the natural sciences, could not resist the challenge. The Medici Grand Duke Francesco I dabbled in alchemy and set up a laboratory for the purpose. It took his craftsmen ten years to perfect their methods and to produce a type of pottery resembling porcelain, which was known as Medici porcelain. It was made from 1576 onwards, but only in very limited quantities, since Francesco reserved it for his own personal use. The residents of the Palazzo Pitti ▲ *288* received a gift of ceramics painted with the Medici coat of arms.

PALAZZO PAZZI-QUARATESI ● *71*

This palazzo, also known as Pazzi della Congiura as a reminder of the Pazzi conspiracy ▲ *131*, is at number 10, Via del Proconsolo. It was built between 1462 and 1472 by Giuliano da Maiano, but based upon original plans by Brunelleschi. Jacopo Pazzi oversaw the construction, only to be executed in 1478 in the violent repression of the conspiracy. The columns of the inner courtyard have remarkable capitals decorated with dolphins and flaming vases. The dolphins come from the Pazzi coat of arms, and the vases mark the fact that on Easter Saturday the family had the right to take holy fire from the high altar of the cathedral. This privilege was a reward to one of the family who had scaled the walls of Jerusalem during the crusades. Opposite, at numbers 5 and 7, Via del Proconsolo, is the 15th-century PALAZZO BALDOVINI.

PALAZZO NONFINITO ● *74*

THE "UNFINISHED" PALACE. Begun in 1593 for Alessandro Strozzi, this palazzo at number 12, Via del Proconsolo, remained incomplete. Bernardo Buontalenti only

The engraving (center) by Giuseppe Zocchi shows the convent, which no longer exists. The little piazza in which the convent stood remains, but only the main door of the church can now be seen. Right, a Kafiri funerary statue from the Institute of Anthropology in the Palazzo Nonfinito. Below, lamp and window of the Ramirez de Montalvo palace. Bottom, the inner courtyard of the Palazzo Pazzi-Quaratesi.

completed the ground floor in his imposing style, but its windows, balcony and columns flanking the main door give the building a powerful grandeur. The large and handsome *cortile* was laid out by Cigoli in 1604. This palazzo has housed the INSTITUTE OF ANTHROPOLOGY since 1869. Now turn right into the Borgo degli Albizzi or left into Dante's quarter.

BORGO DEGLI ALBIZZI ★

This narrow, shady street lined with magnificent palazzi and dominated by their impressive cornices has retained an air of great nobility. The *borgo* follows the route of a Roman road and used to lead from the first city wall to the eastern suburbs. The palazzo of the PAZZI DELLA COLOMBARIA is at number 28. It was built in the second half of the 16th century. At number 26 stands the PALAZZO RAMIREZ DE MONTALVO, dating from 1568 and designed by Ammannati. Its façade was decorated with *sgraffiti* (from the Italian *sgraffiato*, meaning "scratched") by Bernardino Poccetti. This is a black and white or polychrome decoration of the wall surface using a technique similar to fresco (see illustration). Ramirez de Montalvo was a Spanish nobleman who came to Florence as page to Eleonora di Toledo and became a favorite of Cosimo I de' Medici. The latter's coat of arms are above the window on the first floor up. The decoration of the façade of number 18, the PALAZZO DEI VISACCI is unusual. It is covered with bas-relief portraits of eminent citizens of Florence including Dante, Petrarch, Boccaccio, Alberti, Vespucci and Guicciardini ● *38*. The PALAZZO DEGLI ALBIZZI, belonging to the wealthy family after whom the street was named, is at number 12. It was built by Gherardo Silvani between 1625 and 1634. Number 15 is one of the oldest palaces in the street, the PALAZZO DEGLI ALESSANDRI, from the 14th century.

THE PORTICO OF SAN PIER MAGGIORE. The route leads into the Piazza San Pier Maggiore, site of a convent demolished in the 18th century and of which only the portico remains. In typical Italian fashion it seems at home in its new and incongruous setting, amid the façades of private houses. Many tower-houses (*case-torri*) ● *64* stood here in medieval times, but only one remains – a 13th-century *case-torri* on the right of the piazza. To return toward Dante's quarter, take the Via del Corso to the tranquil VIA PANDOLFINI, with its fine palaces concealing courtyards and even gardens.

"SGRAFFITI"
Sgraffiti were produced by covering the wall with a tinted plaster base, over which was applied a thinner layer of plaster. The decoration would then be made by scraping off parts of the top layer to reveal the color of the plaster beneath. During the Renaissance the technique rivaled the fresco in northern

Italy, Austria and Bohemia. It then fell from favor and was not seen again until the 19th and 20th centuries.

DANTE'S QUARTER

VIA DEL CORSO. This is a lively and attractive street with courtyards and little side streets leading off beneath archways to either side. Once the Roman *decumanus* ● *62,* today it is one of the busiest shopping streets in Florence. In medieval times it echoed to the hoofbeats of galloping horses in a race that was once one of the finest sights in Florence. The victor was awarded a standard (*palio*) of dark red brocade worked with the arms of the city – a gilded lily and a red cross on a white field. In times of war this race was transferred to the field of battle, or even held beneath the enemy walls, as at Arezzo in 1289 ● *47.*

PALAZZO PORTINARI-SALVIATI. The Banca Toscana now has its headquarters in this palace, at number 6, Via del Corso. It conceals a remarkable little courtyard decorated in the Mannerist style. On the corner opposite, where the Corso crosses the Via Santa Margherita, stands the TORRE DONATI.

THE CHURCH OF SANTA MARGHERITA IN SANTA MARIA DE' RICCI. This church is on the same side as the Palazzo Portinari-Salviati. It dates from 1508, but the façade by Gherardo Silvani was added a century later, including the loggia with its fine columns closed by a delicately worked wrought-iron grille.

MEDIEVAL TOWER-HOUSES ● *64.* Most of the city's medieval tower-houses are to be found clustered in this area. They were built by noblemen as their residences during the 12th and 13th centuries. There is a group of these towers where the Via Santa Elisabetta runs into the Via del

Corso. In the righthand corner is the TORRE RICCI and on the left are two towers belonging to the Ghiberti family. Turning to face the Via Cerchi, the CASA LAPI can be seen. Its original plans were drawn up by Brunelleschi. Not far away, on a little piazza in Via Santa Elisabetta, stands the round TORRE LA PAGLIAZZA, which is now a luxury hotel.

VIA DE' CERCHI. The Cerchi family was one of the most powerful in medieval Florence. Between 1300 and 1311 they were deeply entangled in the internal Guelf conflicts, leading the "Blacks" against the "Whites" ● *34,* ▲ *312.* The family was of peasant origin, but gained enormous wealth through banking and commerce to become one of the richest in Florence. The street contains a number of their residences, including the tower on the corner of the Via del Canto alla Quarconia, which dates from 1292–8 and, most impressive of all, the PALAZZO CERCHI, a marvelously preserved medieval palace which is arguably among the finest in the whole city. It is on the corner of the Via della Condotta, on the right.

BIZZARI ★. At number 32, Via della Condotta, is a most unusual shop which specializes in an extraordinary range of materials. All kinds of products for artists and craftsmen are on sale here (including the dragon's blood resin that gives violins their gleaming red-orange surface), as well as chemicals, essential oils, medicinal herbs and cooking spices.

Torre de' Cerchi.

VIA DANTE ALIGHIERI. On the corner of the Via Dante and the Via Santa Margherita is a reconstruction of the house in which Dante may well have been born, although this is by no means certain. The original building has gone, to be replaced by a mock-Gothic house built between 1875 and 1910. There is also a little museum.

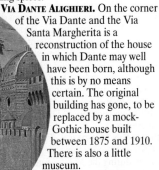

AN UNKIND FATE ● 38. Dante Alighieri was born in 1265 into an impoverished though noble family. He was educated at the University of Bologna, studying philosophy and astronomy. When he was twelve years old his family decided that he should marry Gemma Donati, and the wedding eventually took place in 1295. But at the age of nine Dante had seen and fallen in love with Beatrice, the daughter of the Florentine nobleman Folco Portinari. Her betrothal was purely political, to cement a family alliance, and in 1283 she married Simone de' Bardi, only to die seven years later.

A POLITICAL CAREER. Having married Gemma Donati, Dante began to take an active part in political life. He was registered in the Guild of Apothecaries as a "poet" and took his turn serving on the various city councils. In 1300 he was sent as ambassador to San Gimignano, to persuade the city to join a Guelf alliance and stand up to Pope Boniface VIII, who was hostile to Tuscany. On June 15 of that year he became one of six priors of Florence, a post he held for two months. He continued to defend the interests of his city against the pope and also attempted to make peace between the rival "White" and "Black" Guelf factions ▲ 312. But Florence fell into the hands of Charles de Valois, brother of the king of France and the pope's ally, and Dante was finally exiled. He wandered

VIA DELLA CONDOTTA
The name derives from an institution, the Ufficiali della Condotta. This was a group of four citizens who paid the city's soldiers. By extension the word *condotta* came to signify the contract between mercenary and city.

SANTA MARGHERITA IN SANTA MARIA DE' RICCI
The entrance lies under the fine loggia

on the Via del Corso. Above, interior of the church.

193

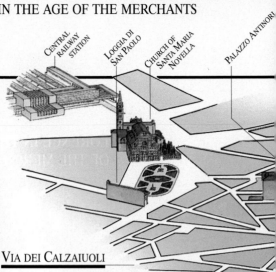

CENTRAL RAILWAY STATION — LOGGIA DI SAN PAOLO — CHURCH OF SANTA MARIA NOVELLA — PALAZZO ANTINORI

THE STATUES OF ORSANMICHELE
At street level the pillars of this building (below) have recesses, most of which are filled by statues of the patron saints of the guilds (the Arti). *Saint John the Evangelist* (above) was done by Baccio di Montelupo.

VIA DEI CALZAIUOLI

This is a busy street that runs between the Piazza del Duomo ▲ *128* and the Piazza della Signoria ▲ *142*. Nowadays it is fortunately free from cars and so has an atmosphere of luxurious calm. The street was widened as part of the large-scale alterations made in the latter half of the 19th century, when many picturesque little streets and alleyways were lost. Its name comes from *calze*, meaning "breeches", after the number of rowdy occupants who were willing to sell you a pair here when they were in fashion in the 14th, 15th and 16th centuries. During the Middle Ages, first cheesemakers and then drapers occupied one end of the street, while the other was lined with *botteghe,* or painters' workshops.

THE CHURCH OF SAN CARLO DEI LOMBARDI. Begun in 1349 to designs by Neri di Fioravante et Benci di Cione, this church was not completed until over a century later. The façade is by Simone Talenti, who also worked on the campanile of the Duomo ▲ *132*.

THE LOMBARD BROTHERHOOD. In 1616 a religious group known as the brotherhood of the Lombards arrived in Florence, bringing with them the relics of St Charles Borromeo, archbishop of Milan. They took over this church, which became known as San Carlo dei Lombardi. It is extremely dark inside, but the chancel has a beautiful *Deposition from the Cross,* by Niccolò di Pietro Gerini (1385–90). The lunettes of the arches have frescoes, which were much damaged by the 1966 flood and which recount the life of St Charles. The painting by Matteo Rosselli above the entrance is the *Apotheosis of Saint Charles* (1616).

ORSANMICHELE   ● 85

AN UNUSUAL HISTORY. The name of this curious looking building goes back to the very first church that stood here from the year 750. It was an oratory built in the

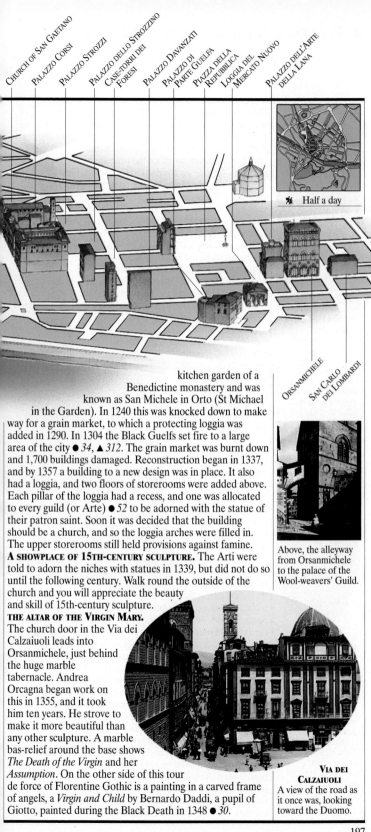

CHURCH OF SAN GAETANO
PALAZZO CORSI
PALAZZO STROZZI
PALAZZO DELLO STROZZINO
CASE-TORRI DEI FORESI
PALAZZO DAVANZATI
PALAZZO DI PARTE GUELFA
PIAZZA DELLA REPUBBLICA
LOGGIA DEL MERCATO NUOVO
PALAZZO DELL'ARTE DELLA LANA

✷ Half a day

ORSANMICHELE
SAN CARLO DEI LOMBARDI

kitchen garden of a Benedictine monastery and was known as San Michele in Orto (St Michael in the Garden). In 1240 this was knocked down to make way for a grain market, to which a protecting loggia was added in 1290. In 1304 the Black Guelfs set fire to a large area of the city ● *34*, ▲ *312*. The grain market was burnt down and 1,700 buildings damaged. Reconstruction began in 1337, and by 1357 a building to a new design was in place. It also had a loggia, and two floors of storerooms were added above. Each pillar of the loggia had a recess, and one was allocated to every guild (or Arte) ● *52* to be adorned with the statue of their patron saint. Soon it was decided that the building should be a church, and so the loggia arches were filled in. The upper storerooms still held provisions against famine.

A SHOWPLACE OF 15TH-CENTURY SCULPTURE. The Arti were told to adorn the niches with statues in 1339, but did not do so until the following century. Walk round the outside of the church and you will appreciate the beauty and skill of 15th-century sculpture.

THE ALTAR OF THE VIRGIN MARY. The church door in the Via dei Calzaiuoli leads into Orsanmichele, just behind the huge marble tabernacle. Andrea Orcagna began work on this in 1355, and it took him ten years. He strove to make it more beautiful than any other sculpture. A marble bas-relief around the base shows *The Death of the Virgin* and her *Assumption*. On the other side of this tour de force of Florentine Gothic is a painting in a carved frame of angels, a *Virgin and Child* by Bernardo Daddi, a pupil of Giotto, painted during the Black Death in 1348 ● *30*.

Above, the alleyway from Orsanmichele to the palace of the Wool-weavers' Guild.

VIA DEI CALZAIUOLI
A view of the road as it once was, looking toward the Duomo.

197

FRESCOES REVEALED. The 14th-century frescoes are in very poor condition. They were painted over in 1770 when they were considered worthless medieval daubs. With all its new ideas, the Renaissance did engender a certain scorn for the preceding centuries, despite an admiration for Giotto. This attitude to the art of the Middle Ages held sway until the 19th century, and even then it was still seen as "primitive". So it was that these frescoes were not uncovered until 1864. They are all of saints. The upper floor is reached through the Palazzo dell'Arte della Lana ▲ *201*, the former headquarters of the Guild of Wool-weavers.

THE RISE OF THE GUILDS ● *52*. There is nowhere better than Orsanmichele to get an idea of the importance of the guilds, or Arti. They date back to the 12th century, and Florence owed its wealth to them. The first association of merchants was the *Societas Mercatorum*, presided over by three consuls. They defended their rights against the *Societas Militum*, which represented the nobles and other well-to-do families. The merchants soon began to have a great deal of influence over trade and politics, and formed their first guild, called the Guild of Calimala. This was for all the trades but, toward the end of the 12th century, groups began to break away to form their own guilds: the money-changers, silkweavers and goldsmiths (known as Por Santa Maria); the wool-weavers, physicians and apothecaries, furriers, and judges and notaries. Calimala came to represent the cloth merchants. Because they were the oldest, these seven were known as the Arti Maggiori, or greater guilds (their arms are shown on the far right).

THE MINOR GUILDS. In 1289 fourteen Arti Minori were founded: the linen-drapers and old clothes dealers; the breeches-makers (*calzaiuoli*); the carpenters and stonemasons; the blacksmiths; the salt, cheese and oil merchants; the butchers; the wine merchants; the innkeepers; the wood merchants; the tanners; the armorers; the locksmiths; the curriers, and last of all the bakers' guild. The Maggiori tended to be wealthy merchants, while the Minori represented the better-off tradesmen. Many who participated in the business life of the city belonged to no guild at all. Into this category fell such tradesmen as fishmongers, as well as artisans, and also the urban and rural laborers.

ANDREA ORCAGNA'S TABERNACLE
Orcagna wanted this to be the finest ever made. It frames a *Virgin and Child* (right) by Bernardo Daddi. Before the loggia arches were filled in it was fully lit by daylight.

THE COAT OF ARMS OF THE CAPTAINS OF ORSANMICHELE
Eight captains made up the Laudesi brotherhood, who were dedicated to the cult of the Madonna delle Grazie, the miraculous virgin. Their emblem has the letters OSM (Orsanmichele) set on a blue ground.

Right, arms of the Arti in terracotta, from the workshop of Luca della Robbia.

How the guilds worked. All the Arti adopted the same structure. The dues paid by the members were high, which kept out the poorer tradesmen and craftsmen. At the head of each Arte were two or four consuls, who were elected for a six-month period, and two councils who shared in the administration. There were also some paid posts, such as treasurers and accountants. The guilds' responsibilities were twofold: they protected their members' interests, but they were also expected to keep up their standards of practice and behavior.

A limited democracy. Guilds were associations of employers, so employees had no say in the running of things. Conditions of work, wages and fees were all dictated from above. Each Arte had its own palace, its own coat of arms and its own standard-bearer. Moreover, each had its own laws and police force. "External officers" were employed to keep an eye on the wages paid and to watch out for signs of discontent or incipient revolt. The two most important guilds, the Calimala and the Arte della Lana, had representatives at the great fairs which were held all over Europe.

A broad intake. The most intriguing thing about the guilds is the variety of professions to be found within each one. For example, doctors, barbers, apothecaries, grocers, sellers of pigments and artists, and haberdashers all rubbed shoulders in the Arte dei Medici e Speziali. The haberdashers sold drugs, so their link with the apothecaries is clear. Less obvious is the presence of pigment sellers, and artists. But recipes for colors were jealously guarded secrets, and their inventors were often the painters themselves.

The power of the Calimala. This was directly linked to the surging development of industry, commerce and banking. At first the Calimala's activity was limited to the processing and dyeing of rough cloth bought at the great fairs of Flanders and Champagne, and resold throughout Europe at a considerable profit. Another trade in which the Calimala specialized was the import of exotic goods, such as spices, scents and expensive fabrics. The guild was also responsible for the export of wheat.

Europe's bankers. Before the Guild of Money-changers came into existence, the Calimala already included money, changers and bankers. It soon became the principal financier of the pope, the kings of France and England, the German princes and those of Burgundy and the Holy Roman

ARMS OF THE SEVEN ARTI MAGGIORI

Money-changers

Calimala

Doctors, apothecaries

Por Santa Maria

Wool-weavers

Furriers

Judges, lawyers

199

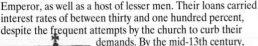

Below, *Distribution of grain at Orsanmichele*.

Emperor, as well as a host of lesser men. Their loans carried interest rates of between thirty and one hundred percent, despite the frequent attempts by the church to curb their demands. By the mid-13th century, twenty-four companies had their share of the international market. Together, families such as the Acciaiuoli, Alberti, Albizzi, Antinori, Bardi, Capponi, Cerchi, Davanzati, Mozzi, Pazzi, Peruzzi, Portinari, Ricci, Strozzi and Tornabuoni held international finance in their grip.

PRIVILEGES. The wealth and power of the Calimala brought its members certain privileges. For example, it was their steel-tipped measuring stick that was taken as the legal unit, or ell, upon which other units of length were also based.

THE GOLD FLORIN. The consuls of the Arti took their place in the governing councils under the Podestà ▲ *188*. With the 1293 "Orders of Justice" ● *29*, they took turns to be elected as governing priors. Their economic power had now earned them a high political position. But the most telling sign of their influence was the international respect for their gold coin, which became standard currency throughout the whole of medieval Europe. Florins were minted in the Zecca (mint), which was next to the Palazzo Vecchio. Goldsmiths kept a careful check on the quality of the workmanship and, more importantly, the purity of the metal used. This was vitally important for the currency to remain stable.

THE ROOTS OF CAPITALISM. The bill of exchange was actually invented by the Genoese, but it was the merchants of Florence who exploited it to most advantage. They had to make long journeys overland and by sea in order to conduct their business. To carry large quantities of gold coin was dangerous so, to avoid this, from early in the 13th century, they began to use bills of exchange. The bill was a legal document which was signed before witnesses; non-payment entailed a fine of double its value. It was an extremely versatile system and was put to four main uses: straightforward buying and selling, transferring funds then available in the local currency, obtaining credit, and dealing in bills whose value would vary from one place to another. Another method of payment, the cheque, dates from this period. Florentine businessmen also invented life insurance and double-entry book-keeping (using two balanced columns, one for debit, one for credit).

DECLINE. Some serious bankruptcies between 1343 and 1346 followed by other problems, worst of all the Black Death, weakened the Florentine economy for many years. It began to recover in the 15th century with new families at the helm, the Medici, the Strozzi and the Guardi in particular. Then, from 1500 they gradually lost ground, and the Germans, Spaniards and Genoese took over as Europe's bankers.

THE GOLD FLORIN
The Florentines used the coin of Pisa, the mark, until 1252. By then trade and banking in the city were expanding so

rapidly that they minted their own florin. On it was John the Baptist, the city's patron saint, and on the reverse was the lily, the symbol of Florence. This was an extremely stable currency, and was used throughout Europe.

PALAZZO DELL'ARTE DEI BECCAI. At 4 Via Orsanmichele stand the old headquarters of the powerful but socially unacceptable Guild of Butchers. They could never escape the stigma of their trade. The goat, a symbol taken from their coat of arms, can be seen high on the façade. The captains of Orsanmichele once lived in this building, but it has long housed the oldest of all art academies, the Accademia delle Arti del Disegno. Inside is a fine fresco and a *sinopia* (sketch) for a *Maestà* by Mariotto di Nardo, who was an important late 14th-century painter.

PALAZZO DELL'ARTE DELLA LANA

TABERNACLE OF SANTA MARIA DELLA TROMBA. This 14th-century tabernacle is now at the corner of the Palazzo dell'Arte della Lana, where the Via Orsanmichele and the Via dell'Arte della Lana cross each other. Originally it stood in the Piazza del Mercato Vecchio, which was demolished in the 19th century in order to make way for the Piazza della Repubblica. It formerly held two paintings of the Madonna by Jacopo Landini, an early 14th-century painter, but they have since been taken down, restored and can now be seen, their colors bright once more, on display at the Bardini Museum ▲ *315*.

FLORENCE, CAPITAL OF CLOTH. During the 14th century the PALACE OF THE GUILD OF WOOL-WEAVERS was the headquarters of one of the most prosperous guilds in the city of Florence. At first their trade simply involved the making of rough wool garments, but soon they mastered new techniques and began to produce the cloth itself, using imported wool from England, Flanders, Spain, Portugal, the Barbary Coast (Algeria and Morocco) and the Near East. The industry expanded with such speed that, by the end of the 13th century, the guild exceeded even the Calimala in importance. Three hundred workshops were producing about 100,000 lengths of cloth each year, and one third of the working population of Florence,

Above, the palace of the Guild of Wool-weavers. At the corner is the tabernacle (empty) of Santa Maria della Tromba.

BILL OF EXCHANGE (below) This is how a bill of exchange might read: "In the year of Our Lord, this sixth day of February 1392. Pay, on this first letter, to Niccolò da Uzano, 103 florins, 12 shillings, 6 pennies *a oro*, in exchange for 100 gold florins".

MAKING A PIECE OF WOOLLEN CLOTH
Transforming the crude fleece into woollen cloth involved washing, carding and spinning.

both men and women, were involved in the work. Production dropped from 1320 to 1330, although the quality accordingly improved. By this time, the number of lengths of cloth being refined by the Calimala was down to about ten thousand a year. Even by mid-century, when the decline had firmly set in, they were still supplying the West with one tenth of all its cloth.

MAKING WOOLLEN CLOTH: A SLOW PROCESS. The wool bought from abroad reached Genoa or Venice by sea, and was then carried overland to Florence. The first stage of the clothmaking process required the wool to be sorted and washed in a mixture of horse urine and detergent. Then it was taken to the *umiliati*, the Benedictines of Ognissanti ▲ *281*, who rinsed it in the Arno or the Mugnone. The wool was then laid out on racks of woven reed and beaten, before being handed on to the *divettini,* who removed the last of the impurities. Next came the combing; each handful receiving ten strokes of the comb, before the long filaments could be separated from the short for spinning. Now the carders (*cardatori*) got to work, originally using the wild thistle (*cardo*) as their tool. Later the job was done with two small boards covered with metal points that were rubbed together. The wool was now fine enough to be spun, usually by women in their own homes. Finally, the spun yarn was woven into cloth, then washed once more and given its finish with a brush made of thistle heads.

THE VITAL ELEMENT. The cloth was now ready to be dyed. Florentine expertise in this craft had become legendary, and sadly the secret has now been lost. It was the particular method of using the mineral alum that made the colors fast. The alum came from Phocaea, a city in Asia Minor, and was shipped to Genoa. The Genoese controlled the supply to the whole of the rest of Europe. But in the early 15th century Turkish invasions threatened this Phocaean source, and anxious cloth manufacturers began to look elsewhere for alum. In 1462 it was found at Tolfa, near Rome, and for a time the Medicis had charge of it. Lorenzo the Magnificent considered it a hostile act when the rival Pazzi family regained control over this key resource.

THE LOGGIA DEL MERCATO NUOVO

A TOURISTS' MARKET. The Via Calimala now leads on to the MERCATO NUOVO (new market). This is an elegant late Renaissance structure with a loggia, by Giovanni Battista del Tasso (1500–55), built between 1547 and 1551. It was

Guilds were also being formed in other regions, particularly in the neighboring province of Umbria. These too chose emblems (shown in the righthand column below). Below left on this page are miniatures taken from a treatise, *L'Arte della Seta*, which give an idea of how silk was manufactured. On the facing page, above, is the Furriers coat of arms; below is the palace of the Guild of Butchers (Arte dei Beccai).

originally a covered market, where silk and gold were sold. A stone set into the floor marks the spot where fraudsters and bankrupts were exposed before being pilloried. But the focal point is the fountain, with its bronze boar statue known as "*il porcellino*". Beneath the loggia, stalls are set out which sell all kinds of goods ranging from straw hats and baskets to furniture and ornaments. Be careful while shopping here, for although some things may be local, many of them are actually cheap imports. The market attracts large numbers of tourists eager for the scarves, ties, leather goods and souvenirs of all kinds that are on sale.

POWERFUL LAWYERS. Although the guilds of the Calimala and Wool-weavers were the most powerful in the city, neither of them ranked first among the Arti Maggiori. This honor belonged to the Guild of Judges and Notaries. In the 13th and

14th centuries notaries were chosen by the Holy Roman Emperor or by the pope (or their representatives) or, in certain cases, by communes that had assumed this imperial prerogative. In industrious medieval Florence the notaries were the intellectuals, thanks to their command of Latin and literary Italian. They performed many functions. They sat on the councils that helped govern the Republic, and assisted the chief magistrates, such as the priors or the "Capitano del Popolo". They helped to administer the Arti and also the judicial system. At trials they acted for the prosecution or the defence, and could be appointed to represent those without means to pay. Notaries were influential and respected citizens, all the more so if they were of noble birth.

LAWYERS AND LITERATURE. The Guild of Judges and Notaries had many members: in the early 14th century there were six hundred of them. These were well-educated men, and their influence on the cultural life of the city was enormous. They were masters of rhetoric, and their command of written and spoken language was

considerable. So it is no surprise to find them among the most important writers and poets of the Middle Ages. In canto 15 of *The Inferno*, Dante meets his master Brunetto Latini ● *38*. He was a Florentine of good birth, a notary, poet, orator and scholar who influenced both Cavalcanti and Dante. Latini was chancellor of the city, but was later exiled and took refuge at the French court in Paris. His encyclopaedic *Livres du Trésor*

THE COATS OF ARMS OF THE UMBRIAN GUILDS
A parchment dating from 1602 showing the emblems of the guilds of the town of Orvieto.

203

IL MERCATO NUOVO
This was an important meeting

place, where news was exchanged about boats in and out of Livorno and Pisa. A word to the wrong person could ruin a carefully planned business transaction and entail great loss. It was forbidden to carry arms here. The bronze boar (*il porcellino*) on the fountain is by Pietro Tacco. Tradition has it that if you rub his snout and throw a coin into the water you will come back to Florence.

were written in French, which was considered the second language of scholars after Latin. In 1266 he was finally able to return home to Florence. Dante had several other notary-poets among his contemporaries: Gianni Alfani, whom Dante considered "the greatest Italian love poet", and Cino da Pistoia (c. 1270–1336), a friend though Ghibelline, whose politics were to cost him three years in exile. On returning to Florence, he held a number of important posts. During his exile he wrote melancholy love poetry, in a style quite different from the other poets, who conformed to the "dolce stil nuovo".

THE "DOLCE STIL NUOVO" ● *38.* The phrase is one of Dante's and cannot be said to represent either a school of poetry or a strict style. Rather, it embraces a range of Tuscan love poetry that was written at the end of the 13th and the beginning of the 14th centuries. What made the poetry so new and so different was that these were direct and passionate declarations of love, rather than rhetorical devices and formulas taken from Latin; this was an age of sincerity, authenticity and introspection. The new approach called for a new language. And the "stil nuovo" had a stong religious vein running through it – woman was an angel who had come down to earth, the incarnation of Good and, like the Virgin, an intermediary between man and God. Virtue was attained through love. But these were men of wide knowledge and interests, and their love poems were easily diverted into philosophy.

PALAZZO DI PARTE GUELFA

THE HEADQUARTERS OF THE GUELF PARTY. Going back up the Via Porta Rossa, there is a little piazza with the old CHURCH OF SANTA MARIA SOVRAPORTA on the left. This is occupied by a university library. On the right are two 15th-century palaces. One of them, the PALAZZO CANACCI, with its curved façade, is decorated with restored *sgraffiti* ▲ *191.* At the far end of the piazza is the PALAZZO DI PARTE GUELFA. The crenellated façade, with its Gothic window overlooking the piazza, dates from the 14th century and is decorated with the arms of the captains of the Guelf party. In the 15th century the palazzo was extended on the side overlooking the Via di

Capaccio toward the Mercato Nuovo. This section was designed by Brunelleschi and completed by Vasari. Most of the interior is taken up by a great hall, the proportions of which have the look of Brunelleschi's work. Go down the Chiasso San Biagio (*chiasso* means "lane") to see the VIA DELLE TERME, a narrow, tranquil street which retains its medieval flavor, with narrow *chiassi* that lead off beneath archways toward the Borgo Santi Apostoli ▲ *270*. Now go back the way you came as far as the Via Pelliceria, which leads back to the Via Porta Rossa.

THE GUELF PARTY. In 1268, after winning a definitive victory over the Ghibellines, the Florentine Guelfs founded the *Parte guelfa* to adminster the confiscated possessions of exiled Ghibellines ● *34*, ▲ *312*. It also carried out some reprisals – destroying all the Uberti properties, for instance, that stood on the site of the Piazza della Signoria. There was an officer whose particular job it was to seek out sympathizers to the Ghibelline cause and bring them before the captains' tribunal. The Guelf party amounted to a state within a state. It had its own palace, its two councils (one of fourteen members, the other sixty), its six captains, its budget and administrative employees. It controlled the economic and political life of the city on the pretext that it was protecting the people's welfare – the Ghibelline strongholds of Pisa and Siena were still functioning, and could come to the aid of their comrades at any time. This state of affairs continued for a long time, with the *Parte guelfa* ruling Florence in a harsh and often quite arbitrary fashion.

THE "CARROCCIO"
This red chariot embodied Florentine patriotism. Pulled by a pair of oxen, it carried the commune's standard-bearers. In times of war it was brought to the Mercato Nuovo ▲ *202* (above), and from there went to the battlefield. The citizens were sworn to defend it, and to die rather than surrender it to the enemy.

PIAZZA DAVANZATI

THE TOWER HOUSES OF THE FORESI. The Via Porta Rossa leads to the Piazza Davanzati, which is surrounded by some of the oldest civic buildings in the whole of the city. There are some very impressive *case torri* which date from the 13th century ● *64*, with ground floors that have dark walls pierced with easily fortifiable doors and tiny windows. Square holes can be seen higher up on the walls. Temporary bridges were fixed into holes these in order to get from one house to another when there were riots or battles going on in the streets below. These particular houses belonged to the Foresi, who were one of the most powerful families living in Florence at that time.

PALAZZO DAVANZATI ★, ● *42*.
Standing opposite these rugged fortified dwellings, the Palazzo Davanzati seems to belong to another world; it has all the peace and opulence that were typical of its period. The palace was built at the beginning of the 14th century for a family of wool merchants, the

A MODEL OF URBAN LIVING
The rooms of the Palazzo Davanzati are full of interesting objects. In the Sala dei Pappagalli, a 16th-century iron casket; in the next room, a chest with an elaborate lock, in the so-called "Room of the Châtelaine of Vergi", a fine late 16th-century wooden trunk. Below, detail of *Joseph taken to Prison* by Granacci, which hangs in the palazzo. Opposite: the *cortile* of the Palazzo Davanzati; the façade; *The Game of Civettino* (15th century) by the Master of the Adimari Cassone.

Davizzi, and then bought by a historian, Bernardo Davanzati, in 1578. It was he who installed the loggia on the top floor. In 1838 the last surviving member of the Davanzati family jumped to his death from a window. The palazzo was then split up into apartments and remained so for many decades. Finally, the art lover, painter and restorer Elia Volpi bought the place in 1904. She restored it and installed her private collection inside. It was opened as a museum in 1910, but remained private until the state decided to take it over and turned it into the *Museo della Casa Fiorentina Antica* (a museum dedicated to Florentine domestic interiors of the past), which was opened to the public in 1956.

A NEW ELEGANCE. The Palazzo Davanzati reflects a change in aesthetic values, and in particular the desire for light. It has lines of fine windows, creating a delightful, airy interior with an atmosphere somewhere between a tower-house and the later grandiose Renaissance palaces of the Medicis or Strozzis. On the ground floor, the large entrances gave access to shops and storerooms. The living accommodation above is set out in quite a new way, around a central courtyard, giving far more light. The huge main room on the *piano nobile* (the "noble floor" because the floor above street level was considered to be the most pleasant, and contained the reception rooms) runs the width of the building. Other rooms were decorated with frescoes, hangings and tapestries. The ironwork on the façade of the building reveals much about everyday life in the city. There are hooks for tying up horses and pack animals, and the bars across the windows served a number of purposes: on special occasions they were hung with colored banners, though normally they were used to hang out skeins of wool or the household washing.

Birdcages and little food safes of woven reed were also hung from these bars, as is charmingly depicted in the *Resurrection of Tabitha*, one of the frescoes by Masaccio and Masolino in Santa Maria del Carmine ▲ 306. There are also attachments for torches and standards.

HOW A WELL-TO-DO FAMILY LIVED. The staircase in the inner courtyard, leading to the floors above, is one of the most impressive in Florence. It has a stone base, and the upper wooden structure has arched supports. Water from the well reached all floors by an ingenious system of pulleys and buckets, and there was even a lavatory on each floor – a great luxury in the 15th century. On the first floor up is the Sala dei Pappagalli (so-called because its walls are painted with parrots), which was the dining room. One of the finest rooms on this floor is the *camera nuziale* (the "nuptual bedroom"), which is decorated with the arms of all the families to which

CONVENIENCES
When the Palazzo Davanzati was built, around 1330, lavatories with drains were still a recent innovation. Those

who lacked such conveniences had to go out and find a quiet corner. Boccaccio describes the most common and basic domestic arrangement, namely two planks set on pieces of wood over a small walled pit. This had to be emptied out from time to time. It is not known whether public latrines existed, as they did at San Gimignano. A decree was passed in 1325 that forbade the emptying of private conveniences directly into the streets and piazzas.

the Davizzi were related. On the next floor there is another dining room with a display of ceramics; the *camera da letto* (the bedroom) has delightful frescoes illustrating a French medieval romance *La Châtelaine de Vergi*. The kitchen on the top floor was obviously both comfortable and convenient, boasting a rudimentary system of running water. Here, as elsewhere in the house, there are traces of scratched writings on the walls, the earliest of which date from 1441 and the most recent from 1516. These are lists, sums, little phrases and even scraps of music.

PALAZZO TORRIGIANI. The palace is now an expensive hotel, the PORTA ROSSA, which stands at number 19. It is unusual in that it has retained its overhanging upper floors. This type of defensive architecture was banned, because it made the already narrow streets unbearably crowded. There are poppies sculpted on the base of the corbelling above, a reminder, along with the motto *"Per non dormire"* (So as not to sleep), of a story featuring the merchant Bartolini Salimbeni, first owner of the palace. One night this cunning businessman gave his rival merchants wine laced with opium, so that he would be the only one up next morning to meet an arriving consignment of goods. He was therefore able to buy them extremely cheaply. It is said that the family's fortune was based on this trick.

Below, a lantern from the façade of the Palazzo Strozzi, by Benedetto da Maiano. Lower down, a gemel window, and bottom, the façade on the Piazza Strozzi.

A NEW STYLE OF "CORTILE"
Built by Cronaca and finished in 1536, this *cortile* contains work that is a mixture of two very distinct styles. The ground-floor arcades, the mixture of *pietra serena* and rough plasterwork, and the rounded windows are all from the early Renaissance; but the pillars, balustrades

and windows betray a classical influence that was partially introduced to Florence by Baccio d'Agnolo.

PIAZZA STROZZI

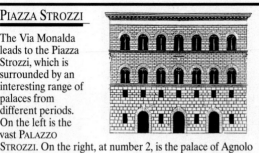

The Via Monalda leads to the Piazza Strozzi, which is surrounded by an interesting range of palaces from different periods. On the left is the vast PALAZZO STROZZI. On the right, at number 2, is the palace of Agnolo and Palla Strozzi, known as the PALAZZO DELLO STROZZINO. It was built between 1445 and 1465, begun by Michelozzo (who also built the Medicis' Palace ▲ *224*) and completed by Giuliano da Maiano, designer of the Palazzo Pazzi-Quaratesi ▲ *190*. The ground floor has the same rough-hewn look as the Medicis', while above it is the more sophisticated style of Maiano. Behind this palace it is worth admiring the façade and foyer of the ODEON CINEMA, an example of the Liberty style (Italian Art Nouveau) influenced by the Viennese school.

PALAZZO STROZZI ● *71*.
It is obvious that this magnificent palazzo was built when Florence was at its zenith. Merchants and bankers no longer kept their wealth under wraps but commissioned the most opulent palaces. Out of the one hundred or so to be built in Florence in the 15th century, the Strozzis' was the largest. In order to obtain the site for its construction, Filippo Strozzi had to buy a dozen separate properties. Benedetto da Maiano (1442–97), brother of Giuliano, was commissioned to build the palazzo, and began work in 1489. In 1497 Simone del Pollaiuolo, known as "il Cronaca" (1457–1508), took over responsibility; the fine jutting cornice and the *cortile* are his. Money ran out before the entablature was completed. The ironwork lanterns, torch-holders, standard-holders and rings for tying horses were all designed by Maiano and Cronaca, and made by the much admired craftsman Niccolo Grosso, called "il Caparra". It was the privilege of a few high-ranking families to have lanterns lit outside their palaces when entertaining in the evening.

AN ARCHITECTURAL MASTERPIECE. The PALAZZO STROZZI marks the high point of Renaissance palace building in Florence. It has three floors, each separated by a band of stone that also forms the sill of the line of windows above. The structure is topped by a massive cornice copied directly from ancient Roman architecture. It is built around a fine colonnaded *cortile* (sadly disfigured by a large metal fire escape), the elegant and delicate appearance of which contrasts sharply with the massive stonework of the exterior.

Right, an old view of the Via Strozzi. In the distance is the arch leading to the Piazza della Repubblica.

A CULTURAL CENTER. Nowadays, this palace is used for commercial events such as fashion shows, and cultural ones too. Important art exhibitions are also held here (which stay open until midnight on certain days). This is the venue of the antique-dealers' "Biennale". The Italian Institute for Renaissance Studies is based here, and the building contains a famous library, the GABINETTO VIEUSSEUX ▲ 272. There is also the PICCOLO MUSEO, which is open to visitors. Its entrance is on the left in the *cortile*, and it covers the history of the Strozzi palace. The original wooden model for the building explains how Cronaca modified the original design.

PIAZZA DELLA REPUBBLICA

The Via degli Strozzi leads to this busy piazza, entering it under an imposing stone arch. With its cafés and kiosks, and the huge central post office, there is always plenty going on here.
A PICTURESQUE QUARTER DESTROYED. The history of this district is more interesting than anything that remains here now. At the end of the 19th century this central area of the city was a collection of narrow medieval streets. They were demolished because they were said to be unhealthy, but what the Florentines really wanted was a grand city center. This is how some of the dwellings of the very oldest families such as the Medici, the Sacchetti and the Brunelleschi came to be lost, as well as the Mercato Vecchio (the old market) and the ghetto. A column in the piazza called *della Dovizia* marks the crossroads of the *cardo* and *decumanus* ● 62, the main roads of the old Roman camp.
IL MERCATO VECCHIO. According to contemporary descriptions, in particular those of the 14th-century poet Antonio Pucci, the old market was the most colorful part of the city. It was a hive of activity. Not just food, but an extraordinary variety of goods and services were on offer here. Everyone was present, from doctors and apothecaries – the Speziali – to notaries, silk merchants to old clothes sellers, sculptors to blacksmiths, not to mention the bookmakers and quacks. There were beggars too, exposing their horrible deformities and wounds;

THE STROZZI FAMILY
There is mention of this family from the 13th century onwards, but their fortune came about a century later, when they took their place among the patriarchs of the city. Their alliances were made with the Albizzi, rivals of the Medicis, and for this they were exiled. Palla Strozzi, a patron of the arts, suffered this fate in 1434. Filippo I, who built the palace, also restored the family's fortunes by starting a bank in Naples. He returned to Florence in 1466. In the 16th century Filippo II led an uprising against Cosimo I. He was defeated and committed suicide in prison.

Madonna and Child by Cosimo Rosselli in the Palazzo Strozzi.

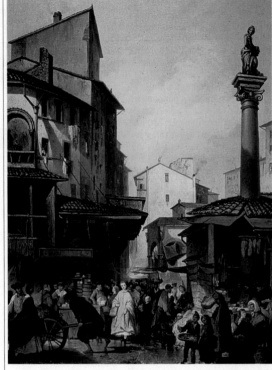

WELL-RESPECTED MEN
Doctors were in demand: there were only about sixty in 1339, in a city then numbering 100,000. They had the right to call themselves *messire* or *sire* and wore special robes like those of judges – a long cloak that came down to their feet, trimmed with fur – and a red hat. Medicine and the law were the two best professions for making money, so doctors were well-off even if they left the fee to their clients' discretion according to the result. Dante mentions the celebrated Taddeo Alderotti in *The Paradiso*. Some Florentine doctors even became well-known abroad. Aldobrandino, for instance, while in Paris in the mid-13th century, wrote some very popular volumes on health matters.

Above, a painting by Giuseppe Moricci de Firenze Pottore (1806–79)which recreates the atmosphere of the Mercato Vecchio, now disappeared. Below, the fashionable Café Paszkowski on the Piazza della Repubblica.

and tumblers; and priests exhibiting holy relics in the hope of obtaining a few coins. A 17th-century painting shows a well-dressed group choosing flowers just a few feet from some poor creature being tortured on the *strappado*. The victim would be drawn up to the top of the gibbet, which was more than 20 feet high, and then left to fall to the ground, only to be drawn up again and have the process repeated.

SURGEONS AND CHARLATANS. Among the many businesses, doctors enjoyed a particularly thriving trade at the Mercato. They belonged to the Arte dei Medici e Speziali, which included a number of different professions ▲ *199*. Plenty has been written, much of it satirical, about their failed attempts at treatment. Their reputation was not helped by the quacks and charlatans, whose skills went little further than peering at urine, cauterizing piles with red hot pokers, and prescribing pigeon dung for dandruff. In fact there were some good doctors carrying out sophisticated treatments. They studied at the university town of Bologna and were taught by some of the best practitioners in Europe. They learned to lance (preferably with red-hot iron), and the art of trepanning. A good doctor could mend a broken bone, arrest a hemorrhage using ligatures, operate on a hernia or a tumor, and reconnect cut nerves. Infant hydrocephalus was treated by draining surplus liquid through a hole in the skull. Patients were anesthetized with a mixture of opium, henbane and mandrake administered on a sponge.

THE "GIUBBE ROSSE", A MEETING PLACE OF INTELLECTUALS.

This was one of the best-known cafés in Italy. It was opened in 1888 by two Swiss brothers, the Reinnighaus, who taught the Florentines to drink beer. At the beginning of this century it became a meeting place for artists and intellectuals. Among them were Giovanni Papini and his friends from *LACERBA,* a Florentine literary review which appeared 1913–15. It was founded by Giovanni Papini (1881–1956) and Ardengo Soffici (1879–1964). Papini was a poet, novelist, essayist and historian, while Soffici, a writer and painter, gave encouragement to the Futurist movement. *Lacerba's* sympathies tended toward the nationalist right wing. Another famous revue, *La Voce,* was founded in 1908. These publications were produced from rooms at the back of the café, and it is said that Lenin met Gorky and other Russian revolutionaries here. Between 1926 and 1936 it was the intellectuals of the revue *SOLARIA* who were to found at the "Giubbe".

"SOLARIA", A HOTBED OF LITERARY TALENT.

This important review introduced the work of Joyce, Eliot, Gide, Rilke and Malraux to Italy. It was in open opposition to the Fascist regime, and published the work of Eugenio Montale and Salvatore Quasimodo.

The Piazza della Repubblica (below) was built on the ruins of the picturesque Mercato Vecchio (bottom).

THE JEWISH GHETTO IN FLORENCE. Italy was the first country in Europe to have an influx of Jews, and it was here that they suffered the least

Montale (1896–1981) is, with Quasimodo and Ungaretti, one of the finest modern Italian poets. In 1929 he became director of the Gabinetto Vieusseux ▲ 272, but was removed by the Fascists in 1939 (the year he published *Occasions*), and they made his life difficult for some years. After the war he went to live in Milan, where he continued his work as poet, translator, critic and painter, being awarded the Nobel Prize for literature in 1975. It was in *Solaria* too that, in 1930, Italians read a first collection of poems by Salvatore Quasimodo (1901–68), a self-educated Sicilian from Syracuse. The next generation to take over the *Giubbe* were the team of *Letteratura,* a review founded in 1937. Although Florence was, according to Mussolini, a Fascist city, the *Giubbe Rosse* remained a stronghold of opposition grouped around the figures of Eugenio Montale and the novelist Elio Vittorini (1908–66), also from Syracuse.

THE CAFÉ PASZKOWSKI. On the opposite side of the square is one of the best-known cafés in Florence. There is a small orchestra, the décor is 1950's and the cakes are delicious. To get back to Via Tornabuoni, take the Via degli Strozzi again.

persecution. The first Jewish colony in Florence was established in the 15th century, and the new arrivals became stiff competition for the town's own powerful moneylenders. They were not allowed to join the guilds, although many of them were doctors. A Jew was easily recognizable by a round piece of cloth sewn on his chest, and by a pointed hat. They were not confined to a ghetto until the papal bull of 1555.

PALAZZO ANTINORI
● *70* (below). Built around 1461 for

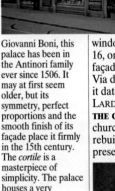

Giovanni Boni, this palace has been in the Antinori family ever since 1506. It may at first seem older, but its symmetry, perfect proportions and the smooth finish of its façade place it firmly in the 15th century. The *cortile* is a masterpiece of simplicity. The palace houses a very fashionable restaurant, the *Cantinetta Antinori*, where wine from the Antinori vineyards is available.

Above, the Cassetti silverware shop and famous *La Giacosa* tearooms, a lively afternoon rendezvous in the Via Tornabuoni.

Horserace in the Piazza Santa Maria Novella, by Antonio Cioci, is in the Museo di Firenze com'era ▲ *250*.

VIA TORNABUONI

A STREET OF PALACES. The Palazzo Stozzi overlooks the most elegant street in Florence. A stroll along it offers a chance to look at the best shops and some fine palaces as well. The PALAZZO GIACONNI is at number 5, built by Gherardo Silvani around 1626 for the poet Giovanni Battista Strozzi. Number 7 is the PALAZZO DELLA COMMENDA DI CASTIGLIONE, built in the 16th century by Ammannati and Giambologna. The 14th-century PALAZZO MEDICI TORNAQUINCI is at number 6. On the corner of the Via della Vigna Nuova is the PALAZZO DEL DUCA DI NORTUMBRIA, part 16th-, part 18th-century, sold by the Rucellai to Robert Dudley, duke of Northumberland. The corner loggia overlooking the Via Tornabuoni is early 20th-century. Florentines find the pâtisserie at no. 83r, *La Giacosa*, worth attention, especially a specialty called *torta della nonna*. Giovanni Battista Foggini designed the palace at number 15, the Palazzo Viviani della Robbia, in 1693: the first floor windows are Mannerist in style. The PALAZZO CORSI, number 16, once belonged to the Tornabuoni family. Its Quattrocento façade was altered in the mid 19th century. On the corner of Via dei Corsi is Cigoli's elegant LOGGETTA DEI TORNAQUINCI; it dates from the early 17th-century. At number 19 is PALAZZO LARDEREL, built by Giovanni Antonio Dosio in 1580.

THE CHURCH OF SAN GAETANO ● *90*. This is an 11th-century church once dedicated to St Michael Berteldi and completely rebuilt in the 17th century. Matteo Nigetti began work on the present structure in 1604, commissioned by Cardinal Carlo

SANTA MARIA NOVELLA
In the piazza are two obelisks supported by bronze tortoises.

de' Medici, and it was completed in 1683 by Gherardo Silvani, who worked on the façade. Inside is a painting by Pietro da Cortona, *The Martyrdom of Saint Lawrence* (c. 1653).

PINOCCHIO. In the narrow Via Rondinelli, at number 7, there is a plaque to show that this was the home of Carlo Lorenzini (1826–90), better known as Collodi, creator of the famous Pinocchio character.

CROCE AL TREBBIO. Going toward the church of Santa Maria Novella, the Via del Trebbio crosses a little piazza with a column. It was erected in 1338 to commemorate the conflict between Catholics and heretic Patarines, and in particular a battle fought here in 1244. The Patarines were a Milanese sect who continued Pope Gregory VII's fight against the accumulation of riches by the higher members of the clergy. At the time, this piazza was not within the city but in an area crossed by ditches that brought water to the industries outside the city walls. Here too were based the mendicant Dominican brothers, doing what they could to help the poor of the outlying villages. And here they built the convent and church of Santa Maria Novella.

THE CHURCH OF SANTA MARIA NOVELLA ● *89*

THE ARRIVAL OF THE DOMINICANS. In 1221, two years after his arrival in Florence, the Dominican Giovanni da Salerno took over a church that stood on the site of the present transept. We know that by 1225 the square could hold large crowds who came to hear the teachings of St Peter Martyr. The new

PINOCCHIO
Between 1881 and 1883 a serial about a puppet appeared in the *Giornale dei bambini*. When Collodi decided to "kill off" his character, Pinocchio, the little readers wrote in to protest. He therefore had to invent a number of additional episodes which were then published in book form in 1883. His success can be put down to the new tone that he introduced to children's literature. Instead of encountering dragons and sorcerers, Pinocchio meets a cricket, a fisherman, and a snake. And though at first so utterly selfish, he turns out to be good at heart. He made a welcome change from the virtuous boy heroes of the writer Edmondo de Amicis. Luigi Comencini's film of Collodi's book, which was made in 1971, is a celebration of freedom and disobedience.

THE SACRISTY
In here are a number of masterpieces, including Giotto's *Crucifix* (below), which was a particularly advanced painting for the late 13th century.

The body of Christ does not have the same hollow slump as earlier figures, particularly that of Cimabue ▲ 261, and this allowed Giotto to follow the rules of proportion that had been given by the Roman architect Vitruvius (in the 1st century). The hands and feet are set in a circle which is centered upon the navel, something which was not possible with the traditional posture of a crucifix. The work used to hang above the high altar of the church. The fine ceramic stoup is by Giovanni della Robbia (1498), the great cupboard was made at the end of the 16th century to a design by Buontalenti, and the sculptures and gilding date from 1693.

In the GONDI CHAPEL, directly to the left of the chancel, is a Crucifix sculpted by Brunelleschi between 1410 and 1425. He did not like the "earthy" quality of Donatello's *Christ* in Santa Croce ▲ 257, and wanted to outdo his friend.

Center, Masacchio's famous *Trinity*.

church was begun in 1278. Its foundation stone was laid by the Dominican Cardinal Latino Malebranca, who was there to make peace between the Guelfs and the Ghibellines. It was he who gave Arnolfo di Cambio the job of building the Duomo and transforming the city. Leon Battista Alberti was able to complete work on the façade from 1458, thanks to the generosity of Giovanni Ruccellai ▲ 276, a merchant. His name can be seen on the cornice, and his emblem, a boat's sail, is on the inlaid friezes.

GOTHIC STYLE. The church is set out according to the rules of Gothic architecture, with a nave including north and south aisles, transept, chancel and sanctuary, with two chapels to either side. It is faithfully copied from the Cistercian churches of Burgundy, but there the similarity with northern models ends. The interior of the building is quite magnificent, with arches picked out in two colors leading gracefully toward the high altar. It is elegant in its simplicity and was much admired by Michelangelo.

A KEY WORK. The *Trinity* (dated 1427) by Masaccio, in the north aisle, represents a very important step forward in Renaissance art. It was the first time that Brunelleschi's mathematical rules of perspective had been put into practice. Space was to be accurately and objectively defined, no longer imposed or simply imagined by the painter. Vasari described it as like looking through a hole in the wall. This was the mystifying effect that Masaccio wanted to achieve. The tomb itself, with recumbent figure, is also a trompe l'oeil. The sense of reality was utterly new at that time, and Masaccio's work had a profound influence. In the foreground are the donor, the judge Lorenzo Lenzi, and his wife.

THE STROZZI CHAPEL. From the north transept a staircase leads up to this chapel, built in honor of St Thomas Aquinas. He is seen on the window with the Virgin Mary. The chapel was decorated between 1350 and 1357 by Nardo di Cione and Andrea Orcagna and shows the rapid success of Dante's *Divine Comedy*. The righthand wall shows *Purgatorio* and *Inferno*, divided into circles as described in the poem. Dante himself can be identified on the far wall among those present at the *Last Judgement*, while *Paradiso* is on

the lefthand wall. The reredos (above) is also the work of
Andrea Orcagna. It was painted after the Black Death and
has a message: Christ in majesty is handing keys of Heaven
and Earth to St Peter and a book to St Thomas Aquinas, who
is dressed in Dominican robes. The Black Death had been
taken as a sign of divine retribution, and the resulting terror
had been exploited by the Dominicans to inspire new
religious fervor with the promise of salvation.

THE CHANCEL AND THE TORNABUONI CHAPEL. The frescoes
behind the high altar were painted between 1485 and
1490 by Domenico Bigordi, known as
"Ghirlandaio", with the help of his pupils, who
included Michelangelo. They are the most
blatant example of frescoes dedicated to the
glorification of a family, and as such they
received Savonarola's outspoken
condemnation. Ghirlandaio (1449–94)
favored realism, and his paintings are an
invaluable record of life in Florence at that
time. The fresco of *The Angel Appearing to
Saint Zacharias in the Temple* contains not
only a portrait of Giovanni Tornabuoni, but
members of his family, his friends and his clients
as well.

GIOVANNI TORNABUONI. Uncle of Lorenzo the
Magnificent, he owed his fortune to the Medicis.
For a long time he was treasurer to Pope
Sixtus IV, who had complete faith in him; for
this reason he was able to help reestablish
peace between Lorenzo and the authorities in
Rome following the Pazzi conspiracy ▲ *131*.
But he was also responsible for causing severe
difficulties for the Medici bank, as he agreed
to make unsafe loans to the sons of Pope
Innocent VIII.

THE FILIPPO STROZZI CHAPEL. Directly to
the right of the chancel and main altar is a
chapel decorated by Filippino Lippi
(1457–1504). The frescoes illustrate
episodes from the lives of St Philip and St
John the Evangelist. They are full of a
strange imagination, and the deliberate
awkwardness and tension of the work
anticipates the Mannerist style.

THE GREEN CLOISTER. Go out of the church and
in again through a wrought-iron gate in the wall
to the left of the façade. The frescoes, much
damaged by damp, are the work of four

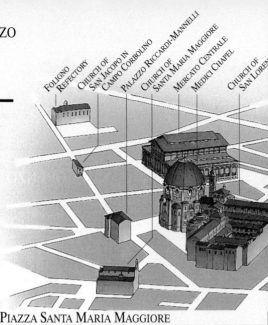

FOLIGNO REFECTORY · CHURCH OF SAN JACOPO IN CAMPO CORBOLINO · PALAZZO RICCARDI-MANNELLI · CHURCH OF SANTA MARIA MAGGIORE · MERCATO CENTRALE · MEDICI CHAPEL · CHURCH OF SAN LORENZO

¾ Half a day

The church of San Jacopo in the Campo Corbolino.

The Riccardi-Mannelli Palace.

SANTA MARIA MAGGIORE
The most interesting decorative feature here is a pilaster on the right as you go in, which features a 14th-century fresco by Mariotto di Nardo. The other pillars have lost their paintings. In the first chapel to the right is a *Communion of Mary Magdalene* (1636) by Domenico Pugliani. The vaulting of the third chapel was decorated in the 16th century by Poccetti with scenes from the life of St Zenobius, bishop of Florence in the 5th century (you will need a flashlight).

PIAZZA SANTA MARIA MAGGIORE

THE CHURCH OF SANTA MARIA MAGGIORE. A couple of steps away from the Duomo ▲ *128* and beside one of the city's busiest shopping streets (Via dei Cerretani), this late 12th-century church is a haven of peace. The building is one of the oldest in Florence, and on the exterior the remains of a 10th-century church are still clearly visible. The interior is austere, the plain columns a reminder that this is one of the earliest examples of Cistercian Gothic. The gloomy light is also not ideal for looking at the Baroque paintings on the altar, though it does lend a certain mystery to the atmosphere. The picture on the high altar was painted in 1700 by Pier Dandini, and represents *The Ecstasy of Saint Francis*. In the chancel are some superb frescoes by Jacopo di Cione, an artist whose work is discussed in the section dealing with his frescoes for San Miniato ▲ *322*. On the right is his *Massacre of the Innocents*, while to the left is *Herod Receiving the Three Wise Men*. A beautiful *Madonna and Child* from the 13th century, attributed to Coppo di Marcovaldo, is in the chapel to the left.

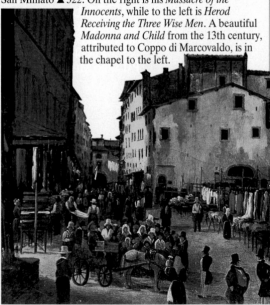

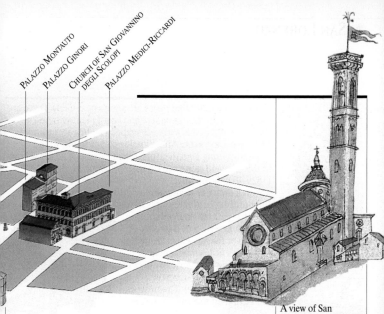

PALAZZO MONTAUTO
PALAZZO GINORI
CHURCH OF SAN GIOVANNINO DEGLI SCOLOPI
PALAZZO MEDICI-RICCARDI

A view of San Lorenzo from the *Codex Rustici*.

PALAZZO ORLANDINI DEL BECCUTO. This is a magnificent palazzo, recently restored, standing at the corner of the Via de' Vecchietti and the Via de' Pecori. Its massive base of honey-colored stone is pierced with heavily barred windows.

AROUND SAN LORENZO

PIAZZA MADONNA DEGLI ALDOBRANDINI. To reach the piazza, take the peaceful Via dei Conti, which features a fine 17th-century palazzo on the left at the point where it meets the Via Zanetti. On coming into the Piazza Madonna degli Aldobrandini, the base of the cupola of the church of San Lorenzo is immediately to the right. Opposite and to the left is a palazzo with frescoes on its façade: this is the PALAZZO RICCARDI-MANNELLI and dates from the 16th century. Above the entrance is a bust of the Grand Duke Francesco I.

VIA FAENZA. To the right of the palazzo, the Via Faenza stretches northwest. Along it, at numbers 37–9, the visitor passes the loggia of the CHURCH OF SAN JACOPO IN CAMPO CORBOLINO. This belonged to the Order of the Knights of Malta, but originally it was the property of the Templars (see right). Its 13th-century Gothic doorway is unique in Florence.

FOLIGNO REFECTORY. At 42 Via Faenza (ring the bell) is the refectory of the old Franciscan convent of San Onofrio, with a beautiful fresco of *The Last Supper*, painted in 1490 by Pietro Vanucci, known as Perugino (1445–1523). It also contains some works by Bicci di Lorenzo.

SAN LORENZO MARKET. The market begins in the Piazza Madonna degli Aldobrandini, and runs the length of the *Vie* del Canto de Nelli, dell'Ariento, Panicale and San Antonino, up to the large esplanade behind the Central Market. Crowds come to buy leather goods, such as bags and

THE TEMPLARS
The Templars were persecuted when they arrived in Florence in 1242. They were not tortured or burned, but their possessions were confiscated in 1312. Without actually siding with them, Dante had some hard words to say of Philip the Fair, and consigned Pope Clement V to the Inferno for abolishing the Templars at the Council of Vienna in 1312.

SAN LORENZO MARKET
Stretching out in all directions from the large hall of the Central Market, this is one of the busiest shopping areas in the whole of the city (except on Mondays) and also a favorite meeting place.

clothes: remember that prices are always negotiable. There are inexpensive silk ties, cashmere and angora knitwear and a thousand other odds and ends snapped up by eager tourists.

MERCATO CENTRALE. After clothing comes food. All the mouth-watering ingredients of Tuscan cuisine ● *58* are set out in this iron and stone market hall. Giuseppe Mengoni (1829–77), the architect who built it between 1870 and 1874, was well aware of local traditions: his ground-floor arcades bear references to some of the city's palazzo doorways.

THE CHURCH OF SAN BARNABA. At the end of the Via Panicale, on the left, is this little church, built in thanksgiving for the victory over the Ghibelline city of Arezzo at Campaldino in 1289. The frescoes are attributed to Spinello Aretino.

The bell tower of San Lorenzo.

HISTORIC PULPITS
It was from one of these two bronze pulpits by Donatello (right) that Savonarola preached his most ferocious sermons.

A view of the courtyard. The houses on the right have been demolished.

SAN LORENZO ● *89*

CONSECRATED BY SAINT AMBROSE. The church of San Lorenzo is one of Florence's most precious treasures. Generations of Medicis put some of the greatest artists to work here – men like Michelangelo and Donatello. The first church, the "Ambrosian Basilica", was consecrated in 393 by St Ambrose, bishop of Milan. In 380 Christianity had been proclaimed the official religion of the Roman empire by Emperor Theodosius I. The sermon that St Ambrose preached is the oldest surviving document belonging to the city. The church was rebuilt in Romanesque style in 1060 and given the status of a cathedral. From 1418 onwards more additions and alterations were commissioned when the important families of the district could agree on the sharing of the expenses.

ENTER THE MEDICIS. Before they had even built their palazzo in the Via Larga (now the Via Cavour), the Medicis commissioned a chapel and what is now called the Old Sacristy. At this time the

The stairway of the vestibule to the Laurentian Library, designed by Michelangelo in *pietra serena* ■ 16.

head of the family was Giovanni di Bicci, father of Cosimo il Vecchio: he commissioned Filippo Brunelleschi, who had just submitted his model for the cupola of the Duomo ● 86, ▲ 128. After Giovanni's death, Cosimo decided to alter the entire church. The high altar was finally consecrated in 1461, but the façade was never completed. The very richness of the church reflects the newly acquired fortune of the Medici family.

WAITING FOR A FAÇADE. It was not for lack of fine ideas that the façade remained unfinished. In 1518 Pope Leo X, son of Lorenzo the Magnificent, commissioned Michelangelo to complete the family shrine. The artist kept coming up with new design models , hesitating over which one to choose, before finally settling on an academic style. The model is on show in the Casa Buonarroti ▲ 263.

A PROJECT FRAUGHT WITH PROBLEMS. The whole undertaking seemed doomed at every step. The pope wanted to use marble from the new quarries at Pietrasanta, land that belonged to Florence. When Michelangelo objected that Carrara marble was much superior, the pope remained adamant. Marquis Alberigo, Michelangelo's friend who operated the Carrara quarries, was outraged and did all he could to scuttle the pope's plan. Then Michelangelo's legendary tightfistedness upset the workmen, who walked out on the project; and when the road was finally built to transport the marble back to Florence, the quarrymen refused to mine the stone! "I am dying of grief," wrote the sculptor in 1518, "it is as though Fate is against me." The pope, infuriated by the delay, finally canceled the contract in 1520. Only the interior façade was completed, in 1531.

BRUNELLESCHI'S PERFECT DESIGN. As you enter San Lorenzo, it is the marvelous balance and proportion of the nave that first catch the attention. Here Brunelleschi decided to abandon traditional forms in favor of mathematical design. He used what is known as *creste e vele*, meaning vaulting in *pietra serena* ■ 16 with plain rough-cast walls that stretched like sails between it, to lend the whole a remarkable feeling of pure, serene majesty.

The cupola of the transept (left) was decorated in 1742 by Vincenzo Meucci (1699–1766), a painter who was trained in Bologna.

"THE MARTYRDOM OF SAINT LAWRENCE" The enormous fresco in the nave of the church (below) was completed by Bronzino in 1565–9. In this work he shows a tendency to conform rather too rigidly to the academic style of the period.

THE TOMBS IN THE NEW SACRISTY
Michelangelo has, with some justification, been called the "Master of the Unfinished". In the 15th century it was rare for a work of art to remain incomplete. But as Vasari well knew, there could be more passion concentrated in a preliminary sketch than in the finished work. Here, the allegorical figure *Dusk* on the tomb of *Giuliano de' Medici* lacks finish. Beyond the obvious reference to the birth and death of the day, there is an overall sense of profound melancholy, present as well in the figures of *Dawn* and *Night*. Below, detail from the *Tomb of Lorenzo II*.

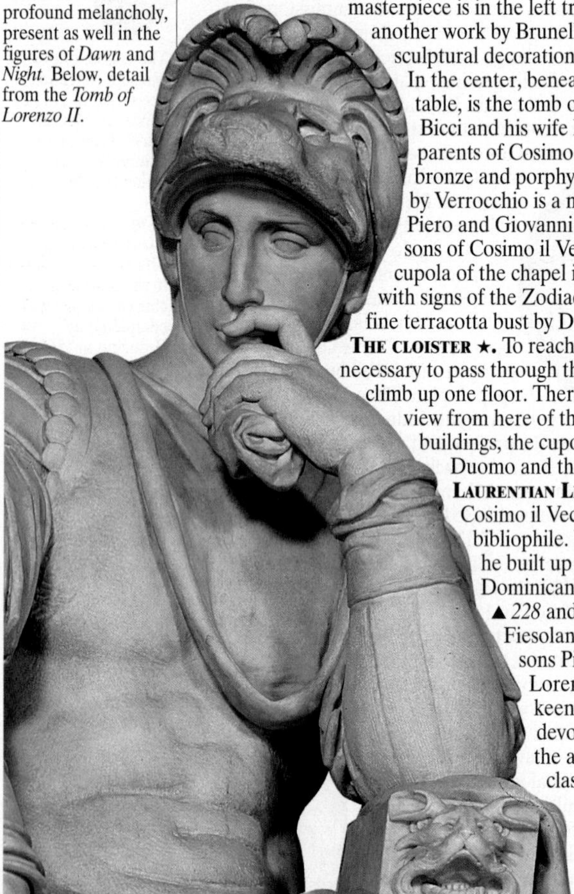

THE GREAT DONATELLO. High among the church's many treasures are two pulpits made by Donatello toward the end of his life, between 1460 and 1466. It was from these that Savonarola used to deliver his fanatical sermons ▲ *143*.
While constructing these works, Donatello was at the very height of his power: the old master refused to soften his work with the fashionable elegance that had brought his young contemporaries such success. The latter are represented in the church by Desiderio da Settignano, who in 1461 made the marble tabernacle (*Pala del Sacramento*) opposite the righthand pulpit. In the nave, at the foot of the high altar magnificently inlaid with *pietre dure* ● *54*, is the tombstone of Cosimo il Vecchio by Andrea del Verrocchio.
MARTELLI CHAPEL. A beautiful *Annunciation* by Filippo Lippi, painted around 1450, is the finest decoration here.
OLD SACRISTY ● *88*. The entrance to this Renaissance masterpiece is in the left transept. It is another work by Brunelleschi, with sculptural decorations by Donatello. In the center, beneath a marble table, is the tomb of Giovanni di Bicci and his wife Piccarda, the parents of Cosimo il Vecchio. A bronze and porphyry sarcophagus by Verrocchio is a monument to Piero and Giovanni de' Medici, the sons of Cosimo il Vecchio. The cupola of the chapel is decorated with signs of the Zodiac, and there is a fine terracotta bust by Donatello.
THE CLOISTER ★. To reach the library it is necessary to pass through the cloister and climb up one floor. There is an excellent view from here of the San Lorenzo buildings, the cupola of the Duomo and the Campanile.
LAURENTIAN LIBRARY ★. Cosimo il Vecchio was a keen bibliophile. While in exile he built up libraries for the Dominicans of San Marco ▲ *228* and for the Badia Fiesolana ▲ *327*. His sons Piero and Lorenzo were no less keen, and the latter devoted himself to the acquisition of classical Greek manuscripts and the development of printing. In consequence

the Laurentian Library contains thousands of works. The vestibule with its massive STAIRCASE is one of Michelangelo's masterpieces. Begun in 1524, it was completed by Vasari and Ammannati. It is a beautiful example of architectural Mannerism: the columns carry no load and the staircase is unusually complex – a revolutionary experiment in the conception of space.

NEW SACRISTY. To find this sacristy, leave the church and go round the back into the Piazza Aldobrandini. It is a funerary chapel containing the famous tombs of a son and a grandson of Lorenzo by Michelangelo. Commissioned in 1521, it was completed by his pupils. The most astonishing figures are the statues adorning the tombs.

THE CHAPEL OF THE PRINCES. In 1568 Cosimo I agreed to build a funerary chapel behind the chancel in San Lorenzo. The project hung fire for a long time, before being taken up by his son Ferdinando I. The first stones were laid in 1605, but it was only in 1962 that the floor was completed. The exterior has suffered through the delays, resulting in a patchwork effect. But the interior is stunning. The craftsmen of the *Opificio delle Pietre Dure* ● 54, ▲ 239 took their skill to its limits, particularly in the arms of the towns of Tuscany. The six tombs of the grand dukes are by Pietro and Ferdinando Tacca. The cupola of the chapel is one of the city's landmarks.

XIMENIANO OBSERVATORY. At 6 Piazza San Lorenzo is Florence's first astronomical observatory. Leonardo Ximenes was a hydraulic engineer, mathematician and geographer to Grand Duke Pietro Leopoldo. He founded it in the mid-18th century and issued a daily bulletin recording seismic movement and details of the weather. A library contains scientific apparatus and astronomical instruments through the ages (visits by reservation only).

VIA DE' GINORI

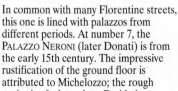

In common with many Florentine streets, this one is lined with palazzos from different periods. At number 7, the PALAZZO NERONI (later Donati) is from the early 15th century. The impressive rustification of the ground floor is attributed to Michelozzo; the rough plaster of the upper stories is of a later date. Beside it at number 9 is the PALAZZO BARBOLANI DI MONTAUTO; the magnificent windows are thought to be by Ammannati. Across the road is the BIBLIOTECA RICCARDIANA MORENIANA,

Above, Chapel of the Princes. Top, cloister of San Lorenzo.

THE OLD SACRISTY
Probably begun in 1422 and finished in 1428, this funerary chapel of the Medicis was by Brunelleschi to an original scheme: it was the first Renaissance room with a centralized design, and conceived as two basic forms, the cube and the sphere. Brunelleschi makes a clear distinction between the architectonic elements and the bare lime-washed walls.

Left, the façade of the Palazzo Ginori.

SAN GIOVANNINO DEGLI SCOLOPI
The façade of this church (1578) is seen below beside the Medici Palace. It was built by Ammannati, who spent his entire fortune constructing it. He is buried here with his wife, the poet Laura Battiferri (above). This church was attached to the convent of the religious order of the *scolopi*. The Ammannati tomb is inside in the second chapel on the left. The picture of *Christ and the Woman of Cana* is by Alessandro Allori.

founded by Count Riccardi in 1600 and housed in rooms that connect with the Medici Palace. There are decorative frescoes by Luca Giordano (1634–1705), one of the masters of Italian Baroque. At number 11 is the PALAZZO GINORI, a 17th-century building with fine ornamental corners. The PALAZZO TADDEI at number 19 is the work of Bartolommeo Baccio d'Agnolo (1462–1543), a pupil of Cronaca and the Sangallos, and one of the great 16th-century architects. It is a typical early 16th-century patrician house, and its design was much imitated. Retrace your steps, and take the Via de' Gori on the left. At the corner with the noisy Via Martelli is the CHURCH OF SAN GIOVANNINO DEGLI SCOLOPI. On the other side is the impressive Medici Palace, now part of the prefecture.

PALAZZO MEDICI-RICCARDI ● 68

AMBITION AND PRUDENCE. Although the family was based in the Mercato Vecchio ▲ 209, Giovanni di Bicci began to buy up property in this area during the 14th century. When Cosimo il Vecchio decided to build his own palazzo, he set about developing the district and opening up the Via Larga (today the Via Cavour): the wide, straight street contrasts strongly with other winding routes from this period. Though he wanted to build an impressive home, he rejected Brunelleschi's design as too opulent: the crafty banker had no wish to arouse the hostility of his fellow citizens. So in 1444 he gave the job to his friend Michelozzo di Bartolommeo, formerly a sculptor and colleague of Donatello, who had followed Cosimo into exile at Venice.
A DOMESTIC FORTRESS. The palazzo is built in a

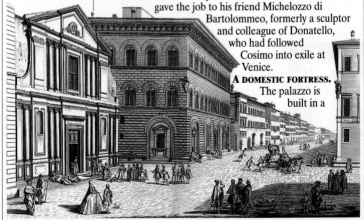

"ENVY IS A PLANT ONE SHOULD NEVER WATER."

COSIMO IL VECCHIO

THE MEDICI CHAPEL
Piero il Gottoso commissioned Benozzo Gozzoli to execute the decorations in 1459. The frescoes on the ceiling are nominally an *Calvacade of the Magi* but in fact represent the Council of Florence of 1439. Gozzoli (whose portrait is shown in the detail above) may not have been a painter of the first rank, but his masterly technique and natural style earn him a place among the great names of 15th-century Florence.

Below, *Cosimo il Vecchio* by Pontormo. Left, the garden of the Medici Palace ornamented with statues.

square around an interior courtyard. The exterior facing is unusual: the ground floor is rusticated in the manner of military architecture, but the first floor up is more refined, and the next even more so, the whole being crowned with a classical cornice that was the first of its kind in Florence. Before it was enlarged in 1670 the palace was cubic in shape and had only ten windows. Its symmetry was to serve as a model for domestic architecture in the 15th century. Behind the *cortile*, looking onto the Via de' Ginori, is a garden full of statues.
A KING WITHOUT A CROWN ● *36.* Born in 1389, Cosimo was forty years old when his father Giovanni di Bicci died. His travels had made him an accomplished connoisseur of refined taste, and he was skilled in financial matters. In addition to his banking activities, he dealt in cloth, dabbled in the slave trade and occasionally organized the sale of *castrati*. His wealthy clients became a close-knit faction that kept him assured of political power, which he was careful to exercise with discretion – Cosimo only held a magistrature for six months, as *gonfaloniere di giustizia*. For the other thirty years of his life he wielded authority through his family connections, friends, and the many people who owed him favors. From behind the scenes he rigged elections and kept a close watch on which men were chosen for important posts. Threats and blackmail were just

🔆 Half a day

THE FRUITS OF PATRONAGE
Cosimo's money made it possible to enlarge the Romano-Gothic church of 1299. Alterations were also made in the 18th century. The convent was entirely rebuilt to match.

The façade of the church of San Marco was put up in 1778–9 by G. B. Paladini.

The interior was remodeled in 1678 by Pier Francesco Silvani.

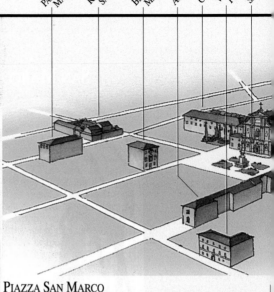

PALAZZO MARUCELLI   REFECTORY OF SANT'APOLLONIA   BIBLIOTECA MARUCELLIANA   ACADEMY OF ART   CASINO MEDICEO   WORKSHOP OF THE PIETRE DURE   SAN MARC

PIAZZA SAN MARCO

The piazza is one of the city's busiest. It is the bus station, so there is a constant roar of traffic (the bus to Fiesole ▲ *328* goes from here); the university is also based in the square and groups of students provide a colorful and lively atmosphere. Solemnly presiding over all this is the Baroque façade of the church of San Marco. Beside it is the entrance to the convent of the same name, which is a haven of peace and tranquillity.

THE CONVENT OF SAN MARCO ● *88*

COSIMO'S PENANCE. It would seem that Cosimo il Vecchio had a number of sins to atone for when he ordered Michelozzo to rebuild the Convent of San Marco. He guaranteed all expenses, no matter how high, including the cost of the furniture, missals, a library and the extension of the church.

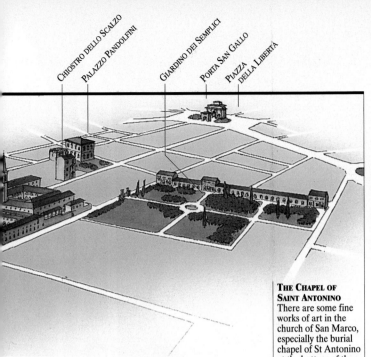

CHIOSTRO DELLO SCALZO
PALAZZO PANDOLFINI
GIARDINO DEI SEMPLICI
PORTA SAN GALLO
PIAZZA DELLA LIBERTÀ

THE RISE OF THE DOMINICANS. Cosimo, always a shrewd observer, had taken note of the growth in popularity of the mendicant orders during the 15th century. He decided to replace the Silvestrine monks, who had occupied San Marco since 1299, with the Dominican friars of Fiesole, who already had a firm base in Florence at Santa Maria Novella ▲ *213*.

SAINT ANTONINO. Some of the most important men in the history of Florence spent time here, including Savonarola ● *31*, ▲ *143*. Perhaps most influential of all was Antonino Pierozzi, now known as Saint Antonino (1389–1459), an honest and wise theologian. He was the founding prior of San Marco and became archbishop of Florence in 1446. Although he and his order benefited directly from Cosimo's generosity, he tried to prevent the inexorable rise to power of the Medicis. He dared to help wealthy citizens ruined by Cosimo's cunningly targeted taxes. He posted warnings on the cathedral doors and made public threats of excommunication in his attempts to stop Cosimo engineering self-interested changes to the constitution.

THE SAN MARCO MUSEUM. The entrance to the convent buildings is at number 1 in the piazza, and leads into the CLOISTER OF SAINT ANTONINO, whose pious life is recounted in twenty-eight frescoes around the walls.

THE ANGELIC TOUCH. The San Marco Museum and the monks' cells on the first floor are a monument to the talent of a great 15th-century Florentine painter, Guido di Pietro (c. 1400–55), known as "Fra Angelico". He started painting relatively late in life, and only received his first commission in 1433. This was the *Linaiuoli Madonna*, to be found in the PILGRIMS' HOSPICE on the ground floor.

THE CHAPEL OF SAINT ANTONINO
There are some fine works of art in the church of San Marco, especially the burial chapel of St Antonino at the bottom of the nave on the left. It contains three excellent Mannerist paintings: left, *The Curing of the Leper* by Francesco Brandi, "Il Poppi", an infinitely better work than the two by him in San Michelino ▲ *247*; center, *Jesus in Limbo*, by Alessandro Allori; right, The *Vocation of Saint Matthew*, by Giovanni Battista Naldini. All would appear to date from the 1580's. The chapel itself is Giambologna's most important architectural work (1580–9).

Portrait of Girolamo Savonarola, in the San Marco Museum.

229

"THE ANGEL OF THE ANNUNCIATION"
From the fresco at the top of the stairs leading to the dormitory cells. The angel's head is bowed in reverence. The angel in the same scene painted in one of the cells is rather more commanding.

"THE SANTA TRINITA ALTARPIECE"
A *Deposition* ordered by Palla Strozzi from Lorenzo Monaco, who only completed the three pinnacles before his death. It was finished by Fra Angelico and is among his masterpieces. In some of the figures he successfully blends two currents in Tuscan art, giving them the weight and solidity of Giotto but enlivened by the vigor of Masaccio.

But the rich use of color (the figure at the extreme right is a good example) is in the Sienese tradition.

"THE ANNUNCIATION"
One of a series of forty-one small panels (thirty-five remain in San Marco) intended for cupboard doors in the oratory of Santissima Annunziata ▲ 242. The cupboard would have held church silver, ex votos made of gold, silver and precious stones. The doors were broken up in 1782.

FRA ANGELICO
Guido di Pietro, or "Fra Angelico", was born in Vicchio di Mugello in about 1400, and died in Rome in 1455. While working in Florence, he was summoned to Rome by Pope Eugenius IV in 1446 with his pupil Benozzo Gozzoli. He painted a number of fresco cycles, most of which have now been destroyed. One that remains is the *Chapel of Niccolo V* in the Vatican. He also worked in Perugia and Orvieto cathedral.

"THE MOCKING OF CHRIST"
A fresco from one of the cells. It dates from 1440–1. Christ's suffering and humiliation are symbolized on either side. It was quite usual in the 14th century to avoid direct representation of insult and injury. Perhaps here it was felt that the monk's meditations could be disturbed by the sight of violent acts.

"NOLI ME TANGERE"
A moving cell fresco showing Christ after the Resurrection, appearing to Mary Magdalene. "Noli me tangere" were the words he spoke (meaning "Don't touch me"). They remain an enigma.

A visit to the Galleria dell'Accademia is essential to a full understanding of Florentine art. Michelangelo's sculptures alone make the visit worthwhile, but the museum also has numerous works by artists usually considered to be of minor importance (Albertinelli, Santi di Tito, Granacci). To study them helps one to appreciate more fully what the great masters achieved. There is also a marvelous collection of 14th-century paintings, which give an ideal opportunity to trace the traditions and the currents of change present in the art of the century preceding the Renaissance.

NARDO DI CIONE
The Trinity between Saint Romuald and Saint John the Evangelist (detail), painted in 1365.

LORENZO MONACO (c. 1370–1425)
Christ in Pietà and Symbols of the Passion. This was a common subject in the Middle Ages: the dead Christ, held by the Virgin and St John, surrounded by symbols of the Passion story. It is the richness of detail that makes this painting interesting. Certain objects, such as the column of the Flagellation or the nails of the Crucifixion, always tended to appear.

A HOST OF SYMBOLS
Other images are more rare. Top left is St Peter's denial, while the kiss of Judas is to the right. Beneath the left arm of the cross, Pilate is seen washing his hands. Beneath the right arm are the ear of Malchus and thirty pieces of silver, the price of Judas' betrayal. The torch is to symbolize Christ's arrest.

FRANCESCO GRANACCI (1469–1543)

The *Virgin of the Sacred Girdle*, a painting from the now demolished church of San Pier Maggiore ▲ *191*. Belief in the Assumption of the Holy Virgin, shown giving her girdle to St Thomas, took many centuries to be accepted. There is no specific scriptural reference to it, but between the 9th and 12th centuries it became an accepted doctrine in the West, largely due to Albertus Magnus and Thomas Aquinas. Only in 1950 was the Assumption declared official doctrine.

MARIOTTO ALBERTINELLI (1474–1515)

The Trinity: a theme that was developed relatively late, probably because of its inherent complexities. To depict one God in three distinct yet equal persons was a puzzle. An early image, first seen in 12th-century France, was the Throne of Grace: Christ on the Cross and above him the Holy Spirit, a dove, and God the Father. It came from the description of the baptism of Christ: "And Jesus, when he was baptized, went up straightway out of the water: and lo, the heavens were opened unto him, and he saw the Spirit of God descending like a dove and lighting upon him: and lo, a voice from heaven saying this is my beloved Son, in whom I am well pleased." (Matthew, III, 16–17).

Right, a detail of the *Annunciation* by Allori.

"DAVID"
Sculpted in 1501, this statue represents the republican spirit of Florence.

THE FOUR UNFINISHED "SLAVES"
These are some of the most disturbing works of art from the whole Renaissance period. Pope Julius II had ordered them for his tomb in 1505: Michelangelo worked on them for forty years without ever finishing them. The tomb, architectural in style like the mausoleums of antiquity, was intended to have had about forty statues. Michelangelo lacked the time (and perhaps also the desire) to complete them.

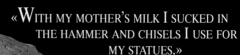

A DRAMATIC EPISODE
Each statue is a scene of intensity – a body trying to emerge from the marble. The fact that they are unfinished makes them all the more tantalizing, the carved marble contrasting with the uncut stone.

MICHEL ANGELO
Michelangelo Buonarroti was born in 1475 at Caprese, near Arezzo. He died in Rome in 1564. Raphael, Titian, Durer, and Cranach the Elder were among his contemporaries.

A SOURCE OF INSPIRATION
His unfinished pieces had an enormous influence on succeeding generations of sculptors, inspired by the idea of the body struggling to escape from the stone. Most fascinated of all by this *nonfinito* was Rodin, who made much use of the technique.

Michelangelo was never satisfied with his work. The "agonies" that he went through epitomized the tortured creative spirit for a generation of Romantic artists.

AUSTERE FRESCOES. In 1438, at the request of St Antonino, Fra Angelico began to paint the cells of the convent, with the help of his pupils. His work was generally much admired, but the frescoes he painted for the monks' cells were extremely plain and severe. There was little of the charming detail seen in his panel paintings. Some of them, like the *Annunciation* in cell number 3, are nonetheless breathtaking. Fra Angelico managed to combine the solidity of form found in Masaccio's work ▲ *307* with a delicacy and grace particular to the 14th century, and epitomized in the work of Lorenzo Monaco.

FAMOUS OCCUPANTS. Cells numbers 12–14 were Savonarola's and they contain several objects belonging to the fanatical monk. St Antonino lived in number 31, and his death mask is on display. Cosimo de' Medici made a retreat in the double cell numbers 38–9, which features a fresco of the *Adoration of the Magi*. The Medicis had a particular liking for this subject, and so it is also to be found in the chapel of the Medici Palace ▲ *224*.

A PHILANTHROPIC MERCHANT. The convent has a beautiful LIBRARY, designed in 1448 by Michelozzo. It was built to house the eight hundred precious volumes accumulated by the merchant Niccolò de' Niccoli (1367–1437).

THE MUSEUM OF MINERALOGY
The museum is at 4 Via Giorgio la Pira and has a number of interesting exhibits, including a topaz from Brazil that weighs no less than 360 lbs, the equivalent of 755,000 carats.

The statue of General Fante in the Piazza San Marco.

THE ACADEMY OF ART

On the Via Ricasoli, just leaving the Piazza San Marco, is the portico of the OSPEDALE DI SAN MATTEO. This was founded in the 14th century by Guglielmo de Vinci. The building was subsequently taken over by the Academy of Art in 1784. At number 60 is the entrance to its famous museum.

THE COMPANY OF SAINT LUKE. Painters had traditionally belonged to the Guild of Physicians and Apothecaries (Arte dei Medici e Speziali) ▲ *199*, but by 1339 they had also formed the Compagnia di San Luca, a guild reserved for artists. In 1563 they took another step forward when a former pupil of Michelangelo, the sculptor and Servite monk Fra Giovannangelo da Montorsoli (1507–63) encouraged them to organize the teaching of drawing, an essential skill for all painters, sculptors and architects.

THE FIRST ACADEMY. The newly formed institution was called an "Academy", inspired by the neo-Platonist philosophy of the time. The founding members included some well-known artists such as Vasari, Ammannati,

> «I WOULD PREFER A PAINTER TO BE EDUCATED, AS FAR AS POSSIBLE, IN ALL THE LIBERAL ARTS, BUT ABOVE ALL I WOULD LIKE HIM TO MASTER GEOMETRY.»
>
> ALBERTI

Bronzino, and Montorsoli himself. Michelangelo was its first head, although he died within a few months.

ART STIFLED BY RULES. Sadly, their ambitious plans proved difficult to carry out. The training soon deteriorated into something not unlike that formerly given in artists' studios: rules and formulas for the production of competent work. The teaching of new scientific subjects gave an impressive, up-to-date image (geometry, perspective, anatomy), but the teaching was all too often little more than pontification. This was particularly true from the 17th century onwards, when Florentine art was in crisis. It proved only too clearly the adverse effects of theories and rigid rules upon creativity.

THE UNIVERSITY

A blank-faced building at 4 Piazza San Marco is the headquarters of the University, where in 1429 Niccolo da Uzzano founded his institute of learning, or *Sapienza*. He was a nobleman, born around 1350, who served both as *gonfaloniere di giustizia* and as ambassador for the Republic. His passion was the pursuit and diffusion of knowledge. The MUSEUM OF MINERALOGY and the MUSEUM OF GEOLOGY AND PALEONTOLOGY are housed in the University building. The entrance is at 4 Via Giorgio La Pira.

IL GIARDINO DEI SEMPLICI

MEDICI BOTANISTS. Cosimo I had his botanical gardens planted in 1550 in order to cultivate exotic plants and exploit their uses. The Giardino dei Semplici became a serious research laboratory for studying the distillation of perfumes, the extraction of essential oils for medicinal use, and possible vegetable antidotes to poisons. This long history today makes it one of Europe's most important botanical gardens. In the 17th century it was the scene of fantastic nocturnal parties given by members of the Medici family. The entrance to the garden is an elegant construction by Niccolò Tribolo in the middle of 3 Via Micheli.

CHIOSTRO DELLO SCALZO

The Via Micheli leads into the busy Via Cavour. At number 69, back toward the Piazza San Marco, is a small 16th-century cloister decorated with frescoes by Andrea del Sarto (right). They were commissioned by the Brotherhood of St John the Baptist, an order known as *dello Scalzo* because its members went barefoot in holy processions. The contract for the work was signed in 1507, but the frescoes were not completed until 1526. Their charm lies in the subtle effects that del Sarto

PALAZZO DELLA LIVIA
This is a beautiful palazzo at 51 Via Cavour, built in 1775 by Bernardo Fallani. He incorporated into its small façade numerous features from 16th-century Florentine architecture.

VISIBLE AND INVISIBLE
The Adoration of the Magi was a potent image in the Christian faith of the Medicis. The Brotherhood of the Magi was one of the most important religious fellowships in Florence under their rule, and Cosimo il Vecchio, Pietro il Gottoso and Lorenzo il Magnifico all presided over it in their time. It included among its members many pious humanists and members of the Platonic academy, such as Marsilio Ficino ● *39*.

In the center, are some of the rare plants and trees in the Giardino dei Semplici.

achieves in monochrome, contriving to give the impression of a series of bas-reliefs. Vasari wrote that his work inspired a whole new school of drawing. The sculptural aspect of *Charity*, a beautiful woman surrounded by three children, underlines del Sarto's interest in this particular medium; in fact the sculptor Sansovino shared del Sarto's workshop and made preliminary models for his paintings. For this work, however, Andrea del Sarto's main influence was Michelangelo, and more specifically his ceiling of the Sistine Chapel in Rome.

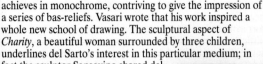

CASINO MEDICEO

Today the law courts are housed inside this palace at 57 Via Cavour. It was built in 1574 by Buontalenti for the Grand Duke Francesco I. *Casino Mediceo* actually means the Medicis' little house, which was a misleading name since it is far from small. At that time, however, the area was on the edge of Florence, almost in the countryside, and the palace was built in what were then the Medici gardens. The Medici porcelain factory was started here ▲ *189*, and the palace held laboratories where new techniques were first experimented with. The main door is magnificent, and in the courtyard on the right is the way up to the next floor, which is decorated with frescoes of great deeds of the grand dukes. In 1662 Matteo Rosselli painted twelve lunettes in the great hall which depicted the military exploits of the last two grand dukes.

ANTICA FARMACIA DI SAN MARCO ★. Opposite, at 146 Via Cavour, is a beautiful pharmacy, which was founded in 1436 (like the convent itself) by St Antonino. Inside the building, the old fittings and decorations are still there, including colored ceramic jars from the della Robbia workshops. If you ask, you may be shown the CROCODILE ROOM, which was formerly a meeting place for the aristocratic intellectuals of Florence, and also the ALEMBIC ROOM, where elixirs and liqueurs are still distilled today.

BIBLIOTECA MARUCELLIANA

Abbot Francesco Marucelli (1625–1703) was born in Florence but moved to Rome once his education was completed. He found favor at the Vatican and was able to devote all his time to amassing an immense number of books, opera libretti, etchings, manuscripts, prints and incunabula.

A DESTRUCTIVE PASSION
The story of Andrea del Sarto's stormy and passionate relationship with his unfaithful wife Lucrezia (her portrait is above) is well known. The king of France, François I, admired his work and invited him to court at Fontainebleau. Andrea del Sarto was happy and successful in France, but Lucrezia was determined to stop that and wrote begging him to come back. He asked permission to visit his home, and the king agreed, asking him to buy some works of art while there. The artist left with a full purse swearing to return, but once home all his promises were forgotten.

PRICELESS MANUSCRIPTS
Here, and opposite, are two valuable

documents from the Biblioteca Marucelliana.

On his death the precious collection of more than thirty thousand items was taken to Florence where, in 1752, it became the foundation of a public library, according to his wishes. The entrance to the magnificent reading rooms is at 43 Via Cavour.

WORKSHOP OF THE PIETRE DURE   ● 54

The entrance to this museum is at 78 Via degli Alfani. The Opificio delle Pietre Dure is a national institution which

specializes in inlaid work with semi-precious stones, or *pietre dure*, also known as Florentine mosaic work. It was founded in 1588 by Grand Duke Ferdinando I de' Medici, and the workshops were originally in the Casino Mediceo. They later moved to the Uffizi and, in 1796 to this palace built by Ammannati in 1577. For three centuries the craftsmen of the Opificio worked on the decoration of palaces and churches, and above all on the Medici tomb, the famous Chapel of the Princes in the church of San Lorenzo ▲ 220. Among its directors there have been a number of famous architects and sculptors, such as Buontalenti, Matteo Nigetti, and Pietro Tacca. Today the work carried out here is mainly of restoration, and the field of expertise has widened to include other techniques such as marquetry and majolica. In the small museum are examples of the Opificio's work, illustrating both its skills and traditions. (A visit could be difficult to arrange because of current renovation work.)

PALAZZO PUCCI · SAN MICHELINO CHURCH · PALAZZO NICCOLINI · PALAZZO SFORZA ALMENI · SANTA MARIA NUOVA HOSPITAL · PALAZZO GRIFONI · BRUNELLESCHI'S ROTONDA · CHURCH OF SS ANNUNZIATA · OSPEDALE DEGLI INNOCENTI · PALAZZO DI SAN CLEMENTE · PALAZZO CAPP...

TEATRO DELLA PERGOLA · ARCHEOLOGICAL MUSEUM

FLORENCE'S HOSPITALS
In the Middle Ages there were some thirty hospitals in Florence containing, in all, about a thousand beds. The citizens took great pride in them, although conditions might now be considered less than adequate. Hygiene was rudimentary, and patients, unless very ill, were two to a bed. The Ospedale degli Innocenti (above) was opened in 1445.

The *Head of the Redeemer* (right) was painted in 1515 by Andrea del Sarto. The old print of Santissima Annunziata (facing page) is by Giuseppe Zocchi.

PIAZZA SANTISSIMA ANNUNZIATA ★

Lined with elegant colonnaded porticoes, this piazza is among the loveliest in Florence. Its architecture conforms perfectly to the Renaissance ideal. An equestrian statue of Ferdinando I by Giambologna is in the center; it was completed by Pietro Tacca in 1608. Tacca also designed the two fountains. There is a long view down the Via dei Servi towards the cupola of the Duomo ▲ *128*.

PALAZZO GRIFONI ▲ *72*. A fine building designed by Ammannati and built between 1563 and 1574. Brick is rarely used in Florence, and the soft rose color gives the palace an unreal appearance set in a piazza that is otherwise so classical and geometrical in design. To add to the effect, the middle-story façade has a small triumphal arch entirely Mannerist in its inspiration.

THE CHURCH OF SANTISSIMA ANNUNZIATA

A SERVITE CHURCH. Seven Florentine noblemen founded the church in 1250, consecrating it to the Annunciation. Twenty years earlier they had given away their possessions and withdrawn to a retreat on nearby Monte Senario, where they dedicated themselves to the cult. They were the founders of the Servants of Mary, the Servite order. On this spot, then just a corner of a field outside the city walls, they built a small oratory. In 1254 it was enlarged, and in the 15th century and Baroque period it underwent major alterations. The church was significant in Florentine life, for until 1750 the Feast of the Annunciation, March 25, was the start of the calendar year.

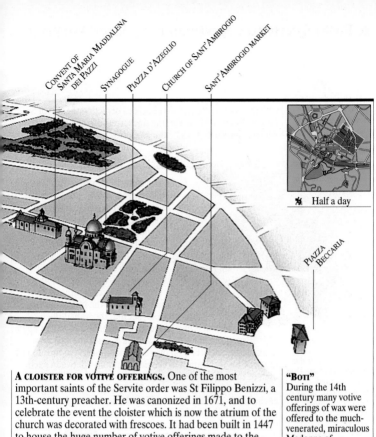

CONVENT OF SANTA MARIA MADDALENA DEI PAZZI
SYNAGOGUE
PIAZZA D'AZEGLIO
CHURCH OF SANT'AMBROGIO
SANT'AMBROGIO MARKET
PIAZZA BECCARIA

✕ Half a day

A CLOISTER FOR VOTIVE OFFERINGS. One of the most
important saints of the Servite order was St Filippo Benizzi, a
13th-century preacher. He was canonized in 1671, and to
celebrate the event the cloister which is now the atrium of the
church was decorated with frescoes. It had been built in 1447
to house the huge number of votive offerings made to the
saint by the people of Florence. There are frescoes by Andrea
del Sarto, Jacopo Pontormo and Rosso Fiorentino. *The
Visitation*, by the young Pontormo, is an early example of the
Mannerist style in painting.

THE TABERNACLE OF THE SANTISSIMA ANNUNZIATA. The
interior is decorated in rich Baroque manner, unusual in
Florence where the style tended to be more restrained. To the
left, on entering the dark and imposing nave, is a little SHRINE.
It was built by Pagno di Lapo Portigiani, based on a drawing
by Michelozzo, to protect a painting of the *Annunciation*
which was thought to be miraculous (see caption, right).

THE CLOISTER OF THE DEAD. The entrance to the cloister is
outside, through the door on the far left of the portico as you
face the church. It was designed by Michelozzo and decorated

"BOTI"
During the 14th
century many votive
offerings of wax were
offered to the much-
venerated, miraculous
Madonna of
Santissima
Annunziata. Then the
grand nobility, both
local and those from
further afield, began
to have their own
likeness made in wax:
life-size, in color,
wearing their clothes,
and often on
horseback. These
were brought to the
Madonna and, at first,
placed on platforms
around the walls of
the church. When
there was no more
room, they were hung
from the vaults of the
nave. In the end they
had to be hung on the
church façade and the
cloister walls. It was
an extraordinary
sight, and became
famous all over
Europe. Many of
these effigies survived
for a surprisingly long
time and there were
still six hundred of
them in the 17th
century. In 1786 they
were all melted down
and used as candles.

Veduta della Piazza della SS Nunziata Statua Equestre di Ferdinando Primo Frati e Logge Latendi

PALAZZO CAPPONI
Below, a detail from the ceiling painting by Matteo Bonechi above the main staircase in the

Palazzo Capponi.
The palace was the home of the scholar and politician Gino Capponi, one of the presidents of the 1848 constitutional government. Today it is the Florentine headquarters of the auctioneers Sotheby Parke Bernet. It has one of the largest private gardens in the city center (top right, facing page). These are private and no visitors are admitted. Below is the plain coat of arms of the Capponi family.

THE ARCHEOLOGICAL MUSEUM
This museum has an exceptional Etruscan collection. Shown here are the bronze statue of a warrior (center), a sarcophagus (top of facing page) and a funerary urn from Montescudaio (far right).

with frescoes by Bernardino Poccetti depicting the life of St Filippo Benizzi. However, the finest fresco is one painted by Andrea del Sarto in 1525: the *Madonna del Sacco*.

OSPEDALE DEGLI INNOCENTI ● 71

COLUMNS BACK IN FASHION. The Guild of Silkweavers ▲ 198 commissioned Filippo Brunelleschi to build the first hospital in the world for foundling children, which he began c. 1419. The guild had been helping the poor for many years, and in 1445 the Ospedale degli Innocenti received its first inmates. For centuries babies continued to be left anonymously at the little revolving door, the *rota*, set into the wall at the lefthand end of the loggia, until it was walled up in 1875. Brunelleschi's building with its elegant colonnade was to influence architects all over Europe, while he in turn found much of his inspiration in classical antiquity. Between each arch of the colonnade is a glazed terracotta medallion from the workshops of Andrea della Robbia. These charming *tondi*, each showing a baby in swaddling clothes, are slightly later than the building itself. The doorway near the lefthand end is the entrance to the Ospedale's church, decorated in 1786, while the central doorway leads to a very pretty cloister.
A MASTER PLAN. Brunelleschi built his hospital on empty land beside the church of Santissima Annunziata. It was the first part of what he planned to be an entirely new and perfectly symmetrical piazza. Sadly, he did not live to complete it, and the other loggias and colonnades were built later. It was, however, the first planned urban construction project of modern times.

VIA CAPPONI

THE HOUSE OF ANDREA DEL SARTO. Up the Via Capponi, on the right on the corner of the Via Giusti is the house of Andrea del Sarto (1486–1530) ▲ 238. Strongly influenced by Leonardo da Vinci and Raphael, he epitomized the final flowering of Florentine neo-classicism.
PALAZZO CAPPONI. At number 26 is the immense Palazzo Capponi, which was built by Carlo Fontana between 1705 and 1708. It is impressive just for the height and length of its façade, not to mention the elegant gardens. The main hall has a fresco by Matteo Bonechi (c. 1669–1726), proof that the French Rococo style had arrived.

PALAZZO DI SAN CLEMENTE OR DEL PRETENDENTE ● 75. At 15 Via Capponi, on the corner of the Via Micheli, stands a fine Baroque building designed by Gherardo Silvani c. 1650. Go back to the Piazza della Santissima Annunziata, under the arch to the Via della Colonna.

THE ARCHEOLOGICAL MUSEUM

The entrance is at 38 Via della Colonna. In addition to rooms dedicated to Greece and Egypt, it houses a large and fascinating collection of Etruscan items.

THE ETRUSCAN AGE. The earliest evidence of Etruscan civilization dates back to the 9th century BC. In the second half of the 8th century, Greek colonies arrived in southern Italy and quickly established contacts with Etruria, drawn by the rich mineral resources of the island of Elba and the region of Campiglia Marittima. From this period, with increased wealth and contacts with the outside world brought by their trade in metals, Etruscan culture and civilization began to develop rapidly. They had their own language, which existed in written form. Trade expanded as far as the Orient, reaching a peak in the 6th century BC. From the 4th century onwards the Etruscans had to exist alongside the Romans, losing much of their independence: Etruria was annexed in 351 BC, and in 90 BC its people became citizens of the Roman empire.

THE DARK AGES. From the 2nd century AD most towns in the region went into decline. During the Dark Ages Etruria, now called Tuscia, was for centuries dominated by the Goths and the Lombards. The region came into the possession of Charlemagne, but the aristocratic Frankish rulers were unable to defend it against the Magyar invasions of 899. Tuscany became a desolate place – the Valdarno a virtual swamp, the Sienese Maremma almost a desert. It was only under the new Germanic domination that it began to flourish again. Tuscia now began to be called Toscana.

THE ETRUSCAN FEAST. The Museo Archeologico has a wonderful collection of funerary urns. One, from Montescudaio, dates from 650–625 BC and has on its lid the dead man at a feast, being served by his slave (right). Feasts and banquets are one of the most ancient and frequently depicted themes in Etruscan art. As with the Greeks

THE "CHIMERA"
The name given to the bronze statue of a mythical beast: a lion with a snake for a tail and the head of a ram on its back. It was discovered in Arezzo in 1553, and tradition says that Benvenuto Cellini restored it. Today the statue is in the Archeological Museum, but it used to be kept in the Palazzo Vecchio. Cosimo I acquired it for his Etruscan collection and invested it with great political significance as a symbol of the enemies of the state, and the peace that he had brought. He offered historical justification for having assumed power over a region that had been united in ancient times. In 1537 Cosimo inherited the title of *Dux Florentiae*, and in 1569 became *Magnus Dux Etruriae*.

▲ FROM SANTISSIMA ANNUNZIATA TO SANT'AMBROGIO

MANNERIST SPIRIT
The work of Pontormo and Rosso is undoubtedly Mannerist in spirit, although it is difficult to pin down precisely what defines them as early exponents of the style. The English art historian Anthony Blunt considered Michelangelo to be the first Mannerist artist because of his formal rejection of Alberti's aesthetic code. Alberti insisted on the faithful imitation of nature, but Michelangelo believed rather that the artist had the right to impose his own vision on what he observed. André Malraux was of the same opinion; in *The Voices of Silence* he wrote that "Art is born from a fascination with things that are not easily expressed, a refusal simply to reproduce what is seen, the need to take forms from a world in which man finds himself a victim, to place them in a world which he controls. That is how form becomes style."

SANTA MARIA DEGLI ANGELI
An illustration from the *Codex Rustici* showing the oratory of Santa Maria degli Angeli in its original setting.

Santa maria degliagnioli

Brunelleschi's Rotonda consists of a central octagonal space surrounded by eight chapels.

and some Eastern civilizations, a funeral ended with a feast to which the deceased was invited.

METALWORKING SKILLS. The earliest metal objects to have been discovered, marking the start of metalworking in Italy, are from the 3rd millennium BC. In the Bronze Age both copper and bronze were much used for all kinds of arms, tools and ornaments. The bronze axes on display in the museum from Campiglia Marittima are fine examples. The Etruscans learned from the Greeks how to solder metal, but they were more particularly expert at making Mannerist vessels by metal casting. Their techniques became so sophisticated that they could also cast sculptures, and the museum contains some remarkable pieces including the *Chimera* discovered at Arezzo, which dates from the 4th century BC and is on display in Room XIV.

BRUNELLESCHI'S ROTONDA

A church formerly called Santa Maria degli Angeli, standing on the corner of Via degli Alfani and Via del Castellaccio.

THE CENTRALIZED PLAN. Renaissance architects particularly admired buildings geometrically disposed around a central point: such a design represented an absolute of balance and beauty. Only in two other projects was Brunelleschi able to put these neo-classical theories into practice: these were the Old Sacristy of San Lorenzo ▲ *222* and the Pazzi Chapel in Santa Croce ▲ *260*. When in 1433 he received the commission from the Arte di Calimala and the monks of the nearby convent of Santa Maria degli Angeli, he modeled his design on an existing Roman building, the Temple of Minerva Medica in Rome.

A MASTERPIECE IN PERIL. The main source of finance was a bequest from the family of a condottiere, but work had to be suspended in 1437 when the Republic appropriated the funds for the war against Lucca. Gradually, bits and pieces were added on and around the Rotonda until the original form was enirely lost to view. Brunelleschi's work was not revealed until five centuries later. It was Rodolfo Sabatini who uncovered the core of the building, restored it and reconstructed the cupola.

MONKS AND SCHOLARS. The priors of the monastery had extremely modern taste to entrust the building of their oratory to Brunelleschi. But these Camaldulian monks were

The tomb of Folco Portinari, father of Dante's Beatrice, which is still in the church of Sant' Egidio.

among the élite of Florence. Cosimo il Vecchio's Platonic academy was in their care at the time when Marsilio Ficino ● *39* was its president. They were also entrusted with giving the Medici children an exemplary education, including Latin, Greek, Hebrew, Arabic and several European languages.

VIA DEI SERVI

A walk along this busy street gives a chance to see several palaces. At number 12, on the corner of Via del Castellaccio, is the PALAZZO SFORZA ALMENI. Designed by Bartolommeo Ammannati, the windows are particularly fine.

PALAZZO NICCOLINI. Standing on the other side of the road at number 15 is a palace designed by Domenico Baccio d'Agnolo and built between 1548 and 1551. It is also called the Palazzo Montauto. On the façade are *sgraffiti* ▲ *191* from 1854. The *cortile* is very pretty, and facing the garden beyond is an unusual loggia with a double row of arcades. In the palace are rooms decorated by Meucci, Volterrano, Gimignani and Colonna. In 1918 the residence was bought by a wealthy scrap-merchant. A few years later it became the headquarters of the Fascist party. On the corner of Via Pucci is the vast PALAZZO PUCCI. Its façade extends all along this street as far as Via Ricasoli.

THE CHURCH OF SAN MICHELINO. A church also known as San Michele Visdomini after the Vicedomini family who had it built in the 11th century. It then stood near the old cathedral of Santa Reparata ▲ *129*, but when the new Duomo was built it was pulled down to make way for part of the chancel. It was reconstructed here a few years later, toward the end of the 14th century, and was substantially altered in 1660. The finest work in the church is in the second chapel on the right: *The Holy Family* (1518) by Jacopo Carrucci, who was known as Pontormo (1494–1556). It is an early work with a nervous energy and anxiety typical of the first generation of Florentine Mannerists. It is far more remarkable than the other works in the church, which date from the late 16th century when Mannerism had run its course. In the third chapel on the left is an *Immaculate Conception* by Francesco

Loggia of S. Maria Nuova Hospital, with the entrance to the church of Sant' Egidio.

PIAZZA SANTA MARIA NUOVA
A print by Giuseppe Zocchi shows the piazza and hospital. On the right, beyond the narrow Via Portinari, is the Convento delle Oblate.

▲ From Santissima Annunziata to Sant'Ambrogio

THE MUSEUM OF PREHISTORY
Founded in 1946, this museum contains well-displayed collections of some varied and

Morandini, known as Poppi (1554–97). He was Vasari's pupil and worked with him on a number of projects. A *Resurrection*, also by him, is in the south transept. His paintings lack force, the compositions are stilted, and the bright colors fail to compensate. The work of Santi di Tito in Florence, and of Caravaggio and the Caraccis in Rome was a reaction to this wilting Mannerism.

THE HOSPITAL OF SANTA MARIA NUOVA ● 75

A MODERN HOSPITAL. This hospital is the oldest in Florence. It dates from 1287, but the façade and wings of the building were added by Giulio Parigi between 1611 and 1618, probably to designs by Buontalenti. The rich banker Folco Portinari, father of Dante's Beatrice, founded the hospital which at first contained just twelve beds. Soon afterwards, in 1296, it was enlarged to take eight hundred beds. The original hospital rules stipulated that "the impoverished sick cared for in the hospital must be visited and comforted, fed, washed and watched over as though Christ lived again in each one." In fact in the Middle Ages this was a rule common to hospitals all over Europe, but Santa Maria Nuova very quickly gained a high reputation because the meals were plentiful and good, with meat and wine, and the standards of hygiene were comparatively high. It was such an exemplary institution that it was regarded as a model as far away as England.

MONNA TESSA. Portinari provided the money to set up the hospital, but the idea was not his own. It was Monna Tessa, a Franciscan tertiary, who persuaded him that he should help the poor in this way. Monna was the Portinari family's governess, and legend has it that she took care of Beatrice. Later she gathered around her a religious community, the

fascinating exhibits. They cover the time stretching from the Paleolithic period to the Iron and Bronze Ages. There are objects from all over the world, including a number of African exhibits, but there is a greater concentration on Italian prehistory. Among the items on display are some extremely early ceramics which are among the first ever made by man, as well as interesting statues of female figures and a human skull from the Paleolithic era. The stone artefacts (top of page) came from a tomb known as "del ponte San Pietro". The vases (above) are called *campianiformi* and *bottoni*.

FLORENCE C. 1480
A magnificent view of the city on show in the Museo di Firenze com'era (Florence as she was). The city wall is clearly visible. Today only the fortified gates remain.

248

«A BOX THEN, AT THE PERGOLA, IS REALLY AN ECONOMICAL AFFAIR . . . IT IS A MOST AMUSING ONE FROM THE VARIETY OF RANKS, NATIONS AND TOILETS THERE REPRESENTED.»

JJ JARVES, 1856

Communità delle Oblate Ospitaliere, who were dedicated to the care of the sick.

THE CHURCH OF SANT'EGIDIO. Beneath the portico of the hospital is the entrance to a 15th-century church at 1 Piazza Santa Maria Nuova. Sant' Egidio was altered by Giulio Parigi in 1611 using Buontalenti's plans of 1575. The ceiling frescoes date from the 18th century and are by Matteo Bonechi and Giuseppe Tonelli. Folco Portinari's tomb is on the right.

THE TEATRO DELLA PERGOLA

INNOVATION IN THE THEATER. A famous old theater stands at nos. 12–30 Via della Pergola. The original wooden one built by Ferdinando Tacca in 1656 caused a revolution in Italian theater design. Moving away from the Roman model, it was ovoid in shape, surrounded by tiers of boxes, and the stage had movable sets, machinery and a painted curtain. Productions reached new heights of fantasy and invention with complicated scenery and sophisticated lighting effects, even including carefully controlled fires. The first musical performance of the musical melodrama *Il Podestà di Colognole* (1657) by Giovanni Andrea Moniglia, with music by Jacopo Melani, marked the birth of comic opera. The theater was rebuilt in 1755, to a design by Giulio Mannaioni.

THE CONVENTO DELLE OBLATE

Opposite the Santa Maria Nuova Hospital, at 21 Via Sant' Egidio, stands a former convent which now houses the MUSEUM OF PREHISTORY along with a number of other municipal institutions. There is also a magnificent and little-

LUIGI DALLAPICCOLA (1904–75) Many of Dallapiccola's works were first performed at the Pergola (below, the auditorium and

entrance), including the opera *Night Flight* (*Volo di Notte*, 1940), based on Saint-Exupéry's novel; and his best-known work, the opera *The Prisoner* (*Il Prigioniero*, 1950). Although much involved in writing twelve-tone music he was never tied to any one musical theory. Dallapiccola (below) was also music critic for *Il Mondo* and for thirty-four years he was professor of piano at the Florence Conservatoire.

FIORENZA

PIAZZA SANT'AMBROGIO TABERNACLE
The majolica figure of St Ambrose was made by Giovanni della Robbia.

BORGO PINTI
Further up the street at number 68, past the Via della Colonna, is the Palazzo Panciatichi-Ximenes, built by Antonio and Giuliano da Sangallo around 1499. Napoleon stayed here in June 1796. At number 80 is the Palazzo Salviati, built in the 17th century but transformed two centuries later by Gaetano Baccani. Lastly, at numbers 97–9, is the Palazzo della Gherardesca. It was built by Giuliano da Sangallo but much altered by Antonio Ferri (1651–1716), who also put the cupola on the church of San Frediano ▲ 310. Ferri designed the handsome façade but Sangallo's 15th-century *cortile* remains unchanged, decorated with grotesques and terracotta bas-reliefs. In the chapel are frescoes by Stradano, a prolific pupil of Vasari.

The interior of the church of Santa Maria Maddalena dei Pazzi (top right). The old Sant'Ambrogio market hall (right).

visited cloister with arcades on three levels; from the top-floor gallery the Duomo can be seen from a new angle.

MUSEO DI FIRENZE COM'ERA. In another part of the old convent, with its entrance at 24 Via dell'Oriuolo, is a rarely frequented museum with a fascinating collection of prints, maps and paintings of the city since the 15th century, displayed in old vaulted rooms. It is a delightful place. In the first room hangs the large view of Florence known as the *Pianta della Catena*: a 19th-century copy of a 15th-century map now in Berlin. Succeeding rooms show Florence as it was (*Firenze com'era*) in drawings, paintings and prints, often of the lively, popular districts. The delicate 18th-century prints of Giuseppe Zocchi are full of human as well as architectural detail. Another delightful series of lunettes by Justus van Utens ● *80* shows the Medici villas with their gardens, today much changed or lost altogether. The collection also contains architectural prints and plans, some for buildings that no longer exist, such as the Convent of San Pier Maggiore ▲ *191*.

BORGO PINTI

PENANCE. At the end of Via Sant'Egidio the narrow and picturesque Borgo Pinti leads out of the city center. The word *borgo* indicates this road was once outside the second circle of medieval walls; it reached the city at the Porta Pinti, pulled down in 1868. "Pinti" comes from *pentiti* (penitents): those repenting a life of debauchery did penance near the gate.

PALAZZO ROFFIA. At number 13 is a late 17th-century palace with an ornate cornice and remarkable windows, among the finest to be seen in this part of the city.

PALAZZO BELLINI. The palace at number 26 is adorned with a bust of Ferdinand I. The sculptor Giambologna lived here, and later Pietro Tacca, one of his most famous pupils, used the palazzo for his academy of painting and sculpture.

PALAZZO NERI. The luxurious Hotel Monna Lisa, with a beautiful coffered ceiling in its entrance hall and a well-tended garden within, occupies the palace where St Filippo Neri ▲ *186* was born.

CONVENT OF S. MARIA MADDALENA DEI PAZZI

PILLAGE. The entrance to the church is at 58 Borgo Pinti. Tradition says that Giuliano da Sangallo designed the nave, but the whole building was substantially altered in the 17th century by Pier Francesco Silvani. Many works of art were carried off by the troops of Napoleon who stayed nearby at the PALAZZO PANCIATICHI-XIMENES (see facing page).

THE CAPPELLA DEL GIGLIO. On the right, before entering the nave, is a 16th-century chapel with frescoes by Bernardino Poccetti on the lives of four saints: Nereus, Achilleus, Bernard and Filippo Neri.

THE CHAPTER HOUSE. Here is one of the masterpieces of Perugino, a *Crucifixion* painted between 1493 and 1495. Standing in a delightful landscape that links the three sections of the fresco, his figures show no sign of emotion, only a sad and serene piety. This is typical of his work: he never allowed violent emotions to upset the harmony of his vision.

THE SYNAGOGUE

Continue up the Borgo Pinti, turn right into Via della Colonna, and on reaching the large and leafy Piazza d'Azeglio turn right into Via Farini. In this street it is easy to recognize the synagogue by its green dome. Jews first arrived in Florence in the 15th century, but this building was begun in 1874 at the instigation of David Levi, a prominent member of the Jewish community and a governor of its university. The foundation stone came from Jerusalem. Designed by Mariano Falcini, Marco Treves and Vincenzo Micheli, it is in Spanish-Moorish style, and the interior is richly decorated with mosaics. There is a small museum on the first floor up.

THE CHURCH OF SANT'AMBROGIO

AN UNDERRATED CHURCH. Via Farina now leads to Via dei Pilastri. Turn left to reach Piazza Sant'Ambrogio. The church which stands opposite dates back to the 5th century when a first building was dedicated to St Ambrose, commemorating his visit to the city in 393 to consecrate the churches of San Lorenzo ▲ *220* and Santa Felicita ▲ *286*. This sanctuary originally stood beside the Roman road to Arezzo. For many centuries it was a country church, and during the Middle Ages

THE CONVENT OF S. MARIA MADDALENA DEI PAZZI
French Augustinians now inhabit the convent, which has among its treasures Perugino's *Crucifixion* (left). The church dates from 1257 and is used by the French community in Florence.

THE FORMER CONVENT OF SANTA MARIA IN CANDELI
The ex-convent at 54 Via dei Pilastri is now occupied by the *carabinieri* (police), but it still contains a *Last Supper* and an *Annunciation* by Francesco di Cristofano, or "Franciabigio".

Mino da Fiesole's *Tabernacle of the Holy Sacrament* in the church of Sant'Ambrogio.

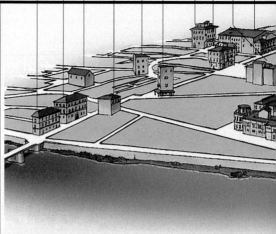

PALAZZO · ALBERTI-MALENCHINI · PALAZZO BARDI DI VERNIO · CHURCH OF SAN REMIGIO · MUSEO HORNE · PALAZZO PERUZZI · ALBERTI TOWER-HOUSE · PALAZZO SALVIATI · PALAZZO COCCHI-SERRISTORI · P. DELL'ANTELLA · TEATRO VERDI

🚶 Half a day

PALAZZO DELL'ANTELLA
21 Piazza Santa Croce once belonged to the Cerchi family and still has its overhanging upper story on stone corbels. Giulio Parigi finished the palace in 1620, and Giovanni di San Giovanni, with pupils, is said to have covered it in frescoes in the space of just twenty-seven days.

Façades that line the Piazza Santa Croce.

PALAZZO COCCHI-SERRISTORI ● 70
One of the most astonishing 15th-century façades in Florence. It seems to expand as it ascends, supported on corner consoles. Twin pilasters at each end of the upper façade stress its width, yet it is set upon a base of three bays only, part of an earlier house. Bramante had this façade in mind when designing the belvedere in the Vatican.

PIAZZA SANTA CROCE

POPULAR AMUSEMENTS. Crowds of people used to gather in this spot long before it was given the name of Piazza Santa Croce. Franciscan friars would preach here beside a small oratory dedicated to the holy cross (Santa Croce). Over the centuries it has remained a favorite location for popular gatherings and events such as jousts, games and festivals of all kinds. *Calcio* (a traditional kind of football) was played here enthusiastically from the 16th century and even under enemy fire, during the siege of Florence in 1529. A marble disk set into the Palazzo dell'Antella still marks the center line of the pitch.

THE CHURCH OF SANTA CROCE ● 84

THE ARRIVAL OF THE FRANCISCANS. Dominicans and Franciscans were the two dominant religious orders in the city. In 1218 Florence became the first town in which the Franciscans established a firm base; this was the

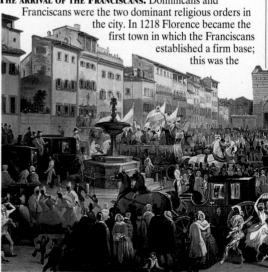

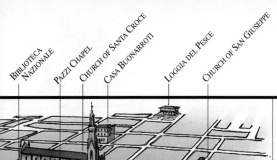

BIBLIOTECA
NAZIONALE

PAZZI CHAPEL

CHURCH OF SANTA CROCE

CASA BUONARROTI

LOGGIA DEL PESCE

CHURCH OF SAN GIUSEPPE

San Gallo Hospital. In the same year the first church of Santa Croce was built, soon to become one of the most active centers of religious life in the city. Miracles were said to take place at the tomb of the blessed Umiliana de' Cerchi, a Franciscan tertiary who died in 1246. The convent attached to the church had a good library, and the Franciscans soon gained a reputation as excellent teachers; many of the best families sent their children to them. The Franciscan creed of universal love suffered its first setback in 1254 when members of the Florentine order undertook to represent the papal Inquisition in the city and surrounding region. The administrator for the province was based at Santa Croce.

A FRANCISCAN EDUCATION. From the early 13th century onwards the larger Franciscan establishments would run two kinds of school: those for young people of all kinds and those for students within the order. Some of the latter came from far afield and would study philosophy, of a limited kind, theology and the Bible. This was the education that Dante received in Florence as a Franciscan tertiary, as did Giovanni de' Medici, son of Lorenzo il Magnifico. The school had famous teachers too, such as Luca Pacioli, master of algebraic theory ▲ 259.

DOUBTS OVER EXPANSION. The little church built in 1228, just after the death of St Francis, was soon far too small for the needs of such a flourishing community. In 1252 the Franciscans enlarged their church in the face of much opposition from Ubertino da Casale, who felt that such worldly expansion went directly against the teachings of St

**THE FRANCISCAN
INQUISITION**
Two armed monks dressed in gray habits went about the city accompanied by a notary, seeking out "heretics". They extracted confessions under torture and inflicted punishments that could vary from a fine to being burnt at the stake; the latter was not uncommon. The Inquisition was much feared. Aristocrats felt particularly threatened, for to the papal authorities the words "Ghibelline" and "heretic" were all too often synonymous, and the inquisitors were very thorough. The possessions of the condemned were divided into three: a third for the pope, a third for the Inquisition and the last third for the city government. This was the money that funded the building of Santa Croce.

PIAZZA SANTA CROCE
A painting (left) by Giovanni Signorini showing the *Carnival in Piazza Santa Croce*. In the oval (above) is a view of the church at night.

255

THE NAVE OF THE CHURCH
The nave (below, right) is 125 feet wide. It is so wide that stone arches could not be used to support the roof, and it had to be supported on wooden beams.

DANTE'S MEMORIAL
Dante was buried in Ravenna. Not until early in the 19th century did Florence pay homage to its great poet by commissioning Stefano Ricci to build a memorial (below). The city would have done better to accept Michelangelo's offer, made three centuries earlier, to erect a monument to Dante himself.

Francis, particularly the vow of poverty. In 1294 the controversy became more bitter still when plans were launched to rebuild the church entirely on an extravagant design by Arnolfo di Cambio. However, severe overcrowding forced a compromise, and it was agreed to replace the existing buildings with a convent. There was certainly a competitive element to the plan, since the Franciscans would not be outdone by the Dominicans, who were now building Santa Maria Novella ▲ 213. On May 3, 1294, the first stone was laid. The entire Signoria was present since, in 1259, the city government had undertaken to contribute a sum for the construction of a basilica. Private chapels had also been reserved in advance by rich families like the Bardis, the Peruzzis, the Baroncellis and the Albertis.

THE QUARATESIS DISAPPOINTED. The work took a long time, and the church was not consecrated until 1443. Even then the façade had still to be erected. The Quaratesi family offered 100,000 florins to pay for it on condition that it feature their coat of arms, like the Rucellais at Santa Maria Novella. But the Franciscans refused, and the front of the church stayed bare until an Englishman, Francis Sloane, paid for a façade in the 19th century.

VAST AND AUSTERE. The church interior is very impressive. It is enormously wide (125 feet), too wide for stone arches and vaulting to be used. In any case, it was the custom for mendicant orders to build churches with wooden roofs, and this was the solution chosen here. The campanile was designed in the Gothic style in 1847 by Gaetano Baccani, copied from a Trecento (14th-century) model.

THE ILLUSTRIOUS DEAD. Although this was the church of an order sworn to poverty, it is full of memorials to the rich and famous. It was an act of extreme humility to be buried here so, paradoxically, in the 13th and 14th centuries

Repentance of Mary Magdalene (right) by Giovanni da Milano.

TANTO. NOMINI. NVLLVM. PAR. ELOGIVM
NICOLAVS. MACHIAVELLI
OBIT. AN. A. P. V. MDXXVII.

ONORATE L'ALTISSIMO POETA

DANTI·ALIGHERIO
TVSCI
HONORARIVM·TVMVLVM
A·MAIORIBVS·TER·FRVSTRA·DECRETVM
ANNO·M·DCCC·XXIX
FELICITER·EXCITARVNT·

NEL VII CENTENARIO DELLA
NASCITA
L'ASSOCIAZIONE'STVDIVM DANTIS
MCCLXV · MCMLXV

Machiavelli's tomb
(left) was sculpted by
Innocenzo Spinazzi.

rich families paid huge sums to
have their dead laid to rest in the
chapels. There are memorials to many
eminent citizens.

MICHELANGELO'S TOMB. In the first chapel on the right
is Vasari's monument (1564). Originally the plan was to
decorate it with the artist's own sculptures, such as the
Pietà in the Museo dell'Opera del Duomo ▲ *138*.
Michelangelo died in Rome, and the pope wanted him
buried there. The Florentines, however, stole his body
back to Florence, where he lay in state in Santa Croce
while crowds filed past for several days.

MONUMENT TO NICCOLÒ MACHIAVELLI. This work by
Innocenzo Spinazzi dates from 1787. It is in the fourth
chapel on the right, after the monuments to Dante and
Vittorio Alfieri. Machiavelli ● *40* was born in 1469 to a
noble family with very little money. He gained his first
important political post in 1498 as second chancellor of
the commune, dealing with war and foreign affairs, and
he was sent on a number of important missions abroad.
Critical of the custom of fighting wars with hired
mercenaries, he believed it would be better to have
soldiers fighting for their own patriotic cause. To this
end, he gained permission to form a national militia for
Florence in 1506. The innovation was short-lived, however.

CONSPIRACY AND DOWNFALL. He remained in his post until the
republic fell and the Medicis returned in 1512. Machiavelli
was willing to work for them, but the following year he was
accused of taking part in a conspiracy. He was imprisoned and
tortured. Eventually his innocence was accepted but on his
release he retired to run the family farm at San Casciano di
Valdipesa, where he spent his time studying the classics.

THE WRITER. Here he wrote his most famous books: *The
Prince* (1513), *La Mandragola* (1518), and *Discourses on the
First Decade of Titus Livius* (1513). Once or twice he returned
to Florence to attend learned meetings in the Casa Rucellai
▲ *276*. In 1520, the year in which he finished the *Art of War*,
Cardinal Giulio de' Medici and his cousin Pope Leo X asked
him to write a history of his city. He began the *History of
Florence*, giving a critical account of the fall of the Roman
Empire. When Giulio became Pope Clement VII, Machiavelli
believed his fortunes would turn: he was made
inspector of the fortifications of Florence in
1526, and entrusted with minor
missions. In 1527, however,
the Medicis were again
removed from
power, and he
found himself
once more out
of favor. He
died on May
22 that same
year.

**DONATELLO'S
"CRUCIFIX"**
In the Bardino
di Vernis
Chapel, at the
end of the north
transept, hangs
the wooden
Crucifix (left) by
Donatello (c.
1411). Vasari
tells us that
Brunelleschi called
it "the body of a
peasant on the
cross", and made a
crucifix of his own,
now in Santa Maria
Novella ▲ *214*.

**BENEDETTO DA
MAIANO'S PULPIT**
The pulpit was
constructed between
1474 and 1480 and is
decorated with

exquisitely detailed
panels (one of which
is shown above)
depicting events from
the life of St Francis:
from right to left they
are *Giving the Rule of
the Order, Trial by Fire
before the Sultan,
Receiving the
Stigmata, Death of
Saint Francis* and
*Saint Francis Praying
for the First Martyrs*.
In the niches between
the consoles are
*Faith, Hope, Love,
Fortitude* and *Justice*.
The staircase leading
up to the pulpit is set
into the pillar.
Benedetto da Maiano
(1442–97) is
considered among the
finest sculptors of the
late 15th century.

STAINED GLASS
The windows of the Bardi di Vernio chapel (below) were designed by Maso di Banco, a pupil of Giotto. At the top are *Saint Sylvester* (left) and the *Emperor Constantine*, below are *Trajan* (left) and

Saint Gregory. They are more austere in style than the windows in the sanctuary by Agnolo Gaddi and Bernardo Daddi.

"THE PRINCE". In Machiavelli's time Italy was a patchwork of small states and principalities. His most renowned work, *The Prince*, dealt with the question of governing a united nation. He regarded a republic as a remote ideal; what was needed initially was a fierce, clever and uncompromising leader. Machiavelli's book takes the form of advice to this imagined leader. It is advice famous for its cynicism, by which the end always justifies the means, however cruel or drastic. But given the fact that the country was then in the hands of a collection of unscrupulous tyrants, his proposed tactics were entirely realistic and expedient.

TOMB OF LEONARDO BRUNI. Toward the end of the nave on the right stands a memorial to one of Florence's great statesmen. The elegant monument was made by Bernardo Rossellino between 1444 and 1445, and became a model for such memorials. Leonardo Bruni (1370–1444) was an early humanist and scholar. He was also actively involved in civic life, and a fierce defender of republican ideals. He was chancellor in 1410 and again from 1427 until his death, greatly respected for his learning, insight and eloquence. He organized the project for Ghiberti's Baptistery doors ▲ *136*, the *Gates of Paradise*. Bruni also wrote a *History of the Florentine People* which was soon translated from Latin into Italian. He portrayed the Florentine republic as the noble heir to Rome and even to Athens, an image long perpetuated. Above all, he did not accept the concept of divine providence. Progress, he insisted, was achieved through man's own efforts, and not imposed by God. Under his influence three great men were recognized as heroes of the city – Dante, Petrarch and Boccaccio.

THE TOMB OF UGO FOSCOLO. At the end of the nave on the right is the tomb of the Venetian poet Ugo Foscolo (1778–1827). As a young man he was filled with admiration for the French Revolution and later he rallied to Napoleon's cause, even writing him an ode. Foscolo joined the French armies, but when the empire fell he had to take refuge in Switzerland and then England, where he ended his days in poverty. In 1871 his remains were returned to the newly united Italy, and he was buried in Santa Croce, a church he had described in his poems. He was one of the great Italian writers of the early Romantic age. His most celebrated work, *Last Letters of Jacopo Ortis* (1802),

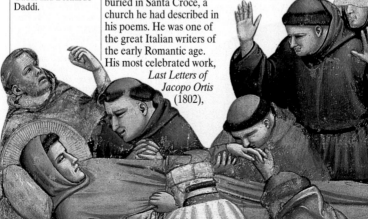

GIOTTO'S "LIFE OF SAINT FRANCIS OF ASSISI"
Giotto's famous frescoes, in the BARDI CHAPEL directly to
the right of the high altar, were painted around 1318. On
the facing page: (top) detail of *Jerome Looking for the
Stigmata*, (center) *Saint Francis Receiving the Stigmata*,
(bottom) *The Death of the Saint* (detail). This page: (right
and center) *Trial by Fire before the Sultan* (details).

was modeled on Goethe's *Werther* and *La nouvelle
Héloïse* by Jean-Jacques Rousseau.

THE BARDI AND PERUZZI CHAPELS. In the chancel are
two chapels decorated by Giotto. The BARDI CHAPEL is
directly to the right of the high altar, and the PERUZZI
CHAPEL is next door. The Bardi Chapel was decorated
by Giotto c. 1318 with scenes from the life of St
Francis. In the 18th century, when medieval art was
regarded as heathen, they were covered in whitewash.
The frescoes were rediscovered in 1852 and,
unfortunately, badly restored.

GIOTTO'S ART. Giotto's work has three key
characteristics. Firstly, it is plain. Most artists at the
time were painting in the International Gothic style,
with complicated architectural structures, stylized
poses and richly ornamented draperies. Giotto's
structures are simple, the poses natural and the
emotions restrained but sincere. There is also a
monumentality about his work: the figures are
solid and well-balanced, with strength rather than
elegance of line. The architectural features too
are large, three-dimensional and
spacious, never cramping the all-important
narrative scene. Finally, Giotto's paintings are
realistic: his contemporaries were amazed by
how true to life his images were, some even
describing his work as illusionistic.

A FAMOUS ADMIRER. In the *Decameron*
Boccaccio wrote: "Giotto's art was of such
excellence that there was nothing in nature
that his pen or paintbrush could not exactly
reproduce, not simply to make a likeness, but
to be the very thing itself. His work was so
perfect that a man standing before it would
often find his visual senses confused, taking for
real what was only painted."

THE PERUZZI CHAPEL. Here the frescoes
include scenes from the lives of John the Evangelist and John
the Baptist. They were also whitewashed in the 18th century
and are so badly damaged that is difficult to appreciate them
fully. This is all the more sad and frustrating as it is the last
surviving cycle that Giotto painted, dating from around 1320.
His later work in Naples has disappeared.

AN ARTIST MUCH IN DEMAND. Giotto di Bondone (1267–1337)
had arrived in Florence in 1311 having already established an
international reputation as a painter. He was in favor with the
pope and had done a number of frescoes, which are now
almost entirely gone, for the church of San Giovanni
Laterano in Rome. He had also decorated the Franciscans'
upper church in Assisi and the Arena Chapel in Padua. When
he came to Florence to undertake the commission at Santa
Croce, he may also have been interested in buying real estate:
he was already the owner of several properties in the city.

AN INFLUENTIAL CITIZEN. On arriving in Florence he
requested a seat on the council of the Podestà ▲ *188*,
although he had not resided in Florence for the
statutory two years. His family was already well
ensconced in the city, and he himself held a high
position in the *Arti Maggiori* ● *52*, ▲ *199*.

**PREACHING BY
PICTURES**
The mendicant orders
owed their success to
the use of images to
illustrate their
sermons. The frescoes
in Santa Croce reflect
this. They wanted to
convey the deeper
significance of the
scriptures and the life
of their founder. The
works exerted a
strong influence on
the development of
western art. From
1280 Cimabue, and
then Giotto, painted
vast fresco cycles
establishing a
narrative tradition
that was to become a
major characteristic
of Italian art.

A portrait of the
mathematician Luca
Pacioli ▲ *255*, who
taught at the
Franciscans schools.

THE PAZZI CHAPEL
Andrea de' Pazzi commissioned the chapel (right) for family tombs. His plans fell through, for after the Pazzi conspiracy ● *31*, ▲ *131* in 1478 the family were all exiled or executed. In his design, Filippo Brunelleschi paid particular attention to light. Where it enters from the side it is filtered by the vestibule, so that the chapel and sanctuary are mainly illuminated by light from the lantern and oculi in the dome which reflects on the white walls. The glazed terracotta medallions of the Apostles are by Luca della Robbia. The Evangelists in the pendentives of the cupola (top of facing page) also come from his workshop, but may have been designed by Brunelleschi himself. The sculpted portico is attributed to Giuliano da Maiano.

A reliquary in the church of Santa Croce. It displays the habit said to have been worn by St Francis.

Giotto was not short of enemies, among them the aristocrat Andrea Albertinelli, and they did their best to spread rumors of dishonesty and the misappropriation of funds entrusted to him for various commissions. However, the painter's eminent connections prevented anyone confronting him openly with such accusations.

THE BARONCELLI CHAPEL ★. At the end of the south transept is a chapel with magnificent frescoes of scenes from the *Life of Mary* painted between 1332 and 1338 by Taddeo Gaddi, a pupil of Giotto. There is also an altarpiece of the *Coronation of the Virgin* from Giotto's workshop.

THE SANCTUARY (CAPPELLA MAGGIORE). In 1348 the Alberti family donated the money with which to decorate the sanctuary, and in 1380 the job was given to Agnolo Gaddi. In the vault are the *Redeemer*, the *Evangelist* and *Saint Francis*, while on the walls is the *Legend of the True Cross*. The rich could not pay to have their dead buried in the sanctuary since it was reserved for the Franciscans. In recognition of the Albertis' generosity, however, the crossed chains from their coat of arms are much in evidence. The frescoes are on the wall behind the high altar, above which hangs a *Crucifix* by Figline, once attributed to Giotto.

THE BARDI DI VERNIO CHAPEL. To the far left of the chancel is a chapel painted with frescoes dating from about 1340 by a pupil of Giotto, Maso di Banco. They relate the life of St Sylvester, set among ancient ruins inspired by real Roman remains. The atmosphere is mysterious, with a dark sky and an absence of shadows giving some interesting effects of light and color that were quite unknown in the work of Giotto.

THE SACRISTY. At the end of the south transept is a door by

Michelozzo which leads into the sacristy corridor. The sacristy itself was built after 1340 by the Peruzzi family. The south wall is painted with a *Crucifixion* attributed to Taddeo Gaddi (c. 1340), a *Road to Calvary* thought to be by a pupil of

Spinello Aretino (c. 1400), and a *Resurrection* by Niccolo di Pietro Gerini (c. 1400). The *Ascension* is thought to be from Gerini's workshop. Niccolo di Pietro Gerini and his son Lorenzo di Niccolo were both working in the late 14th century and tried hard to emulate the sensitivity and sincerity of Giotto in their work. The Rinuccini Chapel is separated from the sacristy by a Gothic grille. The chapel is covered in frescoes of the life of the Virgin and the life of St Mary Magdalene, which were begun around 1365 by Giovanni di Milano, a painter known to have been in Florence from 1346 to 1369. The lower frescoes are by another hand, probably a painter of Orcagna's school. Giovanni di Milano was one of the great artists of the 14th century, and he was trained in the north of Italy: his subtle and delicate use of color betrays his Lombard origins. There is a refinement about his work that seems to show the influence of the Sienese school and also underlines his importance in the development of the International Gothic style.

THE PAZZI CHAPEL ● 89. Outside the church, a door to the right of the façade leads to the cloisters, the Pazzi Chapel and the museum. As you enter the first cloister, on the right there is a small monument to Florence Nightingale, who was born in Florence. The chapel can be seen standing at the end of the cloister (above). Brunelleschi began his design in 1430, and construction started in 1443. As at San Lorenzo ▲ 220, he was able to put into practice his desire to build on a centralized plan. Here he created a chapel of even more remarkable beauty, a perfect example of the confident simplicity of Quattrocento architecture. Romanesque and Gothic architects had mastered geometry, but their creations were often complex, whereas in the bold squares and circles of Renaissance design there is a striking force and clarity. Brunelleschi died leaving the façade unfinished, and it was completed in 1478.

BRUNELLESCHI'S CLOISTER. This is an extremely elegant and tranquil cloister which was designed by Brunelleschi just before his death in 1446, and then built in 1453.

CIMABUE'S "CRUCIFIX"
On November 4, 1966, the Arno broke its banks and flooded the city of Florence ▲ 173. Cimabue's *Crucifix* (c. 1287–90) was "the flood's most famous victim", in the words of Pope Paul VI, who went to pray before it that Christmas at the Limonaia Laboratory, in Boboli. The masterpiece, an early landmark in the history of Florentine art, had lost most of its paint. What remained was peeling off.
Professor Umberto Baldini, entrusted with its restoration, began by removing what paint was left and then cleaning off the varnish which had previously given the painting a greenish tinge. The color had to be removed from the wood and canvas backing in order for certain special treatments to be applied. The surviving paint restored, he decided not to recreate the missing bits but to replace them with a neutral color that blended with the general tone. The image above shows the crucifix in its damaged state and, below, after restoration.

Right, the interior of the church of San Giuseppe.

CASA BUONARROTI
There are a number of preparatory clay studies on display which give an insight into one of Michelangelo's constant preoccupations: capturing the way in which a body, even just the torso alone, can be expressive. Rodin was fascinated by fragments of ancient statuary for the same reason. A torso without a head, arms or legs could still convey much by its line, shape and muscular detail.

Below, Michelangelo's clay study for *Hercules and Cacus*.

MUSEO DELL'OPERA DI SANTA CROCE. In this second cloister, also by Brunelleschi, is the entrance to the museum which contains a number of important works. In the old refectory hangs Cimabue's *Crucifix* (c. 1287–8), badly damaged in the

1966 flood ● *33*, ▲ *173*, but since restored. Here too are fragments of an astonishing fresco of the *Triumph of Death*, by Andrea Orcagna, which used to decorate the nave. They were much damaged by the flood and wonderfully restored. The waters here reached a height of over 16 feet. On the end wall are frescoes by Taddeo Gaddi dating from about 1333, including a *Last Supper* and *Tree of the Cross*. The latter is perhaps the most famous illustration for the book *The Tree of Life*, by the Franciscan St Bonaventura. It shows how medieval thought was permeated with symbolism. St Bonaventura sits writing at the foot of the cross while St Francis kneels embracing it, looking up at Christ. The cross sprouts into the Tree of Life, symbolizing redemption through sacrifice. At the end of each branch an Old Testament prophet holds a parchment inscribed with a prophecy of the coming of the Messiah. At the top of the cross sits a pelican with her young, a symbol of maternal sacrifice.

VIA SAN GIUSEPPE

THE CHURCH OF SANTA MARIA DELLA CROCE AL TEMPIO. The Neri brotherhood who founded the church in the 14th century made it their mission to bring comfort to condemned men. This church has a 15th-century fresco by Bicci di Lorenzo.
THE CHURCH OF SAN GIUSEPPE. Although the church was built to a design by Baccio d'Agnolo in 1519, its appearance was altered completely in the 18th century. A façade was added in 1759 and the interior elegantly decorated in late Baroque style with frescoes by Sigismondo Betti (1754). In the second chapel on the right is a painting of *Saint Francis of Paola*, by Cigoli, and in the third chapel is a *Nativity* (1564) by Santi di Tito. There is also a 16th-century crucifix that accompanied the condemned to their execution, near today's Piazza Beccaria ▲ *252*.

Narcissus at the Pool, a fresco in the Casa Buonarroti.

CASA BUONARROTI

From Piazza Santa Croce go up the Via delle Pinzochere to the Via Ghibellina. The Casa Buonarroti is on the far side of this crossroads, on the corner of Via Buonarroti. It is an intimate and charming museum in which one gains a greater understanding of Michelangelo, the artist and the man. He bought the property in 1508. Later in the century the three existing dwellings were transformed into this modest palazzo following plans drawn up by Michelangelo himself.

EARLY GENIUS. The collection was begun by Michelangelo's nephew, who gathered works by his famous uncle, mostly drawings, studies for pieces of sculpture, portraits and early works. *The Madonna of the Steps* (c. 1492) would seem to be his earliest surviving work, a bas-relief carved when he was sixteen or seventeen. Donatello's influence is clear in the rejection of idealized beauty. The carved relief of the *Battle of the Centaurs* is from the same period but the style is very different. In this complex scene the young artist's heroic fantasy is in full flight. His mastery of light and shade is sophisticated and he already makes conscious use of the unfinished. Another early work is the *Crucifix,* for which he used a youthful corpse as his model.

QUESTIONS OF FAITH. The life of Michelangelo Buonarroti (1475–1564) was one of torment and frustration. He has become the archetypal genius, dominating his age with a combination of vision and technique: there was no sculptor to match him. Perhaps his spiritual anguish can be explained by the profound religious upheavals of the period: the Protestant Reformation put an end to spiritual complacency by raising fundamental and unavoidable questions of conscience. When Michelangelo was working for the popes he must have been all too aware of the religious revolt taking place in northern Europe, and he probably felt sympathy for Luther's stand against the pomp and corruption of Rome. There is no doubt that his *Last Judgement* in the Sistine Chapel was intended as a warning.

PIAZZA DEI CIOMPI

FLEA MARKET. The Via Buonarroti leads on to the Piazza dei Ciompi, a lively square filled with stalls selling all kinds of intriguing secondhand and antique goods, including ornaments, books, uniforms and coins. Behind it stands Vasari's *Loggia del Pesce* which once stood on the site of Piazza della Repubblica ▲ *209*, and was moved here during the major urban redevelopments of the 19th century. The *Ciompi* ● *30* were the cloth workers who rebelled in 1378.

"NOLI ME TANGERE"
A painting by Bronzino, but a copy of one by Michelangelo now lost. The original painting had an interesting history. Michelangelo was active in the defense of Florence during the siege ● *31* by imperial troops in 1529–30. He kept the assailants at bay with his machines placed on the battlements. When, after eight months, the city finally fell, Michelangelo hid in the bell tower of San Niccolò oltr'Arno ▲ *316*, convinced that his hours were numbered. The pope pardoned him, however, on condition that he finish the Medici Chapel at San Lorenzo ▲ *223*. It must have been as a rather malicious joke that a general of the imperial army commissioned this painting *Noli me Tangere*, meaning "Don't touch me".

THE TEATRO VERDI
A theater that is not only the largest in Florence, but among the biggest in Italy. It was opened in 1854 and has always been the venue for an enormous variety of entertainments, including ballet, opera, plays and films. It is also well

THE ORATORIO DI SAN NICCOLÒ AL CEPPO. Returning to the Via Ghibellina, turn right to reach the Via Verdi, right again, and on the corner of the Via Verdi and the Via de' Pandolfini is a small oratory built in 1561 to a design by Giambologna. Inside are old wooden choirstalls and a trompe-l'oeil ceiling.

TEATRO VERDI

ON THE RUINS OF THE "STINCHE". In 1854 the largest theater in Florence was built, with three thousand seats. The site chosen was that of the notorious *Stinche* prison, demolished

in 1838. All that remains is a tabernacle containing a fresco that used to stand at the corner of the Via Isola delle Stinche and the Via Ghibellina, now under the care of the Institution of Fine Arts.

A NOTORIOUS PRISON. The *Stinche* was built in 1301 on land then lying outside the city that had been confiscated from exiled Ghibellines, the Ubertis ● *34.* It had high, windowless walls and was surrounded by a moat, which explains the description *isola* (island). At first it was intended that the prison should take political prisoners and prisoners of war, and it got its name in 1304 from some prisoners taken defending the Cavalcanti castle, known as "delle Stinche". But soon thieves, prostitutes, debtors and murderers were locked within its walls, alongside more illustrious inmates such as Machiavelli, Giovanni, Villani and others.

known for its musical shows and popular concerts: Frank Sinatra, Ava Gardner, Ella Fitzgerald and Keith Jarrett have all had their successes here. Classical concerts, too, have filled the hall, with artists like Zubin Mehta, who particularly likes its accoustics, Sviatoslav Richter and Rostropovich. In 1984 the theater was seriously damaged by fire and it remained closed until 1988.

The *Stinche* prison (top) which was replaced by the Teatro Verdi (above). The façades of the Palazzo Salviati (right, top) and that of the Teatro Verdi (bottom).

CRIME AND PUNISHMENT. The Florentine system of justice did not differ fundamentally from those found elsewhere in Italy, except that it was particularly harsh. Confessions were extracted under torture, and the guilty could have their eyes put out, their tongue cut off, or a limb amputated. Relatively minor crimes were cruelly punished: a practising homosexual would be castrated, burglars would be beheaded or hung, thieves lost an ear for a first offense and could be hanged for a second, those guilty of fraud or arson were generally burned, and if shown mercy would only lose a hand.

PALAZZO SALVIATI

On the corner of the Via Isola delle Stinche and the Via della Vigna Vecchia is one of the best-preserved examples in Florence of a 14th-century dwelling. The Palazzo Salviati still has its overhanging upper story, supported on massive stone corbels. It was later forbidden to build houses with this feature because they made the streets below too dark and narrow.

> "ITALIANS ARE ENTIRELY ACCUSTOMED TO CATHOLICISM,
> IT IS A PART OF THEIR EYES, THEIR EARS,
> THEIR IMAGINATION AND THEIR TASTE."
>
> HIPPOLYTE TAINE

STREET-CORNER TABERNACLES

Florence is not unique in having tabernacles. Many other Italian towns and cities also have them dotted about their streets. They are particularly common here, however, and worth special attention for their great beauty, detail and variety. In the Catholic religion the word "tabernacle" refers to the small niche or cupboard in which the Holy Sacrament is kept. In the Italian language it is also used to describe a niche or tiny chapel set onto or into the wall of a building and usually placed at the crossing of two streets. They are often decorated with miniature columns, and contain a votive image of the Madonna or a saint. In Florence these small landmarks of popular worship can date from as early as the 14th century and have always been a sign of the very strong religious spirit of the city.

BARDIS AND PERUZZIS
Two of the richest families in 14th-century Florence. Edward III of England borrowed 900,000 florins from the Bardis, and 600,000 from the

Peruzzis (in 1349 the king of France bought Montpellier for 133,000 florins). But he went bankrupt waging war on France, causing a number of companies to fail, among them the Acciaiuolis and Peruzzis in 1343 and the Bardis in 1345.

Two views of the Palazzo Peruzzi (above) and windows of the Palazzo Corsi-Alberti, which houses the Museo Horne.

"VIVOLI" ICE-CREAM PARLOR. The most famous ice-cream parlor in Florence is at 7 Via Isola delle Stinche. The flavors are delicious, and especially enjoyable on a summer evening sitting in the nearby Piazza Santa Croce.

THE CHURCH OF SAN SIMONE AND SAN GIUDA

This is a 13th-century church which was redesigned by Gherardo Silvani in 1630. Inside, the decoration features a ladder motif which comes from the coat of arms of the Galilei family. There is an ornate wooden ceiling and on the left, just beyond the fourth altar, is a remarkable bust of a woman. It dates from the 15th century and must be one of the earliest examples of realism in the genre.

THE BORGO DE' GRECI DISTRICT

The network of streets and alleys around the Borgo de' Greci is one of the most ancient and charming areas in the city.
VIA TORTA. The street is curved because the houses were originally built into the remains of a huge Roman amphitheater, dating from 124–30 AD, large enough to hold twenty thousand spectators. The Via Bentaccordi continues the curve, crossing Borgo de' Greci.
BORGO DE' GRECI. The street leads from Piazza San Firenze to Piazza Santa Croce. It is one of the oldest in the city. In Roman times it linked the theater (now Via de' Gondi) with the amphitheater. At number 12 is the PALAZZO D'UBALDINO PERUZZI, with a façade built by Gherardo Silvani in 1640. Number 3, the PALAZZO PERUZZI-BOURBON DEL MONTE DI SANTA MARIA, dates from the 13th and 14th centuries.
PIAZZA DE' PERUZZI. Walk south round the curve of the Via Bentaccordi to a piazza dominated by the PALAZZO PERUZZI, a tall, imposing 14th-century building with a curved façade.
THE CHURCH OF SAN REMIGIO. The Via de' Rustici, with palaces on either side, leads to the church of San Remigio, overlooking a tiny piazza. The first building here, a pilgrims' hospice, was put up in the 11th century. The present church was built in the 13th and 14th centuries and decorated in Tuscan Gothic style. To the left of the high altar is a painting of the *Immaculate Conception* by Empoli (1551–1640). The Via de' Rustici continues south to Via de' Neri. Turn left to reach Via de' Benci, a main road taking traffic to the PONTE ALLE GRAZIE. On the corner with Borgo Santa Croce is the 13th-century CASA-TORRE

ALBERTI, with a 15th-century loggia. The Borgo Santa Croce is a dark, narrow street leading to the buildings of Santa Croce. Turn right into Via Antonio Magliabechi.

THE BIBLIOTECA NAZIONALE. The façade looks onto the Piazza dei Cavalleggeri, which has a fine view of the Oltrarno. It houses a priceless collection of some three million works, including prints, rare manuscripts, many of them illuminated, sea charts and early printed books. Enormous damage was done by the 1966 flood ● *33*, ▲ *173*. The Corso dei Tintori now leads back to the Via de' Benci.

MUSEO HORNE

PALAZZO CORSI-ALBERTI. The palace at 6 Via de' Benci was built for the Alberti Family in 1490, probably by Simone del Pollaiuolo (il Cronaca). It later belonged to the Corsi family and late in the 19th century was bought by the English architect and art historian Herbert Percy Horne (1864–1916). He installed his private collection of furniture and works of art from the Renaissance period. He bequeathed the palazzo and its contents to the nation, and in 1922 it was opened as a museum. It is a typical early Renaissance palace, a place of business as well as a dwelling. Outstanding are the capitals of the two central pillars in the colonnaded *cortile*, by Andrea Sansovino.

TASTE AND DISCERNMENT. Horne was not rich but he was a dedicated and knowledgeable collector. A painting of *Saint Stephen*, by Giotto, is probably his most rare and valuable item. He also loved furniture, and there are some exquisite pieces including a late 15th-century walnut credenza with delightful marquetry work, and an inlaid sacristy bench among the finest surviving examples of 15th-century work.

PALAZZO BUSINI-BARDI

The palace opposite the museum, at 5 Via de' Benci, is generally accepted as having been built c. 1430 to a design by Brunelleschi.

THE "CAMERATA DE' BARDI" ● *50*. Giovanni Bardi, count of Vernio (1534–1612), was a model Renaissance man: a patron of the arts, humanist scholar, mathematician and composer. He gathered together a group dedicated to poetry and music who would meet in this palazzo and were known as the *Camerata Fiorentina* or the *Camerata de' Bardi*. Among its members were Vincenzo Galilei, composer of madrigals and father of the astronomer, Ottavio Rinuccini, poet, Jacopo Peri, composer, and Giulio Caccini, singer. Through their experiments at setting classical drama to music, to intensify its emotions, they can be said to have invented opera around the year 1600.

Remigio. The event was the object of such intense devotional attention that in the 16th century Eleonora de' Medici founded the Order of the Immaculate Conception. Iconography of the Virgin became more and more widespread and the *Immaculate Conception* became far more than the illustration of an episode; it was the symbol of a profound belief.

▲ From Santa Trinita to the Cascine

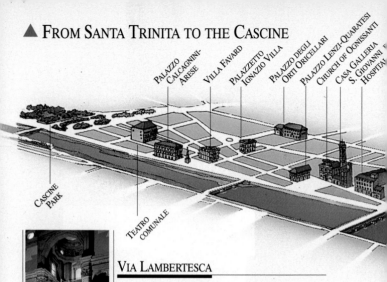

PALAZZO CALCAGNINI-ARESE
VILLA FAVARD
PALAZZETTO IGNAZIO VILLA
PALAZZO DEGLI ORTI ORICELLARI
PALAZZO LENZI-QUARATESI
CHURCH OF OGNISSANTI
CASA GALLERIA S. GIOVANNI
HOSPITAL

CASCINE PARK
TEATRO COMUNALE

INTERIOR OF SANTO STEFANO AL PONTE
The high altar was made by Giambologna (1591) for the church attached to the Santa Maria Nuova Hospital, and moved here in 1885 at the same time as Buontalenti's staircase from Santa Trinita. On the left of the nave is a bronze bas-relief of the *Stoning of Saint Stephen* (1656) by Ferdinando Tacca, who redesigned the interior of the church in 1649. There are also works by both Santi di Tito and Jacopo di Cione.

Santo Stefano al Ponte: detail of a window and the main doorway.

VIA LAMBERTESCA

A winding medieval street that leads west from the Ufizzi ▲ *153* from beneath a grand arch.
THE CHURCH OF SANTO STEFANO AL PONTE. Turn left into the Via Por Santa Maria and left again to reach the tiny hidden piazza on which the church stands. In medieval times Florence was full of such piazzettas, and this has retained its atmosphere. The church of Santo Stefano al Ponte itself is extremely old, founded in the 11th century. In 1378 Boccaccio gave readings here from Dante's *Divine Comedy* ● *39*, ▲ *194*. The façade and doorway are 13th-century, and the interior, which can only be seen during rehearsals and concerts, was altered in the 17th century. Leading up to the raised chancel is an extravagantly Mannerist flight of steps and balustrade (1574) by Buontalenti, brought here from Santa Trinita in 1894. In the cloister is a small room where the goldsmiths of the city used to meet.
VIA POR SANTA MARIA. The oldest street in the city gave its name to the Silkweavers' Guild ▲ *198*. In the days of the republic it was lined with their shops. Today it remains an important road, linking the Duomo with the Ponte Vecchio.

BORGO SANTI APOSTOLI

THE MEDIEVAL CITY. The street dates back to the 11th century and it follows the route of an even older Roman road. It used to lie outside the city walls, hence *borgo*, and in the Middle Ages it led to the shrine of the Holy Apostles (*Santi Apostoli*). A number of narrow streets called *chiassi* lead north from here to pass under archways into the Via delle Terme ▲ *205*.

On the corner of the Via Por Santa Maria is the CASA TORRE BALDOVINETTI, a 14th-century tower. At 6 Borgo Santi Apostoli is the PALAZZO BUONDELMONTI, the oldest palace to have belonged to this family. On the other side of the Chiasso delle Misure is the CASA TORRE ACCIAIUOLI, a 13th-century tower (number 8), next door to the PALAZZO BONCIANO. Number 19 is the PALAZZO ROSSELLI DEL TURCO, built by Baccio d'Agnolo in 1507. Its side wall, with a bas-relief of *Madonna and Child* by Benedetto da Maiano (1442–97), faces onto the Piazza del Limbo, where unbaptized babies were once buried. Here stands one of the oldest churches in Florence.

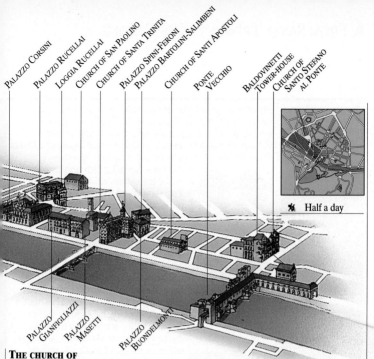

PALAZZO CORSINI
PALAZZO RUCELLAI
LOGGIA RUCELLAI
CHURCH OF SAN PAOLINO
CHURCH OF SANTA TRINITA
PALAZZO SPINI-FERONI
PALAZZO BARTOLINI-SALIMBENI
CHURCH OF SANTI APOSTOLI
PONTE VECCHIO
BALDOVINETTI TOWER-HOUSE
CHURCH OF SANTO STEFANO AL PONTE

PALAZZO GIANFIGLIAZZI
PALAZZO MASETTI
PALAZZO BUONDELMONTI

✷ Half a day

THE CHURCH OF

SANTI APOSTOLI. Only the
Baptistery ▲ *132* and San Miniato ▲ *320* equal this
church in age. Already mentioned in 1075, it is thought to
date back to the 10th century, built into the remains of
Roman baths. From the baths came the capitals of the first
two columns in the nave, on which the rest were modeled.
The wooden ceiling has marvelously preserved 14th-century
decoration. To the right of the church is the PALAZZO of the
archbishop ALTOVITI, which faces onto the Lungarno
Acciaiuoli. It was built in 1512 by Benedetto da Rovezzano, as
was the archbishop's tomb in the church of Santi Apostoli.
The pleasant Borgo Santi Apostoli now leads into Piazza
Santa Trinita.

PIAZZA SANTA TRINITA ★

A small piazza at the heart of a fashionable and elegant
district (the Via Tornabuoni ▲ *212* runs north from here). At
its center stands the COLUMN OF JUSTICE (see following page),
while around it stand handsome palaces. Tasteful lighting
makes it worth a visit after dark.
PALAZZO BARTOLINI-SALIMBENI ● *72.* (1 Piazza Santa
Trinita.) The palace was built by Baccio d'Agnolo
between 1517 and 1520 for the merchant
Giovanni Salimbeni and is very similar in design
to Raphael's Palazzo Pandolfini ▲ *240*. It was
not universally admired, and many considered
it too imitative of Roman architecture.
Carpere promptius quam imitari ("It is easier
to find fault than to imitate") was Baccio
d'Agnolo's touchy response. He had it
inscribed above the door.
A PRELUDE TO MANNERISM. It is a building of
tremendous character, a rare example of High
Renaissance palatial architecture. Earlier, more
rigid, architectural conventions were giving way to
a more experimental style, putting greater emphasis
on contrasting shapes and effects of light and shade.

SANTI APOSTOLI
Inside the church is a
precious 15th-century
silver and gilt carrier
for the holy fire that
is taken to the
Baptistery to set off
the *Scoppio del
carro* ● *47*.

▲ From Santa Trinita to the Cascine

The Column of Justice (below left) and the Palazzo Spini-Ferroni; (right) detail of the Palazzo Buondelmonti façade.

The Ponte Santa Trinita (above). The façade of the Palazzo Bartolini-Salimbeni (below).

THE COLUMN OF JUSTICE
A column from the Terme di Caracalla in Rome, erected to commemorate the Battle of Marciano (1554) in which Cosimo I defeated the Sienese. Francesco del Tadda made the porphyry statue of *Justice* in 1581.

Jean-Pierre Vieusseux and his Father (right).

There is a marked Mannerist tendency, with new features such as the niches on the façade. In the *cortile* are some fine *sgraffiti* ▲ *191* and a pretty loggietta with triple arcade.

PALAZZO BUONDELMONTI. The 15th-century façade at 2 Piazza Santa Trinita, perhaps by Baccio d'Agnolo, masks several dwellings from the 13th century owned by the Buondelmonti family.

THE GABINETTO VIEUSSEUX. From 1820 the famous literary and scientific circle founded by the Swiss Jean-Pierre Vieusseux (1779–1863) used to meet in the Palazzo Buondelmonti. Its members were linked with the then powerful current of Tuscan patriotism, and their cultural influence was immense. They began to publish a number of journals: *L'Antologia, La Nuova Antologia,* the *Giornale Agrario,* the *Archivio Storico Italiano,* with contributions from some of the best writers of the time. *L'Antologia,* with its message of moderate reform, appeared from 1821 to 1833 and involved some of the most famous figures of 19th-century Tuscan life, such as Gino Capponi, Raffaele Lambruschini, Cosimo Ridolfi and Niccolò Tommaseo.

THE EUROPEAN DIMENSION. The Gabinetto Vieusseux had close links with literary and political life in England, France, Germany, Switzerland and Belgium. In the words of Piero Bargellini, it was "a center of European culture". Vieusseux himself was an enormously influential figure and commanded great respect in the city. The grand duke obviously sensed competition, for in 1833 he banned *L'Antologia,* a relatively harmless publication. It was at this time that the Gabinetto moved to a new base in the shelter of the colonnades of the Palazzo Strozzi courtyard ▲ *208.*

PALAZZO SPINI-FERONI. When building began on this palace in 1289 the site was chosen for its strategic advantages; it stretches from the piazza to the PONTE SANTA TRINITA, which it once overlooked from a corner tower beside the river. The tower has now gone, demolished in 1824 to make way for traffic, and the palazzo underwent extensive restoration in the 19th century. Nevertheless, the impressive fortress-like construction is one of the largest medieval palaces to survive in Florence. It can be seen as it once was in a fresco by Ghirlandaio in the church of Santa Trinita, *Miracle of the Boy Brought back to Life.* Today the ground floor is occupied by luxury shops such as Ferragamo.

A FORGOTTEN SCULPTOR. In the entrance way, which has been carefully restored, is a remarkable bas-relief of *The Fall of the Titans* (1705) by the little-known artist Giuseppe Piamontini. He worked with Foggini on the Chapel of Andrea Corsini in the church of Santa Maria del Carmine ▲ *306.* Opposite the Palazzo Spini, at 1 Via Tornabuoni, is the PALAZZO GIANFIGLIAZZI, another grand medieval structure.

PONTE SANTA TRINITA

Via Tornabuoni leads almost immediately to the river and onto the graceful bridge (see facing page) decorated with two statues at either end. A bridge was first built across the Arno at this point in 1257, but several constructions were washed away by floods, the worst being in 1333. In 1557 Ammannati built a new bridge. He may have based his design on ideas from Michelangelo, for the same exquisite curve of the arches is seen on the Medici tombs in San Lorenzo ▲ *220*. The Ponte Santa Trinita was bombed by the Germans in 1944, and an identical replacement was built between 1954 and 1957.

THE CHURCH OF SANTA TRINITA ● *90*

The original church dates back to 1077, being the first in Florence of the Vallombrosan Order. It was substantially altered in the 13th century, probably by Nicola Pisano, who was famous for the pulpit in the Pisa Baptistery (1260), and then altered again in the 14th century. The façade was added from 1593 to 1594 by Bernardo Buontalenti.

THE VALLOMBROSAN ORDER. The abbey was at Vallombrosa, southwest of Florence. The monks were active in city life, both religious and civic, and sat on governing councils.

A MIRACULOUS CRUCIFIX. The founder of the order was St John (Giovanni) Gualberto, a Florentine of noble birth. His brother Ugo was murdered, and Giovanni determined to avenge his death. On Good Friday he and his companions, all armed, marched up the hill to San Miniato. They soon found the murderer, who begged for mercy in the name of Christ. Giovanni Gualberto pardoned him and went into San

INSPIRED ENGINEERING
The river bed was at its narrowest here.
The bridge

had very solid pillars but a fine superstructure to offer the least resistance to floods.

No doubt Ammannati also found such delicate lines pleasing. Dante is said to have first seen Beatrice Portinari at the Ponte Santa Trinita.

THE DESTRUCTION OF AUGUST 4, 1944
▲ *184*. The bridge served no strategic purpose. One-sixth of the original stones were recovered from the river bed and reused. The new *pietra forte* ■ *16* came from old quarries which were specially reopened in the Boboli Gardens. The head of the allegorical statue of *Spring*, by Pietro Francavilla, was not found until 1961. The other statues are by Giovanni Caccini (*Summer* and *Fall*) and Taddeo Landini (*Winter*); they were placed on the bridge for the marriage of Cosimo II to Maria Maddalena of Austria in 1608.

SIBYLS IN THE SASSETTI CHAPEL

A surprising feature taken directly from Greek mythology, these legendary prophets were incorporated into Christian imagery in the 15th century, backing up an attempt to create links between ancient Greece and Christianity. The philosopher Marsilio Ficino was particularly keen to find ways of fitting the Greek and Christian worlds together, and he was responsible for resuscitating the sibyls. They vary in number and can be as many as twelve.

Detail (below) from Ghirlandaio's *Miracle of the Boy Brought back to Life* in the church of Santa Trinita (above right).

Miniato to pray before a crucifix that is now in the FICOZZI CHAPEL of Santa Trinita. Legend has it that the Christ nodded his head in thanks for his mercy. He became a Benedictine monk and in 1012 founded the Vallombrosan Order.

THE SASSETTI CHAPEL. The second chapel to the right of the the chancel was decorated by Domenico Ghirlandaio. He began work on the *Scenes from the Life of Saint Francis* in 1483. The banker Francesco Sassetti, having just finished building himself a splendid villa at Montughi, decided to fund the decoration of a small chapel that would do his vast fortune justice and would equal the

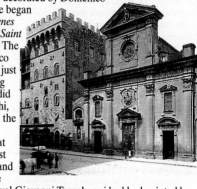

one which his rival Giovanni Tornabuoni had had painted by Ghirlandaio at Santa Maria sopra Minerva in Rome. His first choice for the family chapel and tombs was Santa Maria Novella, which was very popular with good families, but difficulties arose and caused him to fall back on his local church, Santa Trinita. Sassetti's humanism is clearly reflected in Ghirlandaio's frescoes. The decoration of the chapel is elaborate and has a pagan aura. Ornamental bands border the frescoes, directly inspired from Roman bas-relief work. The black porphyry sarcophagi of Sassetti and his wife, thought to be by Giuliano da Sangallo, have Latin inscriptions surrounded by bucranes, (sculpted ox-skulls also borrowed from antiquity). And above in the vault are painted four sibyls.

AN INJUDICIOUS BANKER. Francesco Sassetti was put in charge of the Medici companies by Cosimo il Vecchio, and was confirmed in his duties by Piero il Gottoso and Lorenzo il Magnifico ● *36*. He did not deserve such confidence and was responsible for the financial difficulties of the Medici banking empire. He chose incompetent men to

THE "ADORATION OF
THE SHEPHERDS"
Antiquity and
Christianity are
deliberately united in
Ghirlandaio's
painting with a
sarcophagus bearing
a prophetic
inscription at its
center.

THE TREASURES OF
SANTA TRINITA
There are many
points of interest to
be seen in the church.
Inside the Strozzi
Chapel, first on
the left, is an
Annunciation in the
gleaming colors of
Jacopo da Empoli
(1603). Another
Annunciation, by
Bicci di Lorenzo, is in
the Davanzati
Chapel, third on the
left, and in the chapel
beyond the left is his
fresco of *Saint John
Gualberto with the
Vallombrosian Saints*.
A wooden statue of
Mary Magdalene is
usually kept in the
fifth chapel on the
left. It was begun in
1464 by a pupil of
Donatello, Desiderio
da Settignano, and
was finished in 1455
by Benedetto da
Maiano.

run parts of the business and failed to keep them in check. A
Portinari put in charge in Bruges lent vast sums of money to
Charles the Bold, the insolvent duke of Burgundy.

SOCIETY PORTRAITS. When painting the fresco of *Saint Francis
Receiving the Rule of the Order from Pope Honorius*,
Ghirlandaio slipped the portraits of some eminent Florentine
contemporaries into the scene. It is set in the Piazza della
Signoria, with the Loggia dei Lanzi ▲ *144* at the center.
Lorenzo il Magnifico is on the right, with Sassetti to his left.
A Mannerist staircase rises into the foreground being climbed
by Angelo Poliziano ● *39*, tutor to Lorenzo's sons who are
with him: next to Poliziano is Giuliano, the future duke of
Nemours, next is Piero who succeeded his father, and then
Giovanni, who became Pope Leo X. Last in the line are Luigi
Pulci and Matteo Franco, both poets and close friends of
Lorenzo. Another fresco, *Miracle of the Boy Brought
back to Life*, shows the Palazzo Spini-Ferroni as it
once was, Santa Trinita before Buontalenti's façade
was added and the old Ponte Santa Trinita, looking
toward the Oltrarno.

LORENZO MONACO. Chapels were not usually
entirely frescoed early in the 15th century, but such
is the case of the BARTOLINI SALIMBENI CHAPEL,
decorated by Lorenzo Monaco around 1423. The
grille dates from a century later. Born in Siena in
1370, Lorenzo Monaco, Fra Angelico's teacher,
made his career in Florence, where he entered the
Camaldolensian Order in 1390. At first he

specialized in illuminating manuscripts: his frescoes
use bright colors reminiscent of illumination. He is a late
exponent of the Italian Gothic style, and it is interesting to
compare these frescoes with those by Masaccio in Santa
Maria del Carmine ▲ *306*, painted only a few years later.

FORGIVENESS. In the FICOZZI CHAPEL, the first on the right, is
the wooden crucifix of St John Gualberto ▲ *321*. It belonged
to a brotherhood called the Compagnia dei Bianchi, who in

*The Tomb of Cardinal
Federighi* (above) is
an exceptionally fine
work by Luca della
Robbia from 1455.

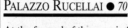
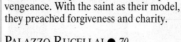

A window in the Palazzo Rucellai (below). San Pancrazio, now the Museo Marini (center left). The handsome Loggia dei Rucellai (center right).

MARINO MARINI
Worked as a painter before becoming more interested in sculpture through his love of antiquity, particularly Greek and Etruscan works. He was a figurative sculptor, and his work, such as *Small Pomona* (top right), is simple and bold. He is best known for his pieces on the theme of horse and rider in the series *Cavalieri* begun in 1936. Among his paintings are portraits of Stravinsky and Henry Miller.

1399 numbered forty thousand, and whose mission was to put an end to acts of personal vengeance. With the saint as their model, they preached forgiveness and charity.

PALAZZO RUCELLAI ● 70

At the far end of the nave in Santa Trinita, on the right, is a door leading out into Via del Parione. At number 7 there is a view into a beautiful colonnaded courtyard. The building belongs to the Law Faculty. Immediately after it, turn right under an arch and into a narrow street which leads to the Via del Purgatorio. Then turn left to reach a small piazza at the junction of the Via della Vigna Nuova, with the LOGGIA DEI RUCELLAI on the right and the PALAZZO RUCELLAI opposite. The narrow, busy Via della Vigna Nuova, dates back to the 13th century, when it acquired its name from the vines that once grew here. Florence in the Middle Ages was a city full of gardens, many of them belonging to the convents and palaces.

THE USEFUL LOGGIA. The Loggia dei Rucellai, designed by Alberti 1463–6, is today enclosed with glass. During the 15th century there were twenty-six such loggias in the city of Florence, each built by noble families near their palaces. They served as a shelter for the watching of organized entertainments, such as jousting or dancing; they were also used for family meetings and for marriage negotiations; and, most importantly, the local people were invited here to eat and drink in celebration of family weddings and christenings.

ULTIMATE ELEGANCE. The palace itself was built for the rich wool merchant Giovanni Rucellai between 1446 and 1458 by Bernardo Rossellino (1409–64) to plans by Leon Battista Alberti (1404–72) ● 39. It still belongs to descendants of the family. The extremely fine façade was quite unlike the usual Florentine palaces of the period. Among the features which were introduced in Alberti's design were the decorative pilasters on the upper stories. Following classical convention, he put capitals of the Doric order on the ground florr, while those of the top story are of the Corinthian. Logically the middle-story pilasters should have had Ionic capitals, but Alberti felt that classical discipline should not rule out creativity, and so he designed his

Ponte alla Carraia seen from the Lungarno Corsini (right).

own, based on the Corinthian. It is interesting to compare this palace with the famous Palazzo Medici ● 68, ▲ 224. The plain bands of stone between the stories were replaced by carved friezes of heraldic emblems. Alberti also had an abhorrence for the Medici rusticated stone. In his work *De Re Aedificatoria* he wrote "only the house of a tyrant can look like a fortress". In his view, palaces should be "open to the world outside, prettily decorated, finely proportioned and elegant, rather than exuding pomposity and arrogance". There is a PHOTOGRAPHY MUSEUM on the ground floor.

THE MUSEO MARINI ★. Take the Via dei Palchetti on the left side of the palace, and then turn right into the Via dei Federighi. In the PIAZZA SAN PANCRAZIO is a very old church of the same name, which was rebuilt in 1752, deconsecrated in the 19th century and is now a sculpture museum and exhibition hall. Marino Marini left these pieces of his work to the city. He and Giacomo Manzu were two of Italy's finest 20th-century sculptors.

CAPPELLA DI SAN SEPOLCRO ★. A chapel set into the church but entered at 18 Via della Spada and open on Saturday afternoons. Alberti redesigned the chapel completely in 1467 to house the marble tomb of "the Holy Sepulcher", a *tempietto* (miniature temple). It is the funerary monument of the Rucellai family. Inside is a block of stone which is said to be the one the angel sat on in Christ's tomb when announcing the Resurrection to Mary. Retrace the route back to the Via del Purgatorio, then turn right into the Via del Parioncino, before crossing over the Via del Parione to reach the Lungarno Corsini.

THE PALAZZO CORSINI ● 75

The palace is vast and imposing, with façades on both the Lungarno Corsini and the Via del Parione (the entrance is here, but visits are by appointment only). The site, then occupied by several houses, was acquired in 1649 by Maria Maddalena Macchiavelli, the wealthy heiress and wife of Filippo Corsini. The Corsini family is one of the grandest in the city of Florence.

POWER AND INFLUENCE. Neri Corsini, who came from Siena, settled in Florence in about 1270. The family fortunes flourished, and a number of his descendants held important positions in the republic. Filippo Corsini was made Count Palatine by Emperor Charles IV in 1371, while in 1730 Cardinal Lorenzo Corsini became Pope Clement XII. During the 19th century a distant descendant, Neri Corsini (1805–59), became one

THE RUCELLAI CHAPEL
Giovanni Rucellai commissioned his funerary monument to be a model of the Sanctuary of the Holy Sepulcher in Jerusalem. But Alberti, rather than imitating its Gothic style, preferred to imagine what it had looked like when it was originally built for the Emperor Constantine. He based his design on the Baptistery ▲ 132, which was then thought to be a building from the late Roman period.

DIPLOMATIC MARRIAGES
A curious motif of three rings interlinked can be seen in the window decoration of the Palazzo Rucellai. It was one of the emblems of the Medici family. Marriage was often the way in which to cement an alliance, and in 1461 Bernardo Rucellai was married to Nannina de' Medici, one of the sisters of Lorenzo il Magnifico.

Ponte alla Carraia (below).

PALAZZO CORSINI
On the ceiling of the Salone del Trono is the *Apotheosis of the Corsini Family* by Antonio Domenico Gabbiani. The statues on the grand

staircase were based on classical models. There is also a spiral staircase built in 1679 by Pier Francesco Silvani, which is one of the finest Baroque stairways in Florence. The Palazzo Corsini (below).

of the leaders of the Florentine liberals: in 1848 he became a minister, but was forced to flee to the Piedmont when Leopold II regained power. When another revolution threatened in 1856, Leopold offered to hand over power to the famous exile, but Corsini declined.

A BAROQUE PALACE. It was the Marchese Filippo Corsini who commissioned this building. He was a friend of Cosimo III de' Medici and a great traveler in his youth: his accounts of his journeys still survive. Pier Francesco Silvani (1620–85) and Antonio Ferri were the architects. The palace was never completed: it was to have extended further to the east. Curiously, the Corsini family never lived here, since they had another palace in the Prato. The huge edifice was therefore used for entertaining and subsequently as a picture gallery.

AN EXTRAVAGANT INTERIOR. The monumental staircase which was designed by Antonio Ferri was installed in about 1690. Upstairs is the Salone del Trono, the magnificent main hall with its ceiling painted by Antonio Domenico Gabbiani, and the gallery of paintings belonging to the family, mainly works from the 15th and 18th centuries. It is the most important private collection in the city, and has long been considered a privilege to visit (see facing page).

LUNGARNO CORSINI

There are some other fine palaces along the lungarno between the Ponte alla Carraia and the Ponte Santa Trinita.
PALAZZO GIANFIGLIAZZI. Number 4, a 15th-century palace, was where the countess of Albany, widow of Charles Stuart

(Bonnie Prince Charlie), received famous writers from all over Europe at her salon. Among the famous names whom she entertained were Alfieri, Foscolo, Shelley, Byron, Stendhal, Chateaubriand, and Von Platen.

PALAZZO MASETTI. This palazzo at 2 Lungarno Corsini was built in the 14th century and modified by Gherardo Silvani in the 17th century. Vittorio Alfieri (1749–1803) died here. Today it houses the British Consulate.

VITTORIO ALFIERI. Having spent his youth traveling across Europe in search of romantic adventure, Alfieri began to write in 1775 and had his first tragedy, *Cleopatra*, performed in Turin in the same year. Two years later, in Florence, he met Louisa of Stolberg, countess of Albany. They fell in love and remained together until his death. They spent much time in Paris, but in 1792 fled from the Revolution, first to England and then back to Florence, where they then remained. Alfieri is considered to be one of Italy's greatest poets and playwrights, doing much to inspire the romantic climate of the Risorgimento. He is buried in Santa Croce ▲ *254*, and when Stendhal came to Florence in 1811, his first visit was to Alfieri's tomb.

THE CORSINI GALLERY
Sophia, wife of the novelist Nathaniel Hawthorne, visited the Palazzo Corsini with friends in 1848. She described the visit in *Notes in England and Italy*: "In one of the saloons we saw a vase of marvelous beauty of design and execution

– bronze, about two feet high. I exclaimed that it must be by Benvenuto Cellini, and the custode said it was so. It represents, in bas-relief, the triumph of Bacchus. Ada tried to draw it on the spot, but in the midst the custode told her she must not do it, for it was forbidden. I suppose the Prince Corsini is afraid that some artist will attempt to imitate it, and then he would not have the only one in the world."

PONTE ALLA CARRAIA

At the far end of the Lungarno Corsini is the PIAZZA CARLO GOLDONI, a major road junction from which the Ponte alla

Carraia leads to the Oltrarno.
A COLORFUL HISTORY. It is the second-oldest bridge in the city, after the Ponte Vecchio, and dates from 1218. In the Middle Ages there was a pillory on the bridge, but it was also a place where plays were performed. Enormous crowds would gather to watch spectacles taking place on the river, and in 1304, during the celebrations of *Calendimaggio* (May) ● *50*, the overloaded bridge collapsed.

AROUND OGNISSANTI

The VIA DEI FOSSI, which leads from the Piazza Goldoni, takes its name from ditches that used to be here in the Middle Ages. The Benedictines occupied this area, then outside the

Grotto in the Palazzo Corsini (above).

279

SHOCK OF THE NEW
The church of
Ognissanti was built
between 1252 and
1255, but much

altered in the 17th
and 18th centuries.
Only the campanile
retains its original
appearance. The
façade was put up in
1637 by Matteo
Nigetti (c. 1560–
1649). It was one of
the very first Baroque
designs to be seen in
Florence, and
contemporaries
found it entirely
"incorrect". It broke
all the rules and flew
in the face of Tuscan
tradition.

The *Last Supper* by
Ghirlandaio (below),
dated 1480, is in a
room off the lovely
cloister whose
entrance is to the left
of the church of
Ognissanti, at
number 42.

city walls, from the 11th century onwards, and gradually
turned it into a center of industry. A number of fast-running
streams, like the Sepiole and the Mugnone, ran down to the
Arno, providing water and power to be used for important
processes in the manufacture of wool ▲ *202*. Another
religious order expert in the work, the *umiliati*, settled in the
area from the mid-13th century. The processes of carding,
weaving and dyeing were all carried out in this suburb, vital to
the trade that was the foundation of Florence's rapidly
increasing wealth. With a population of ten thousand, it was
one of the principal Italian cities at this time.

LISIO, TESSUTI D'ARTE. A thriving
business at 45r Via dei Fossi,
founded in 1906, specializes in
reproducing old fabrics and
making costumes, mostly
for historical dramas.
The best-selling fabric is
a brocade based on
Botticelli's *Primavera*.

**THE CHURCH OF SAN
PAOLINO.** Turn left
into the Via Spada to
reach a piazza, on the
left, where San Paolino
stands. It is decorated in
the Baroque style.

BORGO OGNISSANTI

To reach the church of Ognissanti
turn right into the Via del Porcellana and
then left into the lively and unpretentious Borgo
Ognissanti.

THE SAN GIOVANNI DI DIO HOSPITAL. Just at the corner of the
Via del Porcellana stands what was a hospital founded by the
Vespucci family in 1382. The hospital church, next door, was
built between 1702 and 1713 by Carlo Andrea Marcellini. The
complex includes the Vespucci house, birthplace of Amerigo
Vespucci. There is a splendid entrance hall.

CASA GALLERIA ● *93*. One of the best designs in Florence in
the Italian Art Nouveau, or *Liberty*, style is the house at
number 26. It was designed by Giovanni Michelazzi
(1879–1920) and has a delightfully original façade with large
windows.

PIAZZA OGNISSANTI. Standing on the piazza is the lovely
PALAZZO LENZI QUARATESI, a 15th-century building restored
in 1887. It has *sgraffiti* ▲ *191* decorations and a corbeled
façade on the Borgo Ognissanti. The palazzo houses the
French Consulate, French Institute and bookshop.

LUNGARNO AMERIGO VESPUCCI. The Piazza Ognissanti is bordered by the river and a stretch of the lungarno named after an Italian famous for his voyages, although it seems possible they were a complete invention. Amerigo Vespucci (1454–1512) had America named after him although he certainly did not discover it. He was a businessman employed in an outpost of the Medici financial empire in Seville. The story of his discoveries is based on two letters he wrote, *Mondus Novus* and *Quatuor navigationes*, describing in accomplished style and vivid detail his discovery of the New World. The letters enjoyed great popularity early in the 16th century and inspired the cartographer Waldseemüller to publish his own version of Vespucci's accounts in 1507, in which he gave the new continent discovered by Christopher Columbus the name of America.

THE CHURCH OF OGNISSANTI

IMPORTATION OF SKILLED WORKERS. The church of "all saints" was attached to the convent of the *umiliati*. In 1239 the republic's governing council had brought monks of this order to Florence from Lombardy. They were specialists in the manufacture of wool ▲ *202* and were to work alongside the Benedictines to help the development of Florence's growing industry. The city leased them land near the Arno, where they could live and build workshops. From the 14th century onwards the *umiliati* diminished in importance, and finally in 1561 their convent and the church of Ognissanti were taken over by the Franciscans from San Salvatore al Monte ▲ *319*.

THE VESPUCCIS IMMORTALIZED. The second chapel on the right is dedicated to the Vespucci family with a fresco by Domenico del Ghirlandaio, the *Madonna of Mercy* (1470). Under her cloak she shelters members of the family, among whom is thought to be Amerigo – the young man with dark hair directly on her right. The young woman beneath her left hand seems to be Simonetta Vespucci, the mistress of Giuliano de' Medici.

AN UNTIMELY DEATH. Simonetta Vespucci was so beautiful that for many of the poets of the time she represented a feminine ideal. She came into contact with the businessmen who handled the Medici financial affairs in 1468, but the details of her liaison with Giuliano de' Medici, Lorenzo's brother, remain unknown. She died of tuberculosis at the age of twenty-three.

"SAINT AUGUSTINE" BY BOTTICELLI
This is a major work by the artist, dating from 1480, which showed the saint in a new light. Instead of the usual studious pose, he has an intense expression and looks worn out with intellectual effort. The painting is ahead of its time, anticipating Leonardo da Vinci's preoccupation with facial expression. It is all the more impressive for being placed opposite Ghirlandaio's *Saint Jerome*, which has a more subdued realism. Botticelli personally despised such lukewarm neutrality.

The interior of Ognissanti (above).

AERIAL VIEW OF THE CASCINE PARK
The plan (right) shows the racecourses and other features. The park lies between the Arno and the Mugnone rivers.

A window (below left) from the Villa Favart (bottom), now used by a department of the university. The Casa Galleria (below right), a fine example of the *Liberty* style, stands on the Borgo Ognissanti.

HUMANISM AND THE CHURCH.
The church eventually accepted the exchange of ideas with humanists, and both St Augustine and St Jerome then came to be considered as key Christian figures and philosophers. The two frescoes *Saint Augustine* by Botticelli and *Saint Jerome* by Ghirlandaio give very different impressions of how these great men interpreted the scriptures. St Jerome is shown as dedicated and studious, while St Augustine is inspired, and surrounded by symbols of humanism such as an astrolabe and a book of theorems by Pythagoras.

CONVENT AND CLOISTER. The convent was founded in about 1251 but underwent many alterations up until the 16th century, so there is quite a mixture of styles. At its center is a wonderfully calm CLOISTER decorated with frescoes of the *Life of Saint Francis*, painted by Ligozzi and Giovanni di San Giovanni between 1616 and 1625.

AROUND THE PRATO

A FASHIONABLE DISTRICT. The *prato* (meadow) was annexed by Florence in 1279 and used for livestock and associated trades. With the major urban developments of the 19th century, it was transformed into a residential area. It lies at the far end of the Borgo Ognissanti.

FASHIONABLE PRATO
This exclusive district lying along the Arno was redeveloped during the 19th century. But the rest of the area never attained the prestige or prices that were anticipated by its developers, although there are some elegant residences to be found on the larger streets. Today Prato's population covers the whole social scale. Businesses are based here too, mainly wholesale and skilled trades, and Prato also has its fair share of prostitutes.

VILLA FAVART ● 93. Giuseppe Poggi took his inspiration from Florentine Mannerism when designing the villa in 1847. It is one of the most elegant neo-classical buildings in the whole city (1 Via Curtatone).

THE PALAZZO CALCAGNINI-ARESE. Poggi built the palazzo, now the United States Consulate, in 1860. It stands on the corner of the Lungarno Vespucci and the Corso Italia.

THE PALAZZETTO OF THE SCULPTOR IGNAZIO VILLA. At the other end of the Via Curtatone, at the junction of the Via Santa Lucia and the Prato, is a house dating from 1850, a unique example of a neo-Gothic palazzo built on the corner of a street. It was designed by Villa himself.

A HISTORIC SHED. Turning down the Prato, away from the city center and just before the PALAZZO CORSINI AL PRATO (see facing page), there is a

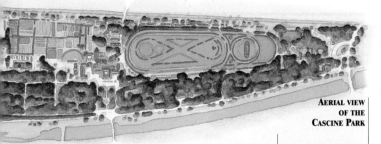

strange-looking building at number 42. It is three stories high with wooden doors, and is the shed in which the cart (*carro*) for the Easter festival of the *Scoppio del carro* is kept ● 47.

THE AMERICAN CHURCH. In the Via Rucellai, at numbers 9–13, is the church of St James, which was built in the neo-Gothic style by Riccardo Mazzanti (1850–1910) and associates between 1908 and 1911.

THE PALAZZO DEGLI ORTI ORICELLARI. The palace at 85 Via della Scala dates from the 16th century and was completely redesigned by Silvani around 1679. It stands in a private garden that goes back to Renaissance times, but which was laid out in the 19th century by Cambray-Digny. In it is a huge statue of *Polyphemus* by Antonio Novelli, from 1650, which is set on a structure of brick. In the 16th century learned gatherings were held in the palace gardens, and attended by Machiavelli.

TEATRO COMUNALE. The principal site for the "Maggio musicale", Florence's music festival, May to July, is the theater at 12–16 Corso Italia. It was designed by Telemaco Bonaiuti in 1862, and the interior was altered in 1961.

THE "MAGGIO MUSICALE". The music festival began in 1931 and is one of the oldest to be held anywhere in Europe. A key feature from the outset was the commissioning of set designs from artists. Giorgio de Chirico's designs for Bellini's *I Puritani* caused a great public scandal, but the policy has done much to encourage interaction between the arts. The 1933 festival had another novelty: Max Reinhardt's production of *A Midsummer Night's Dream* in the Boboli Gardens. Many famous artists have been involved in the "Maggio musicale", including Kokoschka, Severini, Savinio and Soffici.

OPERA AT ITS BEST. The 1953 May festival saw a revival of Cherubini's *Medea* with Maria Callas performing in the title role and conducted by Vittorio Gui, founder of the festival. Some of the great names of the time took part that year: Von Karajan, Böhm, De Sabata, and Furtwängler. In 1958 Pabst directed a production of Verdi's *Il Forza del destino*, which was conducted by Dimitri Mitropoulos. At the

PALAZZO CORSINI AL PRATO
The 16th-century palace, at number 58 on the Prato, has a majestic loggia by Bernardo Buontalenti dating from around 1594. Gherardo Silvani designed the lovely garden. During the 19th century the palazzo was entirely renovated, with a new façade by Ulisse Faldi (1860). A bank now occupies part of the building.

PORTA AL PRATO
Il Prato ends at a 14th-century gate which was originally part of the third circle of city walls.

Via della Regina in the Cascine (above), fashionable at the turn of the century.

283

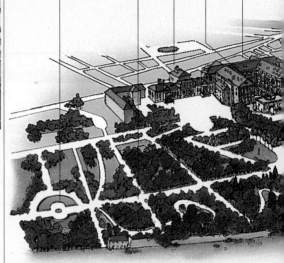

ISOLOTTO   VIOTTOLONE   PALAZZINA DELLA MERIDIANA   ARTICHOKE FOUNTAIN   PALAZZO PITTI

A PRIVATE PASSAGE
The elegant portico of Santa Felicita supports the Corridoio Vasariano as it makes its way from the Palazzo Vecchio to the Palazzo Pitti. In the piazza is a column recording a battle between Catholics and Patarines.

SANTA FELICITA
Between 1736 and 1739 the interior was redesigned by Ferdinando Ruggieri (c. 1691–1741) in strictly classical style, although this was the Baroque period. The pilasters, window frames, arches and architraves are of blue-gray *pietra serena* ■ *16* that contrasts with the white walls, not unlike some of Brunelleschi's work. The nave (above) is seen from the gallery in the Corridoio Vasariano, where the Medicis could attend mass unseen.

The esplanade in front of the Palazzo Pitti (right).

The Ponte Vecchio crosses over the river away from the city center to the Oltrarno. From here take the Via Guicciardini that leads to the Piazza Santa Felicita, on the left. The Corridoio Vasariano ▲ *175* runs in front of the church and is attached to it.

THE CHURCH OF SANTA FELICITA ★

AN EARLY CHRISTIAN SANCTUARY. The first church to stand on this site was built during the 4th century on a Christian burial ground. It stood well outside the city, for the Roman town did not extend as far as this bank of the Arno. The church was rebuilt in the 11th and 14th centuries. When the grand dukes took up residence in the Palazzo Pitti, it was here that they attended mass by using their own safe route along the Corridoio Vasariano, which passes above the portico.

MANNERIST STYLE. The CAPPONI CHAPEL, first on the right, was built by Brunelleschi around 1410. It once had a cupola on which he is said to have later based his design for the Duomo ▲ *130*. It was later destroyed during 18th-century rebuilding work. The chapel was decorated from 1525 to 1528 by Jacopo da

Pontormo (1494–1557). There are four tondos of the Evangelists in the pendentives of the cupola, an airy fresco of the *Annunciation*, and his celebrated *Deposition* above the altar, which is considered to be one of the finest paintings of the period. It is a key early Mannerist work. The vivid colors show little concern for realism and, unlike the Tuscan masters

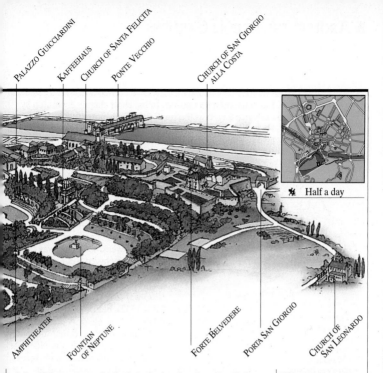

🐾 Half a day

of the 15th century, who had worked so hard to give their paintings depth, Pontormo shows no such interest.

VASARI UNIMPRESSED. Expressing his poor opinion of the work, Vasari found it "lacking areas of shade, and painted in such pale, flat colors that any variations in light are almost indistinguishable, and any sense of depth is lost". He went further, accusing Pontormo of having been inspired by Dürer prints. This was to imply that he had abandoned the Tuscan style, which was built on harmony and carefully constructed composition, for the more troubled German Gothic style. Although Pontormo was very much influenced by Dürer, this is not a copy of German art; the sharp, light colors and subtle rhythms are quite original. Michelangelo, unlike Vasari, greatly admired Pontormo's use of color. Indeed, he thought at one point of asking Pontormo to reproduce his own drawings in color.

PONTORMO'S STRANGE PERSONALITY. According to Vasari, Pontormo's house was like a wild beast's lair in which he lurked, eccentric and unsociable. He was extremely neurotic, locking himself away and even drawing up the wooden steps to his room when he did not want to be disturbed. He only worked when he felt like it, but spent the last ten years of his life painting a series of frescoes in the chancel of San Lorenzo, hoping to be considered as great as Michelangelo. Sadly, the frescoes were destroyed in the 18th century. One of his most characteristic works is the strange and atmospheric *Supper at Emmaus*, painted in 1525. It was originally intended for the Certosa del Galluzzo ▲ *334*, but the fresco is now in the Uffizi.

"DEPOSITION FROM THE CROSS"
An extraordinary work by Jacopo da Pontormo from 1528. It is a landmark of early Florentine Mannerism; the composition is complex and intense, the colors sharp and pale. The painting is in the Capponi Chapel in Santa Felicita.

PALAZZO PITTI
The Piazza Pitti (below), an engraving by Buontalenti. The façade onto the

gardens (detail, below right) includes a courtyard, enclosed on the lower level. This Mannerist creation was designed by Ammannati. The capitals of the columns follow the classical order, with Tuscan at the bottom, going up to Ionic above and then Corinthian. However, the columns are formed differently on each level. Those at the bottom consist of rings of stone set one on top of the other. On the first story up these are alternated with projecting square blocks, contrasting with the curves of the Ionic capitals, and on the top story these projecting blocks are rounded. The stones of the columns blend with those of the façade at each level, which goes against the classical rule that architectural elements should be clearly distinguishable.

On the facing page: the *Artichoke Fountain* (top) with courtyard behind; the palace (center) seen from the amphitheater in the Boboli Gardens.

FRANCESCO GUICCIARDINI. In the choir chapel, decorated by Ludovico Cigoli, is the tomb of a great Florentine historian. He was born in 1483 and began his career as a lawyer. In 1511 he was sent as ambassador to the court of King Ferdinand of Spain. He then entered the service of Pope Leo X, who made him governor of Modena, Reggio, Parma and finally Bologna. Following the sack of Rome, Guicciardini found himself unemployed. He therefore took service under Alessandro de' Medici, which lasted until 1537, when this weak nobleman was murdered by his cousin Lorenzaccio ● *36*. He then decided to retire to his property at Arcetri and wrote a *History of Italy* (covering the years 1494–1532), before dying in 1540.

A PESSIMISTIC OUTLOOK. While Machiavelli ● *39* believed that Italy could be united, Guicciardini took a rather more dismal view, seeing nothing but hypocrisy and deceit. He describes with great insight and clarity the passions, intrigues and entanglements that characterized the period, and his prose is among the finest in the language.

PALAZZO PITTI

Continue along the Via Guiccardini, past the **PALAZZO GUICCIARDINI**, which was restored in the 17th century. On the site of number 18 once stood the house of Machiavelli.

A VAST FAÇADE. The Palazzo Pitti, its façade over 670 feet long, is undoubtedly the grandest of all Renaissance palaces. It stands on slightly raised ground, which renders it still more impressive. The construction took place in several distinct phases. In 1457 the merchant Luca Pitti commissioned a palace; this initial residence now forms only the middle seven bays. The plans, thought have been drawn up by Brunelleschi, were for a square structure with three doorways on the ground floor and two rows of seven windows above. Brunelleschi seems to have first offered the design to Cosimo I, who refused it as being too ostentatious.

FROM PITTI TO MEDICI. It is said that Brunelleschi, in a fit of great pique, then offered his designs to Luca Pitti, who was absolutely delighted for a chance to get one over on his business rival. Although it was still unfinished when Pitti died in 1472, the palace was already

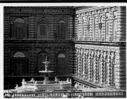

being greatly admired for its size and fine proportions. In 1549 it was bought by Eleanora of Toledo, the wife of Cosimo I, and Ammannati was brought in to enlarge the building. He created a magnificent CORTILE opening onto the garden. In 1620 another campaign of building work was begun by Giulio Parigi, which would triple the length of the façade, to be completed some twenty years later by Alfonso Parigi the Younger. For three centuries the palace was the residence of the grand dukes of Tuscany and, at the time of Napoleon ● *32*, of Elisa Bacciochi. King Victor Emmanuel also lived in the palace during Florence's brief period as the capital of Italy.

A WEALTH OF ART. The palace is full of the most fabulous works of art: there are no fewer than eight museums and collections in all, with works from the 16th and 17th centuries being the best represented. The GALLERIA PALATINA is the major gallery, containing the collection that once belonged to the grand dukes of Tuscany. These paintings, which date from the Renaissance and

Baroque periods, have been on show to the public since 1828. They are presented in a magnificent but rather disorganized manner; not much attempt has been made to arrange the paintings according to period or country. It is of little consequence, however, and a visit to the gallery is still highly recommended. Apart from the many extremely famous works on display, there are also painters and movements to be seen here that are poorly represented in the Uffizi Gallery ▲ *153*: Titian and Andrea del Sarto, for example, and above all the 16th- and 17th-century Florentine painters such as Cigoli, Carlo Dolci, Santi di Tito, Salvatore Rosa, Volterrano and Giovanni di San Giovanni.

PRE-ROMANTIC SPIRIT. The SALA DI PSICHE is given over to the work of Salvatore Rosa (1615–73), a Neapolitan artist who spent ten years in Florence. His paintings, mainly battle scenes and landscapes,

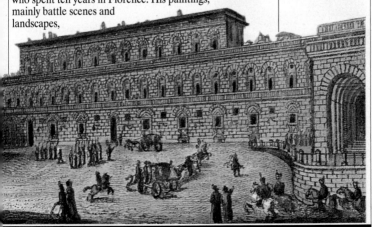

THE ART OF RAPHAEL
La Donna Velata
(above) dates from
1516. It is clear that
Raphael had studied
the Venetians from
his subtly glowing
colors and the
delicate texture of the
young woman's face.
According to Vasari,
she was Raphael's
mistress. Below,
*Portrait of Agnolo
Doni.*

anticipated the Romantic mood and made a great
impression in Florence. The landscapes have the
dreamlike quality that was to become such a
feature of European Romantic painting from the
late 18th century.

SICKLY SWEET PIETY. The work of Carlo Dolci
(1616–86) veers from extremely good to very bad.
When he was young he painted some fine
portraits, a number of which can be seen on
display in the SALA DI VENERE. But the
commissions more often went to the
Flemish court painter Joost Susterman,
who was famous for his *Portrait of
Galileo*, among others. When Dolci
turned his talents to religious
painting, his work quickly deteriorated. He
now started to produce paintings of
exaggerated piety, mostly of saints in ecstasy
like the *Saint Rose of Lima* in the SALA DI
SATURNO. Whatever their merits, his paintings
were in considerable demand. Grand Duke
Cosimo III, part of the weak and ineffective
tail-end of the Medici dynasty, liked them
especially.

SOBER CLASSICISM. By the time Santi di Tito
(1536–1603) began painting, Mannerism had
become a rather stale convention. Time spent in
Rome showed him new possibilities of
refinement and elegance, but he soon
adopted the classical models that were
dominant in the early 16th century, the
style laid down by Raphael.

EARLY BAROQUE. Ludovico Cardi, a painter
and architect known also as "Cigoli"
(1550–1613), was the creator of a number
of the famous Medici spectacles. His
paintings are very dramatic, employing
techniques of light and shade that can
now be recognized as the first signs of
an emerging Baroque style. *Ecce Homo*
in the SALA DI ULISSE is a very good
example.

A VEILED SENSUALITY. Francesco Furini
(1600–46) was a
priest in the
parish of San
Ansano in
Mugello. He had
a wealthy
clientèle which
was very partial
to his langorous
female nudes.
These paintings
had little in
common with the
current
disciplines of
Tuscan realism.

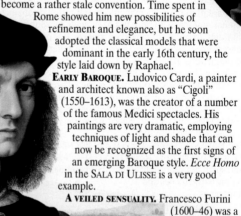

His work is an unusual and interesting mixture of idealism and high-class eroticism which went down well with his rich patrons. In the SALA DI ULISSE is an oval painting, *Faith* by Furini. The mellow tones, which had been learned from Leonardo da Vinci, are also a characteristic of this artist.

YOUNG GENIUS OF THE RENAISSANCE. The Galleria Palatina is particularly well known for its paintings by Raphael. Raffaello Sanzio (1483–1520) was born in Urbino. He was a pupil of Pietro di Cristoforo Vannucci, "il Perugino", and worked in Florence 1504–8, returning frequently to Umbria where he was also working at Perugia. He learned a great deal from Florentine art in these early years, especially the work of Leonardo da Vinci, Michelangelo and Fra Bartolommeo. Da Vinci's influence is quite obvious in a painting in the SALA DI SATURNO, the *Madonna del Granduca* (1504), owned and much loved by Grand Duke Ferdinando III.

SUCCESS IN ROME. In 1508 Raphael was invited to Rome by Pope Julius II. His career took off, and he painted many works including frescoes in the Vatican. *The Madonna della Seggiola* (of the chair), in the Sala di Saturno, dates from this period. The simple, naturalistic style that had been seen in Florence now gained a Roman sophistication. Raphael was a gifted portraitist, as can be seen from those of *Agnolo* and *Maddalena Doni*, painted in about 1506, also in the Sala di Saturno, and above all the painting of a young woman, *La Donna Velata* (c. 1516), which is hanging in the SALA DI GIOVE. When this is compared with the earlier portraits, the development of his style is evident, both in the way he handles colors, much more in the style of Titian, and in the sense of depth that he achieves.

FAMILY TREASURES. The Palazzo Pitti contains a number of other collections which are well worth visiting, although it is frustrating that they are often temporarily closed. The MUSEO DEGLI ARGENTI contains not only silverware, as its name suggests, but all kinds of beautiful things, mostly the precious possessions of the Medici family. It is set out on the ground floor and mezzanine, and four of the lower rooms are decorated with remarkably attractive 17th-century frescoes. There are examples of household silver and gold

Above, *Death of Lucretia* by Filippino Lippi. Center left, Raphael's *Madonna della Seggiola* (1512).

THE ART OF TITIAN
Portrait of a Gentleman (below) is one of the masterpieces of Venetian portraiture. He was far less concerned than the Florentine artists with the disciplines of draftsmanship seen, for instance, in Raphael's two *Doni* portraits painted while he was working in Florence. Titian allowed the painting to take its own shape. As a result his portraits are much more subtle and deft. Raphael's work came to have something of this same quality (as in the *Velata*). There was a third genius who influenced them both in the art of portraiture. This man was Leonardo da Vinci, whose contemporaries were amazed by the nuances of expression captured in paintings like the *Mona Lisa* and *Saint John the Baptist* (both in the Louvre, Paris).

PORCELAIN COLLECTION

At the top of the Boboli Gardens where, in the 17th century, Cardinal Leopoldo created a garden of rare plants, stands the *Casino del Cavaliere*. It was built by Cosimo III as a retreat for his son Gian Gastone, and now houses the Museo delle Porcellane. The first room has French and Italian porcelain, the second Viennese, and in the third are pieces from Meissen and Berlin. Below, the tortoise butter dish and the tankard with *Hausmalerei* were made in Meissen between 1720 and 1735.

A room in the Galleria del Costume (top right).

"THE TUSCAN MAREMMA"

This painting by Giovanni Fattori is in the Galleria d'Arte Moderna, Palazzo Pitti.

dinner services, reliquaries and caskets, embroideries, carpets, fine pieces of furniture and objets d'art made of crystal, amber, ivory and painted glass. One of the finest displays is Lorenzo il Magnifico's collection of sixteen vases in *pietre dure*, and the exquisite cameos include one with a portrait of Cosimo I and his family. This is the astounding collection of a very wealthy and extremely privileged family who acquired it, often with some discernment and occasionally with very bad taste. Also within the Palazzo Pitti complex are separate MUSEUMS OF CARRIAGES, COSTUMES AND PORCELAIN. These last two collections are entered directly from the Boboli Gardens.

GALLERIA D'ARTE MODERNA. Nineteenth-century Florentine art seems to have become overshadowed, and more so than that of the two preceding centuries, by the memory of the Medici Renaissance. It may not have had a Michelangelo, but there were some very good painters all the same. The GALLERIA D'ARTE MODERNA contains exhibits from the end of the 18th century to the beginning of the 20th. Rooms covering the more recent decades are still being arranged. The collection is on the top floor which offers a splendid view over the Boboli Gardens and up the hill.

NEO-CLASSICAL DISCIPLINE. Toward the end of the 18th century there was a reaction to Rococo extravagance all over Europe. Stress was laid instead upon drawing skills and the study of anatomy. Art was now to be of noble inspiration, and once again artists turned toward antiquity in search of sufficiently virtuous and heroic deeds to be their subjects. Color, which had played such a vivid and vital part in Baroque art, was now rather subdued and seen as of only secondary importance. Luigi Mussini was among the Florentine artists of this period. There is a painting by him on display in ROOM 4 called *Eudore e Cimodoce*, which was inspired by Chateaubriand's book *Les Martyrs*.

ROMANTICISM. Things began to change in the 1820's. The new Romantic spirit encouraged more freedom of expression, and art began to show more

The Rotonda of the Bagni Palmieri
(1866) by Giovanni Fattori.

movement, energy, grandeur and mystery. It was a descent
from the high ideals and rarified atmosphere of neo-
classicism into a more cloudy and turbulent era. The subjects
chosen tended to come from more recent times: *Farinata degli
Uberti at the Battle of the Serchio* by Giuseppe Sabatelli, for
example, in ROOM 3. But the greatest changes were seen in
landscape painting. Landscapes were less tied by formal
constraints and academic conventions than history paintings,
although they were also considered of minor importance.
ROOM 14 has fine examples of some very original works from
the mid-19th century. The most innovatory landscape artists
were those working in Tuscany, known as
the *Macchiaioli*.

THE "MACCHIAIOLI". The name
comes from the word *macchia*
which means a "spot" or "blob".
Like the term "Impressionism", the
word *Macchiaioli* was invented as a
less than favorable description by a
critic from the *Gazzetta del Popolo*,
in 1862. He was talking about a
group of painters who had begun to
make a mark in about 1855,
breaking with academic traditions
and flirting with the new realism of
Corot and Courbet. Leading
figures in the group were Giovanni

Fattori (1825–1908), Silvestro Lega (1826–95) and Telemaco
Signorini (1835–1901) ● *104*. These artists were no doubt
inspired and liberated by the revolutionary atmosphere of the
period, which encouraged their defiant reaction to neo-
classicism.

A FERTILE SEAM. The painters of this group used to meet at
the Café Michelangelo in the Via Larga, now the Via Cavour.
They would return from trips abroad with new discoveries to
share, and these foreign influences certainly inspired new
developments in Italian art. Paintings by the Barbizon school
impressed them greatly, in particular those of Constant
Troyon. The effect is clear in a painting such as *The Tuscan*

THE BOBOLI GARDENS

New plants and methods were tried out, such as the exotic *patata*, the potato. The gardens contain a wide variety of species: mulberry trees, dwarf pears and many more, including unknown fruits and plants brought back from all corners of the world.

FOUNTAINS

The *Jupiter Fountain* (top left), the *Neptune Fountain* (top right), and the *Fountain of Bacchus* (below), designed by Valerio Cioli after 1560. The latter is not in fact Bacchus but

Cosimo I's favorite dwarf, unkindly nicknamed "Morgante" after the giant in a poem by Luigi Pulci.

One of the lunettes (right) by Justus van Utens ● *80*, showing the Palazzo Pitti and the Forte Belvedere.

Maremma by Fattori. They developed a characteristic technique. According to Diego Martelli, a critic who allied himself to the group, "an object is represented in three dimensions upon the canvas by a combination of light and shade, and this combination can only be correctly recreated by making spots and strokes that copy it exactly". It would be hard to formulate an argument that was more directly opposed to the dogmatic academic insistence on drawing as the means of representing shapes and objects. *The Rotonda of the Bagni Palmieri* (1886) by Fattori is a wonderful example of how a scene can be recreated using color and light. The young women sitting in the shade are painted with great clarity, simplicity, and a refreshing lack of superfluous detail.

GIOVANNI FATTORI. Fattori came from Livorno to study in Florence with Giuseppe Bezzuoli, a painter in the Romantic mold whose splendid work *The Entrance of Charles VIII into Florence* can be seen in Room 10. Fattori remained under his influence for many years, but in the late 1850's he began to meet other artists at the Café Michelangelo, and gradually his own style emerged. *The Italian Camp after the Battle of Magenta* (1861–2) in Room 18 marks the turning point. His later works were often small and rectangular, like the *Rotonda Palmieri*, particularly suited to his experiments with contrasting bands of color. Fattori was made professor at the Florence Academy in 1869.

THE BOBOLI GARDENS

LUXURIOUS GREENERY. The gardens climb the Boboli hill that rises behind the Palazzo Pitti and are one of the finest examples of Italian landscaping. The grandeur of the amphitheater, the cypress avenue, the island and the fountains, is mixed with charming copses, grottoes, half-hidden statues and

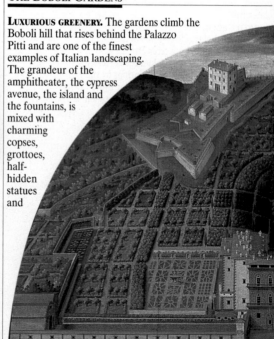

forgotten corners, making the Boboli Gardens a magical
place. There are many surprises, like the MUSEO DELLE
PORCELLANE at the top of the hill in the *Casino del Cavaliere*,
and the Rococo KAFFEEHAUS, a café open in summer, built by
Zanobi Del Rosso in 1776. From there it used to be possible
to reach the Forte Belvedere through a nearby gate. This is
now closed, forcing the visitor to go round by the main
entrance.

MANY CONTRIBUTORS. When Eleanora of Toledo, wife of
Cosimo I, bought the Palazzo Pitti in 1549, she also acquired
lands on the adjoining hillside, largely belonging to the Boboli
family. Designs for a garden were immediately drawn up by
Niccolo Pericoli (c. 1500–50), a pupil of Michelangelo known
as "Tribolo". He had already worked for Cosimo I ten years
before when he designed the gardens of the Villa
di Castello ▲ *324*, but died before he
could complete the Boboli Gardens.
Ammannati was brought in
from 1560, but it is
uncertain whether he
made his own designs
or followed those
of his
predecessor.
From 1583 to
1588

Buontalenti's grotto
and the *Artichoke
Fountain* (below).

Ceres features among
the many statues in
the gardens, a pagan
goddess of fertility
and the harvest,
shown squeezing her
breasts. There is one
Ceres, probably a
copy of a statue by
the Greek sculptor
Phidias, standing with
two other Roman
statues at the far end
of the amphitheater.

THE AMPHITHEATER
An open-air theater modeled on a Roman circus. It was built from 1618 by Giulio and Alfonso Parigi, and restored in the 18th century. The

granite basin came from the Baths of Caracalla in Rome, and the obelisk (1500 BC) was from Luxor, via Rome.

Following the central line of the amphiteater, the view goes up to the huge statue of *Abundance*, begun by Giambologna, who took for his model the Grand Duchess Joanna of Austria. The statue, which was originally intended for the Piazza San Marco, was finished by Pietro Tacca in 1636.

The *palazzina* (right), built in the style of the Medici villas, stands on the Forte Belvedere. There is a view from the terrace over the whole city.

Bernardo Buontalenti made a number of additions. A lunette painted by Justus van Utens in 1599 shows that the gardens did not then reach as far as the Porta Romana. In 1628 Alfonso Parigi the Younger began embellishments and enlargements that were to last until 1656.

A FOREST OF STONE. There are hundreds of statues in the Boboli Gardens, and this was soon to become an established feature of the Italian garden. It was a new idea in the 16th century, however. Bramante set the fashion by arranging a courtyard in the Vatican with a large part of Pope Julius II's collection of statues. He was imitating the gardens of antiquity which were known to have been decorated with statues. The pieces in the Boboli Gardens are of mixed styles and periods, but there are a number of grotesques and many pastoral pieces, such as the groups showing traditional games.

FOUNTAINS. Not merely another feature borrowed from antiquity, the Florentine fountains of Giambologna and Tribolo can be counted among the finest in the whole history of the art. The principal fountains of the Boboli Gardens are the *Artichoke Fountain* (1641) by Francesco Susini and Francesco del Tadda, the *Fountain of Bacchus* (1560) by Cioli, near Buontalenti's grotto, the *Fountain of Neptune* (1565) by Stoldo Lorenzi, and the famous *Fountain of Oceanus* (1576) by Giambologna, which is in the middle of the *Isolotto*. Descending toward this is the long *Viottolone*, a straight avenue lined with cypresses and ornamented with statues.

EARLY OPERA. The Palazzo Pitti and the Boboli Gardens, in particular the amphitheater, were the scene of many festivities and rich spectacles. Some important early experiments in opera took place here. A lyrical drama was performed in 1589 called *La Pellegrina*, for the wedding of Ferdinando de' Medici

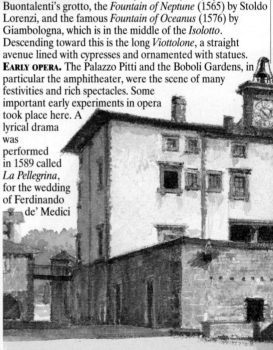

and Christine of Lorraine, with contributions by Giulio Caccini, Cavalieri and Jacopo Peri. In 1600 Peri set a tragedy by the poet Rinuccini to music: *Euridice* was performed in the gardens, with Peri himself singing Orpheus, on the occasion of the marriage of Maria de' Medici to Henry IV of France: it is the first opera for which the music has survived intact.

ANOTHER ORPHEUS. The duke of Mantua was present at the performance and returned home to commission his favorite musician, Claudio Monteverdi, to write a piece in this new dramatic style. The result was *La Favola di Orfeo*, performed in Mantua in 1607.

"L'ACCADEMIA DEGLI ELEVATI". But Monteverdi had to share his glory with Marco da Gagliano (1582–1643), a talented Florentine whose *Dafne* was performed in Mantua in 1608. Gagliano was the first to introduce a *sinfonia* (overture) at the rising of the curtain to whet the audience's appetite. Also in 1607 he founded the *Accademia degli Elevati*, a group of singers, musicians and composers, such as Peri and Giulio Caccini, who experimented with lyric drama and for many years were in charge of composing the music for all the organized spectacles at the Palazzo Pitti. Such music was never printed and has therefore not survived. From about 1625 Florence seemed to lose its musical energy, and Rome and Venice took over as centers of creativity and innovation. The Medici dynasty was losing its vitality too, and there were fewer and fewer grand occasions with their accompanying performances.

FORTE BELVEDERE. The elegant fortress at the top of the gardens is also known as the Forte di San Giorgio. It was built by Buontalenti between 1590 and 1595 for Ferdinando I, and represents a high point in 16th-century military architecture. The fortress is surmounted by a three-story *palazzina*, today used as an exhibition center, mostly for

The *Fountain of Oceanus* (above) by Giambologna stands in the middle of the *Isolotto*. Left, an old photograph of the avenue of cypress trees called the *Viottolone*.

SPECIES OF TREE
The cypress is one of the trees most commonly found in Italian parks and gardens, along with the umbrella pine, the holm oak, plane tree, elm and maple. All these species were already here in Roman times and no longer seemed very exotic by the 16th century. The central avenue is of cypress trees, but at the Hemicycle, near the Porta Romana to the west, plane trees predominate. They are planted around two granite columns topped by ornamental vases.

FORTE BELVEDERE
This fort was built to protect the whole city, and above all the Palazzo Pitti. Its panoramic view of Florence (below) was of great strategic importance: any popular uprising had to be caught early and repressed, with cannon if neccessary.

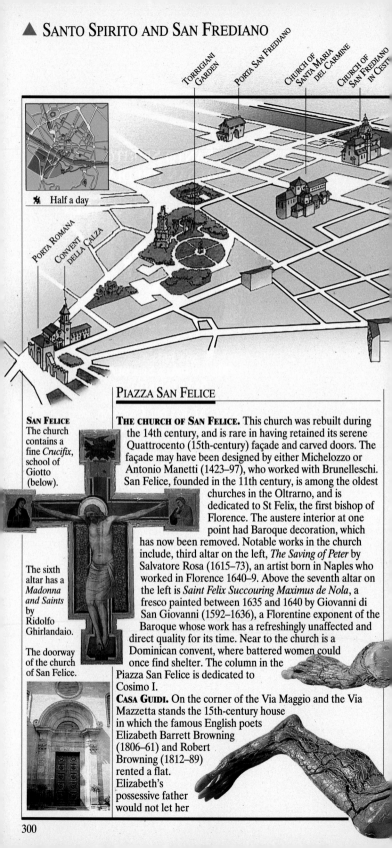

TORRIGIANI GARDEN

PORTA SAN FREDIANO

CHURCH OF SANTA MARIA DEL CARMINE

CHURCH OF SAN FREDIANO IN CESTE

✱ Half a day

PORTA ROMANA

CONVENT DELLA CALZA

PIAZZA SAN FELICE

SAN FELICE
The church contains a fine *Crucifix*, school of Giotto (below).

The sixth altar has a *Madonna and Saints* by Ridolfo Ghirlandaio.

The doorway of the church of San Felice.

THE CHURCH OF SAN FELICE. This church was rebuilt during the 14th century, and is rare in having retained its serene Quattrocento (15th-century) façade and carved doors. The façade may have been designed by either Michelozzo or Antonio Manetti (1423–97), who worked with Brunelleschi. San Felice, founded in the 11th century, is among the oldest churches in the Oltrarno, and is dedicated to St Felix, the first bishop of Florence. The austere interior at one point had Baroque decoration, which has now been removed. Notable works in the church include, third altar on the left, *The Saving of Peter* by Salvatore Rosa (1615–73), an artist born in Naples who worked in Florence 1640–9. Above the seventh altar on the left is *Saint Felix Succouring Maximus de Nola*, a fresco painted between 1635 and 1640 by Giovanni di San Giovanni (1592–1636), a Florentine exponent of the Baroque whose work has a refreshingly unaffected and direct quality for its time. Near to the church is a Dominican convent, where battered women could once find shelter. The column in the Piazza San Felice is dedicated to Cosimo I.

CASA GUIDI. On the corner of the Via Maggio and the Via Mazzetta stands the 15th-century house in which the famous English poets Elizabeth Barrett Browning (1806–61) and Robert Browning (1812–89) rented a flat. Elizabeth's possessive father would not let her

marry Robert,
so they eloped in 1846
and ran away to Florence. There
they lived and worked happily until
Elizabeth's death in 1861.

MUSEO DELLA SPECOLA. Palazzo Torrigiani, at 17 Via
Romana, houses the ZOOLOGICAL MUSEUM, opened in 1775
and also known as the Museo della Specola because it
contained an astrological observatory set up by Grand Duke
Pietro-Leopoldo of Lorraine. Giuseppe Martelli (1792–1876)
added the *Tribuna di Galileo* in 1830 in honor of the great
Tuscan astronomer. It consists of a vestibule, topped with a
curious cone-shaped iron lantern, leading to a square room
with semicircular alcove, decorated with frescoes of the life of
Galileo. The museum has a unique and bizarre collection of
anatomical wax models, about six hundred in all, showing
every detail of the human body and its organs in strikingly
realistic colors. They were made between 1775 and 1814.

PALAZZO DEI GUADAGNI

From the Piazza San Felice it is
best to take the Via Mazzetta
toward the Piazza Santo
Spirito as the traffic in the Via

Maggio is very
heavy. The palazzo on the
corner of the Via Mazzetta and the
Piazza Santo Spirito is attributed to Simone

WAX MODELS IN THE SPECOLA
An astoundingly
accurate encyclopedia
of anatomy. Some of
the models have a
remarkable grace
despite their crude
state. The reclining
figure (below), worthy
of Michelangelo, is
known as *lo scorticato*
("skinned"), and
shows the lymphatic
system. It was made
by the artist Clemente
Susini, who worked
with anatomist Felice
Fontana to make most
of the models.

301

del Pollaiuolo, "il Cronaca", and was built in 1503. It represents a great change in palatial architecture, with the heavy classical cornice being replaced by an airy top-floor loggia. It is decorated with *sgraffiti* ▲ *191*. The palazzo served as a model for many others, notably the Palazzo Ginori in the Via de' Ginori ▲ *224*.

THE CHURCH OF SANTO SPIRITO

A CARDINAL POINT. As in many other Italian cities, religious orders settled in Florence during the 13th century. The Franciscans had staked their claim in the east with Santa Croce ▲ *254;* in the west were the Dominicans at Santa Maria Novella ▲ *213;* Santissima Annunziata ▲ *242* in the north was the base of the Servites, and the Augustinians took the south.

AUGUSTINIANS AND HUMANISTS. The Augustinians were one of the oldest religious orders, their foundation going back as far as the 4th century AD, and their Rule was based on the teachings of St Augustine. Begun in 1250, within a few decades the new convent complex was the most important in the Oltrarno. It included schools, libraries, pilgrims' hostels, refectories for the poor, and a hospital. The first church was built around 1260, and was enlarged as needs expanded. At the end of the 14th century the convent became an important center of scholarship when the humanists began to use it for study and instruction. Its lay resources continued to

ART WORKS IN SANTO SPIRITO
In the right transept, *Madonna and Child with Saints* by Filippino Lippi (above). In the fourth chapel on the right is *Jesus Expelling the Money-changers* by Giovanni Stradano (1572), and in the next chapel a *Coronation of the Virgin* by Gherardini. In the chancel, on the right, is a 14th-century polyptych by Maso di Banco, one of the finest painters of Giotto's circle. Also in the chancel, by Alessandro Allori, are *Christ and the Adultress* (1577), and the *Martyred Saints* (1574). The left transept has a marble altar (c. 1490) by Andrea Sansovino.

The cupola of Santo Spirito (below).

The Palazzo dei Guadagni.

grow, helped by such additions as the library bequeathed by Boccaccio ● *38*.

FILIPPO BRUNELLESCHI, ARCHITECT. Today's church goes back to the 15th century. It was such a costly project that the monks set an example over many years by giving up one meal a day as their contribution. The architect, Filippo Brunelleschi, wanted the church to look out over the Arno, which would have meant the demolition of many buildings between church and river. A number of powerful families stepped in to object to his project, and Brunelleschi had to give up: he died before he could complete the building. The bell tower (1503) is by Baccio d'Agnolo, and the cupola, with its double shell, was built by Cronaca and Salvi d'Andrea from 1479 to 1482.

A PLAIN AND ELEGANT FAÇADE. The present façade dates from the 18th century and is now covered in plain plaster, whereas before it was more elaborately decorated with painted pilasters. Nothing remains of Brunelleschi's original plans but the two volutes. Neither are the flanks of the church as he envisaged them, for he wanted the curve of the chapels to be visible. Inside, however, his vision remains intact: the harmonious proportions and the simple contrast between the white walls and the architectural features in grey anthracite *pietra serena* ■ *16* are both impressive and uplifting.

AURELIO LOMI: REFINED MANNERISM. Most of the paintings in the church date from the 15th and 16th centuries. One particularly worth studying is the *Adoration of the Magi* (1592) by Aurelio Lomi, at the back of the chancel on the righthand side. Lomi (1535–1607) was one of the better painters of the Italian late Mannerist period, after 1580. The composition is overburdened, and the chilly light, emphasizing the delicate artificiality of the scene, falls randomly here and there showing no concern whatsoever for the realism that had so preoccupied the 15th-century Florentine artists.

FILIPPINO LIPPI: REALISM. The painting in the third chapel at the end of the right transept is entirely different. Filippino Lippi's *Madonna and Child with Saints* (1488) is evenly lit, and the composition is carefully structured using regular architectural elements (in Lomi's painting these are lost in shadow). In the background is San Frediano, and the precise detail of the buildings and even the street scenes show the strength of Flemish influence on Florentine painting in the late 15th century.

THE SACRISTY. The door to the sacristy is on the lefthand side of the nave beyond the fifth chapel. It was built between 1488

A detail from Bernardino Poccetti's *Last Supper*.

SAINT THOMAS OF VILLANEUVA
With the Counter-Reformation emphasis was put on

acts of charity; they were frequently depicted, as in Rutilio Manetti's *Saint Thomas of Villanueva Giving Alms*. It was important to show learned intellectuals of the church (St Thomas had preached before the Emperor Charles V) helping the poor and needy. He was taken up as one of the figures of charity.

▲ SANTO SPIRITO AND SAN FREDIANO

TRADITION AND INNOVATION
The sacristy of Santo Spirito continues the conventions of the early Renaissance: *pietra serena* ■ *16* standing out against white walls, twin pilasters, arcades on the ground floor, window pediments. All are reminiscent of Brunelleschi. The octagonal shape echoes the Baptistery ▲ *132* which Giuliano da Sangallo wished to emulate. But he introduced new features too: the three levels, separated by monumental lintels, are linked by the repeated structural motifs of the pilasters and the wall ribs rising to the cupola. Michelangelo used the same technique at San Lorenzo ▲ *220*.

and 1492 following plans which were drawn up by Giuliano da Sangallo and Cronaca (who also worked on the cupola). It can be considered one of the masterpieces of late 15th-century architecture. The vestibule, with its coffered barrel vaulting, has little in common with the work of Brunelleschi, seeming instead to anticipate the Roman Renaissance style. The contrast is quite considerable between this confident

new look and the octagonal sacristy itself, which was built in homage to Brunelleschi.

CLOISTERS AND REFECTORY. The vestibule of the sacristy leads also to the first cloister of the convent, built around 1600 and decorated with frescoes, most notably by Cosimo Ulivelli. The architects were Giulio and Alfonso Parigi. The second cloister (1564–9), designed by Ammannati, has frescoes by Bernardo Poccetti. Leave the church to visit the refectory: its entrance is at 29 Piazza Santa Spirito. This is the only room to have survived of the original 14th-century buildings. Two frescoes still decorate the walls: a *Crucifixion* and a *Last Supper* attributed to Orcagna or one of his pupils, painted around 1360. There is a little museum, which was funded by a donation from the art dealer Salvatore Romano, and which has some interesting exhibits, including angels and caryatids by Tino da Camaino (c. 1285–c. 1337).

PIAZZA SANTO SPIRITO. A colorful market adds to the charm of the piazza each morning. On Sundays there are secondhand stalls and antiques.

AROUND SANTO SPIRITO

PALAZZO COVERELLI. Just behind the church of Santo Spirito, on the corner of the Via dei Coverelli and the Via di Santo Spirito, is a 15th-century palace, restored in the 19th century, and decorated with *sgraffiti* ▲ *191* by Bernardino Poccetti.

VIA DI SANTO SPIRITO. A narrow street lined with the blackened façades of ancient palaces, and still occupied mainly by artisans. At numbers 11–13 is the PALAZZO FRESCOBALDI, with its 16th-century façade. At 39–41 is the PALAZZO RINUCCINI.

Madonna and Child with Saints by Bicci di Lorenzo, in the tabernacle on the corner of the Via Santa Monaca and the Via dei Serragli.

Ludovico Cardi, called "Cigoli" (1559–1613), is said to have designed the façade in the late 16th century; it is one of his finest achievements. The PALAZZO MANETTI, built around 1400, stands at number 23, while at number 58r is the elegant PALAZZETTO MEDICI. The street leads into the Piazza Sauro, with the long Via dei Serragli running off to the left.

VIA DEI SERRAGLI

There are some fine buildings along this street. The PALAZZO AMERIGHI, at number 8, has an elegant *cortile* with statues, and the rounded Spanish-style iron work on the windows is unusual. Number 17, the PALAZZO ROSSELLI DEL TURCO, is also handsome.

TABERNACLE. On the corner of the Via Santa Monaca stands the PALAZZO MAZZEI. This palace has a tabernacle with a fresco by Bicci di Lorenzo that dates from 1427. Those who enjoy walking can now continue up to the Piazzale di Porta Romana.

CONVENTO DELLA CALZA. Just before the Porta Romana is the Piazza della Calza, with a convent whose entrance is at 6 Via dei Serragli. There is a curious trapezoidal cloister, and the refectory has a beautiful *Last Supper* (1514) by Francesco di Cristofano, or "Franciabigio" (c. 1482–1525).

THE PORTA ROMANA. Built in 1326, this gate was part of the third city wall. It is in the center of a busy road junction. Go back to Via del Campuccio and turn left.

THE TORRIGIANI GARDEN. The two entrances are at 144 Via dei Serragli, and 53 Via del Campuccio. The garden of the Palazzo Torrigiani del Campuccio was begun in 1815 by Giuseppe Cambray-Digny, and finished in 1830 by the architect Gaetano Baccani. He also designed the neo-Gothic tower (1821), in which there is an observatory.

GOLDONI THEATER COMPLEX. On the corner of the Via dei Serragli and the Via Santa Maria is the ex-convent of Santa Chiara, founded in 1356. At the beginning of the 19th century it was

PIAZZALE DI PORTA ROMANA
This turn-of-the-century photograph shows a steam tram. Its line ran past the Porta Romana, a vestige of the third wall built around the city in 1333.

GARDEN OF PALAZZO TORRIGIANI
This is a model of 19th-century garden design but it is not easy to get permission to visit.

turned to a more worldly use, popular entertainment, and a theater seating fifteen hundred people was installed.

SANTA MARIA DEL CARMINE

CARMELITE CONVENT AND CHURCH
These are worth a visit. In the sacristy is a polyptych by Andrea da Firenze and frescoes of the *Life of Saint Cecilia*, possibly by Bicci di Lorenzo. The chapter house has an informative exhibition on how frescoes are painted. A lovely cloister (right) leads to the refectory, decorated with a *Last Supper* (1582) by Alessandro Allori. In the apse of the church is the 16th-century monument to Piero Soderini (below) by Benedetto da Rovezzano.

BRANCACCI, PATRICIAN AND DIPLOMAT. Carmelite monks began the building of the church and cloisters of Santa Maria del Carmine in 1268. The greater part was destroyed by fire in the 18th century, after which the church was reconstructed, a cupola added, and the interior decorated in late Baroque style by Giuseppe Ruggieri and Giulio Mannaioni. The church contains the Brancacci family chapel. In 1423 the wealthy Felice Brancacci, just returned from a spell as the republic's ambassador to Egypt, commissioned Tommaso di Cristofano, called "Masolino da Panicale", to decorate it. Masolino (c. 1383–1440) had worked with Ghiberti on the bronze Baptistery doors ▲ *133, 136*.

FREQUENT INTERRUPTIONS. Masolino started work in 1424 with the young Masaccio (1401–28). Masaccio then worked alone for three years while Masolino returned to Budapest, where he was court painter. Masolino returned in 1427, but stopped work again in 1428 when he left for Rome, followed a few months later by Masaccio, who died there in strange circumstances. The cycle of frescoes was completed by Filippino Lippi 1480–5.

THE BRANCACCI CHAPEL. These magnificent frescoes, crucially important in the development of Renaissance art, have only survived by a series of lucky escapes. In 1680 the Marchese Franceso Ferroni wanted to take over the patronage of the chapel. Not impressed by the decoration, he proposed to "get rid of these ridiculous men in their cassocks and old-fashioned outfits". Only the immovable opposition of Vittoria della Rovere, the grand duchess married to Ferdinando II, prevented their removal. In 1771 a terrible fire burned down most of the church, but the chapel somehow survived. Only the massive gilt frames between the frescoes caught fire, blackening the edges of the paintings. The chapel is dedicated to the Virgin Mary, and the decoration has also suffered some damage from all the candles that have burnt there.

THE FRESCO TECHNIQUE. Fresco is wall painting done with pigments of mineral origin (clays and silicates) mixed with water and used on a freshly applied and still damp plaster base, hence the term *a fresco*. The colors are extremely long lasting because the pigments filter into the plaster itself, but they can alter over the years, particularly if affected by damp.

"ARRICCIO" AND "SINOPIA". The fresco technique is difficult to master. The wall is first rough-plastered, then a finer layer of plaster, the *arriccio*, is applied. Next the sketch is made with a stylus; this is the *sinopia*, called after the red pigment used. Work progresses slowly over the surface, so it is divided into *giornate* (days), sections that can be completed in a day's work. One person can cover 30–35 square feet in a day.

"INTONACO". The painter then spreads on a layer of *intonaco*, a smooth plaster mix of sand and lime. He spreads each day only the portion that will be covered in the seven hours of painting. Any area of plaster not covered must be cut away, ready to start afresh the next day. The artist cannot see the exact colors as he works, for the final tones only appear when the surface has dried, gaining an added luminosity from the crystals in the surface mortar. Great advances in fresco technique were made in the mid-15th century, but these came too late for Masaccio and Masolino. The fresco method was frustrating because subtleties of tone could be lost when the colors changed as they dried, and corrections were difficult. The *a secco* technique, which involved applying pigments to dry plaster, did not have these problems and was also much much quicker, but it lacked luminosity and the lasting quality of *buon (*or true) *fresco*.

Scenes from the Life of Saint Cecilia. These frescoes in Santa Maria del Carmine are in the style of Bicci di Lorenzo.

THE FRESCOES OF MASACCIO
These are of key importance in the history of painting. The compositions have great intelligence and considerable narrative power. Màsaccio was not interested in grace and beauty. Instead, the faces of his Apostles are stern and rugged, along the lines of Donatello. His Adam and Eve are quite different from those painted by Masolino. The delicate vision of the older artist could not be further removed from these expressions of intense torment.

CAPPELLA BRANCACCI
The work of Masolino (left, top panel), Masaccio, and Lippi (left, bottom) is the very highest expression of the art of fresco.

"SAINT PETER FREED FROM PRISON" by Filippino Lippi (details). While the guard sleeps (below), an angel comes to release Peter (facing page, bottom right), thrown into prison by Herod.

"EXPULSION FROM PARADISE"
One of the works in which Masaccio most clearly breaks with tradition. This is a scene of intense psychological drama. The figures, loosely based on classical models but direct and uncompromising in their execution, are in marked contrast to Masolino's graceful and harmonious Adam and Eve in *The Temptation*, on the opposite wall of the chapel. Masaccio uses light and shade to give his figures a much stronger form and presence, most markedly in the case of Adam.

"THE HEALING OF THE CRIPPLE AND THE RAISING OF TABITHA" by Masolino. The background seems to be by Masaccio.

"SAINT PAUL VISITING SAINT PETER IN PRISON" Filippino Lippi painted this fresco around 1485 and included himself (left). It was quite common to include a self-portrait in religious scenes.

RESTORATION In the 1980's a huge restoration project was carried out on these frescoes, under the direction of Ornella Casazza. It was sponsored by the Olivetti company.

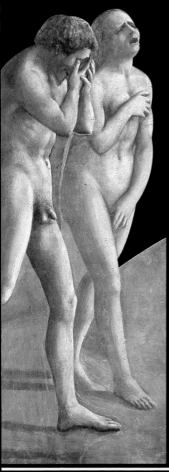

"SAINT PETER FREED FROM PRISON" One of the frescoes by Filippino Lippi. He copied Masaccio's style so faithfully that it took until 1838 for his work to be recognized.

The cupola of the church of San Frediano (right).

ASSUMPTION OF THE VIRGIN
Paintings on this theme show the moment when Mary rose into heaven, like Christ, after her death. The episode is not described in the scriptures, but gradually gained popular credence. The Apostles are often depicted gathered around the Virgin's empty tomb.

In this work by Curradi, Mary has risen to Paradise and is surrounded by angels and saints. The Virgin was also taken up as a symbol of the struggle against heresy.

Sgraffiti on the Palazzo Lanfredini (above).
The interior of the cupola, San Frediano church (right).

AROUND SAN FREDIANO

PORTA SAN FREDIANO. Take the Via dell'Orto and turn right into the Viale Ariosto, which will lead to the Porta San Frediano, built in 1333. Through this gate the French king Charles VIII led his troops to take the city in 1494. The young king had decided to capture the throne of Naples and had descended on Italy taking everyone by surprise ● *31*. Piero de' Medici negotiated with Charles, without consulting the citizens of Florence. To avoid bloodshed in Tuscany he handed Florence over to the French, and they entered the city unopposed. The enraged population threw Piero out. They accepted the conqueror, nevertheless, encouraged by Savonarola ● *31,* who saw the king of France as a great liberator who would free the city at last from the grip of the Medicis.

THE FRENCH IN FLORENCE. On November 17, 1494, the French troops entered the town. They did so in an awe-inspiring procession. The column was led by soldiers carrying drums and trumpets, followed by ten thousand foot soldiers, then thirty or forty cannon, eight hundred knights in armor, a company of archers and finally the king himself. He was an undersized and ugly youth of twenty-four, mounted on a black charger, brandishing his lance, and surrounded by a bodyguard one hundred strong. The doors of the Porta San Frediano were opened wide, and part of the city wall was taken down to admit them. Florence welcomed Charles like a great liberator with open arms. After a brief stay at the Medici Palace, he continued his march toward Naples.

THE CHURCH OF SAN FREDIANO IN CESTELLO. The Borgo San Frediano now leads to the church. First the property of the Carmelites, the convent and church passed into the hands of the Cistercians through a forced exchange. In 1628 the pope asked them to hand over their convent of Santa Maddalena dei Pazzi to the Carmelites. The façade of San Frediano is plain, but it has a magnificently decorated interior, designed by a Roman architect, Antonio Cerruti, in about 1680. The cupola was added in 1698 by Antonio Maria Ferri (1668–1716). On the inside, the cupola is painted by Antonio Domenico Gabbiani (1652–1726).

"BIANCA CAPPELLO HAS AN AGREEABLE, IMPOSING FACE, A LARGE BUST AND BREASTS THE WAY THEY LIKE THEM HERE. SHE SEEMED CAPABLE OF HAVING BEWITCHED THIS PRINCE AND OF BEING ABLE TO MAINTAIN HIS DEVOTION." MICHEL DE MONTAIGNE

LUNGARNO GUICCIARDINI

PALAZZO LANFREDINI. The riverside walk along the lungarno gives a good view of the buildings on the opposite bank, in particular the Palazzo Corsini ▲ 277. There are also some fine palaces on the Lungarno Guicciardini itself. The PALAZZO LANFREDINI, number 9, was built by Baccio d'Agnolo in the 16th century. It has one of the best-conserved façades in the city, decorated with *sgraffiti* ▲ 191 by Andrea Feltini. At number 7 stands the 17th-century PALAZZO GUICCIARDINI.

SAN FREDIANO IN CESTELLO

In the first chapel on the right is an altarpiece of *Santa Maria Maddalena dei Pazzi* by G.C. Sagrestani (1702); the frescoes are by Matteo Bonechi, that in the cupola showing

The PALAZZO DI LUDOVICO CAPPONI is at number 1. It dates from the 16th century and in its main hall are frescoes by Bernardino Poccetti depicting glorious moments in the family's history (1585). The lungarno comes to an end at the Ponte Santa Trinita, with the PALAZZO DELLE MISSIONI ● 75, built in the first half of the 17th century by Bernardino Radi. It has busts of the grand dukes.

VIA MAGGIO

ROMANTIC ENTANGLEMENTS. At 26 Via Maggio is the PALAZZO DI BIANCA CAPPELLO, which was built around 1570 and had alterations made to the ground floor by Buontalenti. The Grand Duke Francesco I had it built for his love, the Venetian Bianca Cappello. At the age of sixteen this girl of good family became pregnant by a Florentine bank clerk posted to Venice, Pietro Bonaventuri. They took refuge in Florence in 1563, and her husband asked Francesco de' Medici for protection. The grand duke fell in love with Bianca. In his own interest the husband accepted that she become Francesco's mistress, and the Buonaventuris lived in the palazzo on the Via Maggio until Pietro was killed, by whom it is not known. In 1579 Francesco's wife conveniently died, and Bianca became grand duchess. Her new husband died of fever in 1587, and Bianca followed eleven hours later.

the *Glory of the Saint.* The next chapel is dedicated to San Frediano and was decorated with frescoes in around 1700 by Antonio Puglieschi. In the third chapel, dedicated to the Virgin, are scenes from the life of Mary. The altarpiece is a *Nativity of the Virgin* by Gherardini; he also decorated the cupola with an *Assumption* (1694) and the pendentives and lunettes with prophets and sibyls. The fourth chapel was painted by Pier Dandini (1689).

Entry of *Charles VIII into Florence by the Porta San Frediano* (above), a painting by Francesco Granacci. The Porta San Frediano (above left).

PONTE VECCHIO · PALAZZO CAPPONI · PALAZZO CANIGIANI · CHURCH OF SANTA LUCIA DEI MAGNOLI · PALAZZO TORRIGIANI · MUSEO BARDINI · PIAZZA DEMIDOF

PORTA SAN GIORGIO · PALAZZO MOZZI

✱ Half a day

SANTA LUCIA
St Lucy was martyred at Syracuse in 303, a victim of persecution by the Roman

emperor Diocletian. The story goes that she was a wealthy Sicilian who refused all offers of marriage and instead gave her fortune to the poor. Denounced as a Christian by one of her suitors, she was decapitated. Her name comes from the Latin word for "light" (*lux*), which is perhaps why she is often invoked in cases of eye disease: fearing his love of her eyes might lead a suitor astray, she plucked them out and sent them to him, so she is often depicted with her eyes on a dish.

VIA DE' BARDI

AN UNEXPLORED STREET. On the southern bank of the Arno (Oltrarno) at the end of the Ponte Vecchio ▲ *172* begins the Via de' Bardi, on the left, which crosses the Piazza Santa Maria Soprarno. This street, which is usually free of tourists, is lined with austere palazzos. At numbers 36–8, the PALAZZO CAPONI DELLE ROVINATE, was possibly built by Lorenzo di Bicci around 1410 for Count Niccolò da Uzzano, the founder of Florence University ▲ *237*. It is in typical early 15th-century style, with its doorway heavily studded with nails. The *cortile* has octagonal columns with capitals derived from 14th-century models.

CHURCH OF SANTA LUCIA DEI MAGNOLI. Formerly known as Santa Lucia delle Rovinate (in ruins), this ancient church is located at the corner of the Via de' Bardi and the Costa Scarpuccia. Standing directly beneath the Costa San Giorgio,

it was often damaged by falling rocks. It was built in the 11th century, but has since been heavily restored. The most significant changes have been made to the façade of Romanesque stone, which was rendered in 1933. The doorway is decorated with a majolica relief (above), *Santa Lucia Venerated by Two Angels*, which is attributed to Benedetto Buglioni. Inside is a painting of *Santa Lucia* (left), dating from around 1332, a fine work by the Sienese artist Pietro Lorenzetti (c. 1280–1348). Though Duccio's International Gothic style dominated early 14th-century Italian art with its studied linear beauty, it was Lorenzetti who first introduced Giotto's monumental style to Siena. On the left of the nave is an *Annunciation* by Jacopo del Sellaio (1442–93), a pupil of Lippi. Opposite the church there used to be a convent where St Francis once stayed.

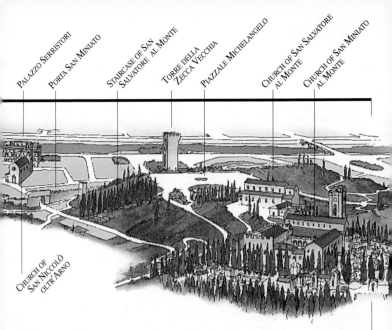

PALAZZO SERRISTORI · PORTA SAN MINIATO · STAIRCASE OF SAN SALVATORE AL MONTE · TORRE DELLA ZECCA VECCHIA · PIAZZALE MICHELANGELO · CHURCH OF SAN SALVATORE AL MONTE · CHURCH OF SAN MINIATO AL MONTE

CHURCH OF SAN NICCOLÒ OLTR'ARNO

PIAZZA DE' MOZZI

PALAZZO TORRIGIANI. The larger of the Torrigiani family palaces was designed by Bartolommeo Baccio d'Agnolo (1462–1543), and the smaller one by his son Domenico (1511–52). The façade was altered in the 17th century.

PALAZZO MALVEZZI. The façade of this other property of the Torrigianis was built by Giulio Parigi in the 17th century.

MUSEO BARDINI. The museum is housed in an unusual palazzo built in 1881 by a famous Florentine antiquarian, Stefano Bardini, on the site of a ruined 13th-century church. Earlier, his collections had been displayed in one of the Mozzi palaces a few yards away, which became too small to hold them all. The museum contains some marvelous works of art from the early Middle Ages to the Baroque, all collected by its founder. Two years before his death in 1923, Bardini bequeathed the collection to the city of Florence, and the addition of a collection of pictures bequeathed by the Corsi family in 1937 greatly enriched the museum. The windows of the palazzo incorporate fragments of altar-stones from a church at Pistoia: ceilings, doors, fireplaces and other features all come from ancient palazzos.

UNDOCUMENTED TREASURES. There is such an abundance of works of art in the Museo Bardini that a comprehensive inventory is still incomplete, neither

The imposing tower of Zecca Vecchia is in the Piazza Giuseppe Poggi. Below left, the Ponte alle Grazie.

STEFANO BARDINI
Born in 1836, Bardini set up in business in Florence as a dealer in fine art, and soon acquired an international reputation. He began by buying Tuscan furniture, and then traveled across Italy and Europe in search of Italian works of art, particularly those from the 15th and 16th centuries. He was operative in helping to found many famous collections, and supplied pictures to museums on both sides of the Atlantic.

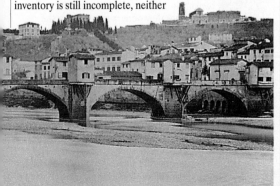

315

THE CHURCH OF SAN NICCOLÒ OLTR'ARNO
Standing in the Via San Niccolò at the corner of the Via del Olmo, this church was founded in the 11th century. It was rebuilt in the early 15th century, thanks to the generosity of the Quaratesi family, and altered in the 16th century. It was badly damaged in the flood of 1966 ▲ 173, but restoration work revealed frescoes which had previously been hidden by 16th-century works.

PALAZZO MOZZI
The plain façade of the palazzo dominates the Piazza de' Mozzi. In spite of its fortified structure, the large windows give it an elegant appearance. Opposite, below left, the riverside façade of the Palazzo Torrigiani.

have the authorities started to promote the museum properly, and there is an urgent need for a catalog. Among its many treasures is a series of drawings by Tiepolo, ceramics, sacristy cupboards, pulpits and fireplaces, together with wooden models of the church of San Firenze ▲ 186 by Gherardo Silvani, and a beautiful *Charity* by Tino di Camaino, who studied sculpture under Giovanni Pisano and who carved the tomb of Bishop Antonio d'Orso in the Duomo. At the entrance are works of art removed from tabernacles and restored, including a beautiful *Maestà* from the tabernacle of Santa Maria della Tromba ▲ 201, which formerly stood at the corner of the Via Orsanmichele and the Via Arte della Lana. An interesting curiosity is a carved plaque from the church demolished to build the palazzo: its chapel was built to celebrate a peace in the feud between the Guelfs and Ghibellines ● 34, and it was called San Gregorio del Pace.

THE MOZZI FAMILY, BANKERS TO THE POPES.
The Mozzis were among the most powerful bankers in 13th-century Florence. For generations they were responsible for the *visdomini*, in other words they were the agents of the bishop of Florence; and were also the pope's financiers for many years. One of their palaces is a few yards away from the Duomo, but the one in the Piazza de' Mozzi is made up of three palaces built between 1260 and 1273. The palazzo used to entertain important guests, such as medieval prelates on their way to Avignon; and it has been the setting for some key scenes in Florentine history, as when Gregory X came here in July 1273 to try to reconcile the Guelfs and Ghibellines. He effected a temporary peace between the leaders of

the two factions, who met on the bank of the Arno a few yards
from the palazzo; and in 1314 the vicar-general of Tuscany,
brother of the king of Naples, signed the treaty of Arezzo
here. The duke of Athens, Walter de Brienne, stayed with the
Mozzis in 1326 when he came to make peace with Florence.
AN AVARICIOUS NOBLEMAN. Walter de Brienne stayed here
again in 1342. Invested now with absolute power as "signore"
for life, he had expensive tastes and never failed to take
advantage of his position by plundering the wealth of
Florence, and importunately confiscating the property of
wealthy clerics. His way of life, cruelty, and the boorish
manners of his entourage soon became intolerable to the
businessmen of Florence: they organized an uprising the

following year and drove Walter out of
the city. He was only missed by the poor,
whose favor he had courted by
exempting them from tax. A painting by
Stefano Ussi in the Galleria d'Arte
Moderna of the Pitti Palace ▲ *292* shows
the duke being ordered to leave
Florence. From the windows can be seen
the tower-houses, massive fortified
dwellings among which the Palazzo
Mozzi stood.
PALAZZO MOZZI. This immense palace is intended to become
the Museum of Decorative Arts, and is a typical nobleman's
house of the 13th century. Constructed at the same time as
severe-looking buildings like the Spini and Gianfigliazzi
▲ *272*, it is a fortified dwelling of roughly dressed stone.
Yet it is rather less cramped and uncomfortable than other
contemporary buildings, and has an altogether more pleasing
appearance, with some large windows and a spacious interior.
This explains why a building now shabby and neglected was
once celebrated as the most luxurious in all Florence.

PIAZZA DEMIDOFF. From the Piazza de' Mozzi take the wide Via de' Renai. At the other end is a pretty square with a garden planted with palm trees and overlooking the Arno. Also in the square is a statue of the philanthropist Prince Nicholas Demidoff. The view from this old-world spot is onto the Biblioteca Nazionale ▲ *267* and the church of Santa Croce ▲ *254*.

PALAZZO SERRISTORI. At 2 Via de' Renai, bordering the Piazza Demidoff, is a palazzo built around 1515 (probably by Baccio d'Agnolo), the façade of which was restored in the 19th century. Before becoming an architect, Baccio d'Agnolo was a wood carver: there were no clear distinctions between different branches of art, as all the Renaissance painters who designed buildings can bear witness. "The *sine qua non* is a mastery of geometry and arithmetic", wrote Luciano Laurana to Federigo da Montefeltro in 1468.

ARCHITECTURE AS AN ARTISTIC DISCIPLINE. Architecture was becoming not so much a practical subject as an abstract conception. Design without a formal code of rules (as had been the practice in Gothic architecture) was now on the way out. The period between 1470 and 1520 was alive with new ideas, and the time soon came when architects became professionals in their own right. "The practice of this art", wrote Vasari in 1550, "was for many years virtually the exclusive province of sculptors and sophists who prided themselves on their knowledge of perspective but lacked the slightest understanding of the most elementary principles." Vasari was talking about just such an architect as Baccio d'Agnolo.

THE CHURCH OF SAN NICCOLÒ OLTR'ARNO. The Via del Olmo leads to this church. It consists of a nave flanked by three absidioles, a style characteristic of the mendicant orders of the 14th century. To the right of the altar is a *Trinity* attributed to Neri di Bicci. It was in the belfry of this church that Michelangelo hid from the invading forces of Charles V. Having taken part in the defense of the city and helped to design its fortifications, he feared for his life.

TORRE DELLA ZECCA VECCHIA. The peaceful Via dei Giardini leads to the Via San Niccolò and the Piazza Giuseppe Poggi. The high crenellated tower ▲ *315* dates from 1324, and is a relic of the third defensive wall that encircled the city. It is the only one of all the towers along this wall to have retained its original height.

PIAZZALE MICHELANGELO

From the Torre San Niccolò there are steps up to a garden which leads to this famous viewpoint. The piazzale was laid out in 1869 to the designs of Giuseppe Poggi (1811–1901), the most important Florentine architect of the 19th century who completed many important urban projects here and in Rome. It is named after the great artist whose famous statue of *David* (a copy) stands here. On the south side is a loggia, called the "Palazzina del Caffè", housing a café-restaurant which is very popular with tourists. The view from the terrace is stunning. From the Duomo ▲ *128* to Forte Belvedere ▲ *297*, from Santa Croce ▲ *254* to the Cascine ▲ *284* and the hill of Fiesole ▲ *328*, the panorama takes in the entire heart of Florence, giving the visitor a clear idea of the topography of the city and of its marvelous colors.

THE CHURCH OF SAN SALVATORE AL MONTE

A world away from the ceaseless traffic on the nearby Viale Galileo, climb the steps behind the loggia between the tall cypress trees.
"BELLA VILLANELLA". Its nickname comes from Michelangelo, who found San Salvatore al Monte one of the loveliest churches in Florence and called it his "pretty country wench". The plans for the church were approved by Lorenzo il Magnifico in 1474, and the work of building was confided to Simone del Pollaiuolo (1457–1508), known as "il Cronaca". Construction began in 1499, and the church was consecrated in 1504. The Arte del Calimala ▲ *198* financed the building, and its symbol of an eagle can be seen on the façade of the church. The spacious interior is simple, reflecting Franciscan piety. The plan is similar to that of San Niccolò sopr'Arno, except that the side walls

▲ San Miniato

FAÇADE OF SAN MINIATO
One of the most exquisite of Romanesque façades, it is clad in white Carrara marble and dark green serpentine known as "Verde di Prato". The design properly belongs to the Florentine "proto-Renaissance", which delighted in delicate inlaid work. The lower story shows the lasting influence of classical models, with half-columns supporting blind semicircular arches. Note the steps formed by the base of the doors, a recurring feature of the Renaissance that is also evident at Alberti's Palazzo Rucellai ▲ 276. The upper part of the façade has a 13th-century mosaic showing *Christ between the Virgin and St Minias*. At the top is a gilded eagle clasping a bale of wool in its talons, the emblem of the Guild of Wool-weavers ▲ 199, whose church it was after 1288.

The site of San Miniato in a 19th-century engraving by Emilio Burci, held by the Gabinetto dei Disegni of the Uffizi.

open onto chapels; but the unusual feature of this church is its use of a two-level structure. The ground floor is classical in style, with pilasters on the arcades in Roman fashion. The windows of the upper story are framed with aedicules, and triangular pediments alternate with curved ones, as in the Baptistery ▲ 132.

ANDREA DA FIESOLE. To the right on entering is a bust of Marcello Adriani, who died in 1521. It was he who signed Savonarola's death warrant. The bust is the work of Andrea Ferrucci, known as "Andrea da Fiesole" (1465–1526).

SAN MINIATO AL MONTE

A LITTLE-KNOWN STORY. The church was built over the tomb of St Minias, martyred at Florence in the reign of Decius around the year 250. According to legend, after being decapitated on the banks of the Arno the saint picked up his head and walked up the *Mons Fiorentinus*, the summit of which was clustered with pagan temples, fragments of which have been found in the crypt of the church. Minias fell dead there, and was buried along with other Christians. There is written evidence that a chapel dedicated to him was built on the site, which seems to have been there since the 4th century, by which time Christians were generally more fortunate. A Benedictine monastery was founded on the spot, around 1013, which was later given over to the Cluniac Order.

A CAMPANILE IN DANGER. The present church was probably built on the same site, though precisely when is unknown. It seems not to have been later than 1207. The campanile is later, the work of Baccio d'Agnolo, whose designs date from 1518. Its top floor was never completed. During the siege of Florence a soldier was placed in the belfry with two small

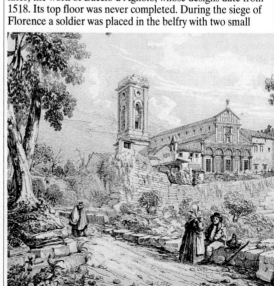

cannon, making it the target of the enemy's artillery. The church and convent were rebuilt after 1373 by the Olivetan Order of Benedictines. The church has known some grim moments in its history: it served as a hospital during the plagues of the 17th century, and then became a refuge for the homeless.

THE CHAPEL OF THE CRUCIFIX. This chapel was built by Michelozzo in 1448. He was the architect of the Medici Palace ▲ *224*, and the chapel was another of his masterpieces. It was commissioned by Piero il Gottoso in order to house the miraculous cross of St John Gualberto ▲ *273*, which was kept at Santa Trinita. The paintings are by Agnolo Gaddi, who died in 1396. Medallions and majolica friezes are from the workshops of Luca della Robbia. Piero did not specify in his commission the inclusion of the family arms for the decoration, but his own crest of three ostrich feathers with a diamond ring and a flying eagle are to be seen in the tondo toward the back of the aedicule.

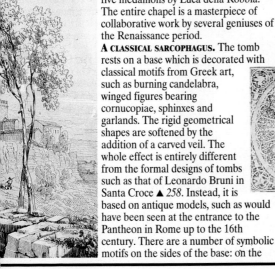

The Medici balls, on the other hand, are tucked away in the scrollwork and so become lost in the vaulted arches.

A NEW STYLE OF TOMB. The monument of Jacopo di Lusitania, cardinal of Portugal, who died in Florence at the age of twenty-five, was sculpted by Antonio Rossellino (1427–79) after 1459. But the chapel itself was the work of Antonio Manetti, a pupil of Brunelleschi, and the picture of Saints Eustace, James and Vincent over the altar is a copy of the Pollaiuolo original, which has been removed to the Uffizi Gallery. In the vault are five medallions by Luca della Robbia. The entire chapel is a masterpiece of collaborative work by several geniuses of the Renaissance period.

A CLASSICAL SARCOPHAGUS. The tomb rests on a base which is decorated with classical motifs from Greek art, such as burning candelabra, winged figures bearing cornucopiae, sphinxes and garlands. The rigid geometrical shapes are softened by the addition of a carved veil. The whole effect is entirely different from the formal designs of tombs such as that of Leonardo Bruni in Santa Croce ▲ *258*. Instead, it is based on antique models, such as would have been seen at the entrance to the Pantheon in Rome up to the 16th century. There are a number of symbolic motifs on the sides of the base: on the

JACOPO DI LUSITANIA
Jacopo was the nephew of King Alfonso V of Portugal, and was sent to study Canon Law in Perugia at the age of nineteen. He became ambassador in Florence but died there in 1459 at the age of twenty-five. Jacopo was acclaimed for his wisdom, beauty, generosity, beauty and virtue. His tomb (above) was carved by Antonio Rossellino.

The hill of San Miniato seen from Forte Belvedere (left).

INLAID MARBLE FLOOR
The first bays of the church are decorated with marble inlays which depict the signs

of the Zodiac. This design was intended as a reminder that real time has no meaning within the House of God.

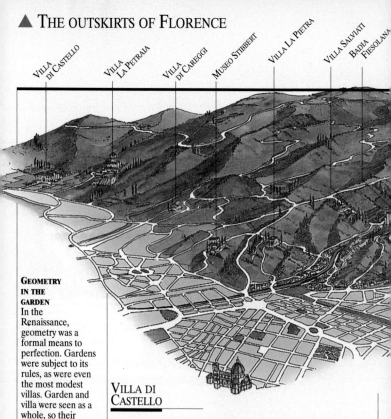

VILLA DI CASTELLO

VILLA LA PETRAIA

VILLA DI CAREGGI

MUSEO STIBBERT

VILLA LA PIETRA

VILLA SALVIATI

BADIA FIESOLANA

GEOMETRY IN THE GARDEN
In the Renaissance, geometry was a formal means to perfection. Gardens were subject to its rules, as were even the most modest villas. Garden and villa were seen as a whole, so their geometrical layout was linked. The garden would be arranged about the central axis of the path that led to the villa's entrance. Secondary lines would cross this main axis to create a characteristic grid-like appearance. The architect Alberti recommended that within this framework various geometrical shapes should be traced, such as squares, circles and arcs.

The Villa di Castello (above), of which only the gardens can be visited.
The Villa La Petraia (right) is topped by a high tower.

VILLA DI CASTELLO

THE WORKS OF COSIMO I. The orginal castle was acquired in 1477 by the great-nephews of Cosimo il Vecchio and then transformed into a country villa. It suffered some serious damage during uprisings against the Medicis in 1527. Cosimo I had the villa restored by Bronzino and Pontormo, and brought in a pupil of Michelangelo, Niccolo Tribolo (c. 1500–50) to redesign the grounds. The entrance to the delightful terraced garden is to the right of the villa. Tribolo laid it out on a geometrical plan, with neat box hedges arranged in complex patterns, lemon trees planted at regular intervals, and set around a tall and delicately shaped fountain. There were once secret bowers to either side, and the central path used to lead into dense greenery concealing another fountain, the *Venus Anadyomene* that is now in the garden of the nearby Villa La Petraia.

SYMBOLIC GROTTO. Now the garden leads to a fantastic grotto decorated with shells and weird creatures. In the "Bear's Den", created by Giambologna, he sculpted a delightful collection of bronze animals. For Cosimo the scene was not just charming, it also had a metaphorical significance. He himself was the unicorn, whose skillful policies had allowed the Florentines, the animals, to drink in safety. On the right side of the grotto an opening

CHURCH OF SAN DOMENICO DI FIESOLE

FIESOLE

PRATOLINO – VILLA DEMIDOFF

VILLA I TATTI

SETTIGNANO

VINCIGLIATA

VILLA GAMBERAIA

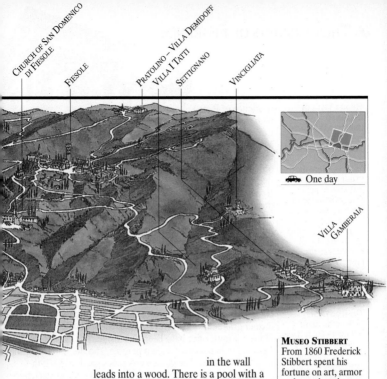

🚗 One day

in the wall leads into a wood. There is a pool with a rocky isle, and rising from it is a figure that would seem to be *Appennino*, or perhaps *Winter*, sculpted by Ammannati.

VILLA LA PETRAIA ● 78

The villa goes back to the 13th century and was originally a castle belonging to the Brunelleschi family. It came into the hands of the Medicis in the 16th century and was completely redesigned by Buontalenti, although he maintained the square structure, the tower, and the 14th-century dungeon. He also planned the large garden. The north and south walls of the courtyard were decorated around 1590 by Cosimo Daddi with grotesques and scenes of *Brave Deeds of Saint Godfrey of Bouillon at the Siege of Jerusalem*. Beneath the side loggias on the east and west walls are frescoes of great moments in the Medici family history, painted by Volterrano between 1636 and 1648. In the 19th century the villa was much loved by King Victor Emmanuel II, and in the garden his favorite tree, a 400-year-old ilex, still contains the tree-house he built. There is a pretty view of Florence framed by greenery from the gardens. On the Via della Petraia, just before reaching the villa, note the splendid Baroque façade of the Villa Corsini ● 75, where Sir Robert Dudley died in 1649.

VILLA DI CAREGGI ● 65

THE FIRST MEDICI VILLA. A fortified dwelling dating from the 14th century at 21 Viale Pieraccini. It was bought by Giovanni de' Medici in 1417 and rebuilt by his favorite architect, Michelozzo. The ramparts on elegant supporting consoles were preserved, and closed in to create a covered walk. This villa was also the favorite rural

MUSEO STIBBERT
From 1860 Frederick Stibbert spent his fortune on art, armor and arms bought on his travels. He built a villa for them and left all to the British government, which gave them to

Florence. The Sala della Cavalcata (above) contains models of fourteen knights and fourteen footmen from the 16th century.

MEDICI VILLA DI BELCANTO
Built by Michelozzo in 1458 for Cosimo il Vecchio, it retains some original features. Here the Platonic Academy gathered to hold dinners in honor of Plato. A visit can also be included in a pleasant walk. From San Domenico di Fiesole take the pretty Via Vecchio Fiesolana past number 62, the villa Il Riposo dei Vescovi (see facing page). The road doubles back to the right, leading to the terrace of the Medici villa with its panoramic view. Return by the steep Via Bandini.

residence of Pietro il Gottoso and Lorenzo il Magnifico ● 36: all three Medici potentates spent their last days here. It was the first of the great Medici villas. Here, as with those that followed, the garden was of prime importance: it was to be a place for quiet reflection and relaxation. According to Alberti, the garden was actually more important than the architecture of the villa itself. At Careggi Lorenzo created a botanical garden that was to become renowned throughout Italy. In it grew basil, pepper, myrrh, frankincense, cloves, jasmin and roses: the effect must have been very similar to the profusion of Botticelli's *Primavera*.

DECLINE. The villa has had a turbulent history, and most of its former grandeur is lost. Only the basement now gives an idea of what it must once have been like inside. The ceiling is frescoed in imitation of a giant pergola, and the floor set with beautiful mosaics. The garden was redesigned in the 19th century along the lines of an English park. Its lawns stretch to the south of the villa, shaded by fig trees, palms, cypresses and many other species.

VILLA LA PIETRA

THE CHURCH OF SAN DOMENICO DI FIESOLE

This is a quite magnificent villa, situated at 120 Via Bolognese, once belonging to the English man of letters Sir

Harold Acton. It is the epitome of elegance, the 17th-century Baroque exterior concealing a much older building within, a square structure around a central courtyard. Scattered about the garden, in glades and bowers, stand numerous statues and pillars framed in greenery. As with most of the private villas, a visit is usually possible if a suitably persuasive letter is written to the owners in advance.

VILLA SALVIATI

The church interior and the cloister of the Badia Fiesolana (below). From the Badia terrace there is a view over the Mugnone valley and the Villa Salviati.

In 1469 this 14th-century palazzo was bought by Alamanno Salviati. It has retained its fortified appearance, with corner towers and some impressive battlements supported by consoles. It was altered around 1470 by Giuliano da Sangallo. The *cortile* is the work of Rustici (1474–1554): it is decorated with *sgraffiti* ▲ 191 and medallions on mythological themes. The chapel too is ornamented with medallions and grotesques, and has an *Annunciation* and a *Virgin and Child* in bas relief by Rustici. The interior rooms have decorations by Francesco Furini. To reach the villa, take the Via Bolognese as far as the junction called "Il Cionfo", which is on the west side of the Mugnone valley.

RUTHLESS VENGEANCE
The Villa Salviati, left, is an elegant building that
still resembles a fortress. It was here in 1638 that
Veronica Cybo gave her husband a New Year's gift
in a linen basket. He opened it, only to find the
head of his lover inside.

BADIA FIESOLANA

THE REMAINS OF SAINT ROMULUS. In the year 313 in the Edict
of Milan, the emperor Constantine finally authorized the
official tolerance of Christianity. Until then worshippers had
been compelled to meet in private houses or outside the city
walls. It was here, close to the tomb of St Romulus, the
evangelist of Fiesole, that the illicit band of Christians used to
gather. Later a chapel was built, which eventually became a
cathedral. During the 11th century, the monks of the order of
St Romuald, who lived here, built an
abbey of which the unfinished façade
may still be seen today. The monastery
became Benedictine in the 13th century,
and in 1439 passed into the hands of the
Augustinian canons of Lucca, who duly
rebuilt it.

ENTER THE MEDICIS. Cosimo il Vecchio
paid for much of the work and also took
an active interest in the architectural
design. Although Vasari attributed the
original plans to Filippo Brunelleschi, it is generally thought
that the designs were the work of Alberti, or else of
Michelozzo, a friend of Cosimo. The building is not laid out
like a basilica, since there are no side aisles or apses. The nave
is simply bordered with chapels, and roofed (rare in Tuscany)
with barrel vaulting. The overall impression is one of
austerity. There are no wall paintings to interfere with
meditation: only *pietra serena* ■ *16* decorates the bare interior,
characteristic of the Early Renaissance.

SAN DOMENICO DI FIESOLE

Not far from the Badia Fiesolana there grew up a Dominican
convent which was founded in 1406 by Giovanni Dominici. It
played an important part in religious life until the monks
moved away to take up residence in the Convent of San
Marco ▲ *228* in Florence. St Antonino and Fra Angelico both
entered monastic life here as novices: the latter was prior
from 1449 to 1452. The church still has a wonderful reredos

**IL RIPOSO DEI
VESCOVI**
Near the church of
San Domenico stands
the villa formerly
called "Bishop's Rest"
(now renamed
"Nieuwenkamp"). Its
old name comes from
the legend that the
bishops of Fiesole,
obliged to live in
Florence, rested here
during their ascent of
the hill of Fiesole. A
pupil of the painter
Gauguin called
Nieuwenkamp lived
here: he was a great
traveler, and sent back
whole ships filled with
statuary, bas-reliefs
and works of art from
the East. Nineteenth-
century alterations
turned the villa into a
curiosity, with
terraced gardens on
the hillside. Large
Etruscan urns are a
relic from
Nieuwenkamp's
excavations in the
ancient theater of
Fiesole.

The Convent of San
Francesco (above).
Fra Angelico's
reredos (1428) in the
church of San
Domenico
di Fiesole (left).

AROUND THE DUOMO
San Romolo (above), the cathedral of Fiesole, is dominated by its tall crenellated campanile. The Piazza Mino da Fiesole (center right) with the church of Santa Maria Primerana, and the columned loggia of the Palazzo Pretorio.

TOMB OF LEONARDO SALUTATI
The tomb is in the Duomo and ornamented with a bust. This style of tomb evolved in the second half of the 15th century. Classical references are obvious: the ancient Roman cult of ancestor worship sparked off a vigorous growth in the production of marble busts, which were often modeled from life.

The Museo Bandini.

by him, *Madonna with Angels and Saints*, which he painted in 1425 at the start of his career. Its background looks wrong for a painting that was executed in the early 15th century, but this was repainted in 1501 by Lorenzo di Credi. The chapter house contains a fresco of the *Crucifixion* by Fra Angelico, which was painted some time around 1430.

FIESOLE

Perched on the top of a hill overlooking the valley of the Arno was a junction in the network of Etruscan, and then Roman, roads. The place has always been enjoyed for its favorable climate, which is much healthier than the plain below, and for its strategic position.

THE CONVENT OF SAN FRANCESCO ★. This stands on the site of an ancient acropolis. The Gothic interior contains many 15th-century works, notably an *Immaculate Conception* by Piero di Cosimo, an early treatment of the subject, which was rare before the 16th century. Through the cloister garden is a small museum of the Franciscan missionaries. At the right of the entrance to the chapel stands the SAN BERNARDINO DORMITORY. A small staircase leads upstairs to the monks' cells.

THE CONVENT OF SAINT ALESSANDRO. The oldest basilica in Fiesole is dedicated to a bishop who was martyred in the year 820. The nave is even older, dating from the 6th century, and the Ionic capitals survive from antiquity, as do the Greek marble pillars. On the orders of Theodoric the Great, king of the Ostrogoths, this ancient temple of Bacchus was transformed into a Christian church. There are also two Etruscan cisterns, showing that this was once a place of sanctuary. The neo-classical façade was built between 1815 and 1819. The broad terrace in front of the church has spectacular views over Florence and the Arno.

THE DUOMO. The cathedral of San Romolo stands in the Piazza Mino da Fiesole on the site of an ancient forum. Built between 1204 and 1208, it was restored in the late 19th century. The bell tower (1213) presents a fortified appearance, and is 138 feet tall. The interior is laid out like a basilica, with three naves. To the right of the choir, the SALUTATI CHAPEL containing the tomb of bishop Leonardo Salutati (1464), the work of Mino di Giovanni da Poppi, known as "Mino da Fiesole". The frescoes are by Cosimo Rosselli (1439–1507). The triptych on the high altar is by Bicci di Lorenzo (1440). To the left of the choir, the *Coronation of the Virgin* (1372) is by Giovanni del Biondo.

THE BISHOP'S PALACE. First built in the 11th century, the palace stands on the terrace opposite the entrance to the

cathedral. It has been altered several times, and the present façade dates from 1675. Beside it stands a seminary that dates from 1637.

PALAZZO PRETORIO. This palace stands at the back of the Duomo. It dates from the 14th century, though its portico and fine columned loggia were built a century later.

THE CHURCH OF SANTA MARIA PRIMERANA. Beside the Palazzo Pretorio on the central piazza is this medieval church with a 19th-century portico. Inside there are 14th-century frescoes which have been attributed to followers of Giotto, and a painted *Crucifix* from the same period.

MUSEO BANDINI. The museum contains some fascinating but little-known collections. As well as furniture and majolica, there is terracotta from the Della Robbia workshops, and 14th- and 15th-century paintings by Bernardo Daddi, Taddeo Gaddi, Lorenzo Monaco and Rico da Cambia. Perhaps the oddest work in the museum is by Jacopo del Sellaio (1442–93), a pupil of Botticelli, entitled *The Triumph of Love*, *The Triumph of Charity*, *The Triumph of Time* and *The Trumph of Divinity*, inspired by the writings of Petrarch.

ARCHEOLOGICAL ZONE. At the foot of the cathedral on the north slope of the hill is an area containing some remarkable remains of the Roman settlement here. Excavated in the 19th century, the THEATER probably dates from the 1st century BC and was rebuilt in the 1st and 3rd centuries AD under Claudius and Septimus Severus. Its terraces have seating for three thousand spectators. The THERMAL BATHS were also built in the early days of imperial Rome and enlarged in the reign of Hadrian (117–38). The arches of these public baths have always been visible, but the springs were only discovered in the 19th century. One of the baths has been preserved, together with the remains of its heating system. Beside a massive Etruscan wall, which gives a good idea of what the original fortifications must have been like, are the foundations of an ETRUSCAN TEMPLE from the 3rd century BC which was altered by the Romans two hundred years later.

COHABITATION
In common with most Etruscan settlements, Fiesole (founded around the 7th century BC) was built on a hilltop. This was for reasons of military security, as well as to avoid the risk of floods and of malaria in the marshland below. Florence and Fiesole have lived together peacefully since 1125, when Florentine troops crossed the borders of Fiesole and destroyed the city, outraged by its arrogant assertion of independence. "They razed it to its foundations", wrote Giovanni Villani, leaving only the Duomo and the Bishop's Palace, so as not to incur the wrath of the pope.

Terraces of the Roman theater at Fiesole.

A NEGLECTED PARK
Nothing remains of
the Buontalenti's villa
built for Francesco I
de' Medici, which was
the favorite resort of
his second wife
Bianca Cappello
▲ *311*: it was blown
up in the early 19th
century. The wealthy
Prince Demidoff

bought the estate in
1872 and began
restoring one of the
villa's buildings as his
private residence
(above). The park
was also partially
restored. When the
Demidoff dynasty
died out the park fell
into utter neglect:
one of its few
remaining treasures is
the colossal carved
figure of *Appennino*
(top right): visitors
can climb up inside
and look out at the
park through the
figure's eyes. The
park now belongs to
the city of Florence,
and is a delightful
place to walk. To
reach it, take the Via
Bolognese to
Pratolino.

**THE ARTISTS' RESORT
OF SETTIGNANO**
This view of the
central square in
Settignano was
painted by Telemaco
Signorini
(1835–1901), one of
the leaders of the
group of artists
known as the
"Macchiaioli" ▲ *293*.

Also go to see the CIVIC
MUSEUM, where many
objects found in the
excavations are on display.

PARK AND VILLA DEMIDOFF

Eight miles from the center
of Florence at Pratolino (bus
25A from Piazza San Marco)
is the enormous park of the
Villa Demidoff. Almost
nothing remains of the
magnificent villa
which was built in
1575 by Buontalenti for Francesco I de' Medici, who decided
that, instead of gardens of geometrical design, it should have
a rural park. Neglected over many years, the now beautiful
and well-tended park has little left to show that it was once a
masterpiece of Tuscan Mannerism.
LOST TOYS. The finest artists of the age (Buontalenti,
Bandinelli, Ammannati, Giambologna and Foggini) were
commissioned to carve statues, fountains and fantastic
grottoes, in which were installed the most amazing hydraulic
automata, but these have long since disappeared. From that
Golden Age all that remains is a huge statue of *Appennino*
carved by Giambologna in 1579–80, 33 feet tall, and a small
hexagonal chapel surrounded by a loggia.

VILLA I TATTI

Near the little river of Mensola stands the villa that once
belonged to the celebrated art historian Bernard Berenson
(1865–1959). He bought it in 1905 and set about restoring it

as it would have looked in the 16th century. He re-landscaped the garden as well. On his death Berenson left his collection of works of art to Harvard University, which now uses the villa as a research center for the study of art history.

SETTIGNANO

The scenic road from Fiesole passes through this lovely village. During the 15th century the village was famous for its "school" of sculptors, which included Desiderio da Settignano (1428–64) and the two Rossellino brothers, Antonio (1427–79) and Bernardo (1409–64). Michelangelo also passed some of his childhood here, in the Casa Buonarroti. In the main square stands the 16th-century Church of the Assumption: the village was almost completely destroyed by the Germans in 1944, and the church is one of the few

surviving ancient buildings. Settignano is also associated with another famous Italian: the poet and novelist Gabriele d'Annunzio (1863–1938) lived in the beautiful Villa Capponcina. **VILLA GAMBERAIA.** Half a mile out of Settignano along the Via

Rossellino is a gorgeous 17th-century villa which boasts what has been described as one of the finest gardens in Europe. House and garden were both badly damaged by fire during World War II, but painstaking work by Marcello Marchi has restored them to their former glory. The magnificent garden, with its sophisticated geometrical design, contains ancient cypress trees and yews which were planted in the 17th century. There is also a small shady terrace with a view that is quite simply unforgettable. The Rhododendron Grotto has walls built out of ancient cobblestones, with niches holding terracotta statues. On the north side of this superb garden is the famous Grotto of Neptune.

THE CONVENT OF SAN SALVI
Standing in the Via San Salvi to the east of Florence, this convent belonged to the Vallombrosian Order and has some of the city's greatest artistic treasures. In the refectory is an important work by Andrea del Sarto, a *Last Supper* painted

in 1527 (top). Excepting Leonardo's fresco in Milan, this is the most famous representation of the Last Supper in the world: its dramatic treatment, bright colors and sense of movement captivate the viewer. The Long Gallery in the convent contains 16th-century altarpieces by Franciabigio, Vasari, and Ghirlandaio's son Ridolfo. The room beyond this houses bas-reliefs from the tomb of St John Gualberto ▲ 273. Not far from the convent is Florence's most important sports ground, the Stadio Comunale ● 94, built by Pier Luigi Nervi in 1931.

The steps of the Villa I Tatti (above), in Ponte a Mensola. The Villa Gamberaia (center left), near Settignano.

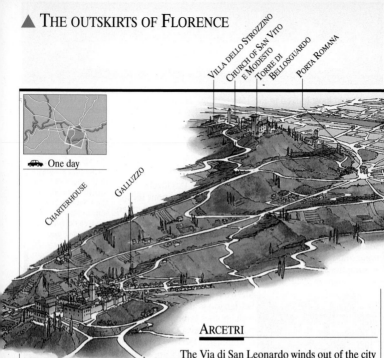

VILLA DELLO STROZZINO
CHURCH OF SAN VITO E MODESTO
TORRE DI BELLOSGUARDO
PORTA ROMANA

🚗 One day

CHARTERHOUSE
GALLUZZO

ARCETRI

The Via di San Leonardo winds out of the city to Arcetri. Here is the astrophysical observatory built by Giuseppe Boccini in 1872, under the direction of the great astronomer Donati. It is well equipped for the observation of the sun. At 42 Via Pian dei Giullari is Il Gioiello, the villa where Galileo spent his last years. The road passes close by the Torre del Gallo, to the charming village of Pian dei Giullari, perched on the top of a little hill, and the Villa Capponi, whose gardens, concealed behind high walls, are among the most beautiful in Florence.

IL GIOIELLO
Galileo ended his days in the Arcetri villa. He finished his *Dialoghi intorno a due nuove scienze*, and, before becoming completely blind, made his last discovery, "the daily and monthly librations of the moon". He worked on with enthusiasm, aided by his long-standing collaborators Viviani and Torricelli, and corresponded with scholars all over Europe.

IL GIOIELLO DI GALILEO

The dome of the astrophysical observatory of Arcetri.

VILLA DEL POGGIO IMPERIALE

MANY ALTERATIONS. The opulent but unprepossessing neo-classical façade of the villa gives no hint of its 15th-century origins. Confiscated from the Salviati family, it was given by Cosimo I to his daughter Isabella, furnished with paintings and statues. The name of Poggio Imperiale came from Maria Maddelena of Austria, wife of Cosimo II, evoking her links with the royal family of Austria. She brought in Giulio Parigi to design an elegant façade crowned with an arcaded belvedere. In the 18th century Pietro-Leopoldo decided to make it his summer residence, and ordered changes to be made by Gaspero Paoletti, who worked on it from 1766 to 1782; his courtyard façades survive. In the early 19th century the last phase of works began: Pasquale Poccianti designed a new façade. It was finished by Giuseppe Cacialli, in 1814.

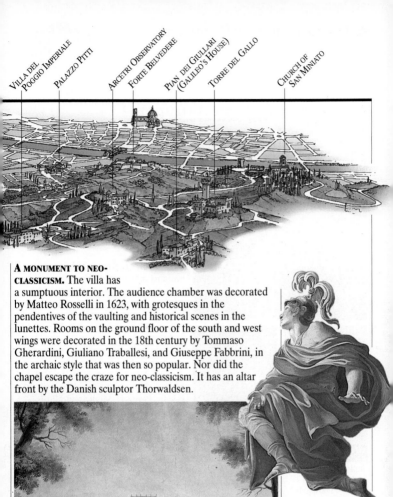

VILLA DEL POGGIO IMPERIALE PALAZZO PITTI ARCETRI OBSERVATORY FORTE BELVEDERE PIAN DEI GIULLARI (GALILEO'S HOUSE) TORRE DEL GALLO CHURCH OF SAN MINIATO

A MONUMENT TO NEO-CLASSICISM. The villa has
a sumptuous interior. The audience chamber was decorated
by Matteo Rosselli in 1623, with grotesques in the
pendentives of the vaulting and historical scenes in the
lunettes. Rooms on the ground floor of the south and west
wings were decorated in the 18th century by Tommaso
Gherardini, Giuliano Traballesi, and Giuseppe Fabbrini, in
the archaic style that was then so popular. Nor did the
chapel escape the craze for neo-classicism. It has an altar
front by the Danish sculptor Thorwaldsen.

BELLOSGUARDO

A rare opportunity for a country walk just minutes from the
center of town is on the hill of Bellosguardo. In this pleasant
setting, Florence can be viewed from a delightful new angle.
It is reached from the Piazza San Francesco di Paola, taking
the tortuous Via di Bellosguardo. Not far from the little
CHURCH OF SAN VITO E MODESTO is the elegant VILLA DELLO
STROZZINO, with loggia and surrounding park. At number 20
is the VILLA BRICHIERI-COLOMBI, where Henry James wrote
The Aspern Papers. Just before reaching the village turn sharp
right into the Via Roti Michelozzi, which will lead past the
VILLA CALAMAI, where in 1813 the writer Ugo Foscolo ▲ *258*
stayed and wrote his poem *Le Grazie*, on to the TORRE DI
BELLOSGUARDO. This villa, the main door of which has a
sculpture by Pietro Francavilla, is now a luxury hotel.

**HENRY JAMES AND
NATHANIEL
HAWTHORNE**
In 1858 Nathaniel
Hawthorne rented a
villa on the hill of
Bellosguardo, later
described by another
American writer,
Henry James: "a
picturesque old villa .
. . a curious structure
with a crenellated
tower, which, after
having in the course
of its career suffered
many vicissitudes and
played many parts,
now finds its most
vivid identity in being
pointed out to
strangers as the
sometimes residence
of the celebrated
American romancer".

stalls date from the end of the 16th century. During the Napoleonic occupation, fearing pillage by French troops, the monks painted them black. The Charterhouse is shown (top) on its hill, with (beneath) the façade of San Lorenzo and the entrance staircase.

The *Crucifixion* (1506) by Mariotto Albertinelli, who taught Pontormo.

THE CERTOSA DI GALLUZZO

A FORTRESS. The village of Galluzzo is just over a mile from the Porta Romana ▲ *305*. The imposing fortress-like building that looks down on the village and Ema valley is a Charterhouse occupied by a few Cistercian monks, who took over from the Carthusians in 1958. With limited means, they do their best to take care of it and show the public round. One of the most generous benefactors of recent times has been the cinema director Luchino Visconti.

PALAZZO DEGLI STUDI. The corner building with Gothic windows and crenellated roof was built in the 14th century to take in young Florentines interested in studying the liberal arts. Its patron was Niccolò Acciaiuoli (1310–65), founder of the Charterhouse. He belonged to one of Florence's wealthy banking families. The Acciaiuolis were high up in the Guild of Money-changers ▲ *198*, along with the Bardis, Peruzzis, Medicis and Pittis. Niccolò was the family's most illustrious member. A friend of Petrarch and Boccaccio, he took an active part in the political life of the city and was several times a prior. He was also governor of Naples. He had gone to the city on business and became a great friend of Caterina, widow of the prince of Tarento and empress of Cosntantinople. Thus it was that he became for twenty years high steward of the kingdom of Naples. One of the rooms in the palace is given over to some fine works of art, among them paintings by Mariotto di Nardo, Dürer and Ghirlandaio.

PONTORMO AND DÜRER. In another room are five detached frescoes by Jacopo da Pontormo, which were painted around 1525. Vasari tells their history in detail, emphasizing Pontormo's admiration for the German artist Dürer (1471–1528). "In 1522 plague broke out in Florence. . . . An opportunity arose for Jacopo to get away from the city when a prior from the Charterhouse asked him to decorate a huge and magnificent cloister set around a lawn. . . . Jacopo came accompanied only by Bronzino. He took a great liking to the life. The peace, the silence and the solitude all suited his temperament and genius well, and he thought it the perfect

chance to demonstrate his progress in a new style. A large number of prints had recently arrived in Florence from Germany, exquisitely engraved by Albrecht Dürer. . . . One series was of *Scenes from the Passion of Christ* . . . and Jacopo decided to repeat the series, convinced that not only he, but the majority of Florentine painters would be pleased with the result, so unanimous were they in their praise of these engravings and the art of Dürer. He worked with such energy that the natural grace and delicacy of his earlier style was quite changed by the force of his effort."

THE CHAPTER HOUSE. There are a number of works here, including a beautiful *Crucifixion* from 1506 by Mariotto Albertinelli (1474–1515), and also the marble tomb of Leonardo Buonafede.

PAINTER TURNED INNKEEPER. Albertinelli was a "character" rather than a great painter. André Chastel has this to say of him: "He would probably have gone into a monastery if he hadn't detested monks, and Savonarola in particular. . . . He lived life to the full, and his amorous excesses were the end of him". Vasari, too, gives a vivid account of his life: "Mariotto Albertinelli was a highly energetic and sensual man, who loved the good things in life; he tired of worrying his head with endless speculation about painting, and putting up with biting criticism from other painters. . . . He decided to devote himself to a less elevated art, not so much trouble and a lot more fun: he opened a fine inn near the Porta San Gallo, and another with entertainment at the old Ponte del Drago. He continued in business for several months, declaring that he had found a profession where he would have no more of muscles . . . and perspective, and above all critics. . . . Then he tired of this new life, ashamed of its vulgarity, and returned to painting."

THE GREAT CLOISTER. The impressive and beautifully proportioned *chiostro grande* encloses an expanse of lawn and at its center a huge well (left). The cloister, built between 1498 and 1516, is surrounded by cells, which can be visited, and also contains a small monks' cemetery. The medallions that decorate the arcades are from the Della Robbia workshops: they are of prophets, sibyls, saints and also of Adam and Eve.

"DEPOSITION FROM THE CROSS"
Vasari liked this work by Pontormo very much: "Despite their Germanic style, the heads of the old men, Joseph of Arimathea and Nicodemus, with their feathery beards, are the finest imaginable." He was much less taken with *Christ in the Garden*: "There is such a strange look on the faces of the soldiers, closely imitating the German style, that the beholder is filled with pity for Pontormo, trying so hard to acquire what others would much rather avoid and forget, all in order to free himself from a better style that was much liked by all". What Vasari failed to understand was that this "better style" was fast becoming a dry academic convention which Pontormo found constricting.

VILLA DEL POGGIO A CAIANO ● 78

🚗 Half a day

POGGIO A CAIANO
The main hall of the villa has a rare and splendid barrel-vaulted ceiling, decorated in 1518. Four scenes evoke great moments from the Roman empire, echoed in the history of the Medici family. The artists were Franciabigio, Andrea del Sarto, Pontormo and, later, Alessandro Allori, who completed the decoration after 1579. Finest of all is Pontormo's lunette of *Vertumnus and Pomona*, an impressively mature Mannerist work.

A MODEL RESIDENCE. This beautiful Medici villa some 11 miles from Florence belonged originally to the Strozzi family ▲ 209. Lorenzo il Magnifico bought it in 1480, and over the next five years Giuliano da Sangallo worked there, creating a colonnaded lower ground floor. Unlike other Medici villas, Poggia a Caiano did not have fortified features. It was a truly gracious villa: just what Alberti had dreamt of. There are only hints of military architecture in the low corner towers and the rough-cut stone at ground level. The classical portico was a new feature, used here for the first time on a secular building, and commissioned by Pope Leo X, Lorenzo's son. Otherwise, later works did not greatly alter the outward appearance of the villa, apart from the 19th-century curved double staircase.

TO THE GLORY OF COSIMO. The interior of the villa is equally handsome. In the dining room is a fresco from 1698, one of the finest works of Antonio Domenico Gabbiani (1652–1726), the *Apotheosis of Cosimo il Vecchio*. His style was much influenced by the great Baroque painter Pietro da Cortona.

UNEXPLAINED DEATHS. In this refined setting, in 1587, the Grand Duke Francesco I and his wife Bianca Cappello ▲ 311 died mysteriously within hours of one another. Bianca Cappello's room can be seen, its decoration unchanged. Most other rooms were redecorated in the 19th century when King Victor Emmanuel II decided to use the villa occasionally.

ARTIMINO ★

In the village of Artimino, perched on a ridge 4 miles south of Poggio a Caiano, is La Ferdinanda, a splendid Medici villa built by Buontalenti for Ferdinando I. Despite its stern appearance with projecting corner towers, there is a great elegance in its design. The many chimneys, like miniature fortresses, are a delightful feature.

PIEVE SAN LEONARDO. A Romanesque church, dating from the 12th century, and one of the best-preserved of its period.

USEFUL INFORMATION

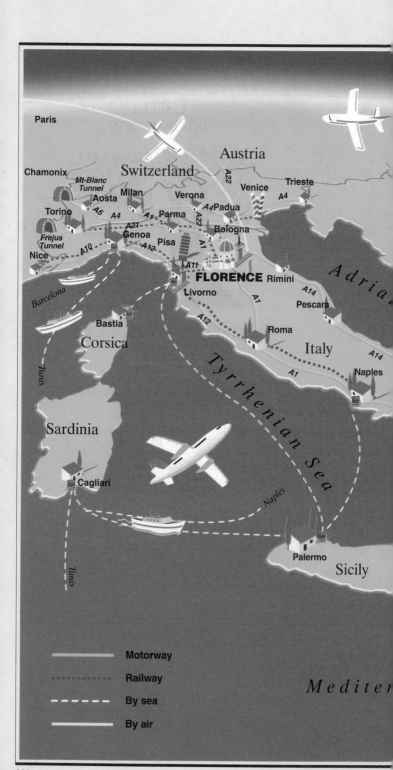

Hungary

Sea

Foggia

A16

Bari

A14

Taranto

A3

Messina

Reggio
di Calabria

Siracusa

nean Sea

BY AIR

There are 2 flights a day from Stanstead to Florence with Air UK, and daily flights from Gatwick with Meridiana. There are no direct flights from the US but you can make connections through Brussels, Rome or Paris from New York, changing to Meridiana, Alitalia or Air France. Vespucci airport at Peretola is 2½ miles from Florence, and mainly caters for domestic flights. Public transport to the town center is complicated, so it is best to take a taxi. Galileo Galilei airport at Pisa–San Giusto is 1¼ miles from Pisa and all international flights arrive here. Take a train from there to Florence; the journey lasts one hour, with departures every 15 minutes.

◆ AIRLINES
–Air UK, London
Tel. 01345 666777
–Meridiana, London
Tel. 0171 839 2222
–Alitalia, Florence
L. no. Acciaiuoli, 10/12r
Tel. 27 888
Open 9am–4.30pm except Sat. and Sun.
–Air France, Florence Borgo Ss Apostoli, 9
Tel. 28 43 04
Open 9am–1pm, 2.30–5pm.

◆ AIRPORTS
–Vespucci airport, Peretola
Tel. 30 615
Galileo Galilei, Pisa
Tel. 050/20 062
(Closed at Christmas.)

BY TRAIN

Take the Eurostar train to Paris, departing from London Waterloo. This service operates hourly throughout the day. Change at Paris and take the overnight train from the Gare de Lyon at 8.09pm, which arrives in Florence at 8.22am the next day.
–British Rail International
Tel. 0171 834 2345
– Eurostar information
Tel. 01233 617575
–Santa Maria Novella Station, Florence
Tel. 28 87 85
Open 9am–5pm.

BY CAR

You can drive across the Continent to Florence via the Mont Blanc tunnel, the Simplon Pass, the Fréjus tunnel or along the motorway "du Soleil" via Genoa. You will need your driving license, vehicle registration documents and international insurance to drive in Italy.

BY COACH

From Victoria Coach Station in London on Sat., Mon., Wed. and

Fri. Departs 12.30pm and takes 28 hours altogether.
–Victoria Coach Stn.
Tel. 0171 824 8657

BY BOAT

The sea crossing from Bastia to Livorno takes 3 hours.
◆ In Florence
–Sardinia Ferries
P. Sauro, 17r
Tel. 28 08 05
Open 9am–1pm, 2.30–6.30pm
– New Tours
Via G. Monaco, 20/a
Tel. 32 11 55
Open 9am–1pm, 2.30–6.30pm.

GETTING ABOUT IN FLORENCE

1.a Duomo

2.a Piazza Signoria
2.b Palazzo Vecchio
2.c Galleria degli Uffizi
2.d Ponte Vecchio

3.a Bargello
3.b Badia Fiorentina

4.a Orsanmichele
4.b Palazzo Strozzi
4.c Church of Santa Maria Novella
4.d Central Post Office
4.e Santa Maria Novella Station

5.a Church of San Lorenzo

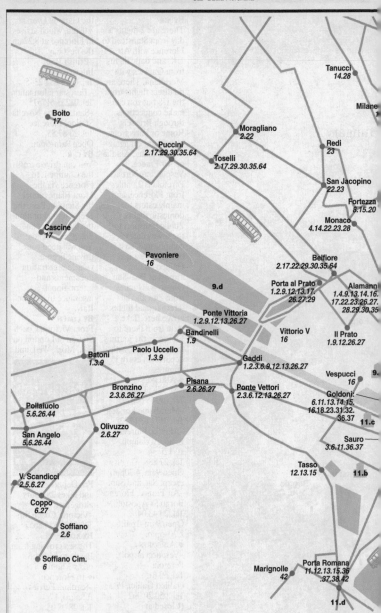

Tanucci
14.28

Milane

Boito
17

Moragliano
2.22

Puccini
2.17.29.30.35.64

Toselli
2.17.29.30.35.64

Redi
23

San Jacopino
22.23

Fortezza
8.15.20

Cascine
17

Pavoniere
16

Monaco
4.14.22.23.28

Belfiore
2.17.22.29.30.35.64

9.d

Porta al Prato
*1.2.9.12.13.17.
26.27.29*

Alamann
*1.4.9.13.14.16.
17.22.23.26.27.
28.29.30.35*

Ponte Vittoria
1.2.9.12.13.26.27

Bandinelli
1.9

Vittorio V
16

Il Prato
1.9.12.26.27

Batoni
1.3.9

Paolo Uccello
1.3.9

Gaddi
1.2.3.6.9.12.13.26.27

Vespucci
16

9.

Bronzino
2.3.6.26.27

Pisana
2.6.26.27

Ponte Vettori
2.3.6.12.13.26.27

Goldoni
*6.11.13.14.15.
16.18.23.31.32.
36.37*

11.c

Pollaiuolo
5.6.26.44

Olivuzzo
2.6.27

Sauro
3.6.11.36.37

San Angelo
5.6.26.44

Tasso
12.13.15

11.b

V. Scandicci
2.5.6.27

Coppo
6.27

Soffiano
2.6

Soffiano Cim.
6

Marignolle
42

Porta Romana
*11.12.13.15.36.
.37.38.42*

11.d

BY BUS
Buses run every day, including Sunday.
◆ The price of a ticket ranges from 1,200 lire for 1 hour (a book of 8 tickets costs 9,000 lire) to 5,000 lire for 24 hours. A weekly (*Carta Arancio*) ticket costs 25,000 lire and can be used on trains and buses in and around Florence. These tickets are sold at tobacconists, in bars and at:
ATAF, Piazza Stazione (in the "Pensilina").
SITA, Via S. Caterina da Siena, 15/r.
LAZZI, Piazza Stazione.
CAP, Via Nazionale, 13.
COPIT, Piazza Santa Maria Novella, 22.
BY TAXI
◆ Socota Radio-taxis Tel: 47 98.
Open 24 hours.
◆ Cotafi Radio-taxis Tel: 43 90.
Open 24 hours.
BY CAR
Cars are not permitted in the city center between 7.30am and 6.30pm Mon. to Sat.

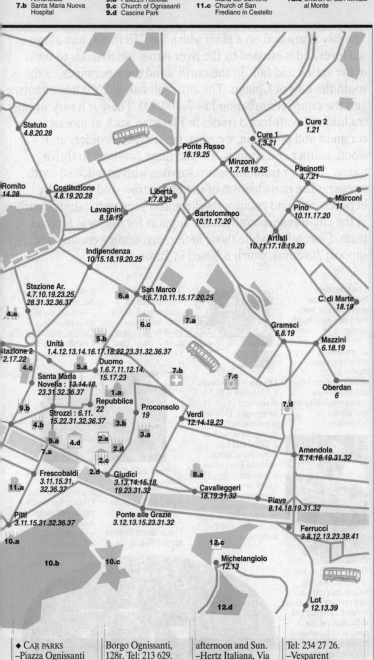

Statuto
4.8.20.28

Cure 2
1.21

Cure 1
1.3.21

Ponte Rosso
18.19.25

Minzoni
1.7.18.19.25

Pacinotti
3.7.21

Romito
14.28

Costituzione
4.8.19.20.28

Libertà
1.7.8.25

Marconi
11

Lavagnini
8.18.19

Bartolommeo
10.11.17.20

Pino
10.11.17.20

Indipendenza
10.15.18.19.20.25

Artisti
10.11.17.18.19.20

Stazione Ar.
4.7.10.19.23.25.
28.31.32.36.37

San Marco
1.6.7.10.11.15.17.20.25

C. di Marte
18.19

4.e

6.a

7.a

Gramsci
6.8.19

Stazione 2
2.17.22

Unità
1.4.12.13.14.16.17.18.22.23.31.32.36.37

5.b

6.c

Mazzini
6.18.19

4.c

5.a

Duomo
1.6.7.11.12.14.
15.17.23

7.b

Oberdan
6

Santa Maria
Novella : 13.14.18.
23.31.32.36.37

1.a

7.c

7.d

9.b

Repubblica
22

Proconsolo
19

Verdi
12.14.19.23

Strozzi : 6.11.
15.22.31.32.36.37

3.b

4.b

9.a **4.d**

2.a

3.a

2.d

Amendola
8.14.18.19.31.32

7.a

2.c

Frescobaldi
3.11.15.31.
32.36.37

2.d

Giudici
3.13.14.15.18.
19.23.31.32

8.a

Cavalleggeri
18.19.31.32

11.a

Piave
8.14.18.19.31.32

Pitti
3.11.15.31.32.36.37

Ponte alle Grazie
3.12.13.15.23.31.32

Ferrucci
3.8.12.13.23.39.41

10.a

12.c

10.b **10.c**

Michelangiolo
12.13

Lot
12.13.39

12.d

◆ CAR PARKS
–Piazza Ognissanti
Open 8 am–8 pm.
–Fortezza da Basso
Open 24 hours.
–Santa Maria Novella Station. Open 5.30 am–10 pm.
◆ CAR HIRE
–Avis Autonoleggio,

Borgo Ognissanti, 128r. Tel: 213 629. Open 8 am–7 pm, Sat 8 am–1 pm, closed .Sun. and holidays
–Europcar-Italia, Borgo Ognissanti, 53r. Tel: 293 444. Open 9am–12.30 pm, 3–6.30 pm except Sat.

afternoon and Sun.
–Hertz Italiana, Via Finiguerra, 33r. Tel: 239 82 05. Open 8 am–8 pm, except Sun. (8 am–1 pm).
◆ BICYCLE AND MOPED
–Ciao & Basta, Lungarno G. Pecori Giraldi, 1

Tel: 234 27 26.
–Vesparent
via Pisani, 103r
Tel: 71 56 01.
–Alinari
via Guelfa 85r
Tel: 29 05 00.
–Motorent, Via San Zanobi, 9r.
Tel: 49 01 13.

341

The city is situated on a plain which lies 150 to 300 feet above sea level and is crossed by the river Arno, which tends to flood in the spring and fall. To the north stand the Apennines, to the south the hills of Chianti. The city itself has 400,000 inhabitants, and the entire conurbation has 7–800,000. There is a very strong tradition of craft-based trades in Florence, such as mosaic, ceramics and porcelain, weaving, tapestry, embroidery and wood, leather and straw-work, and these continue to thrive today. Another tradition which survives with as much strength as ever is the parochialism of the Florentines and the rivalry between city- and country-dwellers. It is seen particularly clearly in the city-dwellers' enthusiastic support for the local football team, Fiorentina, while those in the surrounding countryside support Juventus, which is based in Turin.

THE ECONOMY

In the 1960's the activity of the post-war years gave way to economic problems as commerce became decentralized, the working classes moved to the outskirts of the city and the historic center was left to less specialized businesses.

Today, despite a crisis in the two leading industries (textiles and tanning), the area around Florence can still count on the success of its small businesses. And the city's status still depends very much on its rich artistic and cultural heritage, which attracts some seven million tourists a year.

ON THE NEWSSTANDS

La Nazione is the main local newspaper. However, some national newspapers, such as *L'Unità* and *La Repubblica*, devote space to Florentine affairs every day. The monthly review *Firenze ieri, oggi e domani* also offers a wealth of information on the city and its history.

THE MARKETS

– Food market: central market and Sant'Ambrogio market, weekdays from 7 am to 2 pm. (In winter the central market also opens on Sat. afternoons.)
– General market: Mercato delle Cascine, Viale Lincoln, every Tues. (8 am–2 pm).

– Flower market: Via Pellicceria, every Thursday (8 am–2 pm) from Sept. to June.
– Craft market: Piazza Santo Spirito, second Sun. in the month except Aug.
– Secondhand market: Piazza dei Ciompi, last Sun. in the month except July.
– Flea market: Piazza dei Ciompi, Tues.–Sat., morning and afternoon.

HACKNEY CABS

This is the most romantic way to discover Florence. Negotiate the price of the ride in advance and avoid rush hours. Leave from the Duomo.

STREET NUMBERING
Starting with the city center and the banks of the Arno, the numbers increase the further you get from the center. An unusual feature is that the houses have black numbers while the shops have red ones.

FESTIVALS AND EVENTS

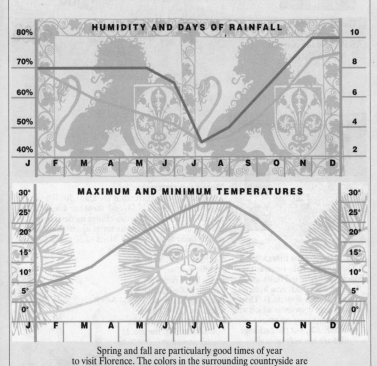

		JANUARY	FEBRUARY	MARCH	APRIL	MAY	JUNE	JULY	AUGUST	SEPTEMBER	OCTOBER	NOVEMBER	DECEMBER
LO SCOPPIO DEL CARRO					●								
FEAST OF THE GRASSHOPPER						●							
FEAST OF ST JOHN						24							
FEAST OF THE RIFICOLONE										7			
THEATER SEASON		●	●	●	●						●	●	●
LYRICAL SEASON		●	●	●									●
MUSIC IN MAYTIME						●							
FIESOLE FESTIVAL								●	●				
FILM FESTIVAL													●
FLORENCE FAIR				●									
FAIR OF SAN GIUSEPPE				●									
FASHION COLLECTIONS				●							●		
DIPLO (ART BOOK FAIR)					●								
LENT FAIR					●								
CRAFT FAIR					●	●							
FLOWER EXHIBITION					●	●							
TEXTILE FAIR										●			
BIRD MARKET										●			
ANTIQUE DEALERS' BIENNIAL EVENT										●			

PUBLIC HOLIDAYS
January 1, January 6 (*la Befana, Epiphany*), Easter Monday, May 1, June 24 (*San Giovanni*), August 15 (*Ferragosto*), November 1 and December 8, 25 and 26.

HUMIDITY AND DAYS OF RAINFALL

80%													10
70%													8
60%													6
50%													4
40%													2

J F M A M J J A S O N D

MAXIMUM AND MINIMUM TEMPERATURES

30°													30°
25°													25°
20°													20°
15°													15°
10°													10°
5°													5°
0°													0°

J F M A M J J A S O N D

Spring and fall are particularly good times of year to visit Florence. The colors in the surrounding countryside are magnificent, and you avoid the summer heat and crowds.

50 LIRE

100 LIRE

50 LIRE
The small coins
are less common.

Prices vary a good deal according to the district. A meal can double in price from one restaurant to another (from 30,000 lire to 60,000 lire for an ordinary meal). Hotels also vary greatly in price, according to their location. For a double room with breakfast, you should allow between 110,000 lire and 185,000 lire a night near the Convent of San Marco, and from 540,000 lire to 675,000 lire at the Excelsior, which has a view over the Arno.

POSTAL RATES
Italian mailboxes are red. The Italian postal system has the reputation of being rather slow.

The rate for sending a postcard within Europe is 700 lire, and the cost of a letter is 850 lire.

AUTOMATIC CASH DISPENSERS
The biggest banks (such as the Banca d'America e d'Italia and the Banca Toscana) now have automatic cash dispensers. There are also cash dispensers which will change your currency automatically, but the exchange rates are not very favorable.

MONEY AND EXCHANGE
The unit of Italian currency is the lira. 1,700 lire are worth a little under US $1, and there are around 2,500 lire to the £ sterling. You can change money at banks, bureaux de change and some travel agents. Banks are usually open Mon. to Fri., 8.20 am –1.20 pm and 2.45–3.45 pm. Banca Nazionale delle Comunicazioni, Santa Maria Novella Station, Tel: 238 1470 (open Sat.). Banca Commerciale Italiana, Via Por Santa Maria, no. 19r, Tel: 239 67 71. Cassa di Risparmio di Firenze, Via Speziali, no. 14r. Bureau de change at station (open 8am–1.20 pm, 2.30–8 pm). Primavera Viaggi, Via Ricasoli, no. 29 (open Sun. am). Tel. 28 20 42

Coffee
1,200 LIRE

Cappuccino
1,500 LIRE

Glass of chianti
from 1,500
to 2,500 LIRE

500

200 LIRE

Phone tokens worth 200 lire are sometimes used in place of money, and, as certain very low-value coins no longer exist, shopkeepers give sweets as change instead!

TELEPHONE
There are phone booths in the city center, but it is easier to make international calls from a public telephone center where you pay at the desk once you have finished your call.

THE PRICE OF A PHONE CALL	
FROM FLORENCE	**1 MIN**
ROME (06)	800 LIRE
FROM FLORENCE	**1 MIN**
GERMANY (00 49)	1,378 LIRE
SPAIN (00 34)	1,524 LIRE
FRANCE (00 33)	1,378 LIRE
GREAT BRITAIN (00 44)	1,524 LIRE
JAPAN (00 81)	4,518 LIRE
USA (00 1)	3,618 LIRE

To call Florence from the UK, dial: 00 + 39 + 55 + the number of the person you are calling. From the US, dial 011 + 39 + 55 + the number you require. To call Florence from another town in Italy, dial 055, and for information, dial 12.

TELEPHONE CARDS
Phone booths take 200 lire coins, tokens and magnetic cards. These cards (5,000 or 10,000 lire) are on sale at post offices, bars, tobacconists' and some kiosks.

SHOP OPENING HOURS
Food shops are usually open 8 am– 1 pm and 5–8 pm (winter 4.30–7.30pm) except Sun. and Wed. afternoon in winter and Sat. afternoon in summer. Other shops usually open 9 am–1 pm and 3.30–7.30 pm. They are closed on Mon. morning in winter and Sat. afternoon in summer (June 15–Sept. 15). Some shops are open for longer hours (10 am–7.30 pm).

Tramezzino (sandwich) from 1,700 to 4,000 LIRE

Admission to museum from 4,000 to 10,000

Inexpensive/expensive meal from 30,000 to 100,000 LIRE

Inexpensive/expensive double room from 80,000 to 210,000 LIRE

Church of Santa Maria Novella. Goldsmiths' shops on the Ponte Vecchio (below).

The Palazzo Vecchio, in the Piazza della Signoria: "When I saw this mass of stones so powerfully rooted in the earth, surmounted by a tower which threatens the sky like the arm of a Titan, the whole of old Florence [...] appeared before me as though I were about to witness the exile of Cosimo il Vecchio."

Alexandre Dumas

9 AM. If you arrive by train, you can start your visit with the church of Santa Maria Novella, which is facing you as you come out of the station. Its façade, the frescoes by Masaccio, Ghirlandaio and Filippino Lippi, and its cloister will give you some idea of the grandeur of the Florentine Renaissance ▲ 213.

10 AM. Follow the Via dei Fossi as far as the lungarni. Ahead of you, one after the other, lie the bridges of Florence, the Oltrarno district, and above all what Palazzeschi called "the civilized beauty" of the surrounding hills. Silhouetted in the distance stands San Miniato al Monte, with its Romanesque façade of white and green marble. Cross the Ponte alla Carraia and follow the Via de' Serragli; if you turn right, you can view the wonderful frescoes of the Brancacci Chapel ▲ 308 in the church of Santa Maria del Carmine. The Via Sant'Agostino will then take you to the Piazza San Felice, near the massive Palazzo Pitti. It is well worth a visit inside to see the many rooms of the Palatine Gallery and linger in front of the Titians and Raphaels ▲ 289; stop for a while in the inner courtyard, which is a jewel of 16th-century architecture. Behind it lie the Boboli Gardens ▲ 294, which you should also make time to visit.

12 NOON. When you leave the palace, go down the Via Maggio ▲ 311 and wander in the adjacent narrow streets, which are full of antique and craft shops. Cross the Arno again, this time by the Ponte Vecchio ▲ 172, to your right. Sip an aperitif at *Rivoire*'s, in the Piazza della Signoria ▲ 142. From there, you can watch the square, the Palazzo Vecchio ▲ 147 and all the other tourists. Rather than eating the usual sandwich for lunch, you may prefer to stop at a *mescita* ◆ 354, like those in the Via dei Tavolini, which will offer you *crostini* with a glass of chianti.

3 PM. The afternoon can be spent walking and shopping in the streets leading from the Piazza della Signoria to the Duomo and San Lorenzo. Here all the traditional Florentine businesses are found side by side with international luxury boutiques selling leather goods, jewelry, clothes and household linen. On the way, do not forget to visit the church of Orsanmichele ▲ 196; when you reach the Piazza del Duomo, the Baptistery and its doors ▲ 134, Giotto's campanile ▲ 132 and the cathedral itself are not to be missed. If it is not too late, continue along to the monumental church of San Lorenzo ▲ 220, where you can pay your respects to Brunelleschi, Donatello and Michelangelo.

8 PM. In the evening go up to the Piazzale Michelangelo ▲ 319, on foot, by car from the Piazza Poggi or by the no. 13 bus, to see the city from above as the sun is setting. Make the most of the spectacular view by having dinner in the loggia. If you are traveling by car, you will be able to go as far as Pian dei Giullari and have dinner at *Da Omero*'s, a typical Florentine trattoria. If you prefer to return to the city center, choose between *Coco Lezzone*, *Latini* and *Sostanza*, which are all typical local restaurants.

DAY ONE. To get off to a good start, spend two hours in the Piazza del Duomo: walk round the cathedral ▲ *128*, and examine the Baptistery doors▲ *134* and Giotto's campanile ▲ *132*. Afterwards, visit the cathedral itself and do not forget to go to the top of the cupola ▲ *130* which gives you a superb view of the city. Then walk down the Via de' Martelli and the Via Cavour, as far as the Convent of San Marco ▲ *228*: the magnificent frescoes by Fra Angelico and Ghirlandaio are worth the detour.

Giotto's campanile and the cupola of the Duomo, seen from a sidestreet in the city center.

12 NOON. Drop into the Museo Nazionale del Bargello on Via del Proconsolo, which has some imposing sculptures by Donatello and Michelangelo. At lunchtime choose a *mescita* ◆ *354*, in the Via dei Neri, where they serve traditional hot dishes: *ribollita* in the winter ● *58, panzanella* in the summer, served with a glass of chianti or Tuscan white wine ■ *22*. You can then choose a delicious ice cream from *Vivoli*, in the Via Torta. Small portions are sufficient: the large ones are truly gigantic.

3 PM. Go to Santa Croce ▲ *254*. Do not forget to visit the cloister and the Cappella dei Pazzi, designed by Brunelleschi ▲ *261*. When you reach the Arno, have a look at the jewelers' shops on the Ponte Vecchio ▲ *172,* then make your way to the Palazzo Pitti ▲ *288*. Have a quick look at the inner courtyard, then go and see Buontalenti's grotto in the Boboli Gardens ▲ *295*. Go down the big cypress-edged pathway as far as the *Isolotto* and leave through the Porta Romana or the Orangery, which is nearer. Come back toward the Arno along the Via Maggio ▲ *311*, the street of antique dealers. The Boboli Gardens close earlier in the winter so you could climb to the Belvedere instead ▲ *297*.

8 PM. Have dinner in the Borgo San Jacopo, at *Cammillo*'s or *Mamma Gina*'s, and finish the evening at the café in the Piazza Pitti.

❝The gardens of the palazzo (Pitti) are extremely pleasant: they are full of mountains, valleys, woods, knolls, flowerbeds and forests, set down at random, without design or sequence, which gives them a real country air.❞
Charles de Brosses

DAY TWO. Start in the Piazza della Signoria, after a hot chocolate or cappuccino at *Rivoire*'s. Admire the statues in the square ▲ *143* (such as that of Cosimo I, shown on the right), then those in the Loggia dei Lanzi ▲ *144*, and go directly to the Uffizi ▲ *153*.

1 PM. Have a snack on the terrace of the Uffizi café ▲ *149*. If you prefer a proper meal, the historic *Antico Fattico* is just a few steps away in the Via Lambertini.

3 PM. Devote the afternoon to Orsanmichele ▲ *196* and the important church of San Lorenzo ▲ *220*, stopping to do some window-shopping along the way.

8 PM. Go up to Fiesole (by car or no. 7 bus): do not forget to climb up to San Francesco and have an aperitif at the *Blu Bar*. If you have a car, stay and have dinner at the *Cave di Maiano*, or go back down into the city near the Sant' Ambrogio market and try *Cibreo*'s restaurant. Spend this last evening tasting Tuscan wines in an *enoteca*, such as *Cantinetta Antinori* or *Cantinone del Gallo Nero*.

View of the "City of the Lily" from the Belvedere.

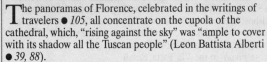

"I climb to the top of the campanile, which affords a unique view of Florence. The outlook over the Duomo itself, with its inspired cupola, is particularly beautiful; an inestimable architectural view."
Hermann Hesse

Views of the church of Santa Croce, the Palazzo Vecchio and Giotto's campanile from the Duomo.

The panoramas of Florence, celebrated in the writings of travelers ● *105*, all concentrate on the cupola of the cathedral, which, "rising against the sky" was "ample to cover with its shadow all the Tuscan people" (Leon Battista Alberti ● *39, 88*).

FROM THE HILLS. From the Via Bolognese, on top of the Costa de la Lastra, like Stendhal and pilgrims from the north before you, you can see Florence, its cathedral and the unusual outline of the hill of Fiesole. Viewed from the terrace of the Convent of San Francesco at Fiesole ▲ *328*, the whole city lies spread out over the plain of the Arno; the best time to go is at dawn or sunset, when you can see clearly the villas, their landscaped gardens and the groups of houses scattered over the hillside between Florence and Fiesole.

FROM THE LEFT BANK OF THE ARNO. The Forte Belvedere ▲ *297*, the Piazzale Michelangelo ▲ *319*, the terrace of San Miniato ▲ *320*, and the hill of Bellosguardo ▲ *333* will give you a low-angled view over the city and its rooftops, since you will be on the same level as the cupola of the Duomo. From the Forte Belvedere or the Piazzale, you will have a quite exceptional view of the Arno, its bridges and the city's monuments, all of which can be seen at a glance. Only the Forte Belvedere allows you to look out over the Boboli Gardens ▲ *294* on one side and see the hills of Arcetri ▲ *332* from the other. You can reach it on foot by the Costa San Giorgio ▲ *298* or the Via dei Bastioni. Wait for sunset in a café in the Piazzale Michelangelo or on the terrace of San Miniato. You can get there by car or the no. 13 bus. On foot, go up by the Via Poggi and down, as far as the Porta San Miniato, along the Via del Monte alle Croci and the *scalee dantesche*, which run parallel to it, to see the city from the gardens. Go for a walk in Bellosguardo: as you turn the corners of the narrow streets and look over the walls of the villas in the Via di Bellosguardo and Via Monte Oliveto, for example, you will see some unexpected views of the city.

FROM THE CENTER. Finally, in the city itself, the tower of the Palazzo Vecchio ▲ *147*, the bell-tower of Orsanmichele ▲ *196* and Giotto's campanile ▲ *132* show very different aspects of the city. Stop at the terrace of the Uffizi café ▲ *149*: it affords one of the finest views of the cathedral and towers of Florence. End your visit with the cupola of the Duomo ▲ *130*, from which there is a panoramic view of all the palaces and monuments of Florence.

S pend a few hours in the Florence painted by Rosai (1895–1957) ● *102*, on the narrow roads lined with walls which hide the villas scattered in the first ring of hills.
NORTH, TO FIESOLE. Begin by following the Via Vittorio Emanuele (bus nos. 31 or 32) as far as the Via Stibbert. Go past the church of San Martino and the Stibbert Museum

STIBBERT MUSEUM
Since 1965 it has housed the collections bequeathed to the city by Federico Stibbert.

▲ *325*; the road becomes narrower and changes its name to Via di Montughi. Notice the Villa Cresci, which used to belong to the Davanzati family, and above all the Villa Alberti, the ancient fortress of the Ughi, which later passed to the Pazzis. The famous conspiracy against the Medicis was plotted there ▲ *131*. Turn left into the Via Bolognese. At the end of a magnificent avenue of cypresses, you will catch sight of the Villa La Pietra ▲ *326*, which belonged to the Capponi, then Harold Acton. If you are on foot, go back down into the city by the Vicolo di San Marco Vecchio, which will take you past some more magnificent villas. At the Via Faentina, right at the end of the street, you can catch the no. 1A bus which will take you back to the city center. You can also cut through and go down by the Via dei Bruni, which offers a very beautiful view of Florence; there are several bus stops in the Piazza delle Cure. If you go by car, it is better to continue along the Via Bolognese as far as the Via Salviati, which runs alongside the villa of the same name, dating from the 14th century ▲ *326*. To go up to Fiesole, turn left before the Ponte alla Badia and continue as far as Pian del Mugnone. Turn right at the traffic lights in the middle of the village and you will arrive at the foot of the Roman amphitheater. Come back along the Via Bolognese Vecchia and, when you arrive at San Domenico, take the Via delle Forbici: rest in the grounds of the Villa "Il Ventaglio". Then you will see the Villa di Camerata, known as "Il Garofano", which belonged to the Alighieri, then the Portinari.
SOUTH, TO PIAN DEI GIULLARI. Leave by the Via San Leonardo, a few steps from the Ponte Vecchio. Stop in its 11th-century church and note no. 49, Ottone Rosai's house ▲ *102*. After crossing the Viale Galileo, you will come to the Pian dei Giullari, then the Piazza Volsanminiato. If you only want a short tour, go and see see the Renaissance villa "La Gallina" in the Via Torre del Gallo, famous for its frescoes by Pollaiuolo. The Via Giramontino leads back to the Viale Galileo. But if you want a longer tour, carry on along the Via Pian dei Giullari and cross the hamlet. You will pass by the villa "Il Gioiello" (no. 42) ▲ *332*, where Galileo died. Turn left into the Via Santa Margherita a Montici to see no. 75, the Villa Ravà, headquarters of Prince Philibert of Orange during the siege of Florence ● *31*. Guicciardini ● *40* wrote his *Storia d'Italia* there. You will arrive at the charming little church of Santa Margherita a Montici and will emerge into the Viale Michelangelo at the Ponte San Niccolò.

This emblem of Fiesole is found on a fragment of the pavement of the Cappella dei Principi of the church of San Lorenzo.

The Teatro della Pergola (right).

For Stendhal, the streets of Florence were "still redolent of the passionate energies of the Middle Ages". "There are a score of odd corners in Florence," he added, "[...] where the traveler may well believe himself to be living in the year 1500." Far from being won over by the ordinary Florentines of his time ("For alas! the present-day citizen of Florence is ignorant of the very semblance of passion"), Stendhal in reality spent his time there conversing with the great men of the Tuscan capital, from Dante to Lorenzo the Magnificent. Below, the tomb of Lorenzo II by Michelangelo, in the New Sacristy of San Lorenzo.

FROM SANTA CROCE TO SAN LORENZO. Go into Santa Croce ▲ *254* and recall Stendhal's impressions: "Within, upon the right of the doorway, rises the tomb of Michelangelo; beyond, lo! there stands Canova's effigy of Alfieri; I needed no *cicerone* to recognize the features of the great Italian writer. Further still, I discovered the tomb of Machiavelli; while facing Michelangelo lies Galileo. What a race of men!" Contemplate the cupola of the Niccolini Chapel: "With my head thrown back to rest against the pulpit, so that I might let my gaze dwell on the ceiling, I underwent, through the medium of Volterrano's *Sybils*, the profoundest experience of ecstasy that, as far as I am aware, I ever encountered through the painter's art." Then go down the present Via Verdi and Via Sant' Egidio to admire the Pergola ▲ *249*, the most cosmopolitan theater of the day. Go as far as the Piazza Santissima Annunziata ▲ *242*, where the writer met again one of his great loves, the young Sienese Giulia Rinieri de' Rocchi, whom he had first encountered in Paris. In the church, Stendhal marveled at the "masterpiece" of Andrea del Sarto. In the Convent of San Marco ▲ *228* the novelist admired the frescoes by Fra Angelico.

From there, make a detour to the Palazzo Pandolfini, designed by Raphael, at Via San Gallo, no. 74 ▲ *240*: every Sunday in July the Marchesina Nencini gave a ball there in her garden, where Stendhal met Dumas again in 1840. Come back toward the Piazza San Marco and take the Via Ricasoli. At the end of the street you will discover the Niccolini Theater, formerly the Teatro del Cocomero, where he first heard *The Barber of Seville*.

FROM SAN LORENZO TO THE FORTE BELVEDERE. Make your way to the church of San Lorenzo ▲ *220*: visit its cloister, library and Michelangelo's chapel. Walk round the Duomo; on the corner of the Via de' Martelli the famous café "Il Bottegone" (now the *Motta* bar) used to stand. Like Stendhal, stroll around the city center: "I began to wander aimlessly about the streets, contemplating, from the wordless depths of my own emotion (with my eyes wide-staring, and the power of speech utterly gone from me), those massive palazzi – those veritable fortresses and castle-keeps – built around the year 1300 by the merchants of Florence." Linger in the Piazza della Signoria ▲ *142*: "Here, on these very stones, Florence had risen a score of times in the name of liberty, while blood had flowed in the cause of an unworkable constitution." Enter "Vasari's noble gallery", then the Uffizi, where Stendhal went every Sunday. He also was a frequent visitor to the hotel in the Via Porta Rossa, which received the guests of the Gabinetto Vieusseux ▲ *272*. Cross the Santa Trinita bridge and make your way to the Palazzo Pitti ▲ *288*, where Stendhal liked to get quietly drunk while reading his favorite works. Lastly, go up to the Forte Belvedere, from where you will get "some notion of the countless multitude of little hills which make up the domain of Tuscany".

"METELLO"

Born into a very poor family and self-taught, Vasco Pratolini (1913–91) liked to paint a picture of working-class Florence in his novels, often taking the scenes of his childhood as background. From *Via dei Magazzini* to *Le Ragazze di San Frediano*, by way of *Il Quartiere*, *Cronache di Poveri Amanti* and *Family Chronicle*, the great representative of neo-realism plunges us back into the atmosphere of the inter-war years.

SANTA CROCE ▲ 253. This is the quintessential Pratolinian district, a working-class area where the streets bear the "names of angels, saints and crafts, and the old names of the rich families of the 14th century". Pratolini was born on the border of Santa Croce, in the Via dei Magazzini, which was "like a silence in the murmur which could be imagined behind it and beyond the palace opposite". Then he lived in the Via del Corno, which was to become the setting for *Cronache di Poveri Amanti*: "It was a short, narrow street, away from the traffic but full of people, noisy, deafening even compared with the Via dei Magazzini, and the stinking of horses and the washing hanging at the windows." Rather than a straight description, Pratolini reproduces the atmosphere of a corner of the city: "We were an island in the river which flowed in spite of everything along the Via Pietrapiana between the carts of the tripe seller and market gardener and the chestnut seller's alcove." Wander through the streets, perhaps along the Via del Pepi and Via dell'Ulivo, where "the women crouched on low chairs", or the Via dei Conciatori, which "gave off a strong smell of leather from its workshops with their wide open doors". But do not forget that the cleaning up mentioned by the author at the end of *Il Quartiere* changed the appearance of the slums and drove away part of the population. Go as far as the lungarno, where the young people used to walk and from which you could watch the holiday fireworks, but where people also worked: Metello's father, Caco, a *renaiolo* by trade (p. 4), was killed there while working during a storm.

SAN FREDIANO ▲ 310. Cross the Arno by the Vespucci bridge to enter another Pratolinian location, that of *Le Ragazze di San Frediano*. Many of these girls were employed at the San Pancrazio factory (the present Marini Museum). San Frediano was "the most unhealthy district in the city. At the heart of streets teeming like ant-hills, were the central garbage dump, the night shelter and the barracks". Lots of small businesses operated there, either out in the street or at home, and some of them still survive today.

TOWARD THE MIDDLE-CLASS DISTRICTS. Return to the Ponte Vecchio, go up the Costa dei Magnoli and the Costa Scarpuccia and have fun looking for the "red villa": as he relates in *Family Chronicle*, Pratolini used to go there every week when he was a child to visit his little brother, who had been adopted by the butler of a baron. Continue along the Viale Galileo to the cemetery of the Porta Santa, where Pratolini is buried.

This novel recreates the years 1875 to 1902: anarchism made way for socialism, and the workers' movement was organized. Mauro Bolognini made it into a film in 1970.

"CRONACHE DI POVERI AMANTI" Private lives are set against a background of political reality: from 1925 to 1926 the Fascist régime strengthened its power, waging a remorseless fight against socialists and communists. The novel was filmed by Carlo Lizzani in 1954.

PALAZZO STROZZI
This elegant 15th-century palazzo is used for fashion shows, art exhibitions and other events.

FLORENCE AND BOOKS
Florence is not only the first city in Italy for libraries (with the Nazionale, Laurentiana, Marucelliana and San Marco), but it also has a large number of bookstores which sell new and secondhand books. Search out the bookstores-cum-antique dealers around the Biblioteca Nazionale or in the streets linking the Duomo with San Marco, which also abound in general bookstores, children's bookstores and secondhand booksellers.

"THE MERCATO DELLE PULCI"
You will find books, uniforms, coins and other ephemera here.

Antiques are sold everywhere in the city, sometimes in the most unexpected places. However, the majority of antique dealers are grouped in a few prestigious streets, such as the Via Maggio and the Borgo Ognissanti. Initiatives such as the biennial antique fair, which takes place in the Palazzo Strozzi, originated here.

BORGO OGNISSANTI: PAINTING AND FURNITURE. You can start from the borgo heading in the direction of the Piazza Goldoni: stop at the *Galleria Vespucci* for 17th-century paintings, at *Romano*'s for 17th- and 18th-century pieces, and at *Fallani*'s for contemporary pictures; do not forget *Guidi*'s in the Via del Porcellana, a street full of small, traditional craft industries. From the Piazza Goldoni, turn left into the Via dei Fossi; look in the windows of *Cei*'s and *Bacarelli*'s, and admire *Frascione*'s drawings and old paintings. Return to the Arno along the street which runs parallel to it, the Via del Moro, which has some smaller antique shops that are full of curiosities. Cross the Arno by the Ponte alla Carraia and go down the Via Santo Spirito. Among a range of shops, you will find the *Galleria Camiciotti*, which specializes in French furniture, and some renowned restorers: *Bellucci* for paintings, a clock workshop for chimes and clocks, and *Ponziani* for furniture. *Albertosi*, in the Piazza Frescobaldi, is an expert on the Empire style. In the Borgo San Jacopo, *Carnevali*'s costumes and old clothes and *Antica Meraviglia*'s dolls are worth a detour.

VIA MAGGIO: A SMALL WORLD OF ANTIQUE DEALERS ▲ *311*. Walk toward the Via Maggio along the Via dello Sprone, where the the highly skilled craftsmen at the *Studio Santo Spirito* restore porcelain and majolica. Make sure you stop at *Astronomi*'s, for its marble and stone sculptures, at *Bartolozzi*'s, which specializes in the *Alta Epoca* (Middle Ages), and at *Piselli*'s, for its paintings and antique textiles. Go into one of the two *Boralevi* antique carpet shops as well (the other one is next to the Palazzo Strozzi, in the Via Monalda). The auction room, called the *Casa d'Aste Pitti*, is also situated in the Via Maggio, in the Palazzo Ridolfi at no. 15 and is worth a visit. In the narrow surrounding streets, *Santoro*'s (Via Mazzetta) sells costumes, antique clothes and paintings; in the Via Maffia, look for *Schinder*'s, where tortoiseshell and pearl fans and other precious objects are sold and restored; watch the skillful restorers of the Borgo Tegolaio at work. Lastly, stroll along the Via dei Serragli, where you should find much of interest.

THE FLEA MARKET ▲ *263*. Follow the lungarni on the other bank of the river as far as the Piazza dei Cavalleggeri. Behind Santa Croce, take the Borgo Allegri, which will lead you to the Piazza dei Ciompi. A flea market is held there every day, and this is also the location of a secondhand market which is held on the last Sunday of every month. On weekdays, poke about in the tiny, eclectic shops in the streets which surround the square: you will find a range of interesting souvenirs and trinkets there.

Florence is famous for fashion design: leather goods, jewelry, accessories, lingerie and ready-to-wear. Small artisans and great couturiers are found side by side. Every year the fashion world gathers in the exhibition hall of the Fortezza da Basso (behind the station), where all the "Pitti" shows take place.

VIA DELLA VIGNA NUOVA AND VIA TORNABUONI. Start your

tour in the Piazza Goldoni: go through the Lungarno Vespucci into *Caponi*'s, which specializes in children's clothes, lingerie and embroidery. Then go up the Via della Vigna Nuova. Among a few small shops (such as the tailor's *Cisternino e Candido* in the Via del Purgatorio), you will find the retail outlets of many of the Florentine designers who are well-known abroad (*Gherardini* for bags, *Coveri* for clothes) as well as those who are less well-known outside Italy (*Italia Bernardini* and *Giulia Carla Cecchi*), alongside the big names of Italian fashion (*Valentino* and *Armani*). Close by, you will find the young designers of the Via del Parione. In the Via Tornabuoni, the international shop window of the city, a number of famous couturiers have established themselves over the last ten years. You must visit the shops of two very famous Florentines: *Gucci* and *Ferragamo*; the latter is in the Palazzo Ferroni, which is worth a visit in itself. *Ugolini*'s, an old shop selling men's accessories, conjures up a picture of what the Via Tornabuoni used to be like twenty years ago. Stroll in front of the windows of the jeweler *Buccellati* and those of *Mantellassi*, the last representative of the luxury Tuscan shoe trade, at the other end of the street.

FROM PIAZZA DELLA REPUBBLICA TO PIAZZA DELLA SIGNORIA. In the Piazza della Repubblica and the Via Roma, *Romano*, *Rossetti* and *Maraolo* offer the best selections of shoes and leather goods. Stop on the corner of the Via Roma and the Piazza San Giovanni, in front of one of the *Raspini* shops, which sell original leather clothes. A little further on, in the Via dei Pecori, the *Casa dei Tessuti* displays an exceptional collection of fabrics. Go down the Via Martelli in order to visit the family palazzo of Emilio Pucci, the couturier who revived fashion in Florence. At the end of the Via Ricasoli, stop at the jewelers' *Torrini* and *Favilli*. For costume jewelry, look in the shops behind the Duomo. Next visit *Beltrami*'s in the Via dei Calzaiuoli, then *Silvi*'s in the Via dei Tavolini, which is known for its trimmings. In the Piazza della Signoria, turn right into the Via Vacchereccia (do not miss *BP Studio*'s woolens) and make your way to the Via Por Santa Maria, where *Cirri* and *TAF* sell embroidery and children's clothes.

TOWARD THE PALAZZO PITTI. Cross the Ponte Vecchio: every jeweler there has a specialty. Follow the Via Guicciardini to the Palazzo Pitti: the European haute couture shows of the 1950's took place in its Sala Bianca; visit the temporary exhibitions on show in the Costume Gallery of the Palazzo Meridiana.

353

The Mercato Centrale.

Wandering tripe-seller of the 19th century.

In Florence, the traditional cuisine appears simple but it is actually very refined.

WINES AND "MESCITE" ◆ *374* . The wine merchants, or *mescite* (from *mescere*, which means to pour), will offer you wine, *crostini* (toast coated with a cream made from chicken livers, capers and anchovies), cooked meats and even hot dishes to eat on the spot. Two of the best are the *Cantinetta dei Verrazzano*, which is at Via dei Tavolini, no. 18 (noted for its *focaccine* cooked over a wood fire), and the *Cantinetta Antinori*, in the Via Tornabuoni. But the most picturesque are the *mescite* in the Piazza dell'Olio and the *Antica Mescita* in the Via del Monte alle Croci. To buy wine, go to *Alessi*'s in the Via delle Oche, *Zanobini*'s in the Via Sant'Antonino, and, above all, to two very well-stocked stores beyond the *Viali*: *Guidi*'s (Viale dei Mille, no. 69r) and *Gambi*'s (Via Monteverdi, no. 72).

BAKERS AND TRIPE BUTCHERS. Taste the *schiacciata all'olio* (very thin crusty bread sprinkled with salt and oil) or the *pandiramerino* ● *60* in the bakery stores. Buy classic *panino con la trippa* from the tripe butchers' vans in the Piazza dei Cimatori, Borgo San Frediano or Mercato Centrale.

MERCATO CENTRALE. The most interesting *pizzicherie* (delicatessens) in the city are on the ground floor, including *Il Forteto* (Alley of Calenzano) and *Baroni* (Alley of the Galluzzo). For classic ravioli with ricotta and spinach go to *Pastafresca* (Alley of Brozzi). As you leave the market, try the fried specialties of one of the few *friggitorie* which still exist in Florence.

GROCERY STORES ◆ *374.* You will find a good selection of traditional products at *Pegna*, a very old shop in the Via dello Studio, and in the shop selling fine foods in the restaurant *Cibreo*, near the Mercato di Sant'Ambrogio. Finally, the *Porta del Tartufo*, at Borgo Ognissanti, no. 133r, sells all sorts of dishes made with truffles, and the little grocery store *Procacci*, in the Via Tornabuoni, sells the famous *panini tartufati* (sandwiches with cream of white truffles).

PASTRY SHOPS ◆ *374.* If you have a sweet tooth, stop at *Robiglio*, in the Via de' Servi and Via dei Tosinghi (try their candied fruit *torta campagnola* or *budino di riso*). Drop into *Sieni*, in the Via dell'Ariento (in front of the Central Market), *Pezzatini*, in the Via dei Cerretani, and *Caponeri*, in the Via Valori. That still leaves *Dolci Dolcezze* (Piazza Beccaria), the most expensive pastry shop in the city.

ICE-CREAM PARLORS ◆ *374.* Do not confuse *gelato*, which is made with milk, and *semifreddo*, which, like *zuccotto*, the traditional dessert of Florence, is made with cream. You should not leave Florence without trying them at *Vivoli* (in the Via Isola delle Stinche).

USEFUL ADDRESSES

- ☀ EXTENSIVE VIEWS
- **C** CENTRALLY LOCATED
- ⊏·· ISOLATED
- � LUXURY RESTAURANT
- ◑ AUTHENTIC LOCAL RESTAURANT
- ○ REASONABLY PRICED RESTAURANT
- 🏛 LUXURY HOTEL
- 🏨 AUTHENTIC LOCAL HOTEL
- ⌂ REASONABLY PRICED HOTEL
- **P** CAR PARK
- 🚗 SUPERVISED CAR PARK
- ⌂ QUIET HOTEL
- 🖵 TELEVISION
- ⌇ SWIMMING POOL
- ▭ CREDIT CARDS ACCEPTED
- ☆ SPECIAL PRICES FOR CHILDREN
- ✖ PETS NOT ALLOWED
- ♫ MUSIC
- 🎺 BAND

	◆ 5,000 L to 30,000 L ◆◆ 30,000 L to 60,000 L ◆◆◆ > 60,000 L	PAGE	VIEW	GARDEN - TERRACE	AIR CONDITIONING	SPECIALTIES	REDUCTIONS FOR CHILDREN	CREDIT CARDS	PRICE
DUOMO									
IL CAMINETTO		360	●	●		N		●	◆◆
IL SASSO DI DANTE		360	●	●		T		●	◆◆
PIAZZA DELLA SIGNORIA									
BUCA DELL'ORAFO		360			●	L			◆◆
CAVALLINO		360	●	●		LNI		●	◆◆
IL FAGIANO		360			●	L		●	◆◆
LA BUSSOLA		360		●		L		●	◆◆
MONKEY BUSINESS		361			●	L		●	◆◆
BARGELLO									
ACQUA AL DUE		362			●	LN		●	◆
DA GANINO		362		●		L		●	◆◆
DA PENNELLO		362				L		●	◆◆
IL BARROCCIO		362				LN		●	◆◆
IL PAIOLO		362			●	L		●	◆◆
PAOLI		362				I		●	◆◆
ORSANMICHELE									
BUCA LAPI		362				L		●	◆◆
CANTINETTA ANTINORI		362				L		●	◆◆
LE FONTICINE		362		●		L		●	◆◆
MARIONE		362	●			L		●	◆
SABATINI		363	●	●		L		●	◆◆◆
SAN LORENZO									◆◆
TRATTORIA MARIO		364			●	L			◆
ZÀ ZÀ		364			●	L		●	◆◆
SAN MARCO									
DON CHISCIOTTE		365	●		●	L		●	◆◆
LA FRASCA		365		●		N			◆
PANE E OLIO		365		●		LN			◆
IL VEGETARIANO		365		●		VI			◆
SANTISSIMA ANNUNZIATA									
OSTERIA IL CHIASSO		366				L			◆
GAUGUIN		366				V		●	◆◆
SANTA CROCE									
CAFFE DEL CIBREO		367	●			I			◆
CIBREO		367				LI		●	◆◆◆
ENOTECA PINCHIORRI		367	●			L		●	◆◆◆
IL FRANCESCANO		367		●		L			◆◆
IL TIRABUSCIO		367				L			◆◆
LA MAREMMANA		367		●		F		●	◆◆
OSTERIA DÈ BENCI		367		●	●	L		●	◆

SPECIALTIES F : fish L : local	N : national I : international V : vegetarian	PAGE	VIEW	GARDEN	AIR CONDITIONING	SPECIALTIES	REDUCTIONS FOR CHILDREN	CREDIT CARDS	PRICE
SANTA TRINITA									
Cocco Lezzone		368				LN			◆◆
Harry's Bar		368				L		●	◆◆◆
Il Cestello (Hotel Excelsior)		368	●		●	L		●	◆◆◆
Il Latini		368	●			L	●	●	◆◆
Il Quattro Amici		369				F		●	◆◆
La Carabaccia		369				L		●	◆◆
Lume di Candela		369				LN			◆◆◆
Oliviero		369		●		L		●	◆◆
Otello		369		●		LF		●	◆◆
Sostanza		369				L			◆◆
PALAZZO PITTI / BOBOLI									
Cammillo		370			●	L		●	◆◆◆
La Sagrestia		371	●		●	L		●	◆◆
Mamma Gina		371	●			L		●	◆◆
SANTA MARIA DEL CARMINE									
Angiolino		371				L			◆
Del Carmine		371		●	●	L		●	◆
Il Cantinone del Gallo Nero		372		●		L			◆
Le Quattro Stagioni		372		●		L		●	◆
Pierot		372				F		●	◆◆
SAN MINIATO									
Bordino		372		●		LI		●	◆
Caponnina di Sante		372		●		F		●	◆◆◆
Da Omero		372				L		●	◆◆◆
La Loggia		372		●		L		●	◆◆◆

◆ < 150 000 L
◆◆ 150 000 L to 250 000 L
◆◆ > 250 000 L

	PAGE	AIR CONDITIONING	T.V. IN ROOM	PARKING	QUIET	VIEW	RESTAURANT	GARDEN - TERRACE	NO. OF ROOMS	PRICE
PIAZZA DELLA SIGNORIA										
DELLA SIGNORIA ★★★	361	●	●					●	27	◆◆
HERMITAGE ★★★	361	●	●	●	●	●		●	22	◆◆
BARGELLO										
CAVOUR ★★★	362	●	●		●	●	●	●	89	◆◆
ORSANMICHELE										
BEACCI TORNABUONI ★★★	363	●	●	●	●		●		29	◆◆
BRUNELLESCHI ★★★★	363	●	●				●	●	94	◆◆◆
CALZAIUOLI ★★★	363	●	●	●	●	●			40	◆◆
CROCE DI MALTA ★★★★	363	●	●		●		●	●	98	◆◆◆
ESPERANZA ★	363				●				8	◆
MINERVA GRAND HOTEL ★★★★	363	●	●	●	●	●	●	●	99	◆◆◆
PENDINI ★★★	363	●							42	◆◆
PORTA ROSSA ★★★	363								84	◆
RESIDENZA ★★★	363	●	●		●	●	●	●	24	◆◆
RIVOLI ★★★★	363		●	●				●		◆◆◆
SAVOY ★★★★	363	●	●		●		●	●	101	◆◆◆
SAN LORENZO										
PULLMAN ASTORIA ★★★★	364	●	●				●	●	36	◆◆◆
GRAND HOTEL BAGLIONI ★★★★	364		●			●	●	●	196	◆◆◆
DÉSIRÉE ★★	364		●		●	●		●	28	◆
JOLI ★★	364		●		●	●			8	◆
NUOVA ITALIA ★★	364				●				21	◆
SAN MARCO										
BASILEA ★★★	365		●	●			●		59	◆
RAPALLO ★★★	365		●		●		●		30	◆
ROYAL ★★★	365	●	●	●	●	●		●	40	◆◆
SPLENDOR ★★★	365		●					●	31	◆
VIENNA ★★	366		●		●				25	◆
SANTISSIMA ANNUNZIATA										
ARISTON ★★	366				●			●	32	◆
LE DUE FONTANE ★★★	366		●		●	●			50	◆◆
LOGGIATO DEI SERVITI ★★★	366		●		●	●			29	◆◆
LOSANNA ★	366				●				13	◆

	PAGE	AIR CONDITIONING	TV IN ROOM	PARKING	QUIET	VIEW	RESTAURANT	GARDEN - TERRACE	NO. OF ROOMS	PRICE
MONNA LISA ★★★★	366		•	•	•			•	34	♦♦♦
MORANDI ALLA CROCETTA ★★★	366	•	•		•			•	10	♦
REGENCY ★★★★★	366	•	•	•	•	•	•	•	35	♦♦♦
SANTA CROCE										
BALESTRI ★★★	367	•	•	•		•		•	50	♦♦
FIORINO ★★★	368				•			•	23	♦
SANTA CROCE ★★	368								10	♦
WANDA ★★	368		•	•					10	♦
SANTA TRINITA										
ANGLO-AMERICAN ★★★★	369	•	•	•	•		•		107	♦♦♦
APRILE ★★★	369		•		•	•		•	29	♦♦
CASA DEL LAGO ★★	369				•	•		•	22	♦
EXCELSIOR ★★★★★	369	•	•	•		•	•		176	♦♦♦
GRAND HOTEL ★★★★★	369	•	•	•	•	•	•		107	♦♦♦
KRAFT ★★★★	370	•	•	•	•	•	•	•	78	♦♦
MONTEBELLO SPLENDID ★★★★	370	•	•	•	•		•	•	43	♦♦♦
PRINCIPE ★★★★	370	•	•	•	•	•		•	50	♦♦
VILLA AZALEE ★★★	370	•	•					•	24	♦♦
VILLA MEDICI ★★★★★	370	•	•	•	•	•	•	•	103	♦♦♦
PALAZZO PITTI / BOBOLI										
CLASSIC HOTEL ★★★	371		•	•	•			•	20	♦
PENSIONE ANNALENA ★★★	371		•					•	20	♦♦
PITTI PALACE ★★★	371	•	•			•		•	72	♦♦
VILLA CORA ★★★★★	371		•	•	•	•	•	•	48	♦♦♦
SANTA MARIA DEL CARMINE										♦
PENSIONE BANDINI ★	372				•	•		•	12	♦
SAN MINIATO	372	•			•					♦♦
PARK-PALACE ★★★★	372	•	•	•	•	•		•	26	♦♦♦
AROUND FLORENCE										
BENCISTÀ ★★★	373			•	•	•	•	•	42	♦♦
DINO ★★★	373		•	•	•			•	18	♦
VILLA LA MASSA ★★★★★	373	•	•	•		•	•	•	62	♦♦♦
VILLA LE RONDINI ★★★	373		•	•	•	•	•	•	43	♦♦
VILLA SAN MICHELE ★★★★	373		•		•	•		•	74	♦♦♦

GENERAL
PRACTICAL DETAILS

STREET NUMBERS
*There are two systems
of street numbering in
Florence: street
numbers are sometimes
in black and sometimes
in red. Streets with a
red numbering system
are indicated here by
the letter "r" appearing
after the name of the
street.*
OPENING HOURS
*The opening and
closing times given here
for museums and
galleries are valid
throughout the summer
months. In winter these
may vary slightly. You
are therefore
recommended to
telephone first to check
the exact opening and
closing times.*
RESTAURANTS
*Except where otherwise
indicated, the restaurant
prices given do not
include drinks.*
SYMBOLS
*The letters "AC" are
given to indicate
establishments which
have air conditioning.*

EMERGENCIES

POLICE
Tel. 113.

**MEDICAL
EMERGENCIES**
Tel. 118.

BREAKDOWNS
Tel. 116.
*Breakdown service is
affiliated to the Italian
Automobile Club, for
which there is a charge.*

LOST PROPERTY
Via Circondaria no. 19
Tel. 36 79 43
Open 9am–noon
Closed Sun.

DUOMO

POSTCODE: 50129.

HOSPITAL
Piazza Duomo no. 20
Tel. 21 22 22.

CULTURE

**MUSEO DELL'OPERA
DEL DUOMO**
Piazza Duomo no. 9
Tel. 230 28 85

Open 9am–7.30pm
In winter 9am–6pm
Closed Sun., Easter,
Christmas and
New Year.

BAPTISTERY
Piazza San Giovanni
Tel. 230 28 89
Open 1–6pm. Public
holidays 9am–1pm.

**CUPOLA OF
BRUNELLESCHI**
Piazza Duomo
Tel. 230 28 85
Open 10am–5pm
Closed Sun. and public
holidays.

**CRYPT OF SANTA
REPARATA**
Piazza Duomo
Tel. 230 28 85
Open 10am–5pm
Closed Sun. and
public holidays.

**CHURCH OF
SANTA MARIA DEL
FIORE (DUOMO)**
Piazza Duomo, 9
Tel. 230 28 85
Open 9am–7.30pm
Public holidays
9am–1pm. Closed Sun.

**CAMPANILE
DI GIOTTO**
Piazza Duomo
Tel. 230 28 55
Open 8.30am–7pm.
Winter 8.30am–
4.30pm

RESTAURANTS

IL CAMINETTO
Via dello Studio
no. 34r
Tel. 239 62 74
Open 11am–4pm,
7–11pm
Closed Wed.
*Pleasant trattoria,
situated close to the
Duomo. Terrace in
summer. Specialty:
bistecca alla griglia.*
30,000 lire–45,000 lire.
◑ ▭ ⊻

IL SASSO DI DANTE
Piazza delle Pallottole
no. 6r
Tel. 28 21 13
Open noon–3pm,
7–10pm
Closed Thur., Fri. and
Dec. 15–Feb.
*Popular with tourists.
Pleasant terrace
immediately opposite
the Duomo.*
25,000 lire–46,000 lire.
○ ▭ ⊻

PIAZZA
DELLA
SIGNORIA

POSTCODE: 50122.

**TOURIST
INFORMATION
OFFICE**
Chiasso dei Baroncelli
no. 17r
Tel. 230 20 33.

POLICE STATION
Palazzo Vecchio
Tel. 28 49 26

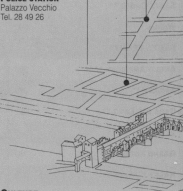

DELLA SIGNORIA
PENDINI

CULTURE

**RACCOLTA D'ARTE
CONTEMPORANIA
A. DELLA RAGIONE**
Piazza della Signoria
no. 5
Tel. 28 30 78
Open 9am–1pm.
8am–1pm public
holidays.
Closed Tues.

**CORRIDOIO
VASARIANO**
Galleria degli Uffizi
Piazzale Uffizi no. 6
Tel. 2 38 85.
*Visits by appointment
only. Work in progress.*

**GALLERIA DEGLI
UFFIZI**
Piazzale degli Uffizi
no. 6
Tel. 2 38 85.
Open 9am–7pm
Public holidays
9am–2pm
Closed Mon.

**MUSEO NAZIONALE
DI STORIA DELLE
SCIENZE**
Piazza dei Giudici no. 1
Tel. 29 34 93
Open Mon. and Wed.
9.30am–1pm, Fri.
2–5pm, Tues., Thur.,
Sat. 9.30am–1pm.
Closed Sun. and public
holidays.

PALAZZO VECCHIO
Piazza della Signoria
Tel. 276 84 65
Open 9am–7pm. Public
holidays 8am–1pm
Closed Sat.

RESTAURANTS

BUCA DELL'ORAFO
Volta dei Girolami no.
28r
Tel. 21 36 19
Open 12.30–3pm,
7.30–11pm. Closed
Sun., Mon. and Aug.
*A basement restaurant
located in a small
vaulted passage.
Pleasant proprietor.
Florentine specialties.
AC.*
23,000 lire–50,000 lire.
◑ ✻

CAVALLINO
Via delle Farine no. 6r
Tel. 21 58 18
Open noon–3pm,
7.30–10.15pm
Closed Wed.
*Terrace with a
delightful view of the
Piazza della Signoria,
the most attractive
square in Florence.
Extremely popular with
tourists.*
32,000 lire–52,000 lire.
◍ ▭ ⊻

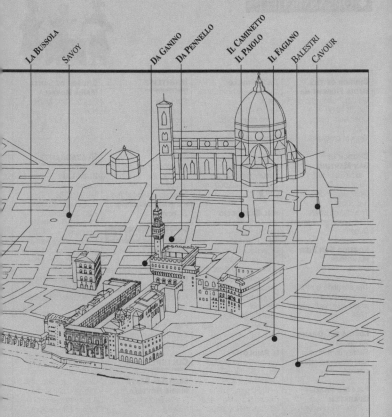

Labels (clockwise from top left): LA BUSSOLA · SAVOY · DA GANINO · DA PENNELLO · IL CAMINETTO · IL PAIOLO · IL FAGIANO · BALESTRI · CAVOUR

★ **IL FAGIANO**
Via dei Neri no. 57r
Tel. 28 78 76
Open noon–3pm,
7.30pm–midnight.
Closed Mon. and Jan.
*The owner is an
inventive and
enthusiastic cook.
Extremely varied and
imaginative menu
(game, fish . . .).
Good wine list.*
35,000 lire–55,000 lire.
◑ ▭ ⊷

LA BUSSOLA
Via Porta Rossa no. 58r
Tel. 29 33 76
Open 12.30pm–2.30am,
Sat. and Sun.
noon–3.30am.
Closed Mon.
*Reasonable but
expensive menu.
One of the few
restaurants in Florence
to stay open late.*
30,000 lire–40,000 lire.
◔ ▭

MONKEY BUSINESS
Chiasso dei Baroncelli
Tel. 28 82 19
Open 12.30–2.30pm,
7.30–11pm
Closed Sun. and Aug.
*The ambience is
established by a*
massive elephant
standing at the entrance
to a "virgin forest".
Excellent cuisine.
Specialties: tagliatelle
with spinach, spaghetti
alla bottarga di
muggine. AC.
43,000 lire–58,000 lire.
◍ ▭

ACCOMMODATION

DELLA SIGNORIA ★★★★
Via delle Terme no. 1
Tel. 21 45 30
Fax 21 61 01.
*The top floors of this
luxurious modern
establishment offer a
fine view of the Ponte
Vecchio. Breakfast and
service on the terrace
included. AC.*
195,000 lire–260,000
lire.
🏛 🅲 ⊿ □ ⌀
▭

★ **HERMITAGE** ★★★
Vicolo Marzio no. 1
Piazza del Pesce
Tel. 28 72 16
Fax 21 22 08.
*This hotel, situated
close to Ponte Vecchio
has the cosy,
comfortable atmosphere
of an old manor house.*
An attractive
honeysuckle-covered
terrace has a view over
the Arno. Breakfast is
included (served on the
terrace in summer).
AC.
190,000 lire–240,000
lire.
🏠 🅲 ⌂ ⊿ □ 🅿
▭

NIGHTLIFE

CAFFÈ RIVOIRE
Piazza della Signoria
no. 5r
Tel. 21 44 12
Open 8am–midnight
Closed Mon. and
2 weeks in Jan.
*This extremely
attractive café has an
interior which is
constructed entirely
from wood, and an
18th-century style
décor. Renowned for
its delicious hot
chocolate.*

TABETA
Vicolo dell'Oro
Tel. 28 94 46
Open 10pm–4am
Closed Sun. and Aug.
*Pleasant piano-bar,
typically frequented by
35–50-year-olds, who*
come here to end the
evening talking and
listening to good Italian
music.
⊷

BARGELLO

POSTCODE: 50122

CULTURE

CASA DI DANTE
Via Santa Margherita
no. 1
Tel. 28 33 43
Open 9am–1pm,
Mon. 9am–1pm and
8–11pm.
Closed Tues.
Entry free.

**MUSEO NAZIONALE
DI ANTROPOLOGIA
ED ETNOLOGIA**
Via del Proconsolo
no. 12
Tel. 239 64 49
Open 9am–1pm Thur.,
Fri., Sat. and the first
three Sun. each month.
Entry free.

**MUSEO NAZIONALE
DEL BARGELLO**
Via del Proconsolo no. 4
Tel. 238 85
Open 9am–2pm
Closed Mon.

CHURCH OF THE BADIA FIORENTINA
Via del Proconsolo no. 1
Tel. 28 73 89
Open 9am–noon,
4.30–7pm.
Work in progress.

CHURCH OF SAN MARTINO
Piazza San Martino
Tel. 21 50 44
Open 9am–noon,
3–6.30pm.
The church where Dante married Gemma Donati.

PORTICO SAN PIER MAGGIORE
Piazza San Pier Maggiore
The entrance is all that remains of the church, which was destroyed in 1784.

LOGGIA DEL GRANO
Via dei Neri.
Former corn market now converted into a cinema.

PALAZZO PAZZI-QUARATESI
Via del Proconsolo no. 10
Closed Wed.
The interior is not open to visitors.

RESTAURANTS

ACQUA AL DUE
Via Vigna Vecchia no. 40r
Tel. 28 41 70
Open 7.30pm–1am
Sat., Sun. 12.30–3pm.
Closed Mon.
Usually packed and buzzing with activity especially late in the evening after the theater. One hour's free parking for patrons. Specialty: "assaggio di primi" gives you the option of tasting the different pastas. AC.
23,000 lire–40,000 lire.
○ ▭ ❧

DA GANINO
Piazza dei Cimatori no. 4r
Tel. 21 41 25
Open 12.30–3pm,
7.30–10.30pm
Closed Sun. and Aug.
A popular, trendy restaurant behind the Piazza della Signoria. Some outdoor tables.
38,000 lire–55,000 lire.
○ ▭

DA PENNELLO
Via Dante Alighieri no. 4r
Tel. 29 48 48
Open noon–2.45, 7–10pm.
Closed Mon. and Sun. evening, Aug. and Christmas.
A good restaurant, frequented by locals.
25,000 lire–40,000 lire.
○ ◑ ▭

★ IL BARROCCIO
Via Vigna Vecchia no. 33r
Tel. 21 15 03
Closed for 10 days in Jan. and in June.
Attractive and quiet little restaurant. Welcoming atmosphere. Specialties: "raviolini alle noci", "bocconcini di ricotta ai formaggi".
26,000 lire–42,000 lire.
◑ ▭

IL PAIOLO
Via del Corso no. 42r
Tel. 21 50 19
Open noon–3pm, 7–10.30 p.m.
Closed Sun., Mon. and 20 days in Nov. and Aug.
Small restaurant offering good, typically Florentine dishes. Specialty: fresh pasta. No à la carte menu. AC.
31,000 lire–60,000 lire.
◍ ▭

PAOLI
Via dei Tavolini no. 12r
Tel. 21 62 15
Open noon–2.30pm, 7–10.30pm
Closed Mar. and Aug.
Superbly decorated, high-class establishment. Formal atmosphere.
25,000 lire–55,000 lire.
◑ ▭

ACCOMMODATION

CAVOUR ★★★
Via del Proconsolo no. 3
Tel. 28 24 61
Fax 21 89 55.
This magnificent hotel was once the residence of a patrician family. Attractive terrace with panoramic views of the city. Some rooms have facilities for the disabled. AC. *Breakfast is included.*
140,000 lire–225,000 lire.
🏠 ▣ ⌂ ⚓ ▢ ▭

NIGHTLIFE

FULL UP
Via della Vigna Vecchia no. 21r
Tel. 29 30 06
Open 10.30pm–4am
Closed Tues., July and Aug.
Revelers of all ages frequent the discotheque. The adjacent piano-bar has a calmer atmosphere.
♫ 🍸

ORSANMICHELE

POSTCODE: 5012.

TOURIST INFORMATION OFFICE
Stazione Santa Maria Novella
Tel. 21 22 45.

POST OFFICE
Via Pellicceria no. 3
Tel. 239 67 11.

CULTURE

MUSEO DI SANTA MARIA NOVELLA
Piazza Santa Maria Novella
Tel. 28 21 87
Open 9am–2pm
Public holidays 8am–1pm
Closed Fri.

PALAZZO DAVANZATI
Via Porta Rossa no. 13
Tel. 238 86 10
Open 9am–2pm
Closed Mon.

PALAZZO STROZZI
Piazza Strozzi no. 1
Tel. 239 80 63
Exhibitions.

CHURCH OF ORSANMICHELE
Via dell'Arte della Lana no. 1
Open 9am–noon, 4–6pm.

CHURCH OF SAN CARLO DEI LOMBARDI
Via dei Calzaiuoli
Open 8.30am–noon, 2.30–5.30pm.

CHURCH OF SAN GAETANO
Via Tornabuoni, on the corner of the Via Corsi
Tel. 21 36 10
Open Sun.
This church has a remarkable Baroque façade.

CHURCH OF SANTA MARIA NOVELLA
Piazza Santa Maria Novella
Tel. 21 01 13
Open 7–11.30am, 3.30–6pm.

RESTAURANTS

BUCA LAPI
Via del Trebbio no. 1r
Tel. 21 37 68
Open noon–2.30pm, 7.30–10.30pm
Closed Sun. and Mon. lunchtime.
Lively atmosphere and good cuisine in a cellar lined with turn-of-the-century posters. Specialties: wild boar and polenta.
30,000 lire–50,000 lire.
◑ ▭

CANTINETTA ANTINORI
Piazza Antinori no. 3
Tel. 29 22 34
Open 12.30–2.30pm, 7–10.30pm
Closed Sat., Sun. and Aug. and Christmas.
A busy restaurant in a former 15th-century palazzo. Good wine list. Specialties: "pappa al pomodoro", "trippa alla fiorentina" (tripe), "fettucine al coniglio" (rabbit).
52,000 lire–60,000 lire.
◍ ▭ ❧

LE FONTICINE
Via Nazionale no. 79
Tel. 28 21 06
Open noon–3pm, 7–10.30pm
Closed Mon., Christmas and Aug.
Not far from the station. Very good pasta dishes.
32,000 lire–65,000 lire.
◑ ▭

MARIONE
Via della Spada no. 27r
Tel. 21 47 56
Open noon–3pm, 7–10pm
Closed Sat., Sun. and Aug.
An extremely lively and welcoming restaurant which is popular with Florentines. Specialties: tripe, "osso bucco" and "baccalà".
18,000 lire–25,000 lire.
Set menu: 18,000 lire.
○ ▭ ⚓ ❧

SABATINI
Via Panzani no. 9A
Tel. 21 15 59
Open 12.30–3pm,
7.30–10.30pm
Closed Mon.
The most renowned restaurant in Florence, offering the ultimate in Florentine cuisine. Specialties: antipasto Sabatini, panzerotti. 65,000 lire–100,000 lire.
⓪ ▱ ⅍

ACCOMMODATION

★ BEACCI TORNABUONI ★★★
Via Tornabuoni no. 3
Tel. 21 26 45
Fax 28 35 94.
*A magnificent hotel in a 14th-century palazzo. Lovely restaurant. Terrace. Breakfast included. AC. 100,000 lire–200,000 lire.
Set menu 35,000 lire.*
🏛 ▣ ⌂ ⅍ ▱ ▱

BRUNELLESCHI ★★★★
Piazza Santa Elisabetta no. 3
Tel. 56 20 68
Fax 21 96 53.
Not far from the Palazzo Vecchio, in a unique architectural setting. Breakfast included. AC. 310,000 lire–420,000 lire.
🏛 ▣ ▱ ▱

CALZAIUOLI ★★★
Via Calzaiuoli no.6
Tel. 21 24 56
Fax 26 83 10.
Renovated hotel in the busiest pedestrian street in Florence. Fine period staircase. Some rooms have an excellent view of the Duomo. Breakfast included. AC. 115,000 lire–190,000 lire.
🏛 ▣ ⌂ ⅍ ▱ ✗
🚗 ▱

CROCE DI MALTA ★★★★
Via della Scala no. 7
Tel. 21 83 51
Fax 28 71 21.
The surprising décor successfully combines concrete, antique columns and neon lights. Garden with swimming pool, restaurant. Breakfast included. AC. 255,000 lire–345,000 lire.
🏛 ▣ ⌂ ▱ ⌇ ▱

ESPERANZA ★
Via dell'Inferno, no. 3
Tel. 21 37 73.
Fax 21 83 64
A small, adequate though rather characterless pensione. Renovated bathrooms. 50,000 lire–90,000 lire.
⌂ ▣ ⌂ ✗ ▱

MINERVA GRAND HOTEL ★★★★
Piazza Santa Maria Novella no. 16
Tel. 28 45 55
Fax 28 45 54.
Well-situated, quality hoTel. the roof pool, veranda and garden make a stay here even more pleasant. 210,000 lire–380,000 lire.
🏛 ▣ ⌂ ⅍ ▱ ⌇
🚗 ▱

PENDINI ★★★
Via Strozzi no. 2
Tel. 21 11 70
Fax 28 18 07.
*Charming pensione next to the Piazza della Repubblica. Reserve in advance by telephone or fax or by Internet. Extremely welcoming. AC.
Breakfast included. 130,000 lire–200,000 lire.*
⌂ ▣ ⌂ ⅍ ▱

PORTA ROSSA ★★★
Via Porta Rossa no. 19
Tel. 28 75 51
Fax 28 21 79.
This 14th-century hotel has had a number of famous guests, including the writers Alphonse de Lamartine, Stendhal and the poet Lord Byron. Superb period decoration. 118,000 lire–174,000 lire.
⌂

RESIDENZA ★★★
Via Tornabuoni no. 8
Tel. 21 86 84
Fax 28 41 97.
Quaint hotel, warm welcome. Clean, airy rooms. Top floor rooms have balconies. Breakfast included. AC. 100,000 lire–215,000 lire.
🏛 ▣ ⌂ ⅍ ▱
🚗 ▱

RIVOLI ★★★★
Via della Scala no. 33
Tel. 28 28 53
Fax 29 40 41.
A former monastery, in the historical center of Florence, which was renovated in 1990 and combines tradition with modernity. Small swimming pool and very pleasant patios. Garden. Breakfast included. 240,000 lire–310,000 lire.
🏛 ▣ ⌂ ▱ ⌇ ✗
🚗 ▱

★ SAVOY ★★★★
Piazza della Repubblica no. 7
Tel. 28 33 13
Fax 28 48 40.
A large luxury hotel in the liveliest piazza in Florence. Breakfast included. AC. 240,000 lire–530,000 lire.
🏛 ▣ ⅍ ▱ ☆
🚗 ▱

CAFÉS AND TEA ROOMS

GIACOSA
Via Tornabuoni no. 83r
Tel. 239 62 26
Open 7.30am–8.45pm
Closed Sun.
Elegant tea room. Ice cream and pastries made on the premises (tea 5,000 lire, cakes 6,000 lire).

GILLI
Piazza della Repubblica no. 39r
Tel. 21 38 96
Open Mon., Wed., Fri. 7.30am–9.30pm.
Open Sat., Sun. 7.30am–12.30am.
Closed Tues.
Founded in 1733, this establishment has a marvelous décor and offers high-quality service. Mainly a tea room, it also serves light meals from noon to 7pm.
⅍ ▣ ▱

GIUBBE ROSSE
Piazza Repubblica no. 13–14r
Tel. 21 22 80
Open 7.30am–1.30pm
Closed Wed.
Florence's literary café, which has enjoyed the patronage of some of the greatest names to visit the city. It serves coffee at 5,000 lire, light meals and mixed ice creams and there is a pleasant terrace.
⅍ ▣ ▱

PASZKOWSKI
Piazza Repubblica no. 12r
Tel. 21 02 36
Open 7am–1.30pm
Closed Mon.
The best-known ice cream parlor and tea room in Florence. Smart and central. Piano-bar which is open all year round and a big band plays on the terrace regularly, from June to Oct.
⅍ ▱

◆ HOTEL PORTA ROSSA ◆

Established in one of the palazzos belonging to the Torrigianis, built in the late 14th century, this hotel welcomed many famous 19th-century writers, often members of the Gabinetto Vieusseux.

SAN LORENZO

POSTCODE: 50123.

CULTURE

**BIBLIOTECA
RICCARDIANA-
MORENIANA**
Via dei Ginori no. 10
Tel. 21 25 86
Open 8am–2pm
Closed Sun. and public
holidays.

**CHURCH OF
SAN LORENZO**
Piazza San Lorenzo
no. 9
Tel. 21 66 34
Open 8am–noon,
3.30–5.30pm.
Open public holidays
3.30–5.30pm

**CHURCH OF SANTA
MARIA MAGGIORE**
Vicolo Santa Maria
Maggiore, no. 1
Tel. 21 59 14
Open 3.30–7.45pm
Public holidays
4–10pm.

**CENACOLO DI
FOLIGNO**
Via Faenza no. 42
Tel. 2 38 85
Open Mon. to Sat.
9am–1pm, 3–5pm.
Open Sun. 9am– noon.
*Visits by appointment
(Tel. 28 42 72)*

MEDICI CHAPELS
Piazza Madonna degli
Aldobrandini no. 6
Tel. 238 85
Open 9am–2pm
Closed Mon.

**PALAZZO MEDICI-
RICCARDI**
Via Cavour no. 1
Tel. 276 03 40
Open 9am–1pm, 3–6pm
Sun and public holidays
9am–1pm.
*Visits to the Cappella
dei Magi (closed Wed.)
available by
appointment.*

RESTAURANTS

TRATTORIA MARIO
Via Rosina, no. 2r
Tel. 21 85 50
Lunchtime only, noon–
3.30pm. Closed Sun.
*A popular trattoria
offering good Tuscan
food at reasonable
prices.*
12,000 lire–20,000 lire
○

ZÀ ZÀ
Piazza Mercato
Centrale, no. 26r
Tel. 21 54 11
Fax 21 07 56
Open noon–3pm and
7–11pm. Closed Sun.
and public holidays.
*A large taverna on the
central market place.
The walls are covered
with photos of famous
people and nearly a
thousand bottles of
chianti. For those with a
sweet tooth the apple
tart with marscapone
cream comes highly
recommended.*
*23,000 lire–42,000 lire.
Menu 20,000 lire.*
◐ ○ ▭

ACCOMMODATION

**PULLMAN
ASTORIA ★★★★**
Via del Giglio no. 9
Tel. 239 80 95
Fax 21 46 32.
*A well-situated 16th-
century palace with a
superb entrance, pre-
1940's décor and
murals. Breakfast
included. AC.*
*260,000 lire–340,000
lire.*
🏛 🄲 ▢ ▭

**GRAND HOTEL
BAGLIONI ★★★★**
Piazza Unità Italiana
no. 6
Tel. 2 35 80
Fax 235 88 95.
*One of the best hotels
in Florence. Top quality*

*service. Breakfast
included.*
*260,000 lire–360,000
lire.*
🏛 🄲 🔆 ▢ ▭

DÉSIRÉE ★★
Via Fiume no. 20
Tel. 238 23 82
Fax 29 14 39
*Small, pleasant hotel
with large rooms. Run
by an old gentleman
who adores animals.
Excellent value.
Breakfast included.*
*95,000 lire–150,000
lire.*
⌂ 🄲 ⌂ 🔆 ▢ ▭

JOLI ★★
Via Fiume no. 8
Tel. 29 20 79
Closed some days in
August.
*Very welcoming
family pensione. The
rooms facing the
inner courtyard are
quieter. Breakfast
included.*
90,000–130,000 lire.
⌂ 🄲 ⌂ 🔆 ▢ ▭

NUOVA ITALIA ★★
Via Faenza no. 26
Tel. 28 75 08
Fax 21 09 41.
*This unassuming but
comfortable hotel is run
by a very friendly
couple. The interior of
the hotel is decorated
with delightful posters.
Breakfast included.*
90,000 lire–135,000 lire.
⌂ 🄲 ⌂ ▭

NIGHTLIFE

MARACANA
Via Faenza no. 4
Tel. 21 02 98
Open 10.30pm–3am
Closed Mon., July
and Aug.
*Brazilian restaurant
which becomes a
discotheque at night.
You eat on a mezzanine
overlooking the dance
floor.*
🔆 ♫ ▭

SAN MARCO

POSTCODE: 50129.

POST OFFICE
Via Cavour no. 71/A
Tel. 47 19 10.

CULTURE

**OPIFICIO DELLE
PIETRE DURE**
Via degli Alfani no. 78
Tel. 29 40 62
Currently closed.

**ACCADEMIA DI BELLE
ARTI**
Via Ricasoli no. 66
Tel. 238 85
Open 9am–1pm
Public holidays
9am–2pm
Closed Mon.

MUSEO SAN MARCO
Piazza San Marco no. 1
Tel. 238 85
Open 9am–2pm
Closed Mon.
Entry free.

PALEONTOLOGY MUSEUM
Via La Pira no. 4
Tel. 23 82 711
Open 9am–1pm, Mon.
2pm–6pm, the 1st Sun.
in the month
9.30am–2.30pm
Closed Fri., public
holidays and August.

CHIOSTRO DELLO SCALZO
Via Cavour no. 69
Tel. 238 86 04
Open 9am–1pm on
Mon. and Thurs.

CHURCH OF SAN MARCO
Piazza San Marco
Tel. 29 69 50
Open 7am–12.30pm,
4–8pm.

CENACOLO DI SANT'APOLLONIA
Via XXV Aprile no. 1
Tel. 238 86 07
Open 9am–2pm
Closed Mon.

RESTAURANTS

DON CHISCIOTTE
Via C. Ridolfi no. 4–6r
Tel. 47 54 30
Open 1pm–2.30pm,
8–10.30pm
Closed Mon. lunchtime,
Sun. and Aug.
*Situated in a beautiful
Florentine palace, this
elegant restaurant
offers an interesting
menu with many Tuscan
dishes. Specialties:
calamari with cheese*
*and roquette, lamb in
spicy sauce. AC.
52,000 lire–65,000 lire.*
▯••

LA FRASCA
Via Faentina no. 70r
Tel. 57 12 44
Open 8–11pm
Closed Tues.
*Specialties of this
restaurant are taken
from all regions of Italy.
28,000 lire–32,000 lire.
Set menus 20,000 lire–
25,000 lire.*
◑ ○ ▯

PANE E OLIO
Via Faentina no. 2r
Tel. 47 01 01
Open noon–3pm,
7.30pm–midnight.

*Riverside restaurant
with a very welcoming
atmosphere. Tuscan
and regional cuisine.
Excellent desserts.
Reservations
recommended. Terrace.
18,000 lire–30,000 lire
(wine included).*
◑ ○

IL VEGETARIANO
Via della Ruote, no. 30r
Tel. 47 03 30
Open 12.30–2.30pm,
7.30–10.30pm.
Closed Mon., Sat. and
Sun. lunchtime.
*Florence's original
vegetarian restaurant.
Excellent, moderately
priced Mediterranean
food. Some vegan
dishes. Terrace.
15,000 lire–25,000 lire.*
○

◆ PIAZZA SANTISSIMA ANNUNZIATA ◆
A perfect illustration of Renaissance architectural
theories, this square, lined with porticos on
three sides, is designed entirely according to
principles of symmetry and unity. The church of
Santissima Annunziata
and the Palazzo Grifoni open onto it.

ACCOMMODATION

BASILEA ★★★
Via Guelfa no. 41
Tel. 21 45 87
Fax 26 83 50.
*Quiet and comfortable
hotel. Breakfast
included.
125,000 lire–190,000
lire. Reductions in low
season.*
▣ 🏠 ▯ 🚗 ▭

RAPALLO ★★★
Via Santa Caterina
d'Alessandria no. 7
Tel. 47 24 12
Fax 47 03 85.
*Large hotel with
remarkable ceilings
and some exceptionally
beautiful pieces of
furniture. Breakfast
included.
121,000 –192,000 lire*
🏛 🏠 ▯ 🚗 ▭

★ ROYAL ★★★
Via delle Ruote
no. 50
Tel. 48 32 87
Fax 49 09 76.
*Large residence full of
character surrounded
by a luxurious garden.
Breakfast included.
140,000–220,000 lire.*
🏛 ▣ 🏠 ☼ ▯
▭ 🅿

★ SPLENDOR ★★
Via San Gallo no. 30
Tel. 48 34 27
Fax 46 12 76
Closed Dec. 1–15.
*This old building, now
renovated and
modernized, is the
ideal place for a
romantic interlude.
Terrace. Breakfast
included.
110,000 lire–180,000
lire.*
🏛 ▣ 🏠 ▯ ▭

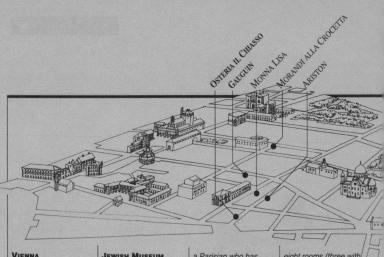

OSTERIA IL CHIASSO
GAUGUIN
MONNA LISA
MORANDI ALLA CROCETTA
ARISTON

VIENNA
Via XXV Aprile no. 14
Tel. 48 32 56
Fax 49 03 42.
*Lovely hotel in a good
location. Warm
welcome. Good value
for money. Breakfast
included.*
*90,000–150,000 lire;
50,000 lire–80,000 lire
in low season.*
⌂ 🄲 ♨ 🖵 ▭

SANTISSIMA ANNUNZIATA

POSTCODE: 50122.

HOSPITAL
Piazza Santa Maria
Nuova no. 1
Tel. 275 81.

POST OFFICE
Via Pietrapiana no. 53
Tel. 21 14 15.

CULTURE

**MUSEO FIRENZE
COM'ERA**
Via dell'Oriuolo no. 4
Tel. 239 84 83
Open 10am–1pm
Closed Thur.

**OSPEDALE DEGLI
INNOCENTI**
Piazza Santissima
Annunziata no. 12
Tel. 247 79 52
Open 8.30am–2pm
Closed Wed.

**MUSEO
ARCHEOLOGICO**
Via della Colonna no. 36
Tel. 247 86 41
Open 9am–2pm
Public holidays
9am–1pm.
Closed Mon.

MUSEO BOTANICO
Via Micheli no. 3
Tel. 275 74 02
Open 9am–noon
Closed Mon., Wed. and
Fri.

JEWISH MUSEUM
Via Farini no. 4
Tel. 24 52 52
Open 10am–1pm,
2–5pm.

**CHURCH OF
SANTISSIMA
ANNUNZIATA**
Piazza Santissima
Annunziata
Tel. 239 80 34
Open 7.30am–12.30pm,
4–7pm.

**CENACOLO DI
SAN SALVI**
Via Andrea del Sarto
Tel. 238 85
Open 9am–2pm
Closed Mon.

**CHIOSTRO DI SANTA
MARIA MADDALENA
DEI PAZZI**
Borgo Pinti no. 58
Tel. 247 84 20
Open 9am–noon, 5–7pm.
Look for the Crucifixion
by Perugino.

**TEATRO DELLA
PERGOLA**
Via della Pergola no. 12
Tel. 247 96 51.
*Visits by appointment
only.*

RESTAURANTS

**OSTERIA IL
TOSCANACCIO**
Via Fiesolana no. 13r
Tel. 24 03 05
Open noon–3.30pm,
7pm– midnight.
Closed Sun. in winter.
*Modest restaurant open
until late. Specialty:
pasta in hare sauce.*
14,000 lire–30,000 lire.
Set menu: 15,000 lire.
○

★ GAUGUIN
Via degli Alfani no. 24r
Tel. 234 06 16
Closed Sun. and Mon.
lunchtime
This restaurant is run by

*a Parisian who has
developed an excellent
and imaginative menu
which is a mixture of
French and Tuscan
cuisine – without meat
or fish. Modern art
exhibitions.*
33,000 lire–37,000 lire.
▭

ACCOMMODATION

ARISTON ★★
Via Fiesolana no. 40
Tel. 247 66 93
Fax 247 69 80.
Closed 10 days at
Christmas.
*Good value for money.
Breakfast included.*
80,000 lire–130,000 lire.
⌂ ♨ 🄳 ▭

LE DUE FONTANE ★★★
Piazza Santissima
Annunziata no. 14
Tel. 21 01 85
Fax 29 44 61.
*Right in the city center,
overlooking the Piazza
Santissima Annunziata.
Breakfast included.*
*130,000 lire–240,000
lire.*
🏛 🄲 ♨ 🖵 🌂 ▭

**LOGGIATO DEI
SERVITI ★★★**
Piazza Santissima
Annunziata no. 3
Tel. 28 95 92
Fax 28 95 95.
*Beautiful 16th-century
building in one of the
most famous piazzas in
Florence. There are
only a few rooms but
they are spacious and
attractively decorated.
Breakfast included.*
*170,000 lire–240,000
lire.*
🏛 🄲 ♨ 🌂 🖵 ▭

LOSANNA ★
Via Alfieri no. 9
Tel. and fax 24 58 40
*A small out-of-the-way
pensione with only*

*eight rooms (three with
en-suite bathrooms)
Attentive manageress.
Tastefully decorated
and quiet. Breakfast
included.*
70,000 lire–96,000 lire.
⌂ ♨ 🄳 🚬

MONNA LISA ★★★★
Borgo Pinti no. 27
Tel. 247 97 51
Fax 247 97 55.
*Elegant Renaissance
palazzo furnished with
genuine works of art
(sculptures by G.
Dupré). Breakfast inc.*
*220,000 lire–350,000
lire. Reductions in low
season.*
🏛 🄲 ♨ 🖵 🚗 ▭
🅿

**MORANDI ALLA
CROCETTA ★★★**
Via Laura no. 50
Tel. 234 47 47
Fax 248 09 54.
*Polite, personal
welcome. Ten very
pleasant rooms. AC.
Breakfast: 18,000 lire.*
96,000 lire–169,000 lire.
🏛 🄲 ♨ 🖵 ▭

REGENCY ★★★★★
Piazza M. d'Azeglio
no. 3
Tel. 24 52 47
Fax 234 67 35.
*A tastefully decorated,
luxury establishment
located in an old villa
alongside a park.
Outstanding cuisine.
Breakfast included.*
*320,000 lire–530,000
lire. Suite: 800,000 lire.
Reductions in low
season.*
🏛 ♨ 🄳 🌂 🖵
🚗 ▭ 🅿

NIGHTLIFE

JAZZ CLUB
Via Nuova de Caccini
no. 3
Tel. 247 97 00

Open 9.30pm–2am
Closed Mon. and mid-
June to mid-Sept..
*Welcoming jazz club,
tends to be packed,
especially late at night.
Orchestra every
evening.*

REX BAR
Via Fiesolana
no. 23–25r
Tel. 248 03 31
Open 5pm–1am
Closed Tues. and
during Aug.
*People come to admire
the blue mosaic décor.
You can also eat
here and drink beer
(5,000 lire) during the
daytime. Livelier in the
evening. Fairly trendy
atmosphere.*

SANTA CROCE

POSTCODE: 50122.

**TOURIST
INFORMATION
OFFICE**
Via Manzoni no. 16
Tel. 234 62 84.

CULTURE

CASA BUONARROTI
Via Ghibellina no. 70
Tel. 24 17 52
Open 9.30am–1.30pm
Closed Tues.
*Michelangelo's family
home.*

**MUSEO DELL'OPERA
DI SANTA CROCE**
Piazza Santa Croce
no. 16
Tel. 24 46 19
Open 10am–12.30pm,
2.30–6.30pm
Closed Wed.
*Cimabue's "Crucifix" is
exhibited here.*

MUSEO HORNE
Via dei Benci no. 6
Tel. 24 46 61
Open 9am–1pm
Closed public holidays.

PAZZI CHAPEL
Piazza Santa Croce
Tel. 24 46 19
Open 10am–12.30pm,
2.30–6.30pm
Closed Wed.

**CHURCH OF
SANTA CROCE**
Piazza Santa Croce
no. 16
Tel. 24 46 19
Open 8am–6.30pm,
Sun. and public
holidays 8am–12.30pm,
3–6.30pm.

RESTAURANTS

CAFFÉ DEL CIBREO
Via Andrea del
Verrocchio, 5r
*Salads, cold dishes in a
1920's-style café.
Superb terrace. Good
range of cocktails all at
around 10,000 lire.
17,000 lire – 34,000 lire.*

CIBREO
Via Andrea del
Verrocchio, 8r
Tel. 234 11 00
Fax 24 49 66
Open 12.50–2.30pm,
7.30–11.45pm.
Closed Sun., Mon.,
Aug., and 1st week in
Jan.
*One of the best
restaurants in Florence
and perhaps the world.
Stylish original décor.*

*Menu includes
delicacies which are
somewhere between
Tuscan dishes and
nouvelle cuisine.
Excellent wine list.
Specialties: pureed
peppers, pigeon stuffed
with mustard. Cibreo is
also a "trattoria" (far less
expensive). See also
Grocery stores.
Restaurant: 60,000
lire–70,000 lire.
Trattoria: 30,000
lire–70,000 lire.*

ENOTECA PINCHIORRI
Via Ghibellina no. 87
Tel. 24 27 57
Fax 24 49 83
Open 12.30–1.30pm,
7.30–10pm
Closed Sun. Mon., Wed.
lunchtime, Christmas
and Aug.
*An outstanding
restaurant with an
established reputation
and a select, regular
clientele prepared to
spend a fortune. AC.
130,000 lire–170,000
lire.
Set menus: 90,000 lire
(lunchtime), 150,000
(dinner).*

IL FRANCESCANO
Via Largo Bargellini
no. 16
Tel. 24 16 05
Open 12.30–3pm,
7.30–10.30pm
Closed Wed. and
Christmas.
*Cosy, welcoming
restaurant not far from

the Piazza Santa Croce,
offering home cooking.
30,000 lire–45,000 lire.
Set menu 15,000 lire.*

IL TIRABUSCIO
Via dei Benci no. 34r
Tel. 247 62 25
Open 12.30–3.30pm,
7–11pm
Closed Thurs.
*Quiet, friendly setting.
Good quality wines.
30,000 lire–43,000 lire.
Set menu: 15,000 lire.*

LA MAREMMANA
Via dei Maci no. 77r
Tel. 24 12 26
Open 12.30–3pm,
7.15–10.30pm
Closed Sun. and Aug.
*This "trattoria" offers set
meals at very
reasonable prices. It
also has a pretty little
indoor garden.
23,000 lire–40,000 lire.*

OSTERIA DÈ BENCI
Via dè Benci no. 13r
Tel. 234 49 23
Open 12.30–3pm,
7.45–11pm.Closed Sun.
*Friendly restaurant
situated between the
Arno and Santa Croce.
Original dishes served
on a little flower-
covered terrace.
Specialty: "spaghetti
degli eretici". AC.
18,000 lire–40,000 lire*

**★ TRATTORIA DA
BENVENUTO**
Via della Mosca, 16r
Tel. 21 48 33
Open 12.30–3pm,
7–10pm.
Closed Wed., Sun. and
Aug.
*Usually crowded,
which is only to be
expected in an
establishment serving
such excellent food at
reasonable prices.
Tuscan specialties.
17,000 lire–36,000 lire*

ACCOMMODATION

BALESTRI ★★★
Piazza Mentana no. 7
Tel. 21 47 43
Fax 239 80 42.
*Very spacious and
comfortable rooms in
this 19th-century
building. Ask for a room*

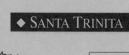

CASA DEL LAGO
MONTEBELLO SPLENDID
PRINCIPE, GRAND HÔTEL
EXCELSIOR, IL CESTELLO
SOSTANZA
LA CARABACCIA

with a view
over the Arno. Friendly
proprietor. Breakfast
included. AC.
130,000 lire–220,000
lire.

FIORINO ***
Via Osteria del Guanto
no. 6
Tel. and fax 21 05 79.
*Neat and tidy rooms
overlooking a flower-
covered terrace.
Breakfast included.
75,000 lire–110,000 lire.*

SANTA CROCE **
Via Bentaccordi no. 3
Tel. and fax 21 70 00.
*A small family hotel.
Breakfast included.
90,000 lire–130,000 lire.
Reductions in low
season.*

WANDA **
Via Ghibellina no. 51
Tel. 234 44 84
Fax 24 21 06
*Rooms have frescoed
ceilings and some have
period mirrors.
Breakfast included.
140,000 lire.*

NIGHTLIFE

RED GARTER
Via dei Benci no. 33
Tel. 234 49 04
Open 8.30pm–1am, Fri.
and Sat. 9pm–1.30am.
Closed Mon. and
Aug.
*An American bar,
popular with tourists
and beer drinkers.
Beer can be ordered by
the glass (½ pint),
the tankard (2 pints) or
even by the barrel
(½ gallon). Banjo
concerts every
evening.*

LIDO
Lungarno Pecori
Giraldi
Tel. 234 27 26
Open every evening
10pm–2am.

SANTA TRINITA

POSTCODE: 50123.

POLICE STATION
Piazza Porta al Prato
no. 6
Tel. 328 31.

POST OFFICE
Via Fininguerra no. 15r
Tel. 21 24 17.

CULTURE

MUSEUM OF PHOTOGRAPHY "ALINARI"
Via Vigna Nuova no. 16
Tel. 21 33 70
Open 10am–7.30pm.
Closed Wed.

MUSEO MARINO MARINI
Piazza San Pancrazio
Tel. 21 94 32
Open 10am–1pm,
3–6pm
Closed Tues.

CENACOLO OGNISSANTI
Borgo Ognissanti
no. 42
Tel. 239 87 00
Open 9am–noon,
3pm–6.30pm. Closed
Wed.–Fri. and Sun.

CHURCH OF SANTA TRINITA
Piazza Santa Trinita
Tel. 21 69 12
Open 7am–noon,
4–7pm

CHURCH OF SANTI APOSTOLI
Piazza del Limbo
Tel. 29 06 42
Open 3.30–5.30pm.

CENACOLO GHIRLANDAIO
Borgo Ognissanti
no. 42
Tel. 239 68 02
Open Mon., Tue., Sat.
9am–noon
Entry free.

PALAZZO CORSINI
Lungarno Corsini
no. 10.
The palazzo houses the
Corsini Gallery.
Entrance at Via del
Parione no. 11.
*May be visited by
appointment.
To make an
appointment:
Tel. 21 89 94 on Mon.,
Wed. or Fri. between
9am and noon.*

PALAZZO RUCELLAI
Piazza Rucellai
Via della Vigna Nuova
*Visitors are not allowed
into the interior of the
palace.*

RESTAURANTS

COCO LEZZONE
Via Parioncino no. 26r
Tel. 28 71 78
Open noon–2.30pm
Closed Sun..
*Typical Florentine,
convivial restaurant.
50,000 lire–65,000 lire.*

HARRY'S BAR
Lungarno Vespucci
no. 22r
Tel. 239 67 00
Open noon–3pm,
7–11pm
Closed Sun., Christmas
and Jan. 6.
*Smart restaurant on
the Arno. Light meals
and cocktails from
5.30pm to midnight.
Specialties: curried
prawns, pasta.
52,000 lire–75,000 lire.*

IL CESTELLO (HOTEL EXCELSIOR)
Piazza Ognissanti no. 3
Tel. 26 42 01
Open noon–3pm,
7–11pm
Closed 10 days in Aug.
*One of the highspots of
Florentine gastronomy
in an extremely elegant
setting.
72,000 lire–103,000 lire.*

★ IL LATINI
Via dei Palchetti no. 6r
Tel. 21 09 16
Open 12.30–2.30pm,
7.30–10.30pm
Closed Mon., Christmas
and New Year.
*One of the most highly
regarded restaurants in*

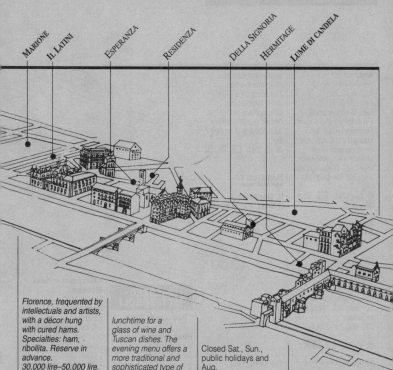

MARIONE · IL LATINI · ESPERANZA · RESIDENZA · DELLA SIGNORIA · HERMITAGE · LUME DI CANDELA

Florence, frequented by
intellectuals and artists,
with a décor hung
with cured hams.
Specialties: ham,
ribollita. Reserve in
advance.
30,000 lire–50,000 lire.
○ ⊡ ♣ ✻

IL QUATTRO AMICI
Via degli Orti
Oricellari no. 29
Tel. 21 54 13
Open 12.30–2.30pm,
7.30–10.30pm
Closed Sun. and Aug.
Modern setting and
cuisine based on fresh
fish. The menu changes
according to the fish
available each day.
38,000 lire–65,000 lire.
◐ ⊡

LA CARABACCIA
Via Palazzuolo no. 190r
Tel. 21 47 82
Open 12.30–2.30pm,
7.30–10.30pm
Closed Sun., Mon.
lunchtime and for 10
days in Aug.
Rather out of the way,
this small restaurant
offers an interesting
choice of Tuscan
dishes. Specialties:
"minestra di farro",
pasta with duck and
pasta with chicken.
32,000 lire–45,000 lire.
◐ ⊡

LUME DI CANDELA
Via delle Terme no. 23r
Tel. 29 45 66
Open noon–3pm,
7.30–11pm
Closed Sun., and 15
days in Aug.
A good place to go at

lunchtime for a
glass of wine and
Tuscan dishes. The
evening menu offers a
more traditional and
sophisticated type of
cuisine. Pasta, ice
cream and homemade
desserts. Specialty:
Mediterranean
swordfish.
45,000 lire–70,000 lire.

OLIVIERO
Via delle Terme no. 51r
Tel. 28 76 43
Open 7.30–11pm
Closed Sun. and Aug.
Luxurious meeting
place for politicians and
artists. Packed after the
theater. Reservations
are essential.
Specialties: duck with
pink pepper, fresh
beans and prawns.
46,000 lire–65,000 lire.
◑ ⊡ ✻

OTELLO
Via degli Orti Oricellari
no. 36r
Tel. 21 65 17
Fax 21 58 19
Open noon–3pm, 7.30–
11pm. Closed Tues.
Just behind the station.
Typical, refined cuisine
in a warm, elegant
setting.
30,000 lire–60,000 lire.
⊡

**SOSTANZA DETTO
IL TROIA**
Via del Porcellana
no. 25r
Tel. 21 26 91
Open noon–2.30pm,
7.30–9.30pm

Closed Sat., Sun.,
public holidays and
Aug.
A small, canteen-like
local restaurant serving
good Tuscan food.
Specialties: chicken
Florentine, "stracotto".
30,000 lire–45,000 lire.
◯ ✻

ACCOMMODATION

ANGLO-AMERICAN ★★★★
Via Garibaldi no. 9
Tel. 28 21 14
Fax 26 85 13.
An immense glass-
roofed entrance hall
and old-fashioned
dining rooms. Spacious,
rooms. Breakfast
included. AC.
202,000 lire–374,000
lire.
🏛 ⌂ ⬦ ▢ P ⊡

★ APRILE ★★★
Via della Scala no. 6
Tel. 21 62 37
Fax 28 09 47.
An abundance of
greenery accompanies
the antique décor and
admirable frescos of a
former Medici palace.
Breakfast included.
140,000 lire–195,000
lire. Reductions in low
season.
🏛 🅲 ⌂ ⅍ ▢ ⊡

CASA DEL LAGO ★★
Lungarno Vespucci
no. 58
Tel. 21 61 41
Fax 21 41 49

A dilapidated old house
which the owners have
made captivating.
Large, airy rooms with a
view over the Arno.
Breakfast included.
50,000 lire–120,000 lire.
⌂ 🅲 ⌂ ⅍ ⊡

★ EXCELSIOR ★★★★★
Piazza Ognissanti no. 3
Tel. 26 42 01
Fax 21 02 78.
The most renowned
palazzo in Florence.
Luxury and comfort are
guaranteed.
See also under
Restaurants and
Nightlife. Breakfast
included. AC.
290,000 lire–490,000
lire. Suite: 1,300,000 lire.
🏛 🅲 ⅍ ▢ ♣ 🚗
⊡

GRAND HOTEL ★★★★★
Piazza Ognissanti no. 1
Tel. 28 87 81
Fax 21 74 00.
Another well-known
palazzo. The rooms are
all either Empire or
Renaissance in style.
Breakfast is served in a
gallery overlooking the
winter garden. AC.
Breakfast: 26,000 lire–
41,000 lire. 360,000
lire–580,000 lire.
Suite: 1,600,000 lire.
🏛 🅲 ⅍ ▢ ♣ 🚗
⊡

KRAFT ★★★★
Via Solferino no. 2
Tel. 28 42 73
Fax 239 82 67.
*Neo-Baroque style.
Founded by the son of
Hermann Kraft, who
created the Excelsior.
Swimming pool on
terrace with panoramic
view. AC. Breakfast inc.
150,000 lire–390,000
lire.*

**MONTEBELLO
SPLENDID** ★★★★
Via Montebello no. 60
Tel. 239 80 51
Fax 21 18 67.
*Refined, elegant hotel
near the Arno.
Restaurant, garden and
fine conference hall.
Garden. AC. Breakfast
included.
280,000 lire–385,000
lire.*
🏠 🏠 📠 □ P ▱ ▱

PRINCIPE ★★★★
Lungarno Vespucci
no. 34
Tel. 28 48 48
Fax 28 34 58
*Superbly situated facing
the Arno. The rooms on
the 4th and 5th floors
have a terrace
overlooking the river.
There is also a pretty
garden. AC. Breakfast
included.
140,000 lire–380,000
lire.*

VILLA AZALEE ★★★
Viale Fratelli Rosselli
no. 44
Tel. 21 42 42
or 28 43 31
Fax 26 82 64.
*In an old house set in a
small garden protected
by high walls. A
romantic hotel, with an
intimate floral décor,
which will charm you
with the warmth of its
welcome. Bicycle rental
in summer. Park. AC.
Breakfast included.
132,000 lire–204,000
lire.*
🏠 C □ ▱

VILLA MEDICI ★★★★★
Via Il Prato no. 42
Tel. 238 13 31
Fax 238 13 36.
*This refined hotel is
situated not far from the
station. It has a*

*swimming pool in a
delightful garden.
Terrace with a stunning
view. Welcoming
atmosphere. AC.
Breakfast: 28,250 lire.
363,000 lire–517,000
lire.*
🏠 🏠 ⚡ □ ▭ P
▱

NIGHTLIFE

**IL DONATELLO
(HOTEL EXCELSIOR)**
Piazza Ognissanti no. 3
Tel. 26 42 01
Open 11am–1pm.

*Tea room in the
daytime, piano-bar at
night. Select
atmosphere in the
setting of the Hotel
Excelsior. Cocktails
from 12,500 lire to
18,500 lire.*
⚡ 🍴

**TAVERNA CLUB
ESKIMO**
Via dei Canacci no. 12r
Tel. 21 06 05
Open 9.30pm–3.30am
Closed Mon.
Italian folk music.
🎺

◆ SANTA MARIA DEL CARMINE ◆

It was in this church, in the early 16th century,
that Masaccio helped to paint the famous
fresco cycle in the Brancacci Chapel.

**PALAZZO
PITTI/BOBOLI**

POSTCODE: 50125.

POST OFFICE
Via Senese no. 40r
Tel. 229 85 11.

CULTURE

PALAZZO PITTI
Piazza Pitti-Portineria
Tel. 21 34 40
Open 9am–2pm
Closed Mon..
**– APARTMENTS OF THE
DUCHESS OF AOSTA**
Tel. 28 70 96
Open Sat. 10.30–
11.30am (by appt.)
**– MONUMENTAL
APARTMENTS**
Tel. 23 88 611
Open 9am–2pm.
Closed Mon.

**– GALLERIA D'ARTE
MODERNA**
Tel. 28 70 96.
Open 9am–2pm.
Closed Mon.
– COSTUME GALLERY
Tel. 29 42 79.
Open 9am–2pm.
Closed Mon.
– GALLERIA PALATINA
Tel. 23 88 611.
Open 9am–2pm.
Closed Mon.
**– MUSEO DELLE
CARROZZE**
Closed at present.
**– MUSEO DEGLI
ARGENTI**
Tel. 21 25 57.
Open 9am–2pm.
Closed Mon.

**CHURCH OF SANTA
FELICITA**
Piazza di Santa
Felicita
Tel. 21 34 40
Open 8.30am–noon,
2.30–6pm
Closed at Christmas.

GIARDINO DI BOBOLI
Palazzo Pitti
Tel. 21 34 40
Open 9am–4.30pm
(9am–7.30pm during
the summer).
Closed the first and last
Mon. of each month.
**– MUSEO DELLE
PORCELLANE**
Tel. 21 34 40.

RESTAURANTS

CAMMILLO
Borgo San Jacopo
no. 57/59r
Tel. 21 24 27
Fax 21 29 63
Open noon–2.30pm,
7.30–10.30pm
Closed Wed., Thur. and
3 weeks Jul.–Aug.

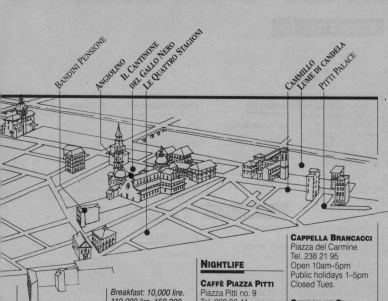

BANDINI PENSIONE
ANGIOLINO
IL CANTINONE
DEL GALLO NERO
LE QUATTRO STAGIONI
CAMMILLO
LUME DI CANDELA
PITTI PALACE

Family-run restaurant. The wine and olive oil come straight from the family estate. The curried prawns are not to be missed. Specialties: truffles and curries (Sept. to Jan.). AC.
32,000 lire–82,000 lire.
◑ ▱

LA SAGRESTIA
Via Guicciardini no. 27r
Tel. 21 00 03
Fax 21 45 67
Open 6.30–10.30pm
Closed Mon. Nov.–Apr.
Gastronomic cuisine in a haven of tranquillity. AC.
28,000 lire–50,000 lire.
Set menu: 20,000 lire.
◑ ▱

MAMMA GINA
Borgo San Jacopo no. 37r
Tel. 239 60 09
Open noon–2.30pm, 7–10.30pm
Closed Sun. and Aug.
Unpretentious trattoria near the Ponte Vecchio in one of the oldest parts of Florence.
40,000 lire–65,000 lire.
◑ ▱

ACCOMMODATION

★ CLASSIC HOTEL ★★★
Viale Macchiavelli no. 25
Tel. 22 93 51
Fax 22 93 53
Small hotel behind the Boboli Gardens with a delightful winter garden. Charming antique furniture.

Breakfast: 10,000 lire.
110,000 lire–150,000 lire.
⌂ C ⌂ ☐ P ▱

PENSIONE ANNALENA ★★★
Via Romana no. 34
Tel. 22 24 02
Fax 22 24 03.
The Orlandini family's former palazzo houses this pensione, named after a princess who was born and married here in 1439. Period decoration and considerable comfort. A variety of different rooms. Breakfast included.
135,000 lire–205,000 lire.
C ⌂ ☐ ▱

PITTI PALACE ★★★
Via Barbadori no. 2
Tel. 239 87 11
Fax 239 88 67.
Modern, comfortable hotel, the latest in a prestigious chain. Beautiful view from the 6th-floor terrace. Breakfast included. AC.
150,000 lire–260,000 lire. Reductions in low season.
⌂ C ⌖ ☐ ▱

VILLA CORA ★★★★★
Viale Macchiavelli no. 18
Tel. 229 84 51
Fax 22 90 86.
Beautifully decorated Renaissance palazzo near the Boboli and swimming pool. Garden and swimming pool. Ferry service from Ponte Vecchio 9am to 6pm. Breakfast inc.
280,000 lire–1,800,000 lire.
⌂ ⌂ ▯⋅ ⌖ ☐ ⌇
◑ P ▱

NIGHTLIFE

CAFFÈ PIAZZA PITTI
Piazza Pitti no. 9
Tel. 239 62 41
Open 10am–1am
Closed Mon.
An excellent place to stop for refreshment and listen to live music. Attractive setting. Light snacks.

SANTA MARIA DEL CARMINE

POSTCODE: 50124.

POST OFFICE
Via Bartolini no. 6
Tel. 21 27 15.

CULTURE

GIPSOTECA DELL'INSTITUTO STATALE D'ARTE
Piazzale di Porta Romana no. 9
Tel. 23 42 427
Open 9am–noon, public holidays 8am–1pm.
Closed Mon.

LA SPECOLA MUSEUM
Via Romana no. 17
Tel. 22 24 51
Open Sun. 9am–1pm, Mon., Tue., Sat, Sun., 9am–noon. Closed Wed. and public holidays.
The museum has two sections: the anatomy section is open Tues. and Sat., and the zoology section is open Mon., Thur. and Fri.

CENACOLO DI SANTO SPIRITO
Piazza Santo Spirito no. 29
Tel. 28 70 43
Open 9am–2pm
Public holidays 8am–1pm
Closed Mon.

CAPPELLA BRANCACCI
Piazza del Carmine
Tel. 238 21 95
Open 10am–5pm
Public holidays 1–5pm
Closed Tues.

CHURCH OF SAN FREDIANO IN CESTELLO
Piazza Cestello
Tel. 23 42 427
Open 9.30am–5.30pm.

CHURCH OF SANTA MARIA DEL CARMINE
Piazza del Carmine
Tel. 21 23 31
Open 7am–noon, 2.30–6.15pm.

CHURCH OF SANTO SPIRITO
Piazza Santo Spirito
Tel. 21 00 30
Open 8am–noon, 4-6pm.
Closed Wed. morning.

CONVENT DELLA CALZA
Porta Romana
Tel. 22 22 87
Open 3.30–4.30pm.
Visits by appointment.

RESTAURANTS

ANGIOLINO
Via Santo Spirito no. 36r
Tel. 239 89 76
Open noon–2.30pm, 7–10.30pm
Closed Sun. evening and Mon.
Each client is greeted like an important guest. Do not hesitate to ask the chef's advice. Specialties: "ribollita" and tagliatelle with mushrooms.
25,000 lire–36,000 lire.
○

DEL CARMINE
Piazza del Carmine no. 18r
Tel. 21 86 01
Open noon–3pm, 7–10.30pm
Closed Sun..

Located behind Santo Spirito. Restaurant with terrace, particularly pleasant in summer. Traditional cuisine.
18,000 lire–32,000 lire.
Set menu: 20,000 lire.
○ ▭

IL CANTINONE DEL GALLO NERO
Via Santo Spirito no. 6r
Tel. 21 88 98
Open noon–2.30pm,
7–10.30pm
Closed Mon., Tue. lunch and 15 days in Aug.
Typical Florentine "enoteca", offering high-quality cuisine at very low prices and a choice of over 500 chiantis.
20,000 lire–26,000 lire.
○

LE QUATTRO STAGIONI
Via Maggio no. 61r
Tel. 21 89 06
Open 12.30–2.30pm,
7.30–10.30pm
Closed Sun. and
15 days in Aug.
Mainly Italian clientèle seeking good local cuisine in a peaceful setting. Specialties: gnocchi with spinach, ravioli with artichokes.
25,000 lire–35,000 lire.
◑ ▭

PIEROT
Piazza Taddeo Gaddi
no. 25r
Tel. 70 21 00
Open noon–2.30pm,
7–10.30pm.
Closed Sun. and last
2 weeks in July.
Reasonably priced fish restaurant. Mainly Florentine clientèle. Speciality: fish soup "Pierot".
28,000 lire–42,000 lire.
◑ ▭

ACCOMMODATION

BANDINI PENSIONE *
Piazza Santo Spirito
no. 10
Tel. 21 53 08
Fax 28 27 61
Set in a 15th-century Florentine palazzo, the Bandini sisters' pensione is a marvel with its majestic loggia and enormous rooms. Breakfast included.
80,000 lire–110,000 lire
(without bathroom)
140,000 lire (with bathroom)
⌂ 🄲 ⌂ ⋯ ⤢

NIGHTLIFE

LA DOLCE VITA
Piazza del Carmine
Tel. 28 45 95
Open 8.30am–2am
Closed Sun.
Open late. Good terrace. Also popular for lunch.

SAN MINIATO

POSTCODE: 50125.

POST OFFICE
Via Giampaolo
Orsini no. 23r
Tel. 68 93 02.

CULTURE

MUSEO BARDINI
Piazza de Mozzi no. 1
Tel. 234 24 27
Open 8am–2pm.
Public hols. 8am–1pm.
Closed Wed.

CHURCH OF SAN LEONARDO
Via di San Leonardo no. 25
Tel. 22 30 84.
No specific visiting times. Ring for admittance.

CHURCH OF SAN MINIATO AL MONTE
Via dei Croci
Tel. 234 27 31
Open 8am–noon,
2–7pm (summer) or
2.30–6pm (winter).

CHURCH OF SAN SALVATORE AL MONTE
Via del Monte alle Croci
Tel. 239 87 00
Open 8am–noon, 4–6pm.

FORTE BELVEDERE
Via di San Leonardo
Tel. 234 24 25
Open 9am–8pm.
No visits to interior.

VILLA POGGIO IMPERIALE
Piazzale Poggio
Imperiale
Tel. 22 01 51.
Visits by appointment only, Wed. 10am–noon.

RESTAURANTS

★ BORDINO
Via Stracciatella no. 9r
Tel. 21 30 48
Open noon–2.30pm,
7.15–10.30pm
Closed Sun.
A friendly restaurant with a small garden, Specializes in delicious Tuscan and Brazilian dishes at very reasonable prices. Lunchtime menu:
10,000 lire or 14,000 lire.
◑ ○ ▭

CAPONNINA DI SANTE
Piazza Ravenna
Tel. 68 83 45
Fax. 68 88 41
Open evenings only.
Closed Sun., and
5 days in Aug.
Fish restaurant. The garden leading down to the Arno is delightful in summer. Local clientèle. Reservation recommended.
80,000–100,000 lire.
▭

◆ SAN MINIATO ◆

The Romanesque church of San Miniato is recognizable from a distance by its façade of green and white marble. It stands on the hill of the same name which offers a superb view of the city.

DA OMERO
Via Pian de'Giullari
no. 11r
Tel. 22 00 53
Open noon–2.30pm,
7.30–10.30pm
Closed Tues. and Aug.
This restaurant, also a "pizzeria", has a good wine cellar. Pleasant, friendly atmosphere.
50,000 lire–70,000 lire.
◑ ▭

LA LOGGIA
Piazzale Michelangelo
Tel. 234 28 32
Open noon–2.30pm,
7pm–midnight. Closed
Wed.
Delicate cuisine and a view over the city. Specialties: fish dishes.
55,000 lire–90,000 lire.
◍ ▭ ⤢ ℗

ACCOMMODATION

PARK PALACE ★★★★
Piazzale Galileo no. 5
Tel. 22 24 31
Fax 22 05 17.
On the left bank of the Arno, away from the city center but comfortable for a quiet stay. Pleasant grounds, restaurant and pool. Breakfast included.
240,000–370,000 lire.
⌂ ⌂ ⋯ ⤢ □
🚗 ⤢ ⋤ ▭

PARCO COMUNALE DI CAMPEGGIO MICHELANGELO
Viale Michelangelo
no. 50
Tel. 68 11 977
Fax 68 93 48
No credit cards.
7,000 lire–15,000 lire.
🚗

AROUND FLORENCE

CULTURE

MUSEO BANDINI
Via Dupré, Fiesole
Tel. 5 94 77
Open 10am–7pm.
Closed Tues.

MUSEO PRIMO CONTI
Le Coste, Via Dupré
no. 18, Fiesole
Tel. 59 70 95
Open 9am–1.30pm
Closed Sun., Mon. and
public holidays.

MUSEO STIBBERT
Via Stibbert no. 26
Tel. 47 55 20

Open 9am–1pm
Closed Thur.
Entry free on Sun.

ROMAN THEATER AND ARCHEOLOGICAL MUSEUM
Via Florentina no. 6
Portigliani 1, Fiesole
Tel. 5 94 77
Open 9am–7pm. l

VILLA MEDICI DEMIDOFF
Via Bolognese-Pratolino
Tel. 47 76 97
Open 10am–8pm Fri.,
Sat., Sun., May–Sept.
Entry free on Fri.

CERTOSA DEL GALLUZZO
Galluzzo
Tel. 204 92 26
Open 9am–noon,
3–7pm. Closed Mon.
*Carthusian monastery
3 miles south of
Florence.*

ACCOMMODATION

CAMPING PANORAMICO FIESOLE
Via Peramonda no. 1
Fiesole
Tel. 59 90 69
Fax 59 186.
*Bar and restaurant.
Bungalows (2 people):
75,000 lire.
Bungalows (3 people):
95,000 lire
Bungalows (4 people):
120,000 lire*
🅿 ▱

★ **BENCISTÀ** ★★
Via Da Maiano
no. 4
50014 Fiesole
Tel. & fax 5 91 63.
*This characterful hotel,
situated on the hill of
Fiesole, offers a superb
panoramic view of
Florence. Half-board
obligatory. Grounds.
200,000 lire–230,000
lire (breakfast + one
meal included).*
🏛 🏠 🖵 🌄 🅿

DINO ★★★
Via Faentina
no. 329
50014 Olmo/Fiesole
Tel. 54 89 32
Fax 54 89 34
*Charming hotel.
Welcoming. Breakfast
included. Tennis court.
90,000 lire–120,000 lire.*
🏛 🌓 🏠 🖵 🌄
🚗 ▱ ▱

VILLA LA MASSA
★★★★★
Via La Massa no. 24
50012 Candeli
Tel. 651 01 01
Fax 651 01 09.
*A self-contained luxury
hotel on an estate not
far from Florence.
Piano-bar and
discotheque in the
basement. Breakfast
included. Ferry service
to Florence. AC.
Breakfast included.
295,000 lire–475,000
lire.
Suite: 750,000 lire.
Reductions in low
season.*
🌄 🏛 🖵 ▱ ▱
🚗 🕺 ▱

VILLA LE RONDINI ★★★
Via Bolognese
Vecchia no. 224
Tel. 40 00 81
Fax 26 82 12.
*Magnificent villa set in
an estate on the
outskirts of Florence.
Facilities include
swimming pool, sauna,
gym and tennis court.
Heliport. Breakfast
included.
90,000 lire–250,000 lire.*
🏛 🏠 🖵 🌄 ▱ ▱
🚗 ▱

★ **VILLA SAN MICHELE**
★★★★★
Via Doccia no. 4
50014 Fiesole
Tel. 5 94 51
Fax 59 87 34.
*Set in a former 15th-
century convent on top
of a hill surrounded by a*

garden. Very expensive.
Breakfast not included.
420,000 lire–1,040,000
lire.
Suite: 1,850,000 lire.
🏛 🏠 🖵 🌄 ▱
🏊 ▱

NIGHTLIFE

BLU BAR
Piazza Mino da Fiesole
no. 39b
50014 Fiesole
Tel. 592 92.
*Favored by fashionable
young Florentines.*

TENAX
Via Pratese no. 46
Tel. 30 81 60
Open 10.30pm–4am
Closed Tues. and
summer.
*Discotheque. African
and reggae music.*
🎵 ▱

◆ **CIVIC MUSEUM, FIESOLE** ◆

The little town of Fiesole, an old Etruscan
settlement, is now an archeological site, with an
antique theater, baths and a temple. The small
museum also contains several remains found in
the excavations carried out here.

ANTIQUE DEALERS

ALBERTOSI
Piazza Frescobaldi 1r
Tel. 21 36 36.

ASTRONOMI
Via Maggio 19–21r
Tel. 29 51 48.

BACARELLI
Via dei Fossi 33r
Tel. 21 54 57.

BARTOLOZZI
Via Maggio 18r
Tel. 21 56 02.

BELLUCCI
Via Santo Spirito 11
Tel. 21 50 64.

BORALEVI
Via Maggio 18r
Tel. 28 17 56

CARNEVALI
Borgo San Jacopo 64r
Tel. 29 50 64.

CASA D'ASTE PITTI
Via Maggio 15
Tel. 28 71 38
Closed Aug.
*See the program in the
"Giornale d'arte".*

CEI
Via dei Fossi 17
Tel. 239 60 39.

CLOCK WORKSHOP
Via Santo Spirito 50r
Tel. 28 29 21.

FALLANI
Borgo Ognissanti 15r
Tel. 21 49 86.

GALLERIA CAMICCIOTTI
Via Santo Spirito 9r
Tel. 29 48 37.

GALLERIA VESPUCCI
Borgo Albizi 72r
Tel. 234 47 19.

PISELLI
Via Maggio 23r
Tel. 239 80 29.

PONZIANI
Via Santo Spirito 27
Tel. 28 79 58.

ROMANO
Borgo Ognissanti 36
Tel. 239 60 06.

SANTORO
Via Mazzetta 8r
Tel. 21 31 16.

SCHINDER
Via Maffia 51r
Tel. 21 77 66.

STUDIO SANTO SPIRITO
Via dello Sprone 19–21r
Tel. 21 48 73.

GROCERY STORES

CIBREO
Via Andrea del
Verrocchio 8r
Tel. 234 10 94.
*Oil, wine, balsamic
vinegar, alcohol,
preserves, recipe
books. Rather
expensive, but very well
presented, good quality
produce. See also
under Santa Croce,
Restaurants.*

PEGNA
Via dello Studio 8
Tel. 28 27 01.
Luxury groceries.

PORTA DEL TARTUFO
Borgo Ognissanti 133r
Tel. 28 75 05.
*Specialties made with
truffles.*

PROCACCI
Via Tornabuoni 64r
Tel. 21 16 56.
*Specialties: "panini
tartufati" (with cream of
white truffles).*

ICE CREAM PARLORS

BADIANI
Viale dei Mille 20r
Tel. 57 86 82.

BARONCINI
Via Celso no. 3r
Tel. 48 91 85.
CAVINI
Piazza delle Cure
19/23r
Tel. 58 74 89.
GELATERIA VENETA
Piazza Beccaria, 7r
Tel. 234 33 70.
PERCHÉ NO?
Via dei Tavolini 19r
Tel. 239 99 69
Open 8am–12.30am
Closed Tue. and low
season.
VIVOLI
Via Isola delle Stinche
7r
Tel. 29 23 34
Open 6pm–1am
Closed Mon., Aug. and
Jan.
*The place to go in
Florence.*

DEPARTMENT STORES

UPIM
Piazza Repubblica 1
Tel. 239 85 44.
COIN
Via dei Calzaiuoli 56/r
Tel. 28 05 31.

BOOKSTORES

**AFTER DARK ENGLISH
BOOKSTORE**
Via del Moro 86r
Tel. 29 42 03
BM BOOKSHOP
Borgo Ognissanti 4r
Tel. 29 45 75
CAPPELLINI
Calle Tintori 27r
Tel. 24 09 89.
EDISON
Piazza Repubblica, 32r
Open 9am–8pm. Public
holidays 10am–
1.30pm, 3.30–8pm.
*The only bookstore
open on Sun.*
FELTRINELLI
Via Cavour 12/20r
Tel. 21 95 24
General bookstore.

GONNELLI
Via Ricasoli 6/14r
Tel. 21 68 35
Antique books.
GOZZINI
Via Ricasoli 49
Tel. 21 24 33
Antique books.
MARZOCCO
Via de' Martelli 22r
Tel. 28 28 73
SALIMBENI
Via Palmieri 14/16r
Tel. 234 09 04
**SEEBER
INTERNATIONAL
BOOKSTORE**
Via Tornabuoni 70r
Tel. 29 43 11.

MARKETS

**MERCATO DELLE
CASCINE**
Viale Lincoln
Open 8am–2pm
Tues. morning.
**MERCATO DELLE
PIANTE**
Under the porticoes of
Via Pellicceria
Open 8am–2pm Thur.
from Sept. to June.
MERCATO PORCELLINO
Via Por Santa Maria

Open 8.20am–6.30pm.
Closed Sun.
**MERCATO DELLE
PULCI**
Piazza dei Ciompi
Daily, am and pm and
last Sun. of each month.
Closed Mon.
Flea market.
**MERCATO DI
SANT'AMBROGIO**
Piazza Ghiberti
Open 7am–2pm
weekdays.
Food and clothes.
MERCATO CENTRALE
Via dell'Ariento
Tel. 21 02 14
Open Mon.–Sat., 7am–
2pm. Public holidays
7am–2pm, 4.20–8pm.
Food.

FASHION

ARMANI
Via Vigna Nuova 51r
Tel. 21 90 41.
BELTRAMI
Piazza Olio, no. 1

Tel. 21 32 90
BP STUDIO
Via Vacchereccia 24r
Tel. 239 89 55.
BUCELLATI
Via Tornabuoni 71r
Tel. 239 65 79.
CAPONI
Lungarno Vespucci 12r
Tel. 21 10 74.
CASA DEL TESSUTO
Via dei Pecori 20r
Tel. 21 59 61.
CIRRI
Via Por Santa Maria 38r
Tel. 239 65 93.
COVERI
Via Tevere, no. 60
Tel. 31 11 35.
FAVILLI
Piazza Duomo 13r
Tel. 21 18 46.
FERRAGAMO
Via Tornabuoni 16r
Tel. 29 21 23.
GHERARDINI
Via Vigna Nuova 57r
Tel. 21 56 78.
**GIULIA CARLA
CECCHI**
Via Vigna Nuova 40r
Tel. 21 33 50.
GUCCI
Via Tornabuoni 73r
Tel. 26 40 11.

ITALIA BERNARDINI
Via Vigna Nuova 26r
Tel. 23 94 40
or Via Tosinghi 14r.
MANTELLASSI
Via Rondinelli 3r
Tel. 29 33 45.
MARAOLO
Via Roma 6r
Tel. 21 38 16.
PUCCI
Via Pucci 6
Tel. 28 30 61.
RASPINI
Via Roma 25r
Tel. 21 30 77.
ROMANO
Piazza Repubblica 22r
Tel. 2 39 68 90.
ROSSETTI
Piazza Repubblica 43r
Tel. 21 66 56.
SILVI
Via dei Tavolini 5r
Tel. 21 31 04.
TORRINI
Piazza Duomo 10r
Tel. 230 24 01.
UGOLINI
Via Tornabuoni 22r

Tel. 21 66 64.
VALENTINO
Via Vigna Nuova 47r
Tel. 29 31 42.
ZEGNA
Piazza Rucellai 4/7r
Tel. 28 30 11.

PASTRIES

CAPONERI
Via Valori 4r
Tel. 58 75 34.
DOLCI DOLCEZZE
Piazza Beccaria 8r
Tel. 23 4 54 58.
RIVOIRE
Piazza della Signoria 5r.
Tel. 21 44 12.
ROBIGLIO
Via dei Servi 112r
Tel. 21 45 01
or Via dei Tosinghi
no. 11r.
SIENI
Via dell'Ariento 29r
Tel. 21 38 30.

DELICATESSENS

BARONI
Central Market.
IL FORTETO
Central Market.

WINES

**CANTINETTA DEI
VERRAZZANO**
Via dei
Tavolini,
18–20r
Tel. 26 85 90.
GAMBI
Via Monteverdi
72/c
Tel. 35 00 04.
GUIDI
Via Paguini 24r.
Tel. 48 02 06
PALAZZO DEI VINI
Piazza Pitti 15
Tel. 28 83 23.
ZANOBINI
Via San Antonino 47r
Tel. 239 68 50.

APPENDICES

◆ BIBLIOGRAPHY

ESSENTIAL
◆ READING ◆

◆ ACTON (H.) and CHANEY (E.): *Florence: A Traveller's Companion*, London, 1986
◆ BURCKHARDT (J.): *The Civilization of the Renaissance in Italy*, London, 1965
◆ HAY (D.): *The Age of the Renaissance*, London, 1967
◆ HAY (D.): *The Italian Renaissance and its Historical Background*, Cambridge, 1961
◆ HUTTON (E.): *Florence*, London, 1966
◆ KING (F.): *Florence: A Literary Companion*, London, 1991
◆ LABANDE (E.R.): *Florence*, London, 1951
◆ MCCARTHY (M.): *The Stones of Florence*, London and New York, 1959
◆ NORWICH (J.J.): *The Italian World*, ed. London 1983
Ruskin (J.): *Mornings in Florence*, London, 1876
◆ SISMONDI (J.C.L. DE): *A History of the Italian Republics*, London, 1907
◆ SYMONDS (J.A): *The Renaissance in Italy*, London, 1875–86

◆ GENERAL ◆

◆ BARET (A.): *Florence Observed*, London, 1973
◆ BORSOOK (E.): *Companion Guide to Florence*, London, 1966
◆ *Firenze e dintorni*, Touring Club Italiano, Milan, 1974
◆ KAUFFMANN (G.): *Florence, Art Treasures and Buildings*, London, 1971
◆ MCCLEOD (J.): *People of Florence*, London, 1968
◆ SABBIETI (M): *Florence from the Air*, London, 1990

◆ HISTORY ◆

◆ ACTON (H): *The Last Medici*, London, 1932
◆ ACTON (H.): *The Pazzi Conspiracy*, London, 1979
◆ ADY (C.M.) : *Lorenzo de' Medici and Renaissance Italy*, London, 1960
◆ BARGELLINI (P.): *Splendida storia di Firenze*, Florence, 1964
◆ BECKER (M.) : *Florence in Transition*, Baltimore, 1967–8
◆ BRUCKER (G.A.): *Renaissance Florence*, New York, 1969
◆ BRUCKER (G.A.): *Florence: 1138–1737*, London, 1984
◆ COCHRANE (E.): *Florence in the Forgotten Centuries, 1527–1800*, Chicago, 1973
◆ CONTI (G.): *Firenze vecchia*, Florence, 1985
◆ CRONIN (V.) : *The Florentine Renaissance*, London, 1967
◆ *Firenze e la Toscana dei Medici nell'Europa del Cinquecento*, Florence, 1980
◆ GUTKIND (C.S.): *Cosimo de' Medici, Pater Patriae*, Oxford, 1938
◆ HALE (J.R.): *Florence and the Medici*, London, 1977
◆ HOLMES (G.): *The Florentine Enlightenment, 1400–50*, London, 1969
◆ MAGUIRE (Y.): *The Women of the Medici*, London, 1927
◆ MARTINELLI (G) ed.: *The World of Renaissance Florence*, London, 1968
◆ MARTINES (L.): *The Social World of the Florentine Humanists*, Princeton, 1968
◆ PAOLETTI (P.), CARNIANI (M.): *Firenze, Guerra e alluvione*, Florence, 1991
◆ ROSCOE (W.): *The Life of Lorenzo de' Medici*, London, 1797
◆ RUBINSTEIN (N.): *The Government of Florence under the Medici*, Oxford, 1966
◆ SCHEVIL (F.): *Medieval and Renaissance Florence*, London, 1961
◆ VANNUCCI (M.): *Storia di Firenze in fotografia dal 1870 al 1990*, Newton Compton, Rome, 1990
◆ VILLARI (P.): *The Life of Savonarola*, London, 1896
◆ VILLARI (P.): *The Life of Machiavelli*, London, 1892

◆ TRADITIONS ◆

◆ ANTONETTI (P.): *La Vie quotidienne à Florence au temps de Dante*, Paris, 1979.
◆ ARTUSI (L.): *Le Arti e i Mestieri di Firenze*, Rome, 1990
◆ ARTUSI (L.) et GABRIELLI (S.): *Le Feste di Firenze*, Rome, 1991
◆ ARTUSI (L.) and GABRIELLI (S.): *Calcio storico fiorentino ieri e oggi*, Florence, 1988
◆ BOJANI (G.C.): *Ceramica e Araldica Medicea*, Città di Castello, 1992
◆ GANDI (G.): *Le Corporazioni dell'antica Firenze*, Florence, 1928
◆ GORI (P.): *Le Feste fiorentine attraverso i secoli*, Giunti, Florence, 1990
◆ LUCCHESINI (P.): *I Teatri a Firenze*, Rome, 1991
◆ PETRONI (P.): *Il Libro della vera cucina fiorentina*, Florence, 1974
◆ SANTINI (A.): *La Cucina fiorentina*, Muzzio, Padua, 1992
◆ TOMMASI (R.): *Il Teatro comunale di Firenze, presenza e linguaggio*, Florence, 1986

ARTS,
◆ ARCHITECTURE ◆

◆ ACKERMANN (J.S.): *The Architecture of Michelangelo*, London, 1961
◆ ANTHONY (F.W): *Early Florentine Architecture and Décoration*, Cambridge, 1927
◆ ARGAN (G.C.): *L'Architettura barocca in Italia*, 1957
◆ ARGAN (G.C.): *Storia dell'arte italiana III*, Florence, 1968
◆ BAJARD (S.) et BENCINI (R.): *Villas et jardins de Toscane*, Paris, 1992
◆ BATTISTI (E.): *Brunelleschi, The Complete Work*, London, 1981
◆ BENEVOLO (L.): *Storia dell'architettura moderna*, Bari,1960
◆ CHASTEL (A.): *Art et humanisme à Florence au temps de Laurent le Magnifique*, Paris, 1982
◆ CRESTI (C.): *L'Architettura del Seicento a Firenze*, Rome, 1990
◆ FANELLI (G.): *Brunelleschi*, Florence, 1988
◆ FANELLI (G.): *La Città nella storia d'Italia*: Bari, 1985
◆ FANELLI (G.): *Firenze, Architettura e città*, Florence, 1973
◆ *Firenze, guida di architettura*, Turin, 1992
◆ GINORI-LISCI (L.): *I Palazzi di Firenze nella storia e nell'arte*, Florence, 1985
◆ GIUSTI (A.) : *Tesori di pietre dure*, Milan, 1989
◆ GOBBI (G.): *Itinerari di Firenze moderna*, Florence, 1987
◆ GOLZIO (V.): *Il Seicento e il Settecento*, Turin, 1968
◆ MAFFEI (G.L.): *La Casa fiorentina nella storia della città*, Venice, 1990
◆ MANDELI (E.): *Palazzi del Rinascimento, dal rilievo al confronto*, Florence, 1989
◆ MARE (A.), SUKUXTER (I. P.J.) et TEMPLE (S.): *Around Midnight: Florence on Decadence*, Harvard Press, 1989
◆ *Il Monumento e il suo doppio: Firenze* (sous la direction de Dezzi Bardeschi (M.)), Alinari Ed., Firenze, 1981
◆ MURRAY (P.): *The Architecture of the Italian Renaissance*, London, 1969
◆ NATALE (D.): *La Cupola di Santa Maria del Fiore*, Universo, 1976
◆ *Raffaello e l'architettura a Firenze nella prima metà del Cinquecento*, Florence, 1984
◆ ROSS (J.): *Florentine Palaces*, London, 1905
◆ SUMMERSON (J.): *The Classical Language of Architecture*, London,1992
◆ VASARI (G.): *Lives of the Painters, Sculptors and Architects*, London, 1927
◆ WITTKOWER (R.): *Art and Architecture of Italy, 1600-1750*, London, 1991

PAINTING AND
◆ SCULPTURE ◆

◆ ANGELINI (A.): *Piero della Francesca*, Florence, 1987
◆ ANTAL (F): *Florentine Painting and its Social Background*, London, 1948
◆ ARGAN (G.C.): *Botticelli*, Geneva, 1989
◆ BARGELLINI (P.): *Città di pittori*, Florence, 1948
◆ BAROCCHI (P.): *Il Rosso Fiorentino*, Gismondi, 1950
◆ BATTISTI (E.): *Giotto*, Geneva, 1990
◆ BAXANDALL (M.): *Painting and Experience in 15th-Century Italy*, Oxford, 1975
◆ BERENSON (B.): *The Italian Painters of the Renaissance*, Oxford, 1957-68
◆ BLUNT (A.): *Artistic Theory in Italy 1450-1600*, Oxford,1940
◆ BOLDINI (U) and

CASAZZA (O): *The Brancacci Chapel Frescoes*, London, 1992
◆ BORSOOK (E.): *The Mural Painters of Tuscany*, London, 1960
◆ CASAZZA (O.), *Masaccio*, Florence, 1990
◆ CELLINI (B.): *Autobiography*, London, 1907
◆ CLARK (K.): *Florentine Painting: 15th Century*, London, 1945
◆ CLARK (K.): The *Florence Baptistry Doors*, London, 1980
◆ DURBÉ (D.) et FOLCINI (C.): *La Firenze dei Macchiaioli*, Rome, 1985
◆ FARA (A.): *Bernardo Buontalenti*, Sagep, 1988
◆ FOSSI (G.): *Filippo Lippi*, Scala, Firenze, 1989
◆ *Frescoes from Florence*, Hayward Gallery, London, 1969
◆ FRUGONI (C.): *Pietro e Ambrogio Lorenzetti*, Florence, 1988
◆ HOLROYD (C.): *Michelangelo Buonarrotti*, London, 1903
◆ *Il Seicento fiorentino*, Florence, 1986
◆ JANSON (H.W.): *The Sculpture of Donatello*, Princeton, 1957
◆ MEISS (M.): *Painting in Florence and Siena after the Black Death*, Princeton, 1951
◆ MORGAN (C.H.): *The Life of Michelangelo*, New York, London 1961
◆ OFFNER (R.): *A Critical and Historical Corpus of Florentine Paintings*, New York, 1947
◆ PADOVANI (S.): *Andrea del Sarto*, Florence, 1986
◆ PAOLIERI (A.): *Paolo Uccello, Domenico Veneziano et Andrea del Castagno*, Florence, 1991
◆ PAOLUCCI (A.): *Signorelli*, Florence, 1990
◆ PONENTE (N.): *Raphael*, Geneva, 1990
◆ POPE-HENESSY (J.): *Italian Gothic Sculpture*, London, 1955
◆ POPE-HENESSY (J.): *Italian Renaissance Sculpture*, London, 1958
◆ ROSSI (F.): *Art Treasures of the Uffizi and Pitti*, London, 1967
◆ ROSSI (M.): *The Uffizi and Pitti Galleries*, London, 1964
◆ WHITE (J.): *The Birth and Rebirth of Pictorial Space*, London, 1957
◆ WILES (B.H.): *The Fountains of Florentine Sculptors*, Cambridge, Mass. 1933

LANGUAGE AND ◆ LITERATURE ◆

◆ ALIGHIERI (Dante): *Italiano Antico e Nuovo*, Milan, 1988
◆ BERENSON (B.): *The Passionate Sightseer*, London, 1965
◆ BOCCACCIO (G): *The Decameron*, London, 1741, and many later translations
◆ CAMPBELL (H.B.): *A Journey to Florence in 1813*, London, 1951
◆ DUMAS (A.): *Une année à Florence*, Éd. François Bourin, Paris, 1991
◆ ELIOT (G.): *Romola*, London, 1863
◆ FORSTER (E.M.): *A Room with a View*, London, 1908
◆ GAUTIER (T.): *Voyage en Italie*, Marseilles, 1979
◆ GIDE (A.): *Journal*, Paris, 1951
◆ GIONO (J.): *Voyage en Italie*, Paris, 1979
◆ JAMES (H.): *Italian Hours*, London, 1909
◆ MONTAIGNE: *Journal de voyage*, Paris, 1983
◆ MUSSET (A. de): *Lorenzaccio*, Paris, 1991
◆ STENDHAL: *Rome, Naples et Florence*, Paris, 1987
◆ WHITFIELD (H.): *Petrarch and the Renaissance*, Oxford, 1943
◆ WILDE (O.): *A Florentine Tragedy*, London, 1895

SPECIAL ◆ INTEREST ◆

◆ BARGELLINI (P.): *Voir Florence*, Florence, 1974
◆ BARGELLINI (P.): *Cento tabernacoli a Firenze*, Florence, 1971
◆ BEFANI (L.): *Firenze, il mercato centrale*, Florence, 1991
◆ BORSOOK (E.): *Ecco Firenze*, Milan, 1972-1983
◆ CANEVA (C.), *Il Giardino di Boboli*, Florence, 1982
◆ CASTELLUCCI (L.) and BARGELLINI (C.): *Firenze, giardini per sognare*, Milan, 1990
◆ *La Chapelle Brancacci*, Paris, 1991
◆ COSTER (L. de) and NIZET (F.): *16 Promenades dans Florence*, PARIS, 1990
◆ *Fresques de Florence*, Paris, 1970
◆ *Florence, un guide intime*, Paris, 1986
◆ *Le Grand Guide de la Toscane*, Paris, 1990
◆ GUARNIERI (E.) and BARGELLINI (P.): *Le Strade di Firenze*, Florence, 1987
◆ GUCCERELLI (D.): *Stradario storico biografico della città di Firenze*, Florence, 1985
◆ GUIDOTTI (A.): *La Badia fiorentina*, Florence, 1982
◆ MICHELETTI (E.): *Santa Croce*, Florence, 1982
◆ ORLANDI (P.S.) *Santa Maria Novella*, Florence, s.d.
◆ PRETI (M.): *Museo dell'Opera del Duomo di Firenze*, Milan, 1989
◆ *Santa Maria Novella* (edited by Baldini (U.)), Florence, 1981
◆ SANTI (B.): *Palazzo Medici Riccardi*, Florence, 1983
◆ SETTESOLDI (E.): *Museo dell'Opera del Duomo di Firenze*, Arte e Natura, 1982
◆ TODOROW (M.F.): *Palazzo Davanzati*, Florence, 1986
◆ WIGNY (D.), *Au cœur de Florence*, Paris, 1990
◆ ZEPPEGNO (L.): *Le Chiese di Firenze*, Rome, 1991
◆ ZIMMERMANNS (K.): *Florence*, Paris, 1990

◆ JOURNALS ◆

◆ *Firenze ieri, oggi, domani*
◆ *Muséart*, n° 1, June 1990
◆ «Toscane, le balcon de la vie»(edited by Tondini (O.)), *Autrement*, hors-série n° 31, May 1988
◆ «Speciale Firenze», *Bell'Italia*, Giorgio Mondadori, Special edition, June 1991
◆ «Toscana», *Meridiani*, Domus, n° 9, May 1990
◆ «Toscane», *Geo*, n° 77, July 1985

◆ FILMOGRAPHY ◆

◆ BLASETTI (A.): *La Cena delle beffe*, 1941
◆ BOLOGNINI (M.): *Metello*, 1970
◆ POGGIOLI (F.M.): *L'Homme à femmes*, 1943
◆ LIZZANI (C.): *Chronique des pauvres amants*, 1953
◆ IVORY (J.): *Chambre avec vue*, 1985
◆ MONICELLI (M.): *Mes chers amis*, 1975
◆ MONICELLI (M.): *Pourvu que ce soit une fille*, 1986
◆ ROSSELLINI (R.): *Paisà*, 1946
◆ ZURLINI (V.): *Les Filles de San Frediano*, 1954
◆ ZURLINI (V.): *Journal intime*,1962

ACKNOWLEDGMENTS
We would like to thank the following publishers or copyright-holders for permission to reproduce the quotations on pages 105–20.

◆ HARCOURT BRACE & COMPANY: Excerpt from *The Stones of Florence*, by Mary McCarthy. Reprinted by permission.

◆ JILL NORMAN, TRUSTEE: THE ESTATE OF ELIZABETH DAVID: Excerpt from *Italian Food*, by Elizabeth David, copyright © 1958 by Elizabeth David. Reprinted by permission of Jill Norman, Trustee, on behalf of The Estate of Elizabeth David.

◆ VIOLET MARY MORTON: Excerpt from *A Traveler in Italy*, by H.V. Morton (Methuen, London 1964). Reprinted by permission.

INDEX